STARS, FAN MAGAZINES AND AUDIENCES

STARS, FAN MAGAZINES AND AUDIENCES
Desire by Design

Edited by Tamar Jeffers McDonald,
Lies Lanckman and Sarah Polley

EDINBURGH
University Press

Edinburgh University Press is one of the leading university presses in the UK. We publish academic books and journals in our selected subject areas across the humanities and social sciences, combining cutting-edge scholarship with high editorial and production values to produce academic works of lasting importance. For more information visit our website: edinburghuniversitypress.com

© editorial matter and organization Tamar Jeffers McDonald, Lies Lanckman and Sarah Polley, 2023, 2024
© the chapters their several authors, 2023, 2024

Edinburgh University Press Ltd
13 Infirmary Street, Edinburgh, EH1 1LT

First published in hardback by Edinburgh University Press 2023

Typeset in 10/12.5 pt Sabon by
IDSUK (DataConnection) Ltd

A CIP record for this book is available from the British Library

ISBN 978 1 3995 0590 1 (hardback)
ISBN 978 1 3995 0591 8 (paperback)
ISBN 978 1 3995 0592 5 (webready PDF)
ISBN 978 1 3995 0593 2 (epub)

The right of Tamar Jeffers McDonald, Lies Lanckman and Sarah Polley to be identified as editors of this work has been asserted in accordance with the Copyright, Designs and Patents Act 1988 and the Copyright and Related Rights Regulations 2003 (SI No. 2498).

CONTENTS

List of Figures   vii
Notes on Contributors   xi
Introduction   1

PART ONE   SINGLE MAGAZINE ISSUES

Part One Introduction   13

1. Never the Twain Shall Meet: Touch, Double-Sidedness and Race in the Pages of *Picture Show*   17
   Joel Casey

2. The Paradoxical Glamour of the Phoney War: Examining the Design of *Picturegoer*   37
   Carolyn Owen King

3. Mid-Century Masculinities: Presentation as Subtext in *Photoplay* January 1955   58
   Lisa Hood

4. Dorothy Dandridge the Invisible Star: Racial Segregation in Hollywood Fan Magazines in the 1950s   75
   Cathy Lomax

PART TWO   FAN MAGAZINES AND REGULAR CONTENTS

Part Two Introduction   97

5. Tyrone Power: International 'Cover Boy'   101
   Gillian Kelly

6.	Leafing Men and Ladies: Fan Magazines and Reading Strategies *Sarah Polley*	121
7.	A Star is Drawn: Media Hybridity and Ordinary Cinephilia in *La Passion de Dora* *Dominic Topp*	139
8.	Wielding the Scissors: Industry Politics and Play in Movie Magazines, 1933–1934 *Tamar Jeffers McDonald*	158

PART THREE   FAN MAGAZINES AND RELATED PUBLICATIONS

Part Three Introduction		179
9.	Universal Horror and *Universal Weekly*: The Visible Invisibility of the Invisible Man *Rahul Kumar*	183
10.	A Performance Studies Perspective On Fan Magazine Images And Silent Film Acting *Jennifer Voss*	200
11.	Context, Content and Form in 1940s British Film Star Fan Club Publications *Ellen Wright and Phyll Smith*	219
12.	The Missing Piece: Imaginary Audiences in the *Ecran* Fan Magazine of the 1940s *María Paz Peirano and Claudia Bossay*	238
13.	The Silver Screen and the Golden Land: Hollywood and 'Hereness' in the Pages of *Film-Nayes* (1936–1938) *Lies Lanckman*	256
Index		274

LIST OF FIGURES

I.1	Advertisement for Palmolive soap. *Motion Picture*, November 1932	5
1.1	Art Supplement, 'The Flower and the Flirt'. *Picture Show*, 28 August 1920	22
1.2	Art Supplement, 'East and West in Screenland'. *Picture Show*, 26 March 1921	25
1.3	Art Supplement featuring *Way Down East* (1920) *Picture Show*, 26 March 1921	26
1.4	Screenshot of Donald Crisp in *Broken Blossoms* (1919)	30
1.5	Screenshot of Lillian Gish and Richard Barthelmess in *Broken Blossoms* (1919)	31
2.1	Front cover featuring Margaret Sullavan. *Picturegoer*, 2 March 1940	40
2.2	Advertisement for Max Factor make-up featuring Rosalind Russell. *Picturegoer*, 2 March 1940	46
2.3	Article 'Between You and Me'. *Picturegoer*, 2 March 1940	48
2.4	Inside back cover advertisements including Vivien Leigh for Lux toilet soap. *Picturegoer*, 2 March 1940	50
2.5	*The Amazing Mr Williams* photospread featuring Melvyn Douglas and Joan Blondell. *Picturegoer*, 2 March 1940	52
2.6	'Personality Parade: Cantor versus Clark'. *Picturegoer*, 2 March 1940	53
3.1	Article 'Tough Softie' about Victor Mature. *Photoplay*, January 1955	58

LIST OF FIGURES

3.2	Article 'The Devil is a Gentleman' about Marlon Brando. *Photoplay*, January 1955	62
3.3	Article 'Rock Hudson's Love Affair with the USA'. *Photoplay*, January 1955	63
3.4	Article 'Purdom – Man on a Tightrope'. *Photoplay*, January 1955	65
3.5	Advertisements accompanying 'Tough Softie' article. *Photoplay*, January 1955	71
3.6	Advertisements accompanying Victor Mature article 'Life Owes You Nothing'. *Photoplay*, April 1942	72
4.1	Dorothy Dandridge's demurely elegant persona is on show in her role in *Bright Road* (1953)	78
4.2	Doris Day cover. *Photoplay*, February 1955	80
4.3	Advertisement for Lustre-Crème Shampoo featuring Doris Day. *Photoplay*, February 1955	81
4.4	Advertisement for Modess sanitary napkins opposite '*Photoplay* recommends *Carmen Jones*'. *Photoplay*, February 1955	85
4.5	Carmen Jones feature. *Picture Show*, 5 March 1955	89
5.1	Tyrone Power and Madeleine Carroll on the cover of *Film Pictorial*, 11 September 1937	108
5.2	Tyrone Power and Norma Shearer on the cover of *MoviePix*, May 1938	110
5.3	Tyrone Power on the cover of *Screen Guide*, December 1943	112
5.4	Tyrone Power and Linda Christian on the cover of *Noir et Blanc*, 2 February 1949	115
5.5	Tyrone Power and Deborah Ann Minardos on the cover of *Gente*, 29 November 1958	118
6.1	Graph of *Picture Show*, 3 September 1955	123
6.2	Graph of *Picturegoer*, 3 September 1955	124
6.3	Graph of *Filmalaya*, August 1955	125
6.4	Graph of *Photoplay* UK, September 1955	126
6.5	Graph of *Photoplay* US, September 1955	128
7.1	'Rocambole' fiction illustrated with photographs. *Ciné-Miroir*, 27 April 1948	142
7.2	Film noir lighting in *La Passion de Dora*. *Ciné-Miroir*, 6 July 1948	147
7.3	Elastic page design in *La Passion de Dora*. *Ciné-Miroir*, 1 June 1948	148
7.4	Behind the scenes of a film in *La Passion de Dora*. *Ciné-Miroir*, 11 May 1948	150
7.5	*Ciné-Miroir* appears in itself: *La Passion de Dora*, *Ciné-Miroir*, 20 July 1948	153

LIST OF FIGURES

8.1	Joan Crawford contest. *Modern Screen*, December 1933	160
8.2	Reconstituting Joan Crawford and Clark Gable from the Joan Crawford contest	161
8.3	Screenshots from *Dancing Lady* (1933)	164
8.4	Article 'Here's what the Censors Took Out'. *Modern Screen*, July 1934	169
8.5	Article 'Let's Fight for Our Movies!' *Modern Screen*, September 1934	170
9.1	Advertisements for *The Invisible Man* (1933). *Universal Weekly*, 9 September 1933	186
9.2	'How Would You Draw or Illustrate the Invisible Man?' *Universal Weekly*, 12 August 1933	188
9.3	Advertisement for *The Invisible Man* (1933). *Universal Weekly*, 4 November 1933	193
9.4	Advertisement for *Werewolf of London* (1935). *Universal Weekly*, 20 April 1935	195
9.5	Advertisement for *Crime Without Passion* (1934). *Motion Picture Herald*, 25 August 1934	196
10.1	'Mae Marsh – Some of her "Thousand Expressions"'. *Picture Show*, 10 May 1919	206
10.2	'The Expressions of Geraldine Farrar'. *Picture Show*, 16 April 1921	207
10.3	'Colleen Moore – The Film Star with the Expressive Eyes'. *Picture Show*, 26 November 1921	210
10.4	'The Expressions of Colleen Moore'. *Picture Show*, 1 July 1922	212
10.5	*Los Angeles Examiner* newspaper clipping, 31 August 1924	213
11.1	A comparative view of several issues of *The International Jean Kent Fan Club Magazine*	220
11.2	A comparative view of several other fan club magazines, devoted to stars Richard Attenborough, Patricia Roc, Michael Rennie and John Mills	227
12.1	'You can use the same make-up as Irene Dunne!' Max Factor Hollywood make-up advertisement. *Ecran*, 6 February 1940	241
12.2	Example of a game that also teaches readers about film culture. 'Puzzle cinematográfico', *Ecran*, 30 January 1940	242
12.3	'Inside the Teatro Real'. *Ecran*, 16 January 1940	246
12.4	'The premiere of *Intermezzo* was attended by a select and numerous audience at the Central Theatre'. 'Día de estreno en el Central'. *Ecran*, 19 March 1940	247
12.5	'En el teatro Real' and 'Notas sociales'. *Ecran*, 16 January 1940	247

LIST OF FIGURES

13.1	Caricatures of famous Hollywoodians in the October 1936 issue of *Film-Nayes*	262
13.2	*Film-Nayes*, November 1937	267
13.3	*Film-Nayes* masthead, October 1936	268
13.4	Advertisement for 20th Century Fox. *Film-Nayes*, October 1936	269
13.5	Suggested reading direction within the 20th Century Fox advertisement	270

NOTES ON CONTRIBUTORS

Claudia Bossay is a historian working as an Assistant Professor in Film Studies at Universidad de Chile (FCEI), with a PhD in Film Studies from Queen's University Belfast, UK. Her research focuses on the study of historical film cultures in Chile, with emphasis on the different cinema house circuits, cinema-going, and mediated industrial culture. She was the lead researcher in the Salas y Butacas project (PAI79170064, CONICYT).

Joel Casey is a DPhil candidate at St Anne's College, University of Oxford. His thesis explores 'performances' of race, racial difference and racial encounter in British interwar cinema and the broader implications of this for conceptions of cinema's relationship to the body, the senses, history and heritage, and other media in British cinema culture. More generally, he is interested in representations of space, setting and architecture, and the body and senses on film.

Lisa Hood is a PhD researcher at the University of Brighton. Her interests include film history, fan magazines, star images and propaganda. She is currently undertaking AHRC-funded research examining the influence of British star images on audience behaviour during World War Two.

Tamar Jeffers McDonald is Professor of Film History, and Dean of the School of Art and Media, at the University of Brighton. A Hollywood historian, Professor Jeffers McDonald is the author of several monographs – on romantic comedy, film costume, stardom, and movie magazines – and wrote the BFI

Film Classic on *When Harry Met Sally* . . . Her next writing project traces the history and impact of the Hollywood movie magazine from 1911 to 1976.

Gillian Kelly is an independent scholar and author of *Tyrone Power: Gender, Genre and Image in Classical Hollywood Cinema* (2021). Her first book, *Robert Taylor: Male Beauty, Masculinity and Stardom in Hollywood* (2019), was shortlisted for best monograph by BAFTSS, and she has contributed to several journals as well as the edited collections *Lasting Screen Stars* (2018) *and Exploring the Spiritual in Popular Music* (2021). Her current research is on Ray Milland and Ida Lupino.

Carolyn Owen King holds a PhD in Film History from the University of Kent. Her thesis, funded by the Consortium for Humanities and Arts South East AHRC Doctoral Partnership, entitled *Haunted Mirror: British Gothic Masculinity in Transatlantic Cinema*, is an exploration of a small group of British male film stars working in Hollywood from the 1920s to the 1950s. Her interests include transatlantic stardom, Victorian Sensation literature and the Gothic aesthetic.

Rahul Kumar is a PhD student in the Film & Media Studies programme at the University of Pittsburgh. He works on the history of cinematic paratexts, especially print paratexts such as film magazines, song-booklets, press books, lobby cards, etc., and the ways in which these get associated with the cinematic text and enhance the audiences' affective engagement with it. His research also engages with questions related to archives and ethnographic media.

Lies Lanckman is a Senior Lecturer in Film at UWE Bristol. She is the co-founder of NoRMMA, the Network of Research: Movies, Magazines, Audiences, and co-editor of *Star Attractions* (2019), an edited collection on methodologies for the study of movie fan magazines of the classic era. The main focus of her research is Hollywood history of the 1920s to 1940s; particular research interests include stardom and fandom, fan magazines, issues of censorship and the career of Norma Shearer.

Cathy Lomax is a PhD candidate at Queen Mary University of London. Her research investigates the role of make-up in the creation and perpetuation of the Hollywood female star image. Publications include 'Ghostly Threads: Painting Marilyn Monroe's White Dresses', in *Film, Fashion and Consumption* (2015) and 'Makeup as Dark Magic: *The Love Witch* and the Subversive Female Gaze', in *Frames Cinema Journal* (2019). Lomax is a practising artist; she won the Contemporary British Painting Prize, 2016, and edits art and culture magazines *Arty* and *Garageland*.

María Paz Peirano is an Assistant Professor in Film and Cultural Studies at Universidad de Chile (FCEI), with a PhD in Social Anthropology from the University of Kent, UK. Her research involves an ethnographic approach to film as social practice, focusing on Chilean cinema and the development of local film cultures. She has published widely on film festivals, exhibition practices, cinemagoing and film audiences and is the co-author of 'Chilefilms, el Hollywood Criollo' (2015) and co-editor of 'Film Festivals and Anthropology' (2017). She is currently the lead researcher of 'Chilean Film Audiences: Film Culture, Cinephilia and Education' (Fondecyt 1211594).

Sarah Polley is an Honorary Fellow at the University of Kent and received her PhD from the same institution. Her primary interests of star studies, fan magazines and audiences are currently being explored in work on 1950s readers of British magazine *Picture Show* and fan magazine fiction in early *Photoplay*.

Phyll Smith researches and teaches in the Department of Film, Television and Media at the University of East Anglia. His work investigates the regulation of cinema and other media and the regulation of their audiences, through the cultural politics and archival objects that shape the narratives of cinemagoing. His work includes 'This is Where We Came In: The Economics of Unruly Audiences from Serial Houses to Grind Houses', in *Grindhouse: Cultural Exchange on 42nd Street* (2016); and (co-written with Ellen Wright) 'Coming Attractions: Tijuana Bibles and the Pornographic Reimagining of Hollywood', in *Mapping Movie Magazines* (2020).

Dominic Topp is a Teaching Fellow in Film Studies at the University of Southampton. He has previously taught at the University of Kent and the Pontifical Catholic University of Chile. His writing has been published in *Projections: The Journal for Movies and Mind* and *Significação: Revista de Cultura Audiovisual*, and in the edited collection *Mapping Movie Magazines: Digitization, Periodicals and Cinema History* (2020). His current research focuses on storytelling strategies in postwar French cinema.

Jennifer Voss is an Early Career Researcher and Archives Assistant at De Montfort University (DMU). Jennifer holds a PhD in Drama Studies and Film History, for an interdisciplinary project combining performance theory and analysis with feminist film historiography and archival research, to explore actor training and women's performances of emotion during the transition from silent to sound cinema in Britain and the US. Jennifer's PhD research was funded by the Midlands 4 Cities DTP.

Ellen Wright is a Senior Lecturer in Cinema and Television History at De Montfort University. Her research expertise is in the leisure industries, consumer culture and broader social contexts surrounding Hollywood cinema in the mid-twentieth century, focusing, in particular, upon representations of gender and sexuality in the material culture of film. She has recently written on the uses and benefits of affect when teaching in the archives in *Transformative Works and Cultures*, and has also published in *Feminist Media Histories*, *Celebrity Studies*, among many other journals.

INTRODUCTION

This edited collection focuses on movie magazines: magazines produced for movie fans from the 1910s onward. Although the first magazine of this type began in the United States, with the publication of *The Motion Picture Story Magazine* in 1911, the phenomenon soon spread around the world. This collection aims to emulate this diversity by bringing together scholars working in a broad range of disciplinary and international contexts, and above all, in joining film history and magazine history, fields which cover similar ground but have nonetheless largely operated in separate spheres before now.

While work on movie magazines is still relatively rare, even rarer is that which focuses on the magazine as an object of material history. Most articles and full-length monographs that examine these colourful and fascinating publications are content to quote from isolated articles, rather than studying items in their full printed contexts. Yet, we contend, the full meaning of any article, editorial, photograph, reader's letter or advertisement can only be grasped when considered in situ: the juxtaposition of these different contents inevitably impacts on their meaning.

Our volume, then, builds upon previous work, but adds a greater emphasis to the visual rather than textual aspects of the magazine. A few scholars have previously addressed design in fan magazines[1] but our edited collection's core focus on the visual aspects of these magazines – one of their key pleasures for contemporaneous and contemporary readers alike – both underlines the importance of studying the fan magazine holistically and provides new and detailed examples of the various ways in which design was employed to engender desire. For these movie magazines use the whole of the designer's toolkit to seduce the reader: with text, they made use of font choice, size and colour, as well as varieties of all of these; with illustration, they engaged line drawings, photos, colour and black-and-white to create interest. Wrapped around the contents, the front and back covers stirred excitement and longing, with their usual combination of glamorous star on the front and full-colour advertisement on the back. And throughout these publications, clustered in the first few pages, accumulated in the rear ones, and interspersed throughout, advertisements invoked yearning and aspiration.

While fan magazines and their *visual* contents are thus at the heart of every chapter, each differs in its specific point of focus. The chapters comprising Part One each investigate a different single issue, variously revealing how the fan magazine could be a conduit for both nationalist and racist ideologies, and gender assumptions, the latter especially significant given the supposed largely female readership of fan magazines. Each chapter also studies specific actors, underlining the crucial role the fan magazines played in raising a performer to the status of a star. This theme is further picked up in Part Two, which analyses regular magazine content. The chapters here examine both specific recurrent items, and the ways in which these items helped shape and promote the personae of particular movie stars. In Part Three the focus is on media inflecting and closely related to the movie magazine, taking in trade publications, newspapers and fan club newsletters, and here, as throughout the volume, scholars present differing national contexts and case studies as well as varied methodologies for future researchers. While some chapters propose new methodological avenues to be explored, particularly in terms of the reading audiences – who they were and how they used these magazines to convey their own views and opinions – others introduce readers to the ways in which fan magazines functioned in international contexts, beyond Britain and America.

Desire and Design in the Movie Magazine

As described above, the movie magazine was a device intended to create desire, for information on or images of a star or a new movie, as well as information and images about products that could, it was claimed, render the reader-viewer-fan into a better version of themselves, and thus one who might have a shot at movie stardom. As both historians and devotees of the pleasures the movie magazine can provide, we are surprised at how relatively overlooked they have been by scholars, since they are clearly an adjunct medium of cinema. The magazine, for all its shared contents with the film, was in several ways almost its opposite: where movies moved, the magazine was inevitably still, yet those moving images were fleeting, while the magazine's pictures endured – at least until the next issue. True fans, therefore, needed both movie and movie magazine in order to worship their idols fully.

It is useful to examine an example of the ways in which movie magazines could generate desire to see a star vehicle and, in turn, benefit from that star's popularity themselves. The pre-Code film *As You Desire Me* (Fitzmaurice 1932) serves this purpose neatly, although many other films could have been chosen as an apt illustration.

In this MGM film, Swedish–US star Greta Garbo plays a woman struggling with her identity; she finds herself caught between two personae, each predicated on a different type of femininity as desired by a different man. As 'Zara', Garbo plays a fatalistic entertainer, drinking and flirting with male admirers, yet cohabiting with cynical author Carl Salter (Erich Von Stroheim). It is, however, soon revealed that she may be suffering from amnesia and could previously have been the demure 'Maria', faithful wife of Count Bruno Varelli (Melvyn Douglas). After various plot exigencies, Garbo's character – whoever she is – vows to Varelli that she will be 'as *you* desire me'.

The narrative of this Garbo vehicle is startlingly self-reflexive, seemingly commenting on the variety of images a performer needs to cultivate to maintain fame and success, and, perhaps especially, how significant it is for female stars to cultivate desirable personae, regardless of who they 'really' are. Garbo was the perfect star to embody this concept contemporaneously, as she was one of the top female stars at the box office during this period.[2] Certainly, editorial teams within the movie magazines seem to have believed she could sell their product: in the year *As You Desire Me* was released, 1932, Garbo appeared on the cover of nine movie magazines and had her name featured on covers a further twenty-three times.[3]

As a further illustration of her contemporary power, we can look briefly at the extraordinary lengths gone to by the editorial team of one movie magazine issue, *Movie Mirror*, to promote Garbo and the film. The film was premiered in May 1932, and thus, given inevitable publication lead-times, August issues of magazines would have been being compiled while the release publicity was freshly available and ready to be disseminated. As well as including eleven photographs of Garbo, this issue of *Movie Mirror* mentions the star no fewer than thirty-two times. These mentions include most obviously a novelisation of *As You Desire Me* which covers nine separate pages, arranged as three double-page spreads in the middle of the issue, and three single pages dispersed, as is usual with follow-on content, to the back of the magazine, including the finale of the story which takes up the entire back page. In addition, Garbo is referenced in pieces on other stars with whom she has had a connection, as in the story on attempts to find true love by John Gilbert, the fiancé she famously jilted, but also where she has no connection, as in the items on fellow actors Robert Montgomery (33) and Ann Harding (84) and, repeatedly, as a point of comparison for Joan Crawford in an essay on the latter (18, 102). In addition, she is mentioned briefly in a 'Hot News' gossip piece (9), extensively in an article on 'How Sex Appeal is Manufactured in Hollywood' (20–1, 23) and fleetingly in 'Who's Getting The Fan Mail Now?' (67), as well as in several letters from readers.

Significantly, then, Garbo's name, first featured in the Table of Contents (4), is carried through the magazine right to the last page, and attains particular prominence, after the three double-pages of novelisation, when one of the continuation pages for that is situated opposite another for the Gilbert article. The whole issue, then, seems to be enlisted to promote Garbo – and this is true despite the fact that she is not on the cover.

In this issue, the editorial team seems to have counted on Garbo being an object of desire for readers, moviegoers and fans. And from at least November that same year, Garboesque desirability was also seemingly available for magazine readers to possess themselves. An advertisement for Palmolive soap appeared in the November 1932 issues of *Motion Picture* (61) and *Movie Classic* (53) as well as in bestselling women's magazine *Ladies Home Journal* (54).

The most prominent text on the page is the bold and capitalised **AS YOU DESIRE ME** which appears at the top left. To its right is a large illustration of a woman pictured from behind. She is seated in front of a mirror and dressed in a flowing sheer gown and slippers. We do not see the woman's face in this advertisement,[4] even in reflection, but her outfit and hairstyle resemble those of Garbo in the scenes from *As You Desire Me* when she is being sweet Maria (only the team behind *Silver Screen* in July that year was brave enough to reproduce an image of Garbo in the silver wig she wore as Zara).

While such magazines were not exclusively read by women, the seemingly handwritten exhortation, 'Keep that Schoolgirl Complexion', suggests that the advertiser was targeting female consumers. Examination of the smaller typed text in the advertisement reveals more detail as to *how* it functions. Using direct address, it urges the reader 'Right now – touch your own skin with your finger tips' and then reflect 'Is it quite as you desire it?' Furthermore, it connects desire to be attractive to the way one is viewed: 'Then think! How can you make it desirable to others?' Luckily, after posing these questions, the advertisement offers a solution: a cake of Palmolive soap. This 'will give your skin that charm – that something that makes you – keeps you desirable'. This points to some of the complexities of the way fan magazine advertisements drew on stars to engender desire. But the Palmolive promotion uses tactile self-assessment along with desire structured around identification with the illustrated figure as an ideal self – a slim white woman who is able to afford nice clothes – whom the reader can become through buying the product.

This analysis of *Movie Mirror*'s commitment to marketing Garbo and *As You Desire Me* stands as an example of the importance of desire to the movie magazines, and how design could be mobilised to create it. Reading across

Figure I.1 Advertisement for Palmolive soap. *Motion Picture*, November 1932. (p. 61)

the magazine and thus equating all contents as providing equal occasions for promoting the campaign, rather than prioritising editorial text, this short case study exemplifies methods used throughout this book, as contributors insist on the importance of design elements in magazines' projects of fashioning desire.

Contents of this Volume

In terms of the design of this collection itself, we have chosen to divide its contents into three parts, which deal, in turn, with single issues of fan magazines, recurrent and regular features present across a range of these magazines, and related publications.

In Part One, contributors each deal with one single fan magazine issue, to permit detailed examinations of these magazines and their societal context. In the opening chapter, Joel Casey examines a 1921 art supplement included with British fan magazine *Picture Show*, which had at its centre stars Lillian Gish and Richard Barthelmess in the US film *Way Down East* (Griffith 1920). Considering this alongside other parts of the magazine which literally touch on these middle pages and comment on cinematic relationships across the East/West divide, Casey connects this image to the stars' earlier film *Broken Blossoms* (Griffith 1919), which featured their characters in an interracial relationship. In doing so, he situates this image within the context of British anxiety about Americanisation and race in the 1920s. Britain's concern with Americanisation is also seen nearly two decades later, as Carolyn Owen King reveals it at work in a 1940 issue of *Picture Show*'s main rival, *Picturegoer*. Delving into matters of structure, gendered address and representation of national identity, important particularly in the context of this early stage of the Second World War, Owen King uncovers some material that supports common assumptions about wartime models of desirable and acceptable forms of femininity and masculinity, but also, importantly, identifies the presence of less conventional forms of desire.

The other two chapters in this section concentrate on dominant US fan magazine *Photoplay* and its representation of particular stars. Here, both Lisa Hood and Cathy Lomax, who each provide a close examination of one 1955 issue of this magazine, usefully engage particularly with Sumiko Higashi's work on the magazine in this decade (see also Polley in this volume). Firstly, Hood investigates the representation in her chosen issue of US star Victor Mature, primarily focusing on one article which asks whether his career is on the wane. By closely analysing the article's design – including the presentation of its images and text, but also its placement within the whole magazine – Hood not only demonstrates how Mature was downgraded by the magazine in comparison to other male stars in the issue, such as Marlon Brando and Rock Hudson, but also emphasises how vital it is to read star pieces in their full context.

While Hood covers questions of de-emphasis, Lomax focuses on issues of exclusion, as she considers black US star Dorothy Dandridge's almost complete absence in the pages of *Photoplay*, in contrast to her frequent presence in mainstream non-fan magazines at this time. Here, Lomax posits that the fan magazine editorial team's dedication to maintaining the political status quo can help explain both Dandridge's invisibility and the abundance of articles on white, and often blonde, stars framed as objects of sexual desire and fan identification, as demonstrated also in product advertisements within the magazine.

Part Two, which deals with recurrent and regular features in movie magazines, begins, aptly, with Gillian Kelly's chapter on the aspect intended to provoke the casual customer at the newsstand to purchase the fan magazine: the cover. Focusing on US male star Tyrone Power, Kelly uses an investigation of a series of international covers published across Power's career to comment on the star's presence across time and place, considering design detail to examine his representation of masculinity at a time when most fan magazines were graced by a cover girl. Moving on to the inner pages of the fan magazine, Sarah Polley focuses on several magazines from late 1955; her approach to these is inspired by Sally Stein's 'exploding' of women's magazines to examine 'the graphic ordering of desire' via the magazines' distribution of editorial material and advertisements. Using this methodology, Polley comments on fan magazine definition as she considers which regular features appear in each title, and examines reading strategies as she analyses how readers are led, through the dispersal of editorial features within the magazine, towards advertising material.

Next, Dominic Topp's chapter addresses the *roman en images*, or illustrated serial feature, *The Passion of Dora* which ran for fifteen issues of the weekly French fan magazine *Ciné-Miroir* in mid-1948. Topp argues that the magazine's story of a fictional starlet and her efforts in working on her very first film not only offered its readers an interesting and inventively presented narrative, but also provided them with information about the postwar French film industry and its promotional methods. In this way, it expanded their knowledge and made them into more expert film viewers, but also fan magazine readers. Closing this section, Tamar Jeffers McDonald examines a contest which ran in the December 1933 and January 1934 issues of US fan magazine *Modern Screen*. Here, readers were invited to cut out and piece together cut-up images of scenes from Joan Crawford's latest film, *Dancing Lady* (Leonard 1933). Placing the competition in its industry context, at a time of fervent debate about the need for narrative and aesthetic restrictions, Jeffers McDonald reveals how the seemingly frothy publication used an ostensibly lighthearted competition to comment on wider political concerns.

The final part of the collection deals with publications related to fan magazines and, through this joint consideration, affords insights into the specificities of both. First, Rahul Kumar's chapter considers trade publicity for the film *The Invisible Man* (Whale 1933). Kumar comments that the need to make invisibility visible in relation to this film was a particular challenge for an industry which often has at its heart sexual desire and/or a focus on ego ideals (see also Jeffers McDonald in this volume). Kumar therefore argues that the advertising strategies used in the context of this film can be best understood in terms of Jeffrey Cohen's formulation of the figure of the monster as one who simultaneously prompts fear and desire. Next, Jennifer Voss draws on a claim by silent US film star Colleen Moore that as an aspiring actress, she consulted fan magazines to learn acting techniques; here, Voss takes a performance studies perspective to trace fan magazines as important sites for actor training. While *Picture Show*'s 1920s coverage frequently included studio portraits of stars (see also Casey), Voss focuses on an important recurring feature which specifically pictured stars performing poses. In this way, she considers the specificities of fan magazines as sources which promoted both the chance of learning acting through their pages and the downplaying of talent in surrounding star discourse.

Relatedly, Ellen Wright and Phyll Smith consider 1940s British fan club magazines in the context of invisible star and fan labour. Though present only in rare archive collections today, these publications help shed light on the variety of ways in which fans engaged with stars in a specific wartime and postwar context. Wright and Smith argue that these publications' simple design (unlike British fan magazines at this time – see also Owen King in this volume) underlined both the manual 'labour of love' and allowed the readers to feel closer to their favourite stars in a less heavily mediated context, reminiscent of social media publicity today. Focusing on this same time period of the 1940s, María Paz Peirano and Claudia Bossay's chapter concerns the Chilean film magazine *Ecran*, and uses this in attempting to create a social history of filmgoing in this non-Anglophone national context. Here, they explore the ways in which the tensions between imagined and real audiences became apparent within the pages of *Ecran*, with messaging about ideal audiences covered in items such as advertisements, but complicated by references to real audiences – and their class identities – elsewhere in the magazine.

Finally, Lies Lanckman analyses the monthly Yiddish-language film magazine *Film-Nayes*, which was published in Poland between 1936 and 1938. By investigating particularly the representation of Hollywood film and its stars in this magazine, Lanckman demonstrates the ways in which both content and design of the publication reflect the particular, in-between space which its editor and readers occupied within their society, both as Europeans interested in Hollywood film and also, crucially, as Yiddish-speaking Jews living in Poland on the eve of the Holocaust. In this way, she demonstrates how historical fan magazines can be useful in expanding our knowledge about this now-vanished film audience.

While contributors spotlight different aspects of desire, across varied publications in time and space, these chapters also function together, opening the magazine page and inviting a deeper understanding of stars, fans and magazines.

Notes

1. See Cowan (2015) on cinephilic puzzles in Europe in the 1920s, Juan (2020) on images of fans in interwar French fan magazines, Keating (2017) on glamour photography, and Higashi (2014) on *Photoplay* in the 1950s.
2. See <https://en.wikipedia.org/wiki/Top_Ten_Money_Making_Stars_Poll> (last accessed 18 November 2022).
3. Garbo covers on sale in North America that year include: *Cine Mundial* (September), *Cinelandia* (March), *Motion Picture* (January), *Photoplay* (January), *Screen Book* (February), *Screen Play* (May), *Screen Romances* (June), *Screenland* (June) and *Silver Screen* (July). In addition to having her name featured on these magazines, as with for example *Motion Picture*'s January cover ('You've been wrong about Garbo . . . she *has* a sense of humor!'), the star's name was also used as a lure for *Hollywood*, *Modern Screen*, *Movie Classic* and *New Movie*.
4. While the November advertisement for Palmolive interestingly did not show the woman's face – permitting the reader to insert herself into the pictured micro-narrative and fostering the fantasy that it could be her own reflection – other iterations of the advert, though they retained the movie tagline and glamorous outfits reminiscent of Garbo's, did make the featured woman's face visible. Her features conform to contemporaneous beauty standards, but do not particularly evoke Garbo; in all, artist Bradshaw Crandell seems to have completed a series of six advertisements using similar text and images.

References

Cowan, Michael. 2015. 'Learning to Love the Movies: Puzzles, Participation and Cinephilia in Interwar European Movie Magazines'. *Film History* 27 (4): 1–45.

Higashi, Sumiko. 2014. *Stars, Fans, and Consumption in the 1950s: Reading Photoplay*. New York: Palgrave Macmillan.

Juan, Myriam. 2020. 'Looking at Movie Fans: On Pictures Published in French Film Magazines of the Interwar Years'. In *Mapping Movie Magazines: Digitization, Periodicals and Cinema History*, edited by Daniel Biltereyst and Lies van de Vijver, 201–20. Cham, Switzerland: Palgrave Macmillan.

Keating, Patrick. 2017. 'Artifice and Atmosphere: The Visual Culture of Hollywood Glamour Photography, 1930–1935'. *Film History* 29 (3): 105–35.

Service, Faith, 1932. 'How Sex Appeal is Manufactured in Hollywood'. *Movie Mirror*, August: 20–21, 23.

PART ONE

SINGLE MAGAZINE ISSUES

PART ONE INTRODUCTION

Scrutinising one issue of a fan magazine, while especially paying attention to design and desire, is admittedly specific. While studies of single films continue to be produced and provide useful insights (including Jeffers McDonald 2017), fan magazine scholars generally do not examine a single fan magazine issue. For example, considerations of particular fan magazine titles – such as Sumiko Higashi on early, and 1950s, *Photoplay* (2017 and 2014, respectively), Jane Bryan and Mark Glancy on *Picturegoer* during both World Wars (both 2011) – cover several issues of these publications. The relatively recent increased access to multiple issues of various digitised fan magazine titles might be presumed to encourage a broader rather than narrower focus. However, the intense single-issue spotlight allows for the truisms which persist about fan magazines to be investigated more effectively. Such detail is sometimes seen in the analysis of discrete fan magazine articles in studies of individual stars. While these may be positioned in the context of coverage about the star appearing in other magazine issues, Tamar Jeffers McDonald's 2013 study of Doris Day also explores how readers are led through single magazine issues by mentions of the star (41). Jeffers McDonald cites Sally Stein's and Ellen McCracken's comments on the structure of women's magazine issues. According to Stein, 'the interruption of articles' causes a reader's attention to spill across the issue and is an 'inconvenient occurrence' (Stein 1992, 149), while for McCracken this delay in completing reading an article is pleasurable (McCracken 1993, 8). Regardless of its emotional effect, Jeffers McDonald resolves that '[t]he placing of an article or picture within a magazine therefore proves to be as potentially significant as what is being said or portrayed' (2013, 42).

Although article placement in an issue is important, there is a variety of ways in which one fan magazine issue can be approached. In addition to intense focus on an article (and its location in a magazine), overall tone, matters of race, gender, stardom, advertising, and so on can be studied. Periodical scholars Robert Scholes and Clifford Wulfman (2010) advocate examining a single issue of a magazine to determine the magazine's implied reader, contents and format. Building up a picture of an implied reader necessitates looking at the magazine issue as a whole and predicting likely characteristics of those at whom the content is aimed by age, sex, economic and intellectual class, race and political position (2010, 146–7). In terms of contents, it is advised that we discern which type occurs most frequently, as well as the ratio of advertising to other forms of text, and what kind of advertising is the most plentiful (2010, 147–8). At a more specific level, format encompasses magazine size and shape and a magazine's employment of visual material – the number of images per page, whether these are photographic or drawn, and if and how colour is used (2010, 148). Scholes and Wulfman also connect visual material to article placement. They suggest that we should note whether this appears as a standalone element or as part of articles and stories (2010, 148). Scholes and Wulfman additionally recommend looking at magazines in terms of circulation, regular contributors, editor and history (2010, 146–8).

The chapters in this opening section therefore focus on single specific issues of various magazines, British and American: Casey investigates the haptic element of design in his examination of an art insert from British fan magazine *Picture Show*'s 26 March issue from 1921; Owen King analyses the different treatment meted out to male and female, and British and American, stars in the British *Picturegoer* of 2 March 1940, finding various forms of contestation around gender, nation and notions of glamour and patriotism. Diverting from the usual attention paid to white female stars, Hood and Lomax, in their individual chapters looking at two successive issues of the American magazine *Photoplay* from 1955, prioritise instead male stars, and the black star Dorothy Dandridge.

Notwithstanding their primarily single-issue focus, writers in this section can contextualise their chapters with one another (for example Hood and Lomax) as well as other academic work (most notably Higashi on 1950s *Photoplay*). Furthermore, contributors' detailed analyses can be pieced together to build a more accurate picture of specific fan magazine titles and to challenge general critical assumptions about fan magazines, and their readers.

References

Bryan, Jane. 2011. '"Shells, Shots and Shrapnel": *Picturegoer* Goes to War'. In *British Silent Cinema and the Great War*, edited by Michael Hammond and Michael Williams, 64–76. London: Palgrave Macmillan.

Glancy, Mark. 2011. '*Picturegoer*: The Fan Magazine and Popular Film Culture in Britain During the Second World War'. *Historical Journal of Film, Radio and Television* 31 (4): 453–78.

Higashi, Sumiko. 2014. *Stars, Fans, and Consumption in the 1950s: Reading Photoplay*. New York: Palgrave Macmillan.

Higashi, Sumiko. 2017. 'Adapting Middlebrow Taste to Sell Stars, Romance, and Consumption: Early Photoplay'. *Feminist Media Histories* 3 (4): 126–61.

Jeffers McDonald, Tamar. 2013. *Doris Day Confidential: Hollywood, Sex and Stardom*. London: I. B. Tauris.

Jeffers McDonald, Tamar. 2017. *When Harry Met Sally . . .* London: BFI.

McCracken, Ellen. 1993. *Decoding Women's Magazines: From Mademoiselle to Ms*. London: Palgrave.

Scholes, Robert, and Clifford Wulfman. 2010. *Modernism in the Magazines: An Introduction*. New Haven, CT and London: Yale University Press.

Stein, Sally. 1992. 'The Graphic Ordering of Desire: Modernization of a Middle-Class Women's Magazine, 1914–1939'. In *The Contest of Meaning, Critical Histories of Photography*, edited by Richard Bolton, 145–61. Cambridge, MA: MIT Press.

1. NEVER THE TWAIN SHALL MEET: TOUCH, DOUBLE-SIDEDNESS AND RACE IN THE PAGES OF *PICTURE SHOW*

Joel Casey

Fan magazine scholarship has become more concerned in recent years with interactivity: the nebulous issue of what readers actually *do* with their magazines. Marsha Orgeron (2009) proposes that thinking about interactivity allows us to look beyond commercial paradigms and explore how fan magazines enabled readers to see themselves as engaged participants and critics. Letters pages in particular have become a means of exploring how these magazines facilitated community building and the creation of codes of behaviour for these communities (Orgeron 2009; Stead 2011; Lanckman 2020). The ways in which magazine readers interacted with publications and, through these, with broader cultures of fandom and cinema have become central to scholarship on the form.

This chapter takes a more close-up view on issues of interactivity by moving beyond textual evidence like the fan letter or competition to think about how magazine design invites material, *tactile* interaction. Sally Stein's important early article on design in women's magazines acknowledges the tangibility of such publications, the way their very non-linear layout and design means that 'we not only will the process to continue by physically turning the pages [. . .] but that we "freely" negotiate a "personal" path through the magazine labyrinth' (1985, 7). More recently, Orgeron suggests that correspondence, competitions and discourses of self-improvement in the fan magazine 'operate within the same framework of empowerment, providing a very tangible, attainable mode of participation for the otherwise potentially disconnected fan' (2009, 9). She concludes by asserting that

> making fans believe that what they said and did mattered was a necessary precondition for a marketplace in which the primary products were as intangible as the movies and the stars who populated them. (2009, 19)

Fan magazines traded on tangibility. Making film performers and film worlds meaningful involved making them material, even touchable, on the magazine page. Yet while scholars have explored in depth the tactile, haptic and intimate possibilities of film spectatorship (Marks 2000; Bruno 2007; Barker 2009), this has not incorporated elements of film and fan culture beyond the film text itself. I therefore argue for the need for close analysis of magazine design and its role in making cinema tangible.

Accordingly, I concentrate on a specific magazine issue to get 'closer' to the question of interactivity: the 26 March 1921 issue of the British fan magazine, *Picture Show*. This allows for close analysis of the features of magazine design that invite tactile engagement and acknowledges the fact that representations and experiences of touch are culturally and historically determined. By analysing a single issue, in fact a single, central 'art supplement' (11–14), I explore the significance of touch to fan magazine and cinema culture in 1920s Britain. Often, questions of interactivity have centred on the American fan magazine. Yet Lisa Stead has argued that British magazines provided British women with an interactive 'platform to express their interpretation of their nationally specific cinematic encounters' and broader issues of femininity and 'restraint' in public space (2011, paragraph 1.1). Restraint is central to thinking about 1920s fan magazine tactility. Stead utilises Christine Gledhill's and Jon Burrows' arguments that 'restraint' or 'reserve' represent a national performance style for 1910s and 1920s British cinema, informed by the influence of theatrical performance practices (Burrows 2003, 28–34; Gledhill 2003, 62–71). Stead's application of this performance style to the conduct of stars and readers interacting with fan magazines reveals its relevance more generally to British cinema culture; certainly, Annette Kuhn (1988) and Lise Shapiro Sanders (2002) demonstrate the ways in which censorship and policing of theatre spaces centred on anxieties about women's respectability and 'restraint'. For Stead, fan magazines provided space for women to explore female stars as emblems of modern femininity, caught between traditional codes of restraint and glamorous, public urban mobility and self-fashioning and self-display (Stead 2011, paragraphs 10.1–11.5). Stead sees the disembodied, dematerialised nature of fan magazine interaction as part of its appeal, offering an alternative to an actual theatre space associated with illicit sexual encounters and uniting women across the country virtually (2011, paragraphs 7.3–7.5). Yet analysing the film magazine as text, as merely a space for letters and photographs, neglects its material role as a physical object designed to be held, and the role of touch in British cinema culture's discourses of restraint.

For Gledhill, restraint is tied to a British cinema 'aesthetic of social decorum and distance between persons' (2003, 19). The geography of the screen separated actors to underline purportedly unchangeable social stratifications. This was reinforced by performed restraint, a denial of 'feeling' that was *sensory* as much as emotional in articulating physical and social distance between performers. Gledhill explores moments of transgressive border crossing in British cinema but argues that the catalysts for this transgression must ultimately be contained and the spatial distinction reasserted (2003, 25–8). Moments of contact between separated groups must not last long. Following Stead's lead in applying Gledhill's and Burrows' work on film texts to fan magazine culture, I suggest that restraint and performed 'decorum and distance' are tied to the very design of fan magazines as objects to be held and thumbed through. Attempting to excavate the actual practices of magazine readers from one hundred years ago inevitably involves speculation. However, close analysis of design and contextualisation within British cinema culture opens avenues to think about how readers may have reflected on the editorial choices of such publications, and how they might have touched, held, folded, crumpled or torn them, as well as read them as texts.

Another recent wave of scholarship on interwar British cinema culture has revealed its inextricability from British *imperial* culture (for example, Stollery 2000, 2011; Jaikumar 2006; Grieveson and MacCabe 2011; Burns 2013; Cinquegrani 2014). The *Picture Show* issue I discuss raises question of racial difference alongside sexuality and contact. Scholars have demonstrated that sexuality and desire are intertwined with boundaries of race and gender that construct colonial space and identity (McClintock 1995; Nagel 2003; Levine 2006; Stoler 2010). Philippa Levine writes that

> [a]ssumptions about the nature and uncouthness of colonial sexualities – always too much, always, potentially, if not actually, out of control – threatened the border between respectability and looseness, between Britain and its subject peoples. (2006, 138)

Ann Laura Stoler develops this thesis to delineate the ways in which policing of sexuality underpinned colonial lawmaking and rule, such that intimacy and touch, or the prohibition of touch, are fundamental to colonial constructions of space and racial difference (2010). Policing of space, identity and intimacy resonates with Gledhill's work on British cinema, suggesting the racial underpinnings of these aesthetics. 'Restraint' is constructed as a white quality in opposition to the racialised unrestraint of colonised or non-white subjects, who reach dangerously and transgressively across colonial and gendered boundaries and divisions. In a British culture defined by its Empire and its racial and geographical distinctions, the 'mapping' of film performers, spectators and fans, on screen and in print, is necessarily informed by Empire and race. The way in which the page is 'mapped' out, permitting or disavowing contact, is fundamentally informed by the mapping of colonial geographies and colonial subjects.

The art supplement on which this chapter focuses contains a large, double-page spread of Lillian Gish and Richard Barthelmess in *Way Down East* (Griffith 1920). The back page is a photo article, entitled 'East and West in Screenland', showing various stills depicting interactions between white and East, South or West Asian characters. I argue that the presence of this photo article *behind* Richard Barthelmess, on the back page of this supplement, creates an important association for knowing fan magazine readers. In March 1921, British filmgoers would not have seen *Way Down East*, which did not premiere in Britain until Monday 5 September that year. They may well have seen, however, and likely would have read about, *Broken Blossoms* (Griffith 1919), Gish and Barthelmess's previous collaboration with D. W. Griffith. This film, set in London's Limehouse district, saw Barthelmess as Cheng Huan, a Chinese migrant to London in love with Gish's white Limehouse waif, Lucy. Even as *Broken Blossoms* is not included on the back page, it is evoked *between* these two pages, representing the meeting of Barthelmess and Gish, East and West. Thus, between the pages, the possibility for interracial eroticism is evoked, even as it is 'officially' contained by the text of the supplement. The design of the supplement conceals the possibility for sexual intimacy and transgression, even as it maps a colonial geography of separation.

I argue, then, that double-sidedness is a crucial feature of fan magazine design. It literally and metaphorically enables multiple readings, perspectives, feelings and ambivalence; it conceals or disguises for the knowing fan magazine reader, and, most importantly, it requires the physical interaction of the reader to activate these differing or disguised perspectives, creating networks between the representation of touch in the magazine and the literal touching of the reader. I begin with a more general exploration of practices of representing touch and inviting touch in *Picture Show*'s art supplements to illuminate the connections between the reader's touch and the intimacy depicted on the page, before closely analysing the 26 March supplement. I then move outwards from *Picture Show* to contextualise this issue within broader critiques of Hollywood cinema's depiction of racial difference and interracial relationships to demonstrate that, while *Picture Show* purports to support these censorious attitudes, the knowing reader was granted the opportunity to *feel* an alternative viewpoint within the double-sidedness of the art supplement page.

Double-sidedness, Desire and Decorum: Representing Touch in *Picture Show*

Picture Show invites interaction as a tangible, tactile object. A pull-out at the centre of the magazine, the art supplement interrupts photographs on the pages either side of it which literally could not be seen without pulling it out. Once removed, the reader can examine this as a separate object and perhaps pin it on the wall if a favourite star is represented, choosing between these photographs and always aware of what is contained on the back of each of them. A weekly column, 'Famous Readers of the "Picture Show"', depicted stars posing with the magazine to emphasise it as something to be held and seen with, and to create a kind of mediated contact with the star through holding the same object. Gledhill and Mark Glancy suggest that stars undermine social boundaries and hierarchies that structure British cinema's aesthetic of social decorum and distance (2003, 82; 2006, 473); these moments which foreground shared touching frame the page itself as a kind of paper-thin boundary that *connects* reader and star, transcending geographical and social distances. This usage of the magazine as a kind of medium connecting and interposing between reader and star recalls Marshall McLuhan's conception of media as prostheses, extensions of our bodies and perception (1964, 6) which, Paul Rodaway argues, include the extension of touch beyond 'the immediate geography of the body' (1994, 53). If correspondence offered a more metaphorical means of 'getting in touch' with the stars, forming communities and interacting with cinema culture to render it tangible, invitations to touch the magazine and picture other readers doing the same facilitated the *sensing* of this community too.

Picture Show invites contact with the magazine and thus virtually with other readers and stars. Its representation of touching in art supplements maintains this concern with the tactile, but also places limits on it, allowing for ambivalent readings of the magazine as both inviting and censoring contact. The middle section is a two-page spread: a publicity still or series of photographs advertising a film. Front and back pages are usually either a star portrait or photo collages on a theme, as with 'East and West in Screenland'. These collages often focus on pairings of male and female stars under headings like 'Flirting on the Film' (8 May 1920), 'The Love Token' (5 June 1920) or 'Flirting with a Parasol' (24 July 1920). The latter two interpose objects between the romantic couple. 'Flirting with a Parasol' depicts five images in which women holding parasols are courted by men. In four of these, the woman looks away and in one, Vivian Martin gazes into Harrison Ford's eyes. Yet the parasol, precluding complete embrace, unites these images of 'flirting'. It functions as a barrier protecting women from men, but also as a tool to 'flirt' with and thus invite sexual contact. One month later, the supplement back page portrays 'The Flower and the Flirt' (28 August 1920) (Figure 1.1), another object interposed

Figure 1.1　Art Supplement, 'The Flower and the Flirt'. *Picture Show*, 28 August 1920. (p. 14)

between bodies to defer the consummation of the relationship and grant women agency through 'flirting'. These images emphasise the reversal of gender roles even further, portraying women not as 'coy' and retiring as the parasol collage does, but as 'teasing', 'coquetting', 'adamant'; they lean forward, using the flowers not as a form of defence but as a kind of extension of touch, a way of reaching across to men without risk of sexual impropriety. The top and bottom landscape images that stretch across the page emphasise this especially: at the top, Gloria Swanson's absurdly long delphinium reaches over to Raymond Hatton who smiles as he holds up his paper in defence, doubling the interposing objects and drawing attention to the role of print publications as one such object, both reaching across the divide and protecting and separating bodies. The centre spread of this issue depicts a portrait of Norma Talmadge, jutting her chin forwards and staring, unusually, directly at the camera. The tilt of her chin and her direct gaze point to the viewer, as if the flowers on the back page are now pointed towards them, as if the star reaches out to the reader rather than her co-star. This focus on mediated contact on the back page underpins, literally and metaphorically, the way in which the reader perceives the main portrait, and both are informed by the literal role of touch in turning the page between them. The representation of touching directly addresses the reader, too, cementing the magazine as mediating presence facilitating physical contact with cinema even as it implies a kind of correct, restrained distance through these mediating objects.

While many supplements depict a single star in a portrait photograph, others around this time use landscape images of couples, as with Gish and Barthelmess in *Way Down East*. Here, the page fold becomes a kind of mediation itself, matching those within the image. In the 6 November 1920 issue, the centre spread depicts William Farnum and Louise Lovely looking down at a photograph of Lovely (12–13). She holds his watch and Farnum holds the photograph, even as they lean into each other. Their mediated intimacy is reinforced by the fold, framing each figure on a separate page. Again, touch is foregrounded even as it is forestalled. In *Picture Show*, the film still delays sexual or romantic consummation, holding protagonists at a distance while inviting the reader to imagine the moment of eventual touch and intimacy. Furthermore, though, it invites readers to *enact* this touch. If Farnum and Lovely sit on opposite pages, frozen in a moment of respectably distanced contact, the magazine permits readers to refold this image, bringing the two into an unseeable embrace or kiss; as Stein argues, turning the page makes narrative from the magazine's collage (1985, 7). This becomes a tactile act, physically engaging with the page and imaginatively enabling romantic, even sexual, touch between stars. Readers can choose how to understand these art supplements, whether they are models for correct, respectable romantic courtship and contact or opportunities to envisage and enact something less restrained and decorous. The magazine's tangible pages, their double-sidedness, evoke and conceal. In line with Gledhill's reading of British cinema's aesthetics of decorum and restraint, the page becomes a separating boundary, yet *as* a boundary, it inevitably invites transgression. It is both a separator and a connective medium, an interposing object or a point of contact, a prosthesis, depending on how the reader interacts with it.

Contact and Concealment in the 26 March 1921 *Picture Show* Art Supplement

The above describes the context in which *Picture Show* readers would have examined, folded, pulled out and pinned up the art supplement from 26 March 1921. As well as inviting readers to touch and imagine contact with and between film stars, this issue introduces racial difference into these illicit intimacies. The presence of a photo collage explicitly about interracial relationships interposes race itself as another social boundary between the film couple to be policed or transgressed. Moreover, this bleeds into the previous centre spread. As Steve Garner explains, whiteness is a 'relational' identity, existing 'only in so far as other racialised identities, such as blackness, Asianness, etc., exist' (2007, 2). This is made tangible in the art supplement as the image of the rural couple of *Way Down East*, depicting ideal, idyllic whiteness, is literally backed by images of racial difference that highlight the couple's whiteness. Richard Dyer has argued that Lillian Gish epitomises connections between stardom, shining light and whiteness in Western cinema (1993). Yet the explicit acknowledgement of this 'behind' her and Barthelmess both draws attention to their whiteness and complicates these connections by recalling their previous collaboration on *Broken Blossoms*.

'East and West in Screenland' (Figure 1.2) depicts interactions between men and women, including famous Japanese actors Sessue Hayakawa and Tsuru Aoki, and white actors made up to perform racist stereotypes. All depict typical frozen images of near-contact, apart from where the white Jack Holt holds Aoki's hand as she looks away. Four of the six stills imply some kind of illicit, dangerous, violent or potentially non-consensual sexual interactions. One man looks down as he literally stretches his arms out towards a terrified Dorothy Dalton. The gazes of the other men upon white women are haptic; we are supposed to imagine their desire to touch, ensnare, or sexually exploit or assault these white women, drawing upon contemporary Hollywood trends for such racist Orientalist narratives in films like *The Sheik* (Melford 1921). This is glossed with a quotation from Rudyard Kipling's poem 'The Ballad of East and West' ([1889] 2006). However, only the first line is quoted: 'Oh East is East and West is West and never the twain shall meet'. This ignores the couplet that follows, declaring 'there is neither East nor West, Border, nor Breed, nor Birth, /

Figure 1.2   Art Supplement, 'East and West in Screenland'. *Picture Show*, 26 March 1921. (p. 14)

When two strong men stand face to face, though they come from the ends of the earth'. The idea that racial and geographical distance might be overcome is omitted from the *Picture Show* article. Instead, the first line is extracted as a truism of British, imperial knowledge, apparently proved in many 'real-life tragedies' and the images that follow. The textual commentary provides the official reading of these images as evidence of incontrovertible, insurmountable racial difference and distance, geographically, culturally and sexually.

However, the alternative to these relationships, the other side of the page, does not provide an appealing alternative. The central spread from *Way Down East* depicts a brooding Barthelmess, looking almost suspiciously or angrily at Lillian Gish who stares into the middle-distance, lips pursed and inscrutable (Figure 1.3). As is typical for the art supplement central spread, the two 'sweethearts' are once again out of contact. Again, the woman stares outwardly and intensely, ignoring the man's gaze. This does not appear to be a 'coquettish' kind of 'flirtation' in the *Picture Show* parlance, but is accentuated further by the fold in the page which aligns with the fence that separates them. Barthelmess stares across the fence and across the page, his hat threateningly poking over this fold as an intrusion into her separate frame. If this is an image of romance between 'sweethearts', it mirrors the discomfort of the images on the 'East

Figure 1.3 Art Supplement featuring Lillian Gish and Richard Barthelmess in *Way Down East* (1920). *Picture Show*, 26 March 1921. (pp. 12–13)

and West' article behind it, images purportedly advocating for the separating of men and women of different races. Indeed, to fold the page and cross the boundary, bringing the two into an embrace, requires revealing the concealed presence of interracial sexuality on the back page. In her work on Orientalism, sexuality and the 'yellow peril' in Hollywood film, Gina Marchetti observes the erotic allure that always accompanies depictions of violent and unrestrainedly sexual 'Oriental' cultures (1993, 1–2). This is perhaps evident between these two pages of the *Picture Show* art supplement, where a photograph of conventional 'sweethearts' contains none of the drama or frisson of the interracial relationships concealed behind Barthelmess.

As Glancy argues, fan magazines invoke the 'glamour of the East' to exoticise and eroticise film stars (2006, 474). This is a kind of 'masquerade', a playing or performing of national and racial difference (Glancy 2006, 470). As such, even as the article claims to depict violent and discomforting forms of contact, it comes in the context of a fan magazine culture which constantly emphasises and advertises the appeal and allure of the 'Orient'. Alice Maurice notes 'the Western tendency to depict or perceive the "Oriental" face *as* a mask', which reflected racist stereotypes of East Asian people as 'inscrutable', emotionally restrained to too great an extent (2013, 138). This, indeed, is the 'art' of the art supplement; art as '[c]unning; artfulness; trickery, pretence' (*OED*, n.d.). In its very doublesidedness, it raises the possibility of 'artfulness' as disguise and concealment. It invites knowing readers, aware of what is missing or what is hidden, to exercise their own craft in 'feeling' between the pages. Perhaps rightfully so, given the marginalised position of many fan magazine readers as working- or lower-middle-class women in a cinema culture intent on surveying and policing them, investigations of interactivity with the interwar fan magazine have focused on its positive, liberatory and community-building possibilities. Given the context of Western fan magazines within colonial Euro-American cultures, however, it is also worth exploring how this 'liberation' is achieved through racist or colonial paradigms, at the expense of cultures and peoples represented or invoked through fan magazine and film practices. The intermixture of Asian actors and white actors 'playing' Asian roles through racist make-up and costume points to the focus on playful concealment and disguise too, located behind the stolid whiteness of Gish and Barthelmess in *Way Down East*. The knowing spectator is aware that Barthelmess has concealed his white identity in his role as Cheng Huan and that Lillian Gish played within the film's narrative by dressing up in Cheng Huan's clothes, spending time in his shop decorated with 'Oriental' silks and fabrics. As readers would not have seen *Way Down East* at the time of the magazine's first publication, this was their only context for viewing Barthelmess and Gish together. *Broken Blossoms* is in fact a film which purports to challenge stereotypes of violent hypersexuality and unrestraint through its Chinese protagonist. Yet by contextualising this act of concealment within the film's reception in

Britain and wider anxieties about depicting racial difference in Hollywood film, it becomes evident that the illicit, exotic appeal of interracial contact and the disguising of this were fundamental to its effect. To understand the ways in which this art supplement invites imagined and physical tactile interaction, I now turn to debates about sexuality, intimacy and race around *Broken Blossoms* and more broadly in British film culture, with which fan magazine discourses and design overlap, interact and undermine.

'THE ART OF THE THING CONSTITUTES ITS DANGER': *BROKEN BLOSSOMS* AND ITS BRITISH RECEPTION

The restraint with which women were required to act according to Sanders and Stead takes on a racialised significance in the 1920s. Film historians have described the moral panic surrounding representations of white women in relation to men of colour on screen in American cinema and the damaging effect this would have on both working-class white women and men of colour in proximity to white women in Britain and British colonies (for example Arora 1995; Chowdhry 2000, 17–38; Sinha 2009; Burns 2013, 79–92). These anxieties centred on American cinema, evidencing political and economic concerns about Hollywood's dominance and the perceived impact of this on British culture and the British economy (Jaikumar 2006, 9). Yet it was expressed in sexual and racial terms and reflected Stoler's arguments about the significance of intimacy and sexuality in racial and colonial policing. Reporting especially on India but also on cinemagoing in 'the East' and 'Africa', newspapers printed correspondence throughout the 1920s from settlers anxious about the dangers of Hollywood films showing 'white women in all sorts of garbs' and 'compromising situations', leading to 'a low opinion of European morals', a damage to 'British prestige' and white women having to change their 'conduct' and dress in public in the colonies (*Daily Mail*, 11 July 1919, 3).[1] A lack of restraint and of 'decorum and distance' on screen instigated a similar unrestraint in the real world surrounding women in public space. As Monika Mehta suggests, this panic is underpinned by colonial constructions, outlined by Stoler, of 'native men as sexually excessive [. . .] degenerate and uncivilized while shoring up a bourgeois, European male identity associated with civility, self-discipline, and sexual restraint' (2011, 29), leading to the careful bounding of colonial space and racial boundaries to inhibit interracial sexual conduct. Stoler asserts further that these constructions entailed the policing of both indigenous men and white women (2010, 59–60). Published for a British audience, these newspaper debates thus interpellated British women in this policing of the possibility of their own 'corruption' by an unrestrained mass of men of colour from whom they needed to protect themselves and the British Empire itself, by conducting themselves with restraint and decorum. Stead's argument that fan magazines provided a space for women to explore restraint, respectability and conduct in public spaces can be nuanced with the context of racialised anxieties about the threat of men of colour to this respectability because of their perceived unrestraint.

Indeed, the concealed presence of *Broken Blossoms* connects these debates to the 26 March 1921 art supplement as a film which catalysed particular concerns about the representation of whiteness and white femininity, and as part of the 'cycle' (Burrows 2009, 282) of British and American films set in London's Limehouse district in the 1910s and 1920s. Limehouse was disproportionately associated with its Chinese population (Seed 2006, 62–7). The presence of Chinese people was characterised as a kind of reverse colonisation, the infiltration of Chinese people, but also values, aesthetics and territory itself, into Britain (Seed 2006, 71–3; Witchard 2009, 71–2). The district formed 'an imaginary cartography, which projects onto the real cityscape its own shadowy ideological antagonisms and fears' (Seed 2006, 76). This imaginary Limehouse thus brings the 'Orient' too close to the West; it 'makes the Orient mobile', relocating it in 'the heart of Western civilization' (Case 2002, 22) and putting it in *touch* with the British imperial metropolis, which is supposed to be distanced from and hierarchically above its colonies and its 'semi-colonies' in its 'informal Empire' like China (see Osterhammel 1986). The Orient's entry point to the West in Limehouse was especially seen to be through white women. Through the dissemination of opium and other drugs, and through purported sexual contact and violence, Chinese men infiltrated and penetrated the metropolitan centre through British white women. Agata Frymus argues that *Broken Blossoms*' depiction of Limehouse should therefore be understood in the context of racist colonial constructions of whiteness as restraint: '[t]he social construct of white (and therefore ideal) manhood relates to the physical stamina, heroism and most importantly, the ability to repress urges seen as inherently masculine, that is to control one's desire for the opposite sex' (2018, 17). The sexual restraint that underpins whiteness and white femininity is thus opposed to a racist construction of East Asian men as unrestrained and uncontrollable, as too proximate, too tactile and liable to undermine the colonial boundaries delineated in Stoler's work.

It should be acknowledged, before exploring how restraint and unrestraint was imagined in relation to the film in Britain, that *Broken Blossoms* claims to challenge stereotypes of sexually unrestrained Chinese men through Barthelmess's Cheng Huan. Huan is presented as a respectful and – crucially – physically distanced lover of Gish's Lucy, and a peaceful, restrained alternative to a violent, masculine British culture embodied in Lucy's father, the boxer Battling Burrows (Donald Crisp) (Hatch 2011, 81). Burrows is represented as a material, tactile threat – a sexual threat according to Julia Lesage (1987) and Anne Veronica Witchard (2009, 234–5) – grabbing, pulling and whipping Lucy, and getting too close to the camera in extreme close-ups before he murders her at the film's conclusion (Figure 1.4). On the other hand, Huan's restraint and desexualised adoration of Lucy is constantly emphasised. In fact, he interacts with her through objects and tactile materials, mirroring the mitigation of touch through mediating objects in fan magazine stills. He dresses her, gives her gifts, and decorates his room in which she rests after being beaten by Burrows. This is most evident when Huan almost seems to give into his unrestrained instincts, approaching Lucy in bed threateningly as the camera intercuts between their faces in close-up. However, just as Lucy is almost abject in terror and he seems to be about to undermine the restraint he has exhibited thus far, he stops, bows his head, and fingers and kisses her dress instead, emphasising through touch his restraint once more (Figure 1.5). Of course, as Kristen Hatch points out, his own relationship with Lucy does not provide an appropriate alternative to Burrows: 'his sexual desire does not signal masculine virility; rather, he assumes a feminine, maternal position in relation to the child', suggesting 'perversion rather than manly self-control' (2011, 81–2) and thus still depending upon racist stereotyping. However, this is articulated through a form of distance, decorum and restraint of touch that accords with British cinema culture's models for appropriate staging and composition of bodies on screen.

Jon Burrows accordingly demonstrates that the critical reception of the film in Britain contains the dangerous potential of representing interracial

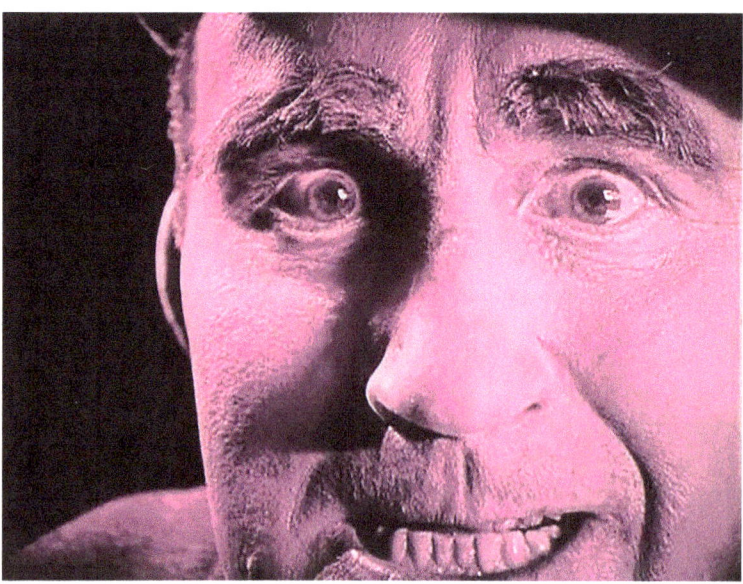

Figure 1.4   Screenshot of Donald Crisp in *Broken Blossoms* (1919).

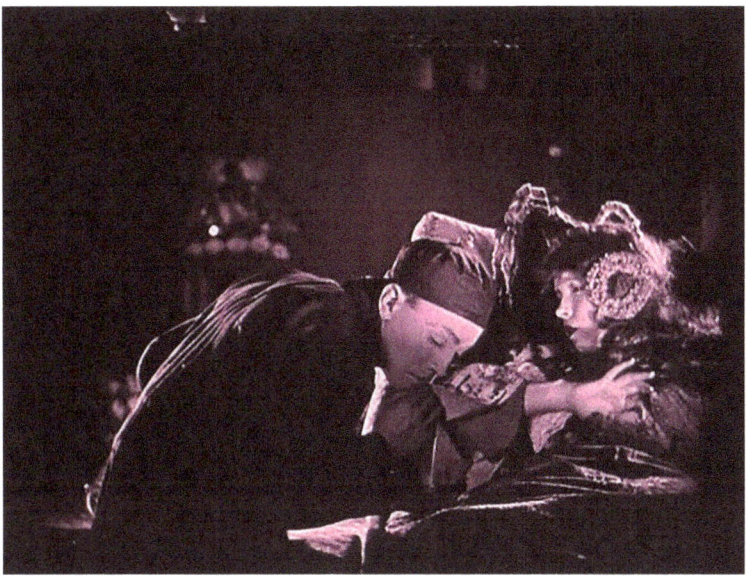

Figure 1.5 Screenshot of Lillian Gish and Richard Barthelmess in *Broken Blossoms* (1919).

relationships for British soil and British women by foregrounding the film's 'artful' direction and acting (2009, 289–95). Burrows particularly highlights the use of soft-focus photography in creating this 'artful' effect by engendering 'contemplative, aesthetic abstraction from reality' (2009, 291), a de-sharpening and dematerialising of the bodies on screen. Yet some contemporary critics contested this narrative, finding in the film dangerously sexualised, bodily effects built upon the anxieties about the representation of racial difference in Hollywood film circulating more widely. Correspondents and critics debated the value of the film and the *deceptive* nature of its artfulness (for example, *The Times*, 23 January 1920, 10; Anderson, 29 January 1920, 4; 'J. P.', 12 April 1920, 6; Lawson, 15 April 1920, 4; Barnard, 17 April 1920, 5). For instance, Australian journalist E. C. Buley wrote for the *Daily Mail* a particularly excoriating review that resonates with the concealment of the art supplement. Buley complains that the film dangerously misrepresented the reality of relationships between Chinese men and white women in portraying Huan's restraint, concluding that '[t]he "new art" of the moving picture has cast its glamour over this abomination', and thus, '[t]he art of the thing constitutes its danger' (9 April 1920, 6). Buley reads the film as a formal embodiment of 'Oriental' artifice and masking, contributing to the actual deception of white 'women who have fallen under the Chinese spell' in Limehouse. Aesthetic distancing merely conceals the 'reality', for Buley and some other critics, of racist stereotypes of Chinese male unrestraint and sexual predation.

However, as Glancy argues, fan magazines offer a different perspective on these debates and anxieties surrounding American cinema (2006, 479). The 'official' text in the supplement, quoting Kipling and asserting the impossibility of interracial relationships, implies that these debates and surveillance of white women and men of colour inflecting British cinema culture still inform the representation of and invitation to touch in the issue of *Picture Show*. Yet the 'art' of the art supplement invites readers to imagine the illicit sensory pleasures of such interracial contact at the same time. For Marchetti, *Broken Blossoms*

> uses spectacle to arouse the sexual interest of the spectator, while narrative structure permits, controls, and legitimizes this arousal by symbolically punishing the principals (and through them the viewer who identifies with them) for their erotic excesses. However, spectacle wins out, and the evocation of an atmosphere, an image, a feeling that stimulates the erotic involvement of the male viewer takes precedence over the moral imperatives of the plot. (1993, 34)

In parallel, the *Picture Show* supplement relies upon the double-sidedness of the page to invoke *Broken Blossoms* and suggest this disavowed spectacle and the disavowed, eroticised sensations of interracial sexual intimacy. Female British readers aware of the debates around the film – which, whether positively or negatively appraising it, deny the pleasures of such relationships – could find an alternative in the pages of *Picture Show* which was not so purely censorious. Depicting such an unappealing intimacy between the white 'village sweethearts' and backing it with images of interracial contact, *Picture Show* uses the very double-sidedness of the page to offer an alternative perspective or way of experiencing the film to critiques levelled by reformers *or* praise of its 'artful' circumventing of interracial sexual intimacy.

Conclusion

We cannot definitively know whether readers would have received this supplement in the context I have described here, and if these debates mattered to them. After all, there was no requirement to pay attention to the photo montage on the back. It is possible that a reader would simply see the still of Gish and Barthelmess as a picture of two stars in an exciting upcoming film, or even fold or tear away one of Barthelmess or Gish so that only the favourite was in view; certainly, the Media History Digital Library's collection of *Picture Show* evidences pages half-torn out, undermining the design decisions of their editors (for example, the art supplement from 5 February 1921). Equally, they may have had no interest in tactile interactions with the page, preferring simply to read about the latest news in British and American cinema, removing the supplement only to access the pages it interrupted.

However, close attention to, and analysis of, the magazine's double-sided design combined with broader examination of specific cinema discourses, criticism and contexts does reveal at least the possibility that these invitations to touch were acknowledged and accepted. *Picture Show* invokes debates about *Broken Blossoms* in Britain between the pages as its own form of artful concealment. As a film which raises the positive, sensual possibilities of an interracial relationship, it is conspicuous by its absence from the 'East and West' article on the back page, and its concealed, inscrutable presence questions the written, textual premise of this article. For the reader aware of Gish and Barthelmess's screen history, the turning of the page becomes an act weighted with illicit appeal, printed and read within a cinema culture in which men of colour and white women's sexuality, restraint and 'decorum and distance' were subject to intense scrutiny. Readers could have thus chosen to display or direct their interest to the danger and allure of East and West on the back page, or pin up the centre spread with the secret knowledge of the more appealing, more illicit kinds of relationship hidden away behind the legitimate but perhaps less exciting relationship between David and Anna in *Way Down East*. By asserting that East and West never meet, the 26 March supplement artfully raises the possibility for the reader of the opposite, for reflecting upon how this meeting *might* be experienced, from their perspective as knowledgeable, active, engaged film fans, not reading but feeling this knowledge in the very pages between their fingers.

Acknowledgement

This chapter is dedicated to my late DPhil supervisor, Professor Laura Marcus.

Note

1. Such articles are too ubiquitous to list comprehensively, and the scholarship cited quotes from a great many of them. However, some of the key articles published contemporarily to the *Picture Show* supplement include *The Times*, 23 February 1920, 12; Atkinson, 14 April 1920, 3; *Sunday Times*, 23 January 1921, 11; Bromley, 21 February 1922, xiv.

References

Anderson, Alder. 1920. 'In Filmland'. *Daily Telegraph*, 29 January: 4.
Anon. 1919. 'White Women Films'. *Daily Mail*, 11 July: 3.
Anon. 1920. 'Broken Blossoms'. *The Times*, 23 January: 10.
Anon. 1920. 'The Film World'. *The Times*, 23 February: 12.

Anon. 1920. Art Supplement 'Flirting on the Film'. *Picture Show*, 8 May: 14.
Anon. 1920. Art Supplement 'The Love Token'. *Picture Show*, 5 June: 14.
Anon. 1920. Art Supplement 'Flirting with a Parasol'. *Picture Show*, 24 July: 11.
Anon. 1920. Art Supplement 'The Flower and the Flirt'. *Picture Show,* 28 August: 14.
Anon. 1920. Art Supplement. *Picture Show*, 6 November: 11–14.
Anon. 1921. 'Film Scandal'. *Sunday Times*, 23 January: 11.
Anon. 1921. Art Supplement. *Picture Show*, 5 February: 11–14. Retrieved from <https://archive.org/details/pictureshowoct1904unse/page/n6/mode/2up?view=theater> (last accessed 18 November 2022).
Anon. 1921. Art Supplement. *Picture Show*, 26 March: 11–14.
Arora, Poonam. 1995. '"Imperilling the Prestige of the White Woman": Colonial Anxiety and Film Censorship in British India'. *Visual Anthropology Review* 11 (2): 36–50.
Atkinson, G. A. A. 1920. 'The Cinema'. *Daily Express*, 14 April: 3.
Barker, Jennifer. M. 2009. *The Tactile Eye: Touch and the Cinematic Experience*. Berkeley, CA and London: University of California Press.
Barnard, Alfred. 1920. 'Films that Damage British Reputation'. *Daily Mirror*, 17 April: 5.
Bromley, Constance. 1922. 'India'. *The Times*, 21 February: xiv.
Bruno, Giuliana. 2007. *Atlas of Emotion: Journeys in Art, Architecture, and Film* (paperback ed.). New York: Verso.
Buley, E. C. 1920. 'Lil White Girl'. *Daily Mail*, 9 April: 6.
Burns, James. 2013. *Cinema and Society in the British Empire, 1895–1940*. Basingstoke: Palgrave Macmillan.
Burrows, Jon. 2003. *Legitimate Cinema: Theatre Stars in Silent British Films, 1908–1918*. Exeter: University of Exeter Press.
Burrows, Jon. 2009. '"A Vague Chinese Quarter Elsewhere": Limehouse in the Cinema 1914–36'. *Journal of British Cinema and Television* 6 (2): 282–301.
Case, Shannon. 2002. 'Lilied Tongues and Yellow Claws: The Invention of London's Chinatown, 1915–45'. In *Challenging Modernism: New Readings in Literature and Culture, 1914–45*, edited by Stella Dean, 17–34. Aldershot: Ashgate.
Chowdhry, Prem. 2000. *Colonial India and the Making of Empire Cinema: Image, Ideology and Identity*. Manchester and New York: Manchester University Press.
Cinquegrani, Maurizio. 2014. *Of Empire and the City: Remapping Early British Cinema*. Berlin: Peter Lang.
Dyer, Richard. 1993. 'A White Star'. *Sight and Sound*, 1 August: 22–4.
Frymus, Agata. 2018. 'Imagining Chinatown: *Broken Blossoms* (1919) in Britain'. *Altre Modernità* 20: 12–37.
Garner, Steve. 2007. *Whiteness: An Introduction*. London and New York: Routledge.
Glancy, Mark. 2006. 'Temporary American Citizens? British Audiences, Hollywood Films and the Threat of Americanization in the 1920s'. *Historical Journal of Film, Radio and Television* 26 (4): 461–84.
Gledhill, Christine. 2003. *Reframing British Cinema 1918–1928: Between Restraint and Passion*. London: BFI.
Grieveson, Lee, and Colin MacCabe, eds. 2011. *Empire and Film*. London: BFI.
Griffith, David Wark (Producer and Director). 1919. *Broken Blossoms* [Motion Picture]. USA: D. W. Griffith Productions.

Hatch, Kristen. 2011. 'Lillian Gish: Clean, and White, and Pure as the Lily'. In *Flickers of Desire: Movie Stars of the 1910s*, edited by Jennifer M. Bean, 69–90: New Brunswick and London: Rutgers University Press.
'J. P.'. 1920. 'White Girls and Yellow Men'. *Daily Mail*, 12 April: 6.
Jaikumar, Priya. 2006. *Cinema at the End of Empire: A Politics of Transition in Britain and India*. Durham, NC and London: Duke University Press.
Kipling, Rudyard. [1889] 2006. 'The Ballad of East and West'. In *Rudyard Kipling: The Complete Verse*, 187–89. London: Kyle Cathie.
Kuhn, Annette. 1988. *Cinema, Censorship and Sexuality, 1909–1925*. London and New York: Routledge.
Lanckman, Lies. 2020. 'Fans, community, and conflict in the pages of "Picture Play", 1920–38'. *Transformative Works and Cultures* 33. Retrieved from <https://journal.transformativeworks.org/index.php/twc/article/view/1745/2203> (last accessed 18 November 2022).
Lawson, Robb. 1920. 'Films that Do the Empire Harm'. *Daily Mail*, 15 April: 4.
Lesage, Julia. 1987. 'Artful Racism, Artful Rape: Griffith's *Broken Blossoms*'. In *Home is Where the Heart Is: Studies in Melodrama and the Woman's Film*, edited by Christine Gledhill, 235–54. London: BFI.
Levine, Philippa. 2006. 'Sexuality and Empire'. In *At Home with the Empire: Metropolitan Culture and the Imperial World*, edited by Catherine Hall and Sonya O. Rose, 122–42. Cambridge: Cambridge University Press.
McClintock, Anne. 1995. *Imperial Leather: Race, Gender, and Sexuality in the Colonial Contest*. New York and London: Routledge.
McLuhan, Marshall. 1964. *Understanding Media: The Extensions of Man*. London: Routledge & Kegan Paul.
Marchetti, Gina. 1993. *Romance and the 'Yellow Peril': Race, Sex, and Discursive Strategies in Hollywood Fiction*. Berkeley, CA and London: University of California Press.
Marks, Laura U. 2000. *The Skin of the Film: Intercultural Cinema, Embodiment, and the Senses*. Durham, NC and London: Duke University Press.
Maurice, Alice. 2013. *The Cinema and Its Shadow: Race and Technology in Early Cinema*. Minneapolis: University of Minnesota Press.
Mehta, Monika. 2011. *Censorship and Sexuality in Bombay Cinema*. Austin: University of Texas Press.
Nagel, Joane. 2003. *Race, Ethnicity, and Sexuality: Intimate Intersections, Forbidden Frontiers*. New York and Oxford: Oxford University Press.
OED. (n.d.). art, n.1, III.11.a. Oxford: Oxford University Press. Retrieved from <https://www.oed.com/view/Entry/11125?rskey=ZWzjQP&result=1> (last accessed 20 November 2022).
Orgeron, Marsha. 2009. '"You Are Invited to Participate": Interactive Fandom in the Age of the Movie Magazine'. *Journal of Film and Video* 61 (3): 3–23.
Osterhammel, Jurgen. 1986. 'Semi-colonialism and Informal Empire in Twentieth-Century China: Towards a Framework of Analysis'. In *Imperialism and After: Continuities and Discontinuities*, edited by Jurgen Osterhammel and Wolfgang J. Mommsen, 290–314. London: Allen & Unwin.

Rodaway, Paul. 1994. *Sensuous Geographies: Body, Sense and Place*. London and New York: Routledge.

Sanders, Lise Shapiro. 2002. '"Indecent Incentives to Vice": Regulating Films and Audience Behaviour from the 1890s to the 1910s'. In *Young and Innocent: The Cinema in Britain, 1896–1930*, edited by Andrew Higson, 97–110. Exeter: University of Exeter Press.

Seed, John. 2006. 'Limehouse Blues: Looking for "Chinatown" in the London Docks, 1900–40'. *History Workshop Journal* 62 (1): 58–85.

Sinha, Babli. 2009. '"Lowering Our Prestige": American Cinema, Mass Consumerism, and Racial Anxiety in Colonial India'. *Comparative Studies of South Asia, Africa and the Middle East* 29 (2): 291–305.

Stead, Lisa. 2011. '"So oft to the movies they've been": British Fan Writing and Female Audiences in the Silent Cinema'. *Transformative Works and Cultures* 6.

Stein, Sally. 1985. 'The Graphic Ordering of Desire: Modernization of a Middle-Class Women's Magazine, 1914–1939'. *Heresies: A Feminist Publication on Art and Politics* 18 (3): 7–16.

Stoler, Ann Laura. 2010. *Carnal Knowledge and Imperial Power: Race and the Intimate in Colonial Rule*. Berkeley, CA and London: University of California Press.

Stollery, Martin. 2000. *Alternative Empires: European Modernist Cinemas and Cultures of Imperialism*. Exeter: University of Exeter Press.

Stollery, Martin. 2011. 'From *Storm Over Asia* to *Dawn Over Africa*: Transnationalism and Imperialism in British Intellectual Film Culture of the Late 1920s and 1930s'. *Transnational Cinemas* 2 (1): 93–111.

Witchard, Anne Veronica. 2009. *Thomas Burke's Dark Chinoiserie: Limehouse Nights and the Queer Spell of Chinatown*. Farnham: Ashgate.

2. THE PARADOXICAL GLAMOUR OF THE PHONEY WAR: EXAMINING THE DESIGN OF *PICTUREGOER*

Carolyn Owen King

By the 1940s, *Picturegoer* was the UK's longest running and most popular film periodical, with an estimated readership of 500,000 per issue (Glancy 2011, 458). Published by Odhams Press, it had started as a weekly magazine in 1913, and after going monthly between 1921 and 1931 returned to weekly frequency in 1931, before merging with *Film Weekly* in September 1939. In this chapter, I will be considering a single issue of *Picturegoer*, from 2 March 1940. On this date, the quiet period of the 'phoney war' portion of the Second World War (1939–1945) ended for Britain, with the bombing of a cargo liner off the Isle of Wight and the loss of more than 100 British lives. By April, the war had begun in earnest. It was a liminal moment, when the transatlantic countries were both on the cusp of the transition to total war.[1] I will be examining this issue of *Picturegoer*, in order to explore its presentation of glamour, assumptions about proper gendered behaviour during wartime, and how these coalesce in the pages of a British film fan magazine, while excavating 'hidden histories' in relation to everyday lives and wider popular culture.

In his 2011 article '*Picturegoer*, the Fan Magazine and Popular Film Culture in Britain During the Second World War', Mark Glancy gives an overview of this movie magazine's historical evolution within the context of cinemagoing in the UK, locating it in relation to its main rival: the less popular British fan magazine *Picture Show and Film Pictorial*.[2] Glancy analyses the effects of the war on all aspects of *Picturegoer*'s content and production. He argues that, although the magazine addresses women, it is the male point of view that dominates, as it was assumed that the masculine voice 'represented a more intelligent and patriotic perspective on films' (Glancy 2011, 459). He analyses the tone, content and significance of the cover images, reviews, editorials, adverts and letters pages, revealing the ways in which the publication mediated between film audiences and the films and their stars. Although he does not directly cite the 2 March 1940 issue of *Picturegoer* in this article, he does mention it elsewhere as revealing much about British treatment of ex-pat Hollywood stars Cary Grant (2020) and Vivien Leigh (2013). Similarly, Lisa Stead's chapter '"There is a War On. Does She Know?": Transatlantic Female Stardom and Women's Wartime Labour in British Film Fan Magazines' (2020) takes part of its title from an article chastising Leigh which appears in the same issue of *Picturegoer*. Stead places the article in the broader context of how *Picturegoer* reflected the negotiation of a new female identity in wartime, exploring the apparently contradictory pressures on women to do war work and run homes in conditions of austerity, while also retaining a film star-like glamour. She observes that '[c]ontent could [. . .] simultaneously exploit and obscure wartime realities, offering readers escapism, but also a variety of means to relate cinema to the war-inflected realities of everyday lives' (Stead 2020, 120).

Existing scholarship on *Picturegoer* therefore neglects detailed focus on particular periods of the war, instead making observations on general trends and especially on the pitting of wartime austerity against the escapism and glamour Hollywood provided, an approach also seen in Jackie Stacey's *Star Gazing: Hollywood Cinema and Female Spectatorship* (1994), which examines British women's memories of cinemagoing and female stars in the 1940s and 1950s. However, austerity was not constant for the entire 1939 to 1945 period: rather it increased over time, especially after the end of the phoney war. Concentrating on this single early wartime edition gives a cultural snapshot of this specific moment in history. I will begin by analysing how – and when – text and image work together in this issue, with particular reference to the arrangement of advertisements and the all-important cover. Significantly, there is an apparent paradox between the images and text: while the former seem to be speaking to women, the latter panders to a male perspective. In this chapter, I also consider the ways in which Hollywood star Rosalind Russell and British star Vivien Leigh are contrasted and used to express underlying assumptions about women and femininity. Finally, I examine the letters pages, among other features, highlighting some surprising expressions of sexuality, gender and race. This last section will be augmented by reference to contemporaneous evidence which is part of the British Mass Observation project which used personal diaries, reports, surveys and other means to chronicle people's experiences during wartime. Citing the Mass Observation archive's report on all the letters *Picturegoer* received over several months in 1940 creates a fuller picture of a portion of the magazine's readers near this time – particularly in relation to gender.

Images and Text: An Overview

By 1940, magazine publishers were already feeling the effects of new wartime restrictions on paper use, and this edition of *Picturegoer* was shorter, now 35 pages as opposed to 60 or more (Glancy 2011, 459). Glancy also states that *Picturegoer* now placed greater emphasis on articles than pictures (458). In '*Picturegoer*: Cinema, Rotogravure, and the Reshaping of the Female Face' (2018), Gerry Beegan argues that *Picturegoer*'s use of the printing technique of rotogravure produced particularly impressive and lifelike visual images that made its cover stand out from its rivals (193), yet images seem to dominate on almost all pages inside the magazine. There are 105 images of women or female body parts, such as hands, in the magazine, carried in photographs, drawings and cartoons, and 66 of men. The latter are mostly photographs of male film stars, as, although there are 28 advertisements, only three contain images of men. Several adverts contain photographs rather than drawings, and they are all of women. Advertisements are generally found after page 22, breaking up the reading experience, offering some delay and disruption of the reading flow, with this interruption forming part of the pleasure of the experience (Jeffers McDonald and Lanckman 2019, 9). Structurally, the first part of the magazine deals with stars and gossip, the second part contains film reviews, fiction, readers' letters pages among some advertising, and the final part has continuation pages, the beauty column, queries and more advertising. Unlike *Picturegoer*'s contemporaneous American counterparts, for example *Photoplay*, *Motion Picture* and *Modern Screen*, where female voices proliferated in features and columns, *Picturegoer*'s writers were almost exclusively men. Only in the beauty column, an occasional advertising feature, and in letters pages, can female voices be detected. The female face, paradoxically, appears on nearly every page.[3]

Cover Girl

The most important page of any magazine is the cover, since this draws in the consumer; for 2 March 1940, in keeping with *Picturegoer* tradition, the cover is of a full-page female face (Figure 2.1). The cover is the periodical's most successful advert. Glancy notes that, throughout the war, the cover of the *Picturegoer* would convey escapist, aspirational fantasy, and glamour 'with an ornate hairstyle and a generous application of make-up [. . .] [c]onspicuous pieces of jewellery often added to the sense of extravagance' (2011, 460). The examples given by Glancy come from post-1940 covers, however; for the issue under investigation here, popular Hollywood star Margaret Sullavan graces the cover. Although she is flawless and beautiful, this is not a portrait of a sophisticated Hollywood star with 'ornate' hair swathed in gauze, draped fabrics and jewels, as in Glancy's examples (2011, 461–3). This portrait of

Figure 2.1 Front cover featuring Margaret Sullavan. *Picturegoer*, 2 March 1940.

Sullavan conveys a simple girlishness: her hairstyle is a gently waving set bob, partly pulled away from the face, a style achievable at home for ordinary women and girls. Although Sullavan's cheek is leaning on a luxurious red satin cushion, there is no detail revealed of her dress. Her nails are polished but cut short and her eye lashes are natural. Her red 'statement' necklace, although eye-catching, does not sparkle with jewels.

Interestingly, this photograph of Sullavan has been recycled. The same picture, tinted differently, had appeared on the cover of *Picturegoer* on 14 January 1939, over a year earlier, before the war. This image, it seems, is then harking backwards to a simple style and fresh-faced look. Indeed, glancing at the *Picturegoer* covers for 1939 and 1940, it seems that the 'high glamour' noted by Glancy has not yet become part of the cover girl appearance. Most stars on the covers in 1939–1940 seem to either be dressed and styled for a particular film role (sometimes in historical costume) or to have hair down and shoulder length. Some cover girls wear hats or furs, but the elaborate hairstyles of later in the war do not seem to be in evidence yet. This implies that the movement towards glamour as the country became mired in austerity was a deliberate move in later issues of *Picturegoer*.

'Inner Cleanliness' and 'Lips Men Adore': Female Duality and Advertising in *Picturegoer*

As if in never-ending reinforcement of the magazine cover, the advertisements inside this issue of the *Picturegoer* are dominated by multiple images of women. There is an unmistakeable stress in advertising features, small and large, on the improvement of women and especially on the female head: teeth, lips, complexion, hair. Most of the images in the advertisements are stylistically similar, with cheaper everyday products aimed at women illustrated with lifelike line drawings, while the more prestige brands employ photography. In fact, in this issue, photographs are used for their products by just five – *American* – companies: Pond's cream (23), Amami setting lotion (22), Max Factor (33), Lux soap (35) and the MGM film *The Women* (Cukor 1939) (2).

There is a clear orientation towards female consumption in the magazine's advertisements, even when the product is effectively genderless. For example, toothpaste and tooth powder are sold as a beauty tool for achieving a 'winning smile' (Odol, 32), which garners the woman in the picture male attention. Painkillers are sold specifically for period pain, as prescribed by an unsmiling, authoritative female nurse (27). Although three advertisements contain male figures, in two cases they are subordinate to a female figure, pushed to the side or behind. There is a reinforcement of the narrative of products making women more attractive to men. For example, the advertisement for Yardley Lavender perfume in this issue shows a smiling woman in coat, gloves and hat, gazing into the distance, with a smiling handsome uniformed escort placed to the side (25). The male figure in the Odol advertisement is likewise shown gazing adoringly at an apparently uninterested woman who is looking away from him. He seems to be drawn to her because 'There's glamour in the Odol Smile' (32). The advert for Val Guitare lipstick is even more explicit, promising to deliver 'lips men adore' (35).

The male figure in the advertisement for Player's tobacco, however, dominates over a quarter of the page on which it appears (30). A bearded sailor looks into the distance, his hat proclaiming his ship to be 'HMS Excellent'. His serious expression, uniform and textual assurances of 'quality' and 'purity' through a male wartime authority figure reinforce the capitalised heading 'SOUND SECURITY'. This could be a concession to *Picturegoer*'s male audience, or perhaps an indication of some reluctance around using images of women to sell cigarettes directly, as smoking might still have been perceived as unfeminine; it should be noted, however, that ads for products credited with beautifying the hand often show female fingers holding cigarettes (for example Snowfire hand jelly, 27, Cutex nail varnish, 26). Whatever the reason, this sudden incongruous large male head and shoulders in a magazine so dominated by a female visual aesthetic gives the reader a jolt.

Although most advertisements are promoting feminine glamour, there are some that seem to be doing the opposite. There is a surprising emphasis on laxatives and an implied cleanliness 'inside'. Andrews Liver Salts are sold as complexion cleansers, as the cartoon drawing of the Andrews tin tells us in a speech bubble: 'inner cleanliness comes first' (30). This delicately euphemistic approach to the sale of the laxative and antacid contrasts with the advert for Milk of Magnesia, which in its small text box, with no image, uses the headline 'Indigestion and Flatulence after meals' (29). The promotion for California Syrup of Figs (32) convolutedly sells its laxative as a cure for children's colds: 'It relieves the system of the germ-breeding poisonous waste and breaks up a cold and cough when other remedies fail'. A postscript also suggests it could be especially 'IMPORTANT TO WOMEN' for ensuring 'complete bowel action without the risk of disturbing functional regularity' (32). Given this advertisement's frank discussion of bowel cleanliness, perhaps it is just as well that once more no image is provided.[4] Similarly, the Milk of Magnesia caption directly addresses at female readers what must be the ultimate in anti-glamorous issues, that of flatulence. Women in *Picturegoer* ads, then, are both unglamorous and glamorous. This is a similar trend to that described by Jane Gaines in her claim that in Hollywood fan magazines:

> Glamour – combining glitter and *amour*, the perfect amalgam of money and love – was absorbed into every topic of interest to women, so that the most 'down to earth' advice [. . .] became imbued with romantic possibilities. (1985, 43)

The world of war work for women also appears in some advertisements. Quickies make-up remover pads are advertised in a simply drawn cartoon where WRENs are shown exclaiming, 'Quick! Skipper's aboard! Another naval occasion for ever-so-cheaper quickies' (28). Women must be able to refresh their glamour in order to get their war work done when surveilled by a male authority figure, although there is some ambiguity over whether the WRENs want to attract or evade the attention of the male skipper. Pond's cream also presents the duality of the working woman showing Lady Kinross, a wartime nurse, in three images, one of which presents her face as 'painting by numbers' (23). The focus on her facial characteristics implies that beauty is an act of creation, with the pale skin of the white female face acting as a blank canvas. Stead's contention that adverts 'promised to help women to balance a worker/domestic identity through physical appearance' is demonstrated here (2020, 121). Kinross's aristocratic title adds a type of allure to the advertiser's message, which extends beyond the glamour/war-work duality to suggest an upper-class/war-work duality. The objectification inherent in the breaking down of women's faces into categories echoes categorisation of women themselves into colour groups which Max Factor adverts had made part of their campaigns since the 1920s, using Hollywood actresses as models.

Beauty Parlour: 'Hitler or No Hitler'

The pre-eminence of feminine beauty as a theme across the advertising features is perhaps unsurprising, but the regular beauty feature is tucked away at the back of the magazine. Its placement alongside the cheaper adverts indicates that it is perceived to be of lesser value than the features and reviews written by men. The title, *Beauty Parlour*, conjures up a glamorous female-only safe space.

Written by Ann Bourn, this section takes up two-thirds of page 32, with the left-hand area, a column divided into two, containing unglamorous adverts for Odol dentifrice and for the laxative California Syrup of Figs. The column is illustrated by a demure image of star Gale Page, head bowed, in a feathered hat. Bourn humorously addresses her audience:

> The very moment the sun begins to shine – and I hope that it will be shining by the time you read these words, most women turn their thoughts to the question of a new hat. I hope that the Chancellor of the Exchequer will not think that I am encouraging extravagance. Even the hardest-hearted man will realise that a new hat is a feminine tonic that positively cannot be denied – Hitler or no Hitler. (32)

The light tone of this piece contrasts sharply with the authoritative, pompous, male voices that dominate the first half of the magazine's articles, as I will show. There is an acknowledgement of the war, but also an encouragement to women to use their appearance as a way of keeping up 'womanly morale' in wartime. Bourn's advice to find the right hat for individual hairstyles creates a particularly gendered tone which seeks to balance the seriousness of war with the apparent frivolity of 'feminine' issues. There is an awareness, at this early stage of the war, of how a woman could negotiate all of the demands that would be made on her through the war years. Appearance becomes playfully entwined with patriotism and morality. In this piece we can hear the echoes of the rhetoric that would, later in the war, surround the lipstick 'weapon' which, far from needing to be wiped off, became part of a woman's uniform (Nicholas 14 June 2018, n.p.)[5] and came itself, in time, to symbolise 'democracy and freedom' (Gaines 1985, 43).

The Women: Advertising Rosalind Russell

By far the most privileged advertisement inside this edition of *Picturegoer* is for the prestige Hollywood film *The Women* (2). This film is unique in its use of an all-female starry ensemble cast, including Norma Shearer, Joan Crawford and Rosalind Russell, and its discussion of female friendships. This advertisement clearly stands out in the magazine for its size (full page) and positioning – it is the only ad in the first half of the magazine. Discrete film advertisements are not seen in every issue during this era of *Picturegoer*, though in this month full-page ones for the Tommy Trinder vehicle *Laugh it Off* (9 March 1940, 24) and *The Wizard of Oz* (23 March 1940, 2) and a small advertisement for *Prisons de Femmes* (16 March 1940, 29) appear. Of course, effectively the whole magazine, with its many film reviews and features about Hollywood and British cinema, works as a huge advert for cinemagoing.

The film is introduced in excessive capital letters, inverted commas and largest font, "THE WOMEN", adding, 'it's all about men!' The glamorous black-and-white photograph of the seven female stars linking arms, walking together, gives an impression of empowering glamour and unity. Interestingly, there is a tension between the text and images used to promote the film, as if there is a nervousness about the film's tone and themes. The snippets taken from reviews all see the film in positive terms and yet women in general are described negatively. The text suggests that women are too stupid to realise that the film is, it is claimed, an 'indictment' of their behaviour but will 'flock' to see it anyway (2). The appeal to men, it seems, will be partly to see a film in which women are denigrated. One reviewer jokingly recommends to his assumed male audience to 'See this film and divorce your wife. Then become a lighthouse keeper'. The only female reviewer quoted calls the movie 'a devastating attack' on women, so it seems that men are directly addressed and pandered to, while the female audience is taken for granted. This advertisement attempts to create a sense of controversy around the film, but the harmonious photograph contradicts the text, and arguably creates a more lasting impression on the reader.

The long review of the film on page 20 also promotes the myth of the film being about fierce rivalry. The idea of an ensemble cast working together is resisted and the review insists on making Russell the leading lady, beginning by proclaiming her the outstanding actress, 'the winnah!' (20). The illustrating photograph, however, once more undercuts the text. It shows Russell's Sylvia in a tall hat with knitting in her hand, smilingly flanked by Norma Shearer's Mary. Here we can perceive a *visual* concern with promoting positive images of women and female relationships, while so often the *text* reveals a negative view of women and a patronising tone towards female readers.

Tamar Jeffers McDonald has theorised about the ways in which fan magazines used what she terms 'star saturation', where a star is promoted through appearing on different separate occasions across a magazine issue (2013, 40). Noting one magazine's return to Doris Day four times, she argues 'that because there are these four different sites for her display, she is actually being highlighted more than if there were only a single sustained article' (40).

Similarly, there is, as we flick through this issue of *Picturegoer*, a truly consistent reiteration of Rosalind Russell's star image; she appears not only in this prestige film advertisement, but also in the privileged film review with photograph attached, and in the series of photographs of stars at the *Gone with the Wind* (Fleming 1939) premiere (12), despite her lack of involvement in the film. Russell's fourth and final appearance in this edition is in a striking three-quarter-page advertisement for Max Factor on page 33 (Figure 2.2).

Smiling, radiant Russell is saying, 'You can give new charm to your beauty with Colour Harmony Make-Up'. She is introduced as 'MGM star of *The Women*', linking to pages 2 and 20. In a time of war, surrounded by adverts that reference women's 'war work',[6] and 'women with busy hands'[7], this advert oozes a luxurious glamour that is firmly positioned in the persona and image of Russell. The advertisement includes a form for readers to fill in to receive free samples of make-up, emphasising the importance of selecting the right colour cosmetics for specific complexions. In the Max Factor ad, women are categorised in four groups based on their hair colour: 'blonde, brunette, brownette and redhead'. The range of complexions graduate along similar lines: 'very light, fair, creamy, medium, ruddy, sallow, freckled, olive'. As Kirsty Dootson has revealed, the system was created to encourage consumers to buy three matching products from Max Factor's brand for a 'colour scheme that was tailor-made to each woman's colouring' (2016, 122). The lack of black hair or any dark skin tones on the list was significant:

> If we understand Factor's cosmetics business to be modelled along Fordist lines, then it should come as no surprise that his customers could have any color, as long as it was white. (Dootson 2016, 123)

Figure 2.2 Advertisement for Max Factor make-up featuring Rosalind Russell. *Picturegoer*, 2 March 1940. (p. 33)

Factor's company had been involved with creating colour make-up for technicolour film since the 1920s, and screen cosmetics were always widely consumed uniquely by women, simultaneously on screen and as physical products sold in pharmacies and beauty salons. This allowed film fans the opportunity to recreate Hollywood glamour relatively cheaply, creating a point of genuine contact with their favourite stars. Increased use of cosmetics coincided with increased interest in cinema, so fan magazines had always been involved in the promotion of cosmetics directly and indirectly (Beegan 2018, 200). Factor had won the well-publicised so-called 'Hollywood Powder Puff Wars', mainly because of his easily applied Caucasian-tinted 'color harmony pan-cake'[8] which made film make-up and make-up in general much more convenient and therefore accessible for ordinary (white) women (Dootson 2016, 120). The entirely positive presentation of Russell as a conveyer of film-star glamour across the pages of the magazine coincides with her appearance in the only two truly prestige advertisements.

Spanking Vivien: British Stars

The treatment meted out to British star Vivien Leigh differs markedly from the attitude to Russell. In Malcolm Phillips's article, the headline draws our attention to a transgression: 'If this is true Vivien should be spanked!', while bullet points underline her sins, noting 'There is a War on' and asking 'Does She Know?' (3) (Figure 2.3). Phillips labels Leigh 'ungrateful' for not agreeing to a photoshoot (3). The magazine then uses capital letters to signify a typographical yell at the extent of her misdemeanour at this point in time: 'IT IS ALSO VERY NAUGHTY OF HER BECAUSE THERE IS A WAR ON' (3). This infantilising language is continued when Phillips calls the twenty-seven-year-old Leigh 'a very lucky young lady' and insists that 'she should be treated like any other spoilt child and soundly spanked' (3). Lisa Stead notes that the 'infantilising and eroticised language posits the unrestrained glamorous star body as a threatening entity that needed to be contained and chastised' (2020, 127). While the text certainly portrays Leigh as somewhat unrestrained, the main glamour in the text is a mention of Leigh 'basking in the warmth of the Californian sun' (3) with the allure actually mostly supplied by the accompanying photograph. This is not of Leigh, but of an unknown starlet, Nell O'Day.[9] Even Phillips admits that 'perhaps [Leigh] has been misrepresented' since she had simply not yet responded to the request to do the shoot (3). Ultimately it is clear that there is no substance to the attack.

By contrast, Leigh's actor peers – male British stars in Hollywood – are treated more gently in relation to the war later in the magazine. Norman Payne merely

Figure 2.3 Article 'Between You and Me'. *Picturegoer*, 2 March 1940. (p. 3)

asks, 'Should the Boys Be Embarrassed?' if they do not sign up for war service (6). Payne's article mildly questions Cary Grant's future role in the war, alongside a half-page portrait of him in uniform. It also places Grant among Hollywood's

Englishmen whom Payne treats in generous terms: they are 'upstanding young screen heroes'; 'young movie idols'; 'fine young fellows' (6).

Leigh is also denied the star saturation afforded to Russell since she is absent from the *Gone with the Wind* premiere photographs in which Russell appears (12). Stead convincingly argues that this was a 'punishment' to 'reprimand her for lack of patriotism' given the 'status' of her role as Scarlett O'Hara in the film (2020, 128). Indeed, while Leigh's co-star Clark Gable is not included in this spread, he is pictured on the same double page in a different context, and at the premiere with his film-star wife Carole Lombard in the gossip section (5). Glancy shows that, while *Picturegoer* had expressed pride when Leigh won the role, her slowness in leaving Hollywood after war had been declared 'made her a target for the fan magazine's scorn' (2013, 149). Leigh had become implicated in a national response to *Gone with the Wind* that was anything other than straightforward, revealing a deeply felt fear of Americanisation, as the film was seen to embody all of Hollywood's most suspicious excesses (Glancy 2013, 149). Scarlett O'Hara and her alter ego Leigh shared an appeal which for wartime cinemagoers and fan magazines seemed to be a hugely desirable commodity, the quality of 'minxishness' (Glancy 2013, 178). It is perhaps unsurprising that Leigh would therefore be suggested to exhibit in 'real life' the spoilt behaviour which is central to her screen character. Thus male and female stars are seen to embody – and be rewarded or condemned for – the characteristics displayed in the gendered roles they have to play on screen. Leigh is read as her selfish Southern belle character, culpable for not evincing the desirable feminine attributes of good behaviour, which, as a star and thus role model, she should display, and this is mapped within the magazine onto a gendered form of patriotism at this historical moment.

In relation to this issue of *Picturegoer*, Stead furthermore says that the absence of Leigh from the premiere photographs allows the 'seedy implications of a "spanked" Leigh to linger in the imagination of the reader moving though the magazine in a linear order' (2020, 128). This is not Leigh's final appearance in this issue of *Picturegoer*, however. There is a photograph of her tucked away on page 35, in an advert for Lux soap (Figure 2.4). This appears on the back inside cover, where her face, photographed from the side, takes a quarter of the page, placed between adverts for Oxo stock cubes, Val Guitare lipstick and the film *Prisons de Femmes*.

Lux seems to be the least prominent brand on the page as the name of the soap is hidden in the text of the speech bubble. While American Rosalind Russell warrants star saturation, high praise, a film advertisement on the inside front cover and a prominent and glamourous Max Factor ad, British Vivien Leigh is chastised, replaced, absent from her own party, with her face only appearing once: in a generic ad for toilet soap on the inside back cover.

Figure 2.4 Inside back cover advertisements including Vivien Leigh for Lux toilet soap. *Picturegoer*, 2 March 1940.

Surprise Elements: Sexual and Racial Difference

While the female address in advertisements and the proliferation of glamorous role models might be expected, there are some surprises within the pages of this issue of the magazine. Within the usual features in this *Picturegoer* we find some expression of alternatives to the dominant white middle-class heteronormativity. In the three photographs on the page devoted to his featured comedy, *The Amazing Mr Williams* (Hall 1939), the usually suave Melvyn Douglas is shown twice in female dress, as the text announces, 'Melvyn is forced to masquerade as a woman' (15) (Figure 2.5). In one photograph, his co-star Joan Blondell is doing his hair, adjacent to the caption that reads, '"my dear, what a lovely hair-do" . . . Joan Blondell maliciously helps in the glamourisation of her he-man co-star' (15).

The final image on the page restores Douglas to a suit and tie, and throughout his moustache is a reminder of his masculinity. In the foregrounded photograph of Douglas having his hair done by Blondell, a mirror image is created of the two in black dresses, trimmed with white. Douglas's decolletage draws the eye, with the dress's V-neckline decorated with a white flower. The reference to the star as a 'he-man' draws attention to the fact that Douglas is really not a macho, muscular Clark Gable-type, but tends towards a more effete Anglicised masculinity, possibly one that could (moustache notwithstanding), look quite appealing in a dress. The text, then, serves to raise questions for a knowing reader about the sexuality of Douglas in this film rather than convince them of his alpha masculinity.

In the photographic feature 'Personality Parade', the nonconformity of usually unspoken desire is seen fleetingly in a shot captioned 'Cantor versus Clark' (12). In an image parodying Judy Garland's 'Dear Mr Gable' performance from *Broadway Melody of 1938* (del Ruth 1937), comedian Eddie Cantor is shown gazing adoringly at a photograph of Clark Gable (Figure 2.6). The photograph is explained as a 'little off-stage fooling between scenes of his new film' (12). This fooling, however, by substituting Cantor for Garland, carries the clear message that a man can have a crush on another man. The image of Cantor on a largely male-dominated page, gazing at a photograph of Gable, suggests a homo-sociability that might veer into same-sex romance, something that could never be hinted at textually. The heading suggesting conflict – 'CANTOR versus CLARK' – is contradicted by the image which depicts Cantor's adoration of Gable.

Fan magazines have traditionally offered, through the letters pages, an opportunity for readers to be part of 'interactive fandom' (Orgeron 2009, 3). In *Picturegoer* the 'idea' of a reader is replaced by actual readers. In relation to fan magazine letters in the US in 1930, Lies Lanckman observes that 'the overwhelming majority' of correspondents were women (Lanckman 2019, 52).

Figure 2.5 *The Amazing Mr Williams* photospread featuring Melvyn Douglas and Joan Blondell. *Picturegoer*, 2 March 1940. (p. 15)

Figure 2.6 'Personality Parade: Cantor versus Clark'. *Picturegoer*, 2 March 1940. (p. 12)

Juxtaposed with the columns of the letters pages of this British fan magazine of 1940 (26–8), are adverts for Cutex nail polish, Snowfire hand jelly and Amami nail varnish, all featuring women's hands. This might give the impression that the majority of the letters have been written by women. In fact, seven are attributed to female names or are prefixed by 'Miss', four others are genderless, giving initials only or claiming to give 'an English viewpoint' (28), three are attributed to male names and one is written by a 'Staff Sergeant' who the context clearly shows to be male. Only 50 per cent then, are credited to women.

A report from the Mass Observation project, which sought to gain insights into everyday people's lives during wartime, focused on *Picturegoer* letters for the period of May to December 1940. Significantly this did not just cover correspondence that was published, but the more than 1500 letters received by the magazine just after the end of the phoney war period. In her work on wartime British female audiences, Stacey cites the report's claim that 59 per cent of letters about stars were from women (1994, 54). The report judges that, in letters concerning *all* subjects, 'roughly 55 per cent come from men and 45 per cent from women' (Mass Observation Report 1940, 1). While Stacey's selective quoting suggests a majority of women readers, and both Glancy and Stead presume female address from the content of the magazine, the matter of actual readers at this earlier part of the war is more complex. It perhaps even suggests a divergence from the gender of writers whose letters were published in the United States as dealt with by Lanckman (2019).

Glancy labels *Picturegoer*'s letters pages a 'pedant's corner', and notes the prevalence of a prudish tone of 'critical righteousness' (2011, 471), which is certainly present in the letters content of this issue. Of the fourteen letters published, only two are *not* complaints about something. Two of the letters complain about stars (Charles Laughton and Ann Sheridan) being given unsuitable roles, and seven protest about Hollywood stars' lurid publicity or evince disapproval of immoral elements in films, such as divorce, torture, or a priest murderer. The Mass Observation report suggests that there was a high incidence of correspondents writing regularly to *Picturegoer* (1940, 1). Some, it suggests, might even have been hard-up journalists in search of the cash prize (1). The extended debate in two letters on page 28 is clearly a continuation of an argument begun in previous issues, and the writer of the main letter, BB Chandhuri, makes it clear that s/he has been published elsewhere. In a letter headed 'Anti-Indian Propaganda?' Chandhuri argues that Hollywood's portrayal of India and Indians reveals a racist agenda. They explain that certain films had been banned officially in India 'for anti-Indian propaganda' and ask, 'Has any film been produced to show the "snobbery, jobbery and robbery of white men in the East?"' Chandhuri's erudite, confident style implies that they might well have been a journalist. The letter expresses some exasperation with the editorial staff of *Picturegoer* which seems to compare unfavourably with other publications, as Chandhuri protests that 'my views had carried some weight in the Indian and American press' (28).

Picturegoer's letters editor 'Mr Thinker' dismisses Chandhuri's argument, protesting, in a tone of outrage, against the writer's implication of racism: 'Why should America or Britain want to make anti-Indian films?' (28). A jingoistic letter from 'an English Viewpoint' further dismisses Chandhuri's views as 'rather pointless' and 'childish', accusing them of being 'a little prejudiced against the British' (28). There is no acceptance of the negative influences of colonialism or real consideration of the arguments, despite Chandhuri's passion. The plea for racial equality and justice is a lone – and unexpected – one in this wartime *Picturegoer*. It is interesting that, among all of the complaints and negativity, this is the only letter that warrants a reply in this edition. The racial Other, like the British woman in Hollywood, comes in for the magazine's most supercilious dismissal.

Conclusion

By casting a spotlight on a single edition of *Picturegoer* from this early stage in the war, I have highlighted the ways in which popular culture reveals the tensions evident in British society at this transitional moment in history. The magazine cover, which in this case expresses a femininity that is youthful and girlish, as opposed to sophisticated and glamorous, is itself a palimpsest of the period immediately before the war. The different ways in which American and British female film stars were framed and approached is illustrated in the disparate treatment of Rosalind Russell and Vivien Leigh. Despite the powerful repetition of the white female face across the magazine, there are unexpected elements that hint at a secret audience that might be non-white, non-heteronormative, non-middle class. Notwithstanding a concern with glamour, there is an unexpected emphasis on bodily functions via laxatives, some hints at alternative sexualities and gendering, and there is a heartfelt argument against institutional racism. While other scholars have recorded the ways in which wartime fan magazines revealed how film culture connected to women's lives (Stead; Glancy; Beegan), I have opened up the discussion to consider some unexpected elements. It is beneficial for us to stand back from general trends evident in fan culture, to look to individual artefacts for coded details that hint at alternative narratives in cultural texts. Every text contains a subtext, and it is there that interesting and revealing truths can emerge about buried histories and unspoken desires.

Notes

1. America was still practising isolationism, although Hollywood filmmakers had begun to show allegiance to the British cause after the release of *Confessions of a Nazi Spy* (Litvak 1939).

2. These two titles merged on 7 October 1939.
3. There are only five pages that contain only male and no female faces.
4. Only these two ads and one exhortation to 'Think of the wounded, Give to the Lord Mayor's Fund' (32) appear with no illustrative images at all.
5. Hitler's violent dislike of red lipstick made it a particularly potent symbol of rebellion (Nicholas, 14 June 2018, n.p.).
6. The Lady Kinross advertisement for Ponds Cream on page 23 comments that nursing is 'fatiguing' war work.
7. An advertisement for Cutex nail polish on page 26.
8. First introduced in Walter Wanger's *Vogues of 1938* according to Dootson 2016, 120.
9. This is not uncommon within *Pictuergoer*. Phillips's headline was not always matched to the accompanying photograph.

References

Anon. 1940. 'An English Viewpoint'. Reader's letter. *Picturegoer*, 2 March: 28.
Anon. 1940. *Picturegoer*, 2 March: front cover.
Anon. 1940. Advertisement for *The Women*. *Picturegoer*, 2 March: 2.
Anon. 1940. Cantor Versus Clark. *Picturegoer*, 2 March: 12.
Anon. 1940. *The Amazing Mr Williams*. *Picturegoer*, 2 March: 15.
Anon. 1940. Review of *The Women*. *Picturegoer*, 2 March: 20.
Anon. 1940. Advertisement for Pond's Cream. *Picturegoer*, 2 March: 23.
Anon. 1940. Advertisement for Quickies make-up remover pads. *Picturegoer*, 2 March: 28.
Anon. 1940. Advertisement for Milk of Magnesia. *Picturegoer*, 2 March: 29.
Anon. 1940. Advertisement for Andrews Liver Salts. *Picturegoer*, 2 March: 30.
Anon. 1940. Advertisement for Player's Tobacco. *Picturegoer*, 2 March: 30.
Anon. 1940. Advertisement for California Syrup of Figs. *Picturegoer*, 2 March: 32.
Anon. 1940 Advertisement for Max Factor Make-Up. *Picturegoer*, 2 March: 33.
Anon. 1940. Advertisement for Lux toilet soap. *Picturegoer*, 2 March: 35.
Anon. 1940. Advertisement for *Laugh it Off*. *Picturegoer*, 9 March: 24.
Anon. 1940. Advertisement for *Prisons de Femmes*. *Picturegoer*, 16 March: 29.
Anon. 1940. Advertisement for *The Wizard of Oz*. *Picturegoer*, 23 March: 2.
Beegan, Gerry. 2018. '*Picturegoer*: Cinema, Rotogravure, and the Reshaping of the Female Face'. In *Women's Periodicals and Print Culture in Britain, 1918–1939: The Interwar Period*, edited by Catherine Clay, Maria DiCenzo, Barbara Green and Fiona Hackney, 185–205. Edinburgh: Edinburgh University Press.
Bourn, Ann. 1940. 'Beauty Parlour'. *Picturegoer*, 2 March: 32.
Chandhuri, BB. 1940. Reader's letter. *Picturegoer*, 2 March: 28.
Dootson, Kirsty. 2016. '"The Hollywood Powder Puff War": Technicolour Cosmetics in the 1930s'. *Film History* 28 (1): 107–31.
Gaines, Jane. 1985. 'War, Women and Lipstick: Fan Mags in the 40s'. *Heresies* 18 (3): 42–7.
Glancy, Mark. 2011. '*Picturegoer*: The Fan Magazine and Popular Film Culture in Britain During the Second World War'. *Historical Journal of Film, Radio and Television* 31 (4): 453–78.

Glancy, Mark. 2013. *Hollywood and the Americanization of Britain, From the 1920s to the Present*. London: I. B. Tauris.
Glancy, Mark. 2020. *Cary Grant: The Making of a Hollywood Star*. New York: OUP USA.
Jeffers McDonald, Tamar. 2013. *Doris Day Confidential: Hollywood, Sex and Stardom*. London: I. B. Tauris.
Jeffers McDonald, Tamar, and Lies Lanckman, eds. 2019. *Star Attractions: Twentieth-Century Movie Magazines and Global Fandom*. Iowa: University of Iowa Press.
Lanckman, Lies. 2019. 'In Search of Lost Fans: Recovering Fan Magazine Readers, 1910–1950'. In *Star Attractions: Twentieth-Century Movie Magazines and Global Fandom*, edited by Tamar Jeffers McDonald and Lies Lanckman, 45–59. Iowa: University of Iowa Press.
Mass Observation. 1940. Report by L[eonard] E[ngland] on *Picturegoer* letters, 8 December.
'Mr Thinker'. 1940. Letters pages. *Picturegoer*, 2 March: 26–8.
Nicholas, Elizabeth. 2018. 'Little Known Lipstick Battle of World War II', 14 June: n.p. <https://theculturetrip.com/north-america/usa/articles/the-little-known-lipstick-battle-of-world-war-ii> (last accessed 1 November 2021).
Orgeron, Marsha. 2009. '"You Are Invited to Participate": Interactive Fandom in the Age of the Movie Magazine'. *Journal of Film and Video* 61 (3): 3–23.
Payne, Norman. 1940. 'Should the Boys be Embarrassed?' *Picturegoer*, 2 March: 6–7.
Phillips, Malcolm. 1940. 'Between You and Me'. *Picturegoer*, 2 March: 3–5.
Picturegoer. 1940. 2 March.
Stacey, Jackie. 1994. *Star Gazing: Hollywood Cinema and Female Spectatorship*, London: Routledge.
Stead, Lisa. 2020. '"There is a War On. Does She Know?": Transatlantic Female Stardom and Women's Wartime Labour in British Film Fan Magazines'. In *Women's Periodicals and Print Culture in Britain, 1940s-2000s: The Postwar and Contemporary Period*, edited by Laurel Forster and Joanne Hollows, 117–32. Edinburgh: Edinburgh University Press.

3. MID-CENTURY MASCULINITIES: PRESENTATION AS SUBTEXT IN *PHOTOPLAY* JANUARY 1955

Lisa Hood

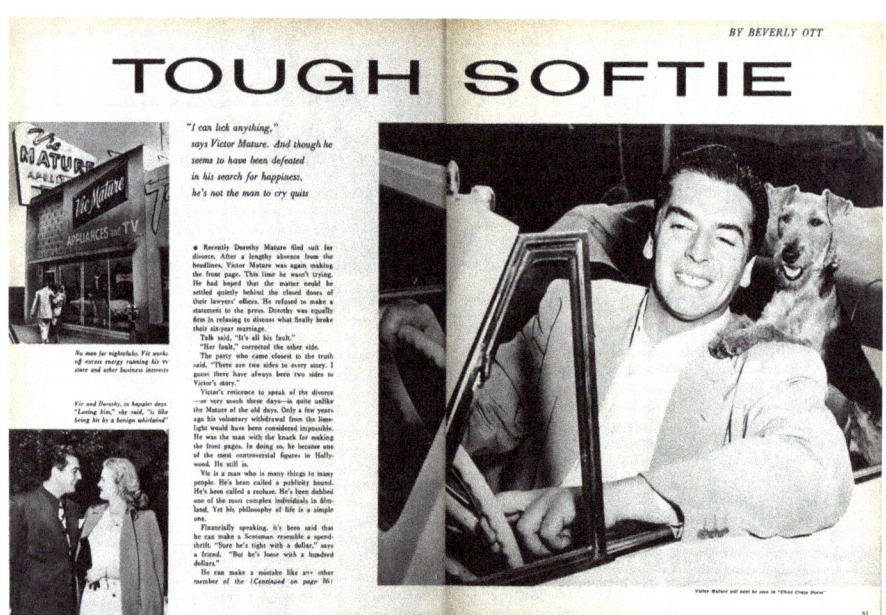

Figure 3.1   Article 'Tough Softie' about Victor Mature. *Photoplay*, January 1955. (pp. 50–1)

The value of fan magazines as historical artefacts has until fairly recently been contentious. In his 2011 article, Mark Glancy discusses the fan magazine's place in popular culture during the Second World War. He notes that historians had been reluctant to use fan magazines as a primary source of historical evidence since they are neither transparent nor neutral in their views. Further, and somewhat more revealing of certain historians' underlying biases, Glancy reports that the readers of the magazines are also found wanting since historians' 'reluctance has stemmed partly from the traditional view of fans as passive, gullible, undiscriminating consumers' (2011, 455).

Similarly, in *Star Attractions: Twentieth-Century Movie Magazines and Global Fandom* (2019) editors Tamar Jeffers McDonald and Lies Lanckman cite Anthony Slide's generally held assumption that the fan magazine was aimed at a reader who was 'an average member of the moviegoing public who more often than not was female' (1). They explain that fan magazines initially 'summarized the plots of particular films in a story format' but widened their content to encompass reviews, news and articles focusing on stars and related gossip (1). Therefore, if we replace the word 'fans' with 'women' in the quote by Glancy and consider this in combination with the seemingly lighthearted nature of fan magazines, it is not unreasonable to infer a gendered bias so entrenched that there was a failure to recognise the value of the magazines as primary historical evidence.

Using articles from a single issue of *Photoplay*, January 1955, this chapter will demonstrate how magazine editors communicated information about stars to their readers via a blend of visual signifiers and subtext. Four male stars are prominent in this issue – Victor Mature, Marlon Brando, Edmund Purdom and Rock Hudson – the presentation of whom demonstrates how editors constructed multilayered profiles avoiding explicit proclamations, but relying upon visual cues and allusions to tropes and stereotypes to hint at various subtexts, confident their skilful readers would pick up on their insinuations.

Victor Mature had a film career which spanned from 1939 to 1984, covering roles in a wide range of genres from hard-boiled *films noir* such as *I Wake Up Screaming* (Humberstone 1941) and *Kiss of Death* (Hathaway 1947), to westerns like *My Darling Clementine* (Ford 1946), musicals including *Wabash Avenue* (Koster 1950) and *Million Dollar Mermaid* (LeRoy 1952) and lavish Biblical epics such as *Samson and Delilah* (DeMille 1949) and *The Robe* (Koster 1953). Despite this versatility and an employability that saw him making forty-nine films in the twenty years between 1939 and 1959, by 1961 he had ceased consistent output.

Although his work still seemed to be flourishing in the mid-1950s, 'Tough Softie' (Figure 3.1) casts doubt on Mature's potential for career longevity. Author Beverly Ott takes stock of the star's career and intimates that it is all but over for the actor, aged forty-two. Ott ostensibly attempts to consider both sides of Mature's purported reputation as either a 'publicity hound' or a 'recluse', using the publicity surrounding his divorce as a springboard into a character analysis. The tone is set in the opening paragraph: Ott notes that he 'was again making the front page. This time he wasn't trying.' Ott's slightly contemptuous tone is underlined by the placement of the article midway through the issue versus the front page he craves, perhaps signalling that the editor – ultimately responsible for all matters, including article placement – is granting Ott's wish to put him in his place.

But was Mature really 'one of the most controversial figures in Hollywood'? (50). His films were popular with audiences: *Samson and Delilah* (1949) 'became the highest grosser in [Paramount's] history to date' (Hall and Neale 2010, 136) and *The Robe* achieved 'a world record box-office gross of $267,000 in its first week' (147–8). Meanwhile, dramas such as *Kiss of Death* and *My Darling Clementine* belied his oft-cited claim to be '. . . no actor and I've got 28 pictures and a scrapbook of reviews to prove it' (Vallance 11 August 1999, n.p.). The *New York Tribune* noted of his performance in *Kiss of Death* that 'Mature has been growing in acting stature so immensely that it is no surprise to find him playing [. . .] with persuasion and finesse' (cited in James McKay 2012, 13). Perhaps his dramatic performances were less problematic than his overt brand of masculinity. Much was made of the actor's appearance, with comments usually celebrating his dark, brooding looks, and he was billed by his studio as 'a beautiful hunk of a man' (Vallance 11 August 1999, n.p.).

Beverly Ott asserts that Mature is a controversial figure in Hollywood, intimating that this is well known by the fan magazine audience. However, is this yet another article in the tradition of 'hot headlines and tepid text'? Tamar Jeffers McDonald (2019) characterises this as a device whereby the headline provides bait to pique the reader's interest but the content either flips the thesis into something less tawdry or avoids answering the question completely. We must consider how the placement of Ott's article within the magazine and its layout promulgates Ott's thesis: does it reinforce the content, replace the argument or provide supplementary information? It is necessary not only to apply a critical eye to the text, but also to interrogate whether the placement of the article within the magazine truly reflects the star power of Mature; for instance, is it significant that it appears midway through the issue, with most of the text in the final third? Similarly, does the selection of pictures, their size, composition and whether they are colour or black and white coalesce to reflect Mature's status in Hollywood at this point? It will also be instructive to compare this magazine with issues of *Photoplay* from 1942, the point at which magazine mentions of Mature peaked.[1]

If we start with the article, it is presented as a generous double-page spread accompanied by one large and two smaller photographs. The headline 'Tough

Softie' is written in fine sans serif capitals which are assertive but not overbearing. Choice of font is used throughout *Photoplay* to provide a rebus-like clue to the intent of the article, as further demonstrated by the article placed before 'Tough Softie', Lola Parmeter's entreaty to young readers, 'Don't Be a Teenage Misfit' (48–9, 76). The headline's quirky font signifies youth and non-conformity, while Parmeter discusses how her subject, Kim Novak, overcame a lack of confidence. This technique is a visual equivalent to onomatopoeia: the combination of the headline and font signifies the tone of the article, allowing the reader flicking casually through the magazine to choose quickly which story to tackle first, providing us with the most immediate example of the use of visual code as shorthand.

The first column of Ott's article launches into the contradictory nature of Victor Mature and the folklore that surrounds him. She alludes to his divorce, noting 'Talk said, "It's all his fault". "Her fault", corrected the other side' (50). This sets up the structure of the article by reflecting the headline: both sides of the argument are presented, ostensibly for even-handedness but, more probably, to give two passes at salacious speculation about the life and career of Mature. Ott goes on to characterise the star as a 'publicity hound', 'complex' (a euphemism for difficult) and 'tight with a dollar', and, although each point is then countered with a positive statement, leading with the criticism gives it greater weight. As was the standard practice of movie and fan magazines, the article opens with a splash towards the front half of the magazine but continues at the rear (86–8). However, it is the impact of the opening two pages of the article which determines whether the reader will continue to the back of the issue, where there is a higher density of advertising, to read more. The headlines must be tantalising, but the visual impact must reinforce their message; the claims may be unsubstantiated, but they are sensational and made with conviction.

It is interesting that the assertions are so emphatic throughout the article yet there is a lack of named and verifiable sources. This is common in fan magazines and does not necessarily indicate poor research; rather it is a technique that could be employed to defend sources and thereby secure more scandalous tales. Jane Corwin's article 'The Devil is a Gentlemen' on page 24 (Figure 3.2) provides further evidence that the magazine is happy to apply creative embellishment to its articles. To demonstrate that Brando is both romantic and quirky, Corwin recounts a scene where Brando arrives to collect his date and calls the telephone exchange from another room within her property. Brando asserts to the operator that he is having problems with the line and asks to be connected to his date's phone. His date is irritated that he is running late and is impatient with him on the phone, but – surprise, he has been here all along! However, the story is told not from the viewpoint of either of the protagonists or as recounted by either one, but with a detached authorial voice. The fiction does no real harm and is intended to enhance the image of Brando by highlighting a playful persona. The story is benign but demonstrates how careful drafting could protect the writer, subjects and sources from censure.

Returning to Ott's article, the relationship between the text and the supporting photographs and their captions conveys important information. The picture to the left of the first paragraph on page 50 is of the successful electrical appliances store owned by Mature. It is captioned 'No man for nightclubs' and intimates that he spends his spare time on his business ventures. This seems innocuous but implies a certain snobbery. One might reasonably expect that an American magazine would celebrate his entrepreneurial success and laud Mature as a true embodiment of the American Dream. However, the caption, coupled with the comments regarding his alleged parsimonious nature, and the fact that he is at this point middle-aged, projects a diminution of his sex appeal, reducing him to a pedestrian businessman. Similarly, the picture of Mature and his wife Dorothy was selected to capture them at their happiest and she is quoted as saying 'Loving him is like being hit by a benign whirlwind', puncturing any allusion to intrigue or bad behaviour. Finally, there is the beaming full-page picture of Mature, undeniably handsome in his open-top sports car, accompanied by his dog. This can be read both as an attempt to visualise Ott's description of Mature as a 'publicity hound', and as lending a less-than-erotic avuncular air to the photo, again serving to neutralise his allure.

Figure 3.2   Article 'The Devil is a Gentleman' about Marlon Brando. *Photoplay*, January 1955. (pp. 24–5)

MID-CENTURY MASCULINITIES

Figure 3.3   Article 'Rock Hudson's Love Affair with the USA'. *Photoplay*, January 1955. (pp. 40–1)

The position of the Mature article within the magazine correlates to his relative star power in 1955. Ott's article commences on page 50, whereas younger stars, Marlon Brando (aged 31), Edmund Purdom (aged 31) and Rock Hudson (aged 29) are placed earlier in the issue, at pages 24, 30 and 40 respectively. Unlike the Mature piece, all the articles examining the younger men are accompanied by a colour portrait suitable to adorn a young fan's dressing table or bedroom wall. The largest photograph in both Brando's and Hudson's articles are classic portraiture. Brando is presented in a head shot and is clean-cut and debonair, which provides a counterpoint to the inference of the article's headline. The smaller photographs on the facing page show Brando in various candid-seeming moments, each of which serves to highlight admirable facets of his character, which the article will draw out.

Similarly, in Ray Manning's article, 'Rock Hudson's Love Affair with the USA' (Figure 3.3), Hudson is presented from just below the waist up. He wears a sports jacket and trousers, not the new more relaxed look then appealing to the teenager. His overall appearance is more aligned to that of the elder-statesman, Mature, than his contemporary, Brando, who is depicted in various more contemporary casual outfits. Indeed, the article plays up Hudson's conservative charm; the article portrays him as the all-American man, and this project

63

begins with a headline incorporating the stars and stripes of the American flag in the font that spells out 'USA'.

A cold reading of the article would suggest it provides an anodyne account of Hudson's recent visit to Europe. Manning portrays the actor as less of a Lothario and more a regular patriotic fellow, homesick, after an extended trip to Europe, for his girl – the Statue of Liberty – and all she symbolises. However, the text and photographs combine to create a loaded subtext. The article is accompanied by three smaller pictures of Hudson with women, none of whom is his girlfriend, while the text explains away – and simultaneously plays up – the romantic unavailability of the confirmed bachelor.

In contrast to Ott's treatment of Mature, within the Manning article there is an absence of overtly snide commentary regarding Hudson; indeed, the first clue to the subtext is the almost obsequious flattery of its subject. There is very little comment on Hudson's physical attributes aside from the well-known fact that he is a 'giant' (41) and 'that smile of his will melt any female' (75). Instead the piece contains anecdotes seemingly designed to reveal his tender heart. Manning notes Hudson's humble beginnings, calling him 'a poor kid in a rich town' which, Manning asserts, meant he had socialised with people from different backgrounds: 'perhaps that helped him get on so well with Europeans' (74). Manning, like Ott with Mature, obliquely references Hudson's relationship to the American Dream by implying that though Hudson had been poor, 'it wasn't the grinding poverty he'd seen abroad. Poverty without hope' (74). Hudson's return to the USA, according to Manning, causes him to recall the 'blind, ragged beggar' in Venice, the 'painfully thin little flower girl' and the 'bent old woman drawing a bucket of water' in Rome (73). These recollections serve to highlight his patriotism – and *sensitivity*. To drive the point home, Manning reveals that Hudson has collected on his travels 'Faience and Wedgwood' for his mother, a camera, silk shirts and cufflinks for himself. Although when questioned about the acquisition of 'perfume', a smiling Hudson confirms he has none (74), the paragraph is so heavily laden with familiar tropes insinuating homosexuality that it was surely intended to allude to his sexuality, without incurring legal costs or the opprobrium of the studio.

Manning notes that Hudson has two glamourous travelling companions; the 'happily' married Barbara Rush (she and Jeffrey Hunter divorced later in 1955) and Betty Abbott. The fact that Manning has chosen to report that Hudson is travelling with two beautiful young women without a whisper of romance surfaces suspicion, and doubt is further raised by the revelation that Betty 'usually calls Rock nicknames like "Father" or "Igor"' (75). This article is an example of drafting to ensure plausible deniability on the part of the magazine, but was close enough to the truth that Hudson's manager Henry Willson undertook a firefighting campaign to protect Hudson which culminated later in 1955 with him sacrificing two other clients, Rory Calhoun and Tab Hunter, and their

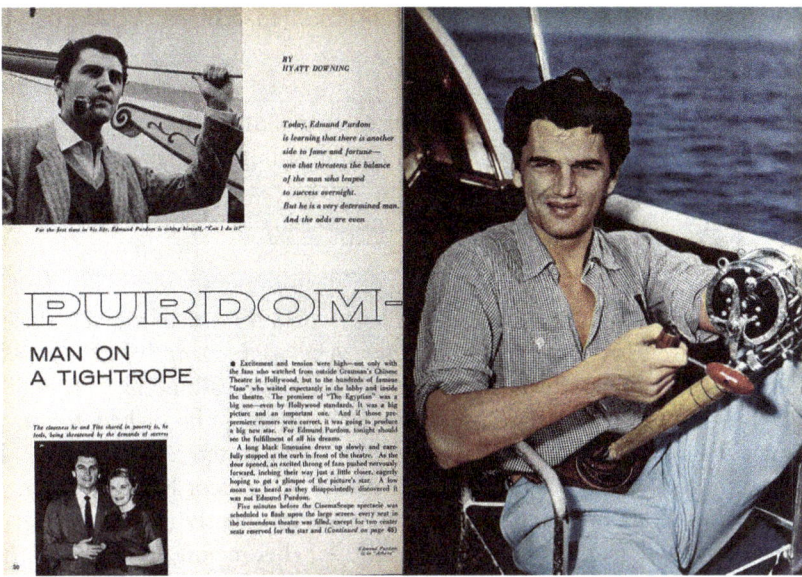

Figure 3.4   Article 'Purdom – Man on a Tightrope'. *Photoplay*, January 1955. (pp. 30–1)

criminal records, in exchange for not revealing all in respect of Hudson (Lang and Kambhampaty May 2020, n.p.).

Moving on to 'Purdom – Man on a Tightrope', whose subject is the English actor Edmund Purdom, Hyatt Downing's article is placed further towards the front of the issue (30–1) than the Rock Hudson piece, reflecting Purdom's current status (Figure 3.4). Purdom had, to this point, embodied the Hollywood 'overnight' success story but as the headline intimates, was now teetering precariously. Downing asserts that Purdom's break came with perfect Hollywood timing when he won a small part in *Titanic* (Negulesco 1953) at $300 per week, which led to him being offered a contract with MGM and the potential for greater opportunities (66). His path crossed with his contemporary, Marlon Brando, when he was offered the small part of Strato in *Julius Caesar* (Mankiewicz 1953) to Brando's Mark Antony. It must have seemed as though their careers were on a similar trajectory when Purdom was called upon to replace Mario Lanza in the light operetta, *The Student Prince* (Thorpe 1954) and achieved leading-man status in two steps (66). The film was a success, and heavily promoted by MGM.

However, the intent of the *Photoplay* article is to call into question Purdom's character and marital fidelity. As previously seen with the Ott piece, there is a surface attempt to present a balanced appraisal of the subject, hence the lauding of Purdom's rise to fame. But the article opens with a description of Purdom's failure to attend the premiere of *The Egyptian* (Curtiz) the previous year. Downing sets out the possible, unsubstantiated, scenarios, none of which is flattering:

> Rumor the next day blamed his absence on a tiff with his wife, which left the young Englishman sulking alone in his room. Others said he was ill. Still others blamed it on 'first-night' jitters.
>
> However, those close to Edmund and his lovely wife Tita do admit that success has changed him. (65)

It would seem that the success of *The Student Prince* had given Purdom an inflated sense of his abilities. In *Heyday: An Autobiography* (1979), MGM Studio Head Dore Schary was dismissive of Purdom, recalling that 'He believed he was responsible for [the *Student Prince*'s success]. He asked for a new contract. We denied it. He asked for a release. We granted it.' (267)

Not only was Purdom presented as egotistical, but according to Downing he was 'nervous, temperamental, frequently upset, frequently ill' (65); the article lays the blame for Tita's decision to petition for divorce on these failings (65). Downing briefly mentions that Purdom was on vacation with Tyrone Power when he received the news that he had a part in *The Egyptian*. This sliver of information is not insignificant. Downing allusively notes that now for the first time the Purdoms' marriage 'faced an intangible problem', financial woes were over, but 'the problem was personal and one of adjustment' (66). The mention of Power is strategic, as Purdom had commenced an affair with Power's wife, Linda Christian, on the set of *Athena* (Thorpe 1954). The star of the film, Debbie Reynolds, recalled that

> [Linda Christian] was a temptress, and right before our eyes we saw the tempted, who was Edmund Purdom. They would go to his little trailer, close the door and be gone for quite a while. (Vallance 16 February 2009, n.p.)

As mentioned, the layout of the first two pages of the Purdom article align with those of Hudson and Brando, and reflects a set *Photoplay* house style. There are two smaller black-and-white photographs on the left and a colour portrait on the right. The text of the headline is all upper case, with the word 'Purdom' dividing the page widthways. The tails of the letters extend to flatten the word and separate the two smaller photos, the first of which sees the actor smoking a pipe, looking pensive, as the caption reads 'For the first time in his life, Edmund Purdom is asking himself, "Can I do it?"' (30). On first appraisal, this appears to be the portrait of a thoughtful man; however, the implication that this is the first time in his life he has encountered doubt alludes to his hubris, reinforcing both Downing's and Schary's assertions that he had become egotistical. Below the dividing line is a picture of Purdom with his wife, the pair arm in arm and smiling. The legend states 'The closeness he and Tita shared in poverty is, *he feels*, being threatened by the demands of success' [my emphasis]. The inclusion of the clause 'he feels' is intended to undermine the plausibility of the statement, as it is actually his infidelity that has strained the relationship. The question of ego is also expressed in the choice of font for 'Purdom': all upper case and large, but hollow. The inference is that, like Purdom, its presence is impactful, disruptive and insubstantial.

The colour print on page 31 is an informal portrait, unlike those of Hudson and Brando. It depicts a relaxed-seeming Purdom fishing from a boat. It portrays a classic, masculine pose reminiscent of Ernest Hemingway. However, this picture does not portray the fisherman in profile. We are not watching him fishing. He is facing us, leaning back with his legs splayed, and his fishing rod resting on his waist extending out of the frame. The sexual connotations are evident, and this photo may be read as an expression of virility. Yet Purdom's gaze glides past the viewer, he is relaxed, not concentrating on the activity, he holds a pipe in one hand and the rod with the other hand and out of shot. Both the pipe and the fishing rod allude to solitary, sensual pleasure. Although this article attempts to give the appearance of journalistic balance, it is clear that the author's opinion was that Purdom's star was already falling because of his arrogance.

So far, all the analysed articles reveal themselves as webs of code, signifiers and tropes. So what of Jane Corwin's article on Marlon Brando? Brando was at this point at the absolute crest of his career and was rewarded with the first feature of the three high-profile men in the first *Photoplay* issue of the year, corresponding to his fame at the time. Jane Corwin, like Beverly Ott, seeks to interrogate her subject's bad boy image in her article. As discussed, this piece serves as an opportunity to reveal anecdotes which uncover Brando as charming and playful. Whereas Ott spins her article from hearsay, Corwin's article quickly shifts from a frivolous fiction to a more journalistic style, quoting Brando's friends Johnny Ray and Harry Belafonte in support of her observations that he is, underneath it all, a good guy, and thereby enhancing the credibility of her assertions (68). Again *Photoplay* emphasises this pictorially, juxtaposing a colour head shot of an urbane Brando with pictures of him casually taking a telephone call, spending time with the child of a crew member of *On the Waterfront* (Kazan 1954) and speaking with a studio security guard. The 'candid' composition of these photos, combined with the use of black-and-white film stock, emphasises the reportage nature of the piece and connotes verisimilitude.

The comical vignette about Brando opens the story, commencing on page 24 and continuing on page 67, where the tone of the article shifts, to introduce friends who may shed some light on his 'true' personality. The text on page 67 only runs for one column, situated on the right-hand page facing the continuation of the Purdom story, and beside an advert for subscriptions to *Photoplay*.

It is both physically and textually the bridge from frivolous to factual. The story then continues on page 68, discussing the fact that Brando had socialised with a real-life 'gang' of stevedores in New Jersey while filming *On the Waterfront*. Using the testimony of Joseph Conepo, one of the gang, Corwin shows via firsthand evidence that Brando is truly a man of the people. The status of Conepo as an outsider to the film industry lends weight to his credibility, as he has no vested interest and can be considered impartial.

If his friendship with gang member Conepo provides an indication that Brando lives his life outside the mainstream, the hint is reiterated via his relationship with Harry Belafonte, with whom he had been friends since they studied together at the Dramatic Workshop. It is important to note at this point that Belafonte was primarily known as a folk singer, having just starred in his breakout film, *Carmen Jones* (Preminger 1954). The magazine signalled both its own and Brando's progressiveness by including Belafonte's words 'I was one of the very few Negro students in the school . . . Marlon was one of the first students to befriend me' (68). The magazine makes capital of the fact that Belafonte is conferred high social standing due to his success in *Carmen Jones*. However, the anecdote itself highlights the uncommon nature of Belafonte and Brando's friendship due to prevailing social norms. Indeed, the magazine is not bold enough to provide an accompanying picture of Belafonte, either with or without Brando.

Both Corwin and Manning have crafted articles which are not so much in the mould of 'Come-on Covers and Climb-down Contents' (Jeffers McDonald 2019) but are somewhat more sophisticated. They both masquerade as embodying this format, but their subtexts do not climb down, instead stealthily bringing to light 'controversial' aspects of their subjects' lifestyles. The text is opaque enough to allow the editors plausible deniability to fend off criticism.

While endorsing journalists sprinkling intrigue about a star within an article to pique fans' interest, the movie magazines seem to be less keen on the technique when it is employed by the star himself. This might be the real 'controversy' embodied by Victor Mature. Magazine articles from 1942 onwards report on Mature's view of himself as an *actor* in both senses of the word: as someone endowed with agency, who takes action, and a performer, even as a product.

Discomfiture with Mature's self-promotion was noted as early as 1942, when prolific Hollywood journalist Frederick C. Othman published his column 'Gall is a Wonderful Thing' in *The Saturday Evening Post* (18 July 1942): he highlighted Mature's self-awareness and ownership of his own publicity campaign as a character flaw. Othman seems to have found Mature's pragmatism combined with his business acumen distasteful: 'he studied all the movie magazines assiduously, with particular attention to the publicity campaigns of the great stars' (18 July 1942, 48). The implication here is that Mature's agency was in some way vulgar. Perhaps it was. If we are to believe that Mature was able to persuade his fiancée, Martha Kemp, to allow him to jilt her at the altar in order to generate publicity for him, as reported by Othman (49), it reinforces the contention that no publicity was bad and to be perceived as slightly rakish only added to the allure of a male star – a ploy which Mature was seeking to exploit.

A 1947 article in *Modern Screen* relays a similar story of Mature's dual roles as product and marketing man for that product. Carl Schroeder, in 'You're All Wrong About Mature!' (July 1947), presents a supposedly candid recollection of '[t]he tall, black haired young man . . .' (46) bursting enthusiastically into his office to request that Schroeder publish his photograph. Mature is portrayed as being very clear that this would stimulate interest in him as a commodity: 'I have it on good authority that if you'll put my picture in your magazine, I will be a cinch to get a job acting' (47). Schroeder says that he advised Mature to go and learn his craft for a couple for years instead; Mature agreed, with the proviso that Schroeder would publish his photograph upon his return.

When Mature did reappear from a period spent with the Pasadena Community Playhouse, Schroeder further relates, the writer kept his word by publishing his picture in an article entitled 'What Hollywood Needs Is a Man' (70). This initiated a run of four months during which Mature's picture was ubiquitous; the inference was that this had been a shrewd move by the pair. However, Schroeder noted that Mature voiced his disappointment at not becoming an overnight success via this initial campaign, and when the writer recommended that he should '[j]ust have a terrific romance' (70), Mature readily agreed. The correspondent in this arrangement was Lana Turner who, apparently, was a willing partner. If we believe that these events played out as Schroeder alleges, Mature saw himself as a business and surrounded himself with those who were able to assist him in achieving his business goals. Mature's pragmatic approach to attracting work was to commoditise, or sell himself, thereby unsettling the reader's attempt to reconcile the archetype of heterosexual masculinity with the more feminine role of sex object.

The various elements of Schroeder's piece written in 1947 foreshadow Ott's article. The earlier piece provides evidence of Mature's agency and pragmatism in characterising himself as a commodity. Mature's candour seemingly undermined the mythology of the overnight success in Tinseltown and set Mature up as an outsider, someone who could possibly draw back the curtain to reveal the 'Wizard'. A feeling that Mature was too artful seems to drive Ott's writing, in contrast to Corwin's piece on Brando. There is no hint that the latter is anything other than authentic, and the 'regular guy' aspects of his personality are easy to find and offset his more difficult aspects, whereas the attempt to manufacture a bad boy image by Mature seems to have backfired. Indeed, Mature must have been aware that his carefully crafted campaign to tread an intriguing line between saint and sinner had been undermined when Louella Parsons exposed him as being 'Mr Stay-At-Home' in *Modern Screen* July 1947, when she queried whether his tours of Hollywood night clubs with young beauties would continue after the release of his next film, implying that she knew this was a ruse to raise publicity (8). Similarly, Hedda Hopper mentioned Mature twice in her 'Myths Stars Believe About Themselves' column in a July 1949 issue of the same magazine, puncturing his carefully cultivated persona. Hopper asserts that he would 'flaunt his florid affairs to be sure they didn't bloom unseen', but insists that he is happier 'as a family man supreme, thoroughly domesticated and loving his role of foster dad' (99). These doyennes of the scandal sheet effectively beat Mature at his own game, by highlighting his naturally avuncular tendencies, not the stuff of glamour and scandal required to sell magazines.

Ott's article rehashes the contradictory tropes regarding Mature without uncovering any new scandal. This is in contrast to Parsons and Hopper who 'exposed' Mature's secret – that he is a kind and well-loved actor; Ott seeks merely to highlight his downward trajectory to the mundane.

In conclusion, this chapter has demonstrated the editorial precision of fan magazines, revealing that editors were reliant upon the audience being sophisticated individuals with a wide range of cultural references to draw on, in order to interpret the subtext of the magazine. Very different from the view that movie magazine readers were the 'passive, gullible, undiscriminating consumers' Glancy references, my careful examination of a single issue reveals an interest in various forms of mid-century masculinity, a dislike of overt self-promotion, and an expectation that readers were adept enough to pick up indirect clues in both text and layout. This issue of a popular movie magazine was carefully crafted so that the content of its various pieces was subtly reinforced by the advertising surrounding them. That Victor Mature was not considered a draw for the teenager is evident, then, not only from Beverly Ott's article but also from the advertisements appearing next to its penultimate page, which were for a maternity fashion brochure, unwanted hair removal cream, and Anacin (87). This contrasts with the advert for the youthful Sweetheart Soap which accompanied the Schroeder article in 1947 (71). Perhaps the ultimate blow to Mature's sex appeal is the rather curious advertisement for a signed miniature reproduction of Liberace's piano (Figure 3.5). The suggestion that the dandyish Liberace appealed to the same audience as Mature seems to emasculate the latter, or at the very least peg him as a heartthrob for the more senior lady.

To underline the authority of this reading, it is useful to return to 1942 which, as mentioned, was a high point for fan magazine mentions of Mature. In the April 1942 edition of *Photoplay* Mature has a feature article by John R. Franchey, 'Life Owes You Nothing'.

This article, like Ott's, was placed in the middle of the magazine (52–3) and neither the portrait nor the text was coloured. While the fact that this was a wartime edition might have restricted paper, font and colour choices, many

Figure 3.5 Advertisements accompanying 'Tough Softie' article. *Photoplay*, January 1955. (p. 87)

colour plates were used elsewhere in the same issue and, therefore, it is valid to query the editorial choice not to use colour in this article. The headline text has a traditional font which chimes with the basis of the article: a discussion of advice given to Mature by his father. In contrast to the article by Ott, the main photo accompanying this one is of a screen idol. This seems at odds with the assertion that the placement of Ott's article is commensurate to the failing popularity of Mature, when the Franchey article, appearing in the year Mature receives most mentions, is in almost the same position. It is the throwaway description on page 53 of Mature as the 'Hero of 1941's biggest comeback story' which provides justification for the placement of the article. In both situations the magazine writers had judged Mature to be unworthy of a colour photograph or a lead story in the issue, but, though they might denigrate him, they could not afford to ignore him, and the article's position was a begrudging acceptance of his popularity.

The adverts here also follow the traditional layout format for mass-market periodicals, again being displaced towards the rear of the magazine alongside the article's continuation columns. The choice of accompanying advertisements also signifies the assumed reader to be a young woman. While not glamourous, the necessary Meds tampon is advertised to the left of the text on page 80, opposite an advert for the glamorous Tangee lipstick on the far right of page 81 (Figure 3.6).

Figure 3.6 Advertisements accompanying Victor Mature article 'Life Owes You Nothing'. *Photoplay*, April 1942. (pp. 80–1)

Both adverts speak to the very essence of the feminine sexuality possessed by the assumed audience, as the embedded photograph of Mature does to virility. It can be no accident that Mature is presented as a primitive hunter, carrying a woman over one shoulder, thrusting spear in his opposite hand. The editorial choice to nestle such a potent demonstration of masculinity between two phallic-shaped items, designed to touch only the most intimate feminine parts, is not subtle. It does, however, reflect the fact that Mature remained vital and his successful comeback at this point was due in some part to his sexual potency.

This contrasts with the adverts around the 1955 Brando article: the magazine's subscription offer, the classifieds and a sinus congestion remedy (67). This might seem to run counter to Brando's contemporaneous fame and persona: it might be imagined that more prestigious adverts would be placed around this article in accordance with his star power. It is more likely, however, that Brando could sell copies of the magazine affecting *all* advertising revenue, whereas other stars earned their place alongside appropriate product placement. Hence the advertising surrounding the Hudson article is suitably reflective of his popularity and the editor's target audience. The eclectic range of items for sale include a solution for restless legs, Ex-lax, teething lotion, potholders (73) and handbags (75). There are no overt nods to sex or desire in this selection of adverts, which conveys a neutrality to sex contrary to Hudson's public persona but aligned with the tenor of the article portraying him as benign rather than erotic. Accompanying Edmund Purdom's article is an advert for Needlecraft Design and another for Elsa Maxwell's *Etiquette Book* (64). Again, these are not titillating. However, the precise placement of the advert for the etiquette book is remarkable. Almost level with the section which speculates on the reasons for Purdom's failure to attend the premiere of *The Egyptian* including those 'first night jitters', is the advert header, 'I was afraid of my shadow'. The article continues 'Today, Edmund Purdom is Hollywood's fastest-rising young star', which is mirrored in the advert's assertion that '. . .now I am the most popular woman in town'. The link between the two is made in the description of Purdom's handsome good looks and crucially, his 'frightfully British accent'. The connotations of class are linked vertically within the article to success, and horizontally to etiquette as a means to acquire class and thereby mirror that success.

Despite the longevity of disparagement regarding the value of movie magazines, which indicates a fundamental distrust of the taste and judgement of its – gendered – audience, recent work on these popular publications has demonstrated that they can be a rich source of historical and cultural information. Juxtaposing content and layout, and analysing both, this chapter has highlighted a seeming willingness on behalf of editorial staff to suspend cynicism about their readers' abilities in picking up subtle intimations and non-verbal clues.

Note

1. Using 'Victor Mature' as search criteria in the Media History Digital Library's Arclight tool reveals that Mature is mentioned 464 times in its collection of 1942 publications.

References

Corwin, Jane. 1955. 'The Devil is a Gentleman'. *Photoplay*, January: 24–5, 67–8.
Downing, Hyatt. 1955. 'Purdom – Man on a Tightrope'. *Photoplay*, January: 30–1, 65–6.
Franchey, John R. 1942. 'Life Owes You Nothing'. *Photoplay*, April: 52–3, 80–1.
Glancy, Mark. 2011. '*Picturegoer*: The Fan Magazine and Popular Film Culture in Britain During the Second World War'. *Historical Journal of Film, Radio and Television* 31 (4): 453–78.
Hall, Sheldon, and Steve Neale. 2010. *Epics, Spectacles, and Blockbusters: A Hollywood History*. Detroit, MI: Wayne State University Press.
Hopper, Hedda. 1949. 'Myths Stars Believe About Themselves'. *Modern Screen*, July: 34–6, 99–100.
Jeffers McDonald, Tamar. 2019. 'Come-on Covers and Climb-down Contents'. In *Star Attractions: Twentieth-Century Movie Magazines and Global Fandom*, edited by Tamar Jeffers McDonald and Lies Lanckman, 29–44. Iowa: University of Iowa Press.
Jeffers McDonald, Tamar, and Lies Lanckman, eds. 2019. *Star Attractions: Twentieth-Century Movie Magazines and Global Fandom*. Iowa: University of Iowa Press.
Lang, Cady, and Anna Purna Kambhampaty. 2020. 'The True Stories Behind Ryan Murphy's New Netflix Series Hollywood'. *Time*, May: n.p. <https://time.com/5828209/hollywood-true-story-netflix> (last accessed 1 November 2021).
McKay, James. 2012. *The Films of Victor Mature*. Jefferson, NC and London: McFarland & Company Inc.
Manning, Ray. 1955. 'Rock Hudson's Love Affair with the USA'. *Photoplay*, January: 40–1, 73–5.
Othman, Frederick C. 1942. 'Gall Is a Wonderful Thing'. *The Saturday Evening Post*, 18 July: 24–5, 48–50.
Ott, Beverly. 1955. 'Tough Softie'. *Photoplay*, January: 50–1, 86–8.
Parmeter, Lola. 1955. 'Don't Be a Teenage Misfit'. *Photoplay*, January: 48–9, 76.
Parsons, Louella. 1947. 'Louella Parsons' Good News'. *Modern Screen*, July: 6–8, 10, 114–15.
Photoplay. 1955. January.
Schary, Dore. 1979. *Heyday: An Autobiography*. Boston: Little Brown.
Schroeder, Carl. 1947. 'You're All Wrong About Mature!' *Modern Screen*, July: 46–7, 70–1.
Vallance, Tom. 1999. 'Obituary: Victor Mature'. *Independent*, 11 August: n.p. <https://www.independent.co.uk/arts-entertainment/obituary-victor-mature-1112009.html> (last accessed 1 November 2021).
Vallance, Tom. 2009. 'Edmund Purdom: Actor who Replaced Brando in "The Egyptian" then forged a new career in Italy'. *Independent*, 16 February: n.p. <https://www.independent.co.uk/news/obituaries/edmund-purdom-actor-who-replaced-brando-in-the-egyptian-then-forged-a-new-career-in-italy-1623022.html> (last accessed 1 November 2021).

4. DOROTHY DANDRIDGE THE INVISIBLE STAR: RACIAL SEGREGATION IN HOLLYWOOD FAN MAGAZINES IN THE 1950s

Cathy Lomax

In 1954 Dorothy Dandridge's career was approaching its peak. After many years playing small roles on screen and singing in theatres and clubs, she was cast as the lead in Otto Preminger's all-Black musical *Carmen Jones*, a role that won her an Academy Award nomination. But while she was a familiar face to readers of Black targeted magazines such as *Ebony* and *Jet*, was extensively featured in European magazines, and appeared in 'mainstream' US publications such as *Esquire* and *Cosmopolitan*, becoming the first Black woman to appear on the cover of the leading US photo magazine *Life* in November 1954, she was ignored by the US fan magazines. Donald Bogle in his substantive biography of Dandridge notes that with the release of *Carmen Jones*

> movie magazines like *Photoplay*, *Modern Screen* and *Motion Picture* chose not to do features on her. *Photoplay* reviewed *Carmen Jones* [. . .] but there were no glamorous photo layouts. No visits to the star's home. No features detailing the star's love life. (Bogle 1998, 313)

Building on Bogle's observations I will be examining how despite being set up as the first Black female Hollywood star, Dorothy Dandridge's exclusion from Hollywood fan magazines in effect rendered her invisible to a large percentage of filmgoers and thereby quashed her chances of a sustained high-profile film career. My focus will be an issue of *Photoplay* from February 1955, where, discretely nestled among the usual colourful content about new babies, feuding stars, happy (and not-so-happy) marriages, glamorous homes, decorative fashion and the latest film releases, is a one-page feature in black and white about *Carmen Jones*. By looking at this, alongside coverage of Dandridge in contemporaneous magazines, I will outline the way in which US fan magazines of the mid-1950s, a time when the civil rights movement was gaining traction, maintained a conservative and essentially racist agenda by only promoting white actors.

Dandridge

Before focusing on *Photoplay* I want to outline Dandridge's importance as a totemic figure. At surface level it would be easy to dismiss her as a minor Hollywood actor, in that her filmography is sparse and the films she made of variable quality. However, as Karen Alexander in her study of Black women in Hollywood asserts, Dandridge was 'the only genuine Black female star Hollywood ever produced, if by star is meant that combination of an immediately seductive image with the larger-than-life projection of a persona, the combination that also produced Marilyn Monroe' (Alexander 1991, 53). Alexander states that Dandridge was known as 'America's first sex goddess of colour' (1991, 47), a tag that somewhat inaccurately paints her as a sexy, dark-skinned counterpoint to the blondeness of Monroe (of whom she was an acquaintance). In actuality, Dandridge's persona was far more complex, and her image went through many iterations before she was promoted as a seductive sex bomb in the lead up to *Carmen Jones*. Pre-Carmen, Dandridge's screen roles are notable for a certain controlled style; sleek nightclub singer, doting wife, respectable schoolteacher, and in *Tarzan's Peril* (Haskin 1951), a principled African queen who is described by *Ebony* as 'dignified and beautiful [. . .] quite different from the black-faced tribal characters seen in the past 35 years of filming the favourite jungle stories of Edgar Rice Burroughs' (April 1951, 48). These roles, as Mia Mask notes, convey an 'air of bourgeois respectability, elegance, and sophistication [which] broadened the image of Black womanhood in the public sphere' (Mask 2009, 14).

The promotion of Dandridge as sexually provocative in the build-up to *Carmen Jones* cast her in a role which had been the preserve of white female stars (such as Monroe) since the earliest days of cinema, a move which might be considered progressive in the racially segregated US society of the mid-1950s, when miscegenation was still forbidden on screen. However, Dandridge's styling, and, as I will go on to discuss, the particular way she was described after *Carmen Jones*, acted to reinforce the clichéd idea of the Black woman as sexualised other, while her absence from fan magazines reflected the queasy uncertainty that society felt about depicting a Black woman as beautiful and desirable. It was, writes Jeremy Tambling in *Opera, Ideology and Film*, a 'mythologising of the dangerous black or mixed race woman, and of her ambivalent "nature"'

(Tambling 1987, 31–2). It is noticeable that commentaries on Dandridge's performances frequently remark on how she is dressed as a factor in her suitability for roles, as if unable to reconcile her appearance with her skin colour. For example, a review of *Porgy and Bess* (Preminger 1959) in *Variety* is of the opinion that, 'Miss Dandridge is perhaps too "refined" in type to be quite convincing as the split-skirt, heroin-shuffling tramp' (Land, 1 July 1959, 6), while a press release issued by Columbia to accompany *Tamango* (Berry 1958) stated

> [i]t is ironic that, although she is one of the most elegantly groomed women in show business, almost all her film roles have called for a drab and tattered wardrobe. No exception is her latest part of a slave girl (Columbia Campaign Book (UK) for *Tamango*, 1959, 2. Quoted by Alexander 1991, 48)

Aside from this disequilibrium between on- and off-screen persona, Dandridge's story of hard-won success was something that aligned her with many other stars. Born in 1922, she began work as a child in a singing duo with her sister, and by the age of twelve she was performing internationally with The Dandridge Sisters trio. In 1940 she had her first credited film role in the race film *Four Shall Die* (Popkin).[1] This was followed by appearances in 'soundies' (short musical films played on video jukeboxes), before graduating to small roles as maids and African natives in mainstream Hollywood films. Throughout her adult life Dandridge continued to perform as a singer, often on variety bills for which she received good, if not outstanding, notices, such as a 1947 show at the Million Dollar Theatre, Los Angeles, with the Floyd Ray orchestra, where her performance was commended for 'solid thrushing'[2] (Hurl, 21 August 1946, 57). This changed in 1950 when, after working with arranger Phil Moore, she emerged with a solo nightclub act which marked her as 'a new and far more glamorous' performer (*The Chicago Defender*, 27 January 1951, 21). Dandridge's new image was celebrated in a series of stylish photographs in the 5 November 1951 issue of *Life*, in which she is said to have 'sung her way from a small Hollywood nightclub to stardom at the Mocambo and a huge success in London' (65).

This high-profile nightclub act brought her new attention from Hollywood producers[3] and in 1953 she was cast in the starring role of a small-town schoolteacher in MGM's majority-Black-cast *Bright Road* (Figure 4.1) (Mayer), a film seen by Otto Preminger, who went on to direct her in the all-Black musical *Carmen Jones*. In 1955 after the completion of *Carmen Jones*, Dandridge's potential was confirmed by Darryl Zanuck, who signed her to a three-year contract with 20th Century Fox. By this point she was an experienced thirty-two-year-old performer who had appeared at nightclubs all over the world and had made over twenty feature film appearances.

Figure 4.1 Dandridge's demurely elegant persona is on show in her role in *Bright Road* (1953).

A Censored Stardom

Although generally well received, *Carmen Jones* was not universally liked, with the film's racial politics criticised by some commentators, notably James Baldwin, who wrote that while the lighter-skinned actors (Dandridge and co-star Harry Belafonte) are depicted as complex and desirable, the darker-skinned characters, who in effect 'do not live in the same world', are sketchily drawn clichés ([1957] 2017, 51–2). Despite this, it is hard to dispute the importance of the film's depiction of the erotic love of an appealing Black couple, and the consequent elevation of the Black actors playing these roles to the lower echelons of stardom. *Jet* (*Ebony*'s sister publication) wrote that Dandridge and Belafonte were Hollywood's first 'love team that does not tax the imagination' (30 September 1954, 60). This was in opposition to previous Black cast films in which the female star was matched with an unlikely romantic partner in order to downplay her sexual appeal. *Jet* notes that in the 1929 Black musical *Hallelujah* (Vidor) 'beauteous Nina Mae McKinney began a long-suffering career of playing opposite males who were a far cry from the "leading man" type' (60).

Carmen Jones was adapted from the 1943, all-Black cast stage musical of the same name, which was itself an adaptation of Bizet's opera *Carmen*. The film's well-regarded producer/director Otto Preminger secured $775,000 from

20th Century Fox to finance the film. The cast was announced in May 1954, and principal photography in DeLuxe Color and the relatively new Cinemascope format completed in early August 1954. In the months around the film's release in October 1954 there is a noticeable shift in the way that Dandridge is depicted, in what appears to be a concerted campaign to promote her as more sexually seductive. Although variations in magazine lead times make it hard to pinpoint the exact dates that features were compiled, notable in this regard is the 'Lady Fair' pin-up, photographed by Philippe Halsman, for the June 1954 issue of *Esquire*. This magazine at the time was a high-profile men's magazine published in US and British editions, which, alongside literary fiction and articles about cars, sport and fashion, included tastefully provocative images of women (often actresses) taken by prestigious photographers.[4]

Other publicity in late 1954 included the cover feature in the 1 November issue of *Life* and on 24 October, four days before the film's opening, a live television broadcast in which Dandridge, the only Black performer, sang two songs to an audience estimated at 60 to 70 million.[5] After the film's premiere *Newsweek* hailed Dandridge as 'an incandescent Carmen, devilishly wilful and feline. She is one of the outstanding dramatic actresses of the screen' (25 October 1954, 102). Louella Parsons in *Cosmopolitan* called *Carmen Jones* 'a work of vitality, compassion, strength, and passion rarely reflected on the screen', with Dandridge 'a beautiful girl who knows how to wear clothes and swing a hot song', (*Cosmopolitan*, December 1954, 4) able to display her acting talent. This publicity continued into 1955 when the film opened in Europe, with Dandridge given the treatment and coverage afforded to any attractive new star in the British publications *Picturegoer* and *Picture Show*, as well as appearing on covers across Europe, including *Der Stern* and *Paris Match*.[6] The rise of her star in Europe was capped by a promotional visit to Cannes where *Carmen Jones* had been selected to close the 1955 Cannes Festival, while back in the US Dandridge's good notices brought her a nomination for the Best Actress Academy Award. With this impressive national and international success, *Ebony* reported in December 1955 that the film had grossed $5,000,000, a figure which would have netted Preminger and Fox an extensive profit (24).

In the light of this information, it seems astonishing that in early 1955, when *Carmen Jones* was showing on screens across the US, and receiving almost universal acclaim, and Dandridge was the subject of numerous articles in Europe, the US fan magazines gave the film only a cursory mention. The February 1955 issue of *Photoplay*, which proclaims itself to be, 'America's largest selling movie magazine',[7] featured Doris Day on its cover as a tie-in for her latest release *Young at Heart* (Douglas 1955) (Figure 4.2). This image of Day in pale pink against a pastel turquoise background is credited (on the contents page) as, 'Color Portrait of Doris Day, currently in Warner's *Young at Heart*, by Six'. *Young at Heart* is further promoted in the issue with a full-page advertisement

Figure 4.2   Doris Day cover. *Photoplay*, February 1955.

Figure 4.3   Advertisement for Lustre-Crème Shampoo featuring Doris Day. *Photoplay*, February 1955. (p. 20)

on page 7, and then again on page 20 in an advertisement for Lustre-Crème Shampoo, which features an image of Day (in which she bears almost exactly the same expression and hair style as in the cover image) accompanied by the credit line 'Doris Day co-starring in *Young at Heart*. An Arwin Production in WarnerColor. Presented by Warner Bros' (Figure 4.3). Day is also mentioned briefly by Sidney Skolsky in his 'That's Hollywood Gossip For You' on page 10. All of this is before the main interview with the star by Ernst Jacobi, 'If you like what you love You're in Luck', on page 48. This accumulation of material is what Jeffers McDonald terms the 'star trail', that is, a series of images and mentions for a star that appear before the main feature, which lead 'the reader to her while magnifying the sense of her importance' (Jeffers McDonald 2013, 39).

As is evident from this wealth of Doris Day content, a star actor's work did not finish when a film wrapped. The extent of this work is outlined by Esther Williams, who in her autobiography, describes the publicity regime that was set in place after production on *Skirts Ahoy!* (Lanfield 1952) was completed,

> the now-familiar pattern proceeded into the next phase and we moved into publicity. The studio shot the stills that would be used for lobby cards and posters [. . .] After that they arranged for the parade of fan magazine writers and photographers to come to the house for interviews and the obligatory home candids. (Williams 2000, 208)

Returning to *Young at Heart*, we should note that although Day was a very popular star, as was her co-star Frank Sinatra, Day's role in the film is not generally considered noteworthy. Bosley Crowther in his *New York Times* review (published on 20 January 1955) calls the film 'a bit flabby and wishy-washy in spots', with Day 'sometimes much too bubbly' (n.p.), while Foster Hirsch describes Day as being 'trapped in a vapid ingenue role' (2010, 154). Of course, the staff responsible for the February 1955 issue of *Photoplay*, which appeared on the newsstands in January and was prepared months before, would not necessarily have been aware of the quality of the film. However, it does highlight how the established status quo is maintained by studio publicity departments, which would have supplied material about Day and offered the star for interview. This treatment of Day and *Young at Heart* is in stark contrast to *Photoplay*'s coverage of Dandridge and the highly acclaimed *Carmen Jones*, which is only mentioned twice in the issue, with product tie-ins and star interviews notable by their absence. We should note that Dandridge was known to the magazine, as she had received a good notice in a June 1953 review of *Bright Road* ('Lovely Dorothy Dandridge, known chiefly as a singer, approaches the business of acting with disarming simplicity.') (Graves 1953, 22). The first mention for *Carmen Jones* in the February 1955 issue is a very short write-up in 'brief reviews' (it was reviewed a little more expansively in the previous issue on page 8) which gives it the highest possible rating, calling it a '[b]rilliant, unusual musical, set in America's South. Dorothy Dandridge, as the temptress, and Harry Belafonte, as the soldier she ruins, head an all-Negro cast.' (12).

The second is a one-page '*Photoplay* recommends' profile of *Carmen Jones* on page 31. This curious feature, which appeared sporadically in *Photoplay* during 1955, highlighted films that might be termed prestige pictures, including *East of Eden* (May 1955, 37) and *Marty* (June 1955, 35). The presentation of the feature suggests it is an advertorial, that is, a paid-for feature used to educate consumers in a credible form by including more detail than an advertisement and tying the promoted product to the magazine with the 'recommends' tag. We might extrapolate that Fox and Preminger thought that the readers of *Photoplay* might not be attracted by (or connect to) the film's standard advertising material (which featured a provocative image of Dandridge) and needed to be persuaded that they should see the film by a special recommendation from a trusted magazine. The feature itself is made up of small black-and-white production images in which Dandridge is shown as part of the film's *mise en scène*. This is in stark opposition to the mostly colour glamour images of Day as a singular star figure apart from the cast of *Young at Heart*. The short text outlines that Dandridge, Belafonte and Pearl Bailey 'have all achieved imposing reputations as night-club stars', and identifies the film as 'an exhilarating, utterly different kind of musical drama'. The words used to describe the film and Carmen/Dorothy, 'different', 'exhilarating', 'unusual', 'temptress', are as telling as the visual treatment it is given. These mark Carmen/Dorothy as other, drawing on the clichés of Black women as sexually charged, thereby marking the film as an oddity, and separating it from the usual Hollywood output in which Black women did not appear in starring roles. Further ignominy for the stars of *Carmen Jones* is apparent in *Photoplay*'s annual awards published in the March 1955 issue and selected by the magazine's readers, in which the only mention for *Carmen Jones* was in the 'Special Award' presented by the magazine to 'talented producer-director' Otto Preminger for his work on the film. The short text notes that '[h]e chose his players (headed by Dorothy Dandridge and Harry Belafonte) shrewdly, guided them unerringly'. There is no image of the film and only a cursory mention for its stars (*Photoplay*, March 1955, 65.)

As Bogle notes, it was not just *Photoplay* that ignored Dandridge (1998, 313). *Modern Screen*'s approach was almost identical, with *Carmen Jones* given a short positive review but not featured in any other way. In December 1954 *Modern Screen*'s regular 'Louella Parsons in Hollywood' section ran to eight pages, with no mention of Dandridge, and her 'I nominate for stardom' accolade awarded to Mitzi Gaynor (12).[8] I mention this because the same writer's December 1954 *Cosmopolitan* feature effusively praised Dandridge (4). Anthony Slide observes that when another of the fan magazines, *Motion Picture*, put Lena Horne on their October 1944 cover, it became the first to feature an African-American cover star.

As Slide notes, '[e]xecutive editor Laurence Reid took the gamble, which was considered a high-risk one, and it resulted in a sales slump. The experiment was never repeated' (2010, 199).

The scope of Preminger and Fox's campaign to promote Dandridge and *Carmen Jones* is apparent in the enthusiastic notices displayed in an advertisement in *Boxoffice* (a publication aimed at theatre owners and film professionals) on 13 November 1954 by the likes of Hedda Hopper, Walter Winchell and Ed Sullivan (11–13). Although these testimonials and reviews were undeniably an important factor in the success of the film, the absence of personal publicity for Dandridge in the mainstream fan magazines was a notable and serious impediment to her personal development as a star. An unattributed article published in *Ebony* in July 1955, 'Dorothy Dandridge's Greatest Triumph', features images of Dandridge presenting an Academy Award alongside a discussion of her thoughts on stardom, her disabled daughter and her failed marriage; exactly the kind of life information that was the staple of fan magazines. It is this mix of glamorous imagery and revelatory background detail about life events that Richard Dyer notes as setting stars up as simultaneously special and ordinary (Dyer 1998, 35) and it is this fundamental component of stardom that was not afforded to Dandridge by white America.

Placement and General Contents

To determine what informed *Photoplay*'s decision – and indeed those of other Hollywood fan magazines – to ignore Dandridge, we need to look at the magazine in more detail. Lies Lanckman's work on the readership of *Photoplay* in the 1930s identifies the average letter writer as a 'young white woman in her early twenties' (Lanckman 2019, 53). The content of the February 1955 issue suggests that little had changed, with white skin presented as the norm, and promoted as desirable, subtly in the editorial and more overtly by the advertising. This tone is set by the very blonde Doris Day on the cover and reinforced on the inside front page with a full-page advertisement for Ivory Soap. Other advertisements in the issue for Helene Curtis Shampoo plus Egg (8), Marchand's Golden Hair Wash (24) and Helene Curtis Suave (11) continue the message in their foregrounding of blonde hair and white skin. The Marchand's Golden Hair Wash advertisement proclaims 'Blondes have a magic . . . Poets through the ages have sung of blonde beauty. With Marchand's Golden Hair Wash, *you* can be a devastating golden-top – safely, easily, right at home.' Aside from the advertisements, a profile of Virginia Mayo on page 34 titled 'Speaking of Angels . . . There's a Girl Called Virginia', is illustrated with a colour image of the very blonde and fair-skinned star in a white satin dress. On page 44 there is another full-colour image of a blonde star, Grace Kelly. Smiling and fresh-faced, aside from the ever-present 1950s red lipstick, her whiteness is

Figure 4.4   Advertisement for Modess sanitary napkins opposite '*Photoplay* recommends *Carmen Jones*'. *Photoplay*, February 1955. (pp. 30–1)

reinforced by the copy, which describes her as being 'fair and beautiful with a couple of bright blue eyes and corn-blond hair' (Cohen 1955, 82).

Among this content, on pages 30 and 31, is the spread which includes '*Photoplay* Recommends *Carmen Jones*' on the right-hand page. Facing it is a full-page colour image of an elegant white woman leaning against a grand piano in a luxurious, full-skirted long white dress, with the caption 'Only New Design Modess gives you the luxury of a new whisper soft fabric covering ... no gauze ... no chafe' (Figure 4.4). Although not immediately apparent because the product is not identified, the inclusion of 'gauze' and 'chafe' are the clues that reveal that the advertisement is for a sanitary product. In this curious pairing of sanitary product with prestige film, the gleaming whiteness of the Modess model acts to highlight the dark skins of the *Carmen Jones* actors on the facing page, a seemingly incongruous piece of magazine layout which could be explained away as a random placement of advertisement and editorial/advertorial. However, this theory is tempered by Darrell Blaine Lucas and Steuart Henderson Britt's 1950 study of advertising psychology, which explains that the positioning of advertising was a well-considered subject.

> Most magazines have some pages which advertisers call preferred positions. The outside back cover has an obvious advantage in advertising

exposure. There are other locations inside of the magazine which have, or are believed to have, a special advantage [such as] the page facing the first important editorial feature. Those who specialize in buying magazine-advertising space put a great deal of emphasis upon the page locations they obtain. (Lucas and Britt 1950, 223)

Although feasible that Johnson & Johnson (the owners of the Modess brand) purchased advertising space in *Photoplay* without regard to where it was placed, Lucas and Britt report that anecdotally over 50 per cent of advertisers requested a particular prestigious space early in the make-up of a magazine (232). Examining Modess's advertising patterns reveals that Johnson & Johnson took out a full-page colour advertisement in the September, October and November 1954 issues of *Photoplay* (which appeared on pages 12, 125 and 113 respectively). In 1955 they advertised in February, April, September and October (pages 30, 113, 9 and 117). Each advertisement features fashion models, in high-quality fashion, as part of what has been called a ground-breaking campaign to destigmatise sanitary products (Henderson, 5 September 2018, n.p.). The seemingly random placement of the advertisement throughout these issues indicates that the company did not receive a regular spot in the running order of the magazine and most frequently appeared in the back pages, where they face run-on copy from earlier articles. It is worth referring back to Lucas and Britt, who note that despite requesting prestigious spots 'as a general rule advertisers have little control over their page location in a magazine' (223). We can assume that the popularity of *Photoplay* (and its young female readership) gave it an upper hand in the finely balanced relationship between advertiser and magazine, which meant it could afford to prioritise prestige and visual appeal over the requests of advertisers. I would suggest that a page facing a promotion for an all-Black film would not have been popular for the very same reasons that Dandridge herself was not featured in the magazine in any meaningful way. That is to say, it would be assumed that images of Black actors would alienate the majority white readership. Therefore, a low-prestige advertisement, which, despite its visual appeal, would always be the categorisation of anything associated with menstruation, was able to be positioned wherever the magazine had a difficult spot to fill.

Black Magazines

I am not suggesting that readers of *Photoplay* were necessarily or knowingly racist; in fact evidence to the contrary is supplied by a letter in the November 1949 issue of the magazine:

> Recently, I've been reading about all the movies being made about Negroes, but all of them such as 'Pinky' have white people as stars [. . .]

> Why don't they make a movie with Lena Horne as the star? She hasn't made any pictures in which she has an acting part. I think she is a beautiful person and she can act. (Orlegard, 4)

Generally, however, it appears that magazines mirrored the segregation that affected so many aspects of American life in the mid-20th century, a position that kept white Americans ignorant and ill-informed about non-white Americans. A 2019 *New York Times* feature about *Ebony* magazine, which was founded in 1945 with an ambition to present African-American issues in a thoughtful and positive light, notes wryly that African Americans were rarely featured in the white press in the 1950s unless they committed crimes (Staples, 11 August 2019, n.p). It is certainly true, as Sumiko Higashi writes, that the absence of women of colour in US fan magazines in the 1950s reflected a repression of racialised women on screen (2014, 2). This is the very reason why the positive if somewhat repressed reception of Dandridge in *Carmen Jones* was so remarkable. To unpick this a little we should note that Black actors had been working in Hollywood since the early days of the film industry but were generally cast in subservient roles, often as maids or railway porters. Exceptions to this were entertainers like Lena Horne, who were admired for their energy and exoticism but (as commented on by the letter writer) remained separate from the main cast of the film, performing instead as speciality acts. The often-repeated reason for this separation of Black musical stars and the absence of Black lead actors in Hollywood films is what Thomas Cripps terms 'the myth of the Southern box office'. This myth suggests that films starring Black performers would not make economic sense because they would be boycotted in the Southern states, thereby losing revenue. Consequently, Black performers, if not playing subservient roles, had to be able to be cut from the film without disrupting the narrative. Cripps repudiates this idea, contending that the Southern box office was notoriously low and would in any case have been offset by increased Black patronage (Cripps 1970, 121–5). This returns us to the maintenance of the racist status quo as the prime motivation for not developing Black stars or financing films starring Black actors.

We should also note that Hollywood did periodically produce Black cast films, generally musicals, such as the already mentioned *Hallelujah*, as well as *Cabin in the Sky* (Minnelli 1943) and indeed *Carmen Jones*. However, these films tended to present Black people in a 'folksy' way, which harked back to the woefully inaccurate popular myth of the idyllic antebellum South. Diahann Carroll, who made her film debut in *Carmen Jones*, noted some of the issues she had with the film (which are also applicable to other examples of the 'Black musical' genre):

> The plot and the characters and situations were every bit as stereotyped as the 'dees', 'dems' and 'dats' that filled the dialogue [. . .] We were the

> only Black people on the lot [. . .] we were outsiders, in town for only a short while to do our 'Black' feature film (there was a 'Black' film every few years), and when it was over we would go back to where we came from and no one would ever see us again. (Carroll 1986, 47–8)

The European Difference

The difference in the treatment of Dandridge by European fan magazines is yet more evidence that highlights the US's suppression of information about its racially segregated society. A 1 January 1955 article in the British fan magazine *Picturegoer* notes:

> She's dynamite all round – but Hollywood is finding this dynamite too tricky to handle. The trouble lies in the colour of her skin. It's coffee-coloured. Yes, Dorothy Dandridge is a negress [. . .] there's no question of a movieland colour bar. The only thing that concerns Hollywood is: would more Negro films be box office? (Hinxman, 5)

This open articulation of the problems Dandridge faced because of her colour is markedly different from the covert approach to issues around race in the US. In another British fan magazine, *Picture Show*, the discrepancy between the treatment of Dandridge (and Belafonte) in Europe and the US is apparent in the magazine's design. In this feature from the 5 March 1955 issue the stars are foregrounded in two solo publicity shots which are surrounded by smaller images from the film (8) (Figure 4.5). This differs sharply from '*Photoplay* recommends *Carmen Jones*', in which the stars are only shown as members of the cast in stills from the film.

Dandridge and *Ebony* as Signifiers of a Black Middle Class

In contrast to her invisibility in the Hollywood fan magazines, Dandridge was a familiar face in the Black press. *Ebony* in particular broke new ground in its focus on members of the African-American middle and upper classes, showing them in their tastefully decorated homes and enjoying the same activities as white people: travel, skiing, tennis, drinking Coca-Cola. Brent Staples contends that, the '[c]orporate advertisers who had previously shunned black ventures warmed to [*Ebony*'s] argument that the black middle class would embrace brands that depicted people of color in advertisements' (11 August 2019, n.p.). The commercial possibilities afforded by this new market of affluent Black middle-class consumers aligns with a significant aspect of Dandridge's persona, which as Mia Mask notes, was that 'she was a star during the instantiation of the black American as consumer' (Mask 2009, 19).

The possibilities of this new market were undoubtedly noticed by the studios who were keen to mitigate some of the losses that the advent of television had wrought, and Dandridge's contract with 20th Century Fox is part of this slow

Figure 4.5 Carmen Jones feature. *Picture Show*, 5 March 1955. (p. 8)

progressive move. However, it was precisely because it was a transitional period that Dandridge faced problems in finding suitable film roles. Discussions about race had been suppressed in the US for so long that inherently conservative producers and stretched film studios, who were still subject to the Production

Code's ban on miscegenation until 1956, were slow to take risks with more liberal projects and casting ideas, and quick to fall back on stereotypes, as Gary Null notes in *Black Hollywood: The Negro in Motion Pictures*:

> the role Dandridge plays in *Carmen Jones* and later in *Porgy and Bess* does not essentially depart from the image of the mulatto woman whose white blood makes her beautiful and whose black blood degrades her and who is doomed to die tragically [. . .] In Hollywood, right up to the present, the beautiful Black woman has always been light-skinned and short-lived. (Null 1975, 169–71)

Ebony magazine was also caught in this double bind, in which its mandate to promote and elevate Black Americans was severely compromised by mixed messages about skin colour. In the 1950s the magazine almost exclusively promoted light-skinned women of colour, such as Dandridge, as aspirational figures of glamour, a position reinforced by prominent advertising for numerous skin lightening products, such as Nadinola Bleaching Cream, which proclaimed that '. . . a lighter, brighter complexion improves your chance for romance' (*Ebony*, February 1955, 14). This direct correspondence with the white-promoting beauty products that appeared in *Photoplay* highlights a hierarchy of light skin that connects to a broader Western history of make-up, which as Richard Dyer notes is a 'history of whitening' (Dyer 1997, 48). Staples goes as far as to extrapolate that *Ebony* in the 1950s was an enterprise that 'encouraged African-Americans to remake themselves as white' (Staples, 11 August 2019, n.p.).

Fading Out

Dorothy Dandridge was an active member of the National Association for the Advancement of Coloured People and had an ambition to transcend stereotypes in her career as a serious actor. Despite this, her rise to prominence in the 1950s mired her in the US's outdated attitudes to race, a problem that proved impossible to surmount, condemning her to be a star defined and confined by her race. Marguerite Rippy concludes that:

> Dandridge was destroyed first by a media obsession with reproducing commodification of white femininity on a Black body and second by the desire to sample Black exoticism without having to confront the national history of exploitation and violence that accompanied that body. (2001, 179)

The realisation of this is the opposition that lies in her promotion by *Ebony* as a glamorous light-skinned Black role model living the Hollywood lifestyle with her white husband (as epitomised by the June 1962 cover story 'The Private World of Dorothy Dandridge'), set against her invisibility to young white women in the Hollywood fan magazines, while at the same time being promoted as the risqué, sexy Carmen Jones in the mainstream white press.[9] The full irony of this, as Nelly Furman notes, is apparent in a close examination of *Carmen Jones*, where rather than a one-dimensional sex bomb we are in fact presented with Carmen 'buying food, cooking, brushing Joe's pants and shoes: in short she is portrayed as a woman with domestic qualities, sensitive, and generous, who sacrifices herself for her man' (Furman 2005, 128). While it is true that Carmen is impulsive and concerned with her own libido, and there is misdirection in her characterisation, such as in the way she is set up as a femme fatale, my reading is that for the most part Carmen is indeed caring, kind and devoted, and it is only her reliance on, in Baldwin's words, the 'mumbo jumbo' of superstition (a folksy quirk attributed to many Black characters on screen) that initiates her uncharacteristic decision to take up with another man (Baldwin [1957] 2017, 53). Furman's conclusion is that 'Preminger presents us with a Carmen close to being an exemplar of middle-class values of female domesticity and self-abnegation so celebrated during the Eisenhower era' (Furman 2005, 128). While this may be seen as an over-simplification which glosses over the film's mixed messages, in many ways Carmen (and Dandridge) *are* closer to the prevailing image of white 1950s femininity than to the barely coded cliché of 'fiery beauty and wild allure' that demarcates the light-skinned Black women, as exemplified by Carmen and Dandridge in the public imagination.[10]

We may see here the connecting thread between Dandridge/*Carmen Jones* and the unmentionable women's product placed alongside each other in *Photoplay*, with both indicative of different kinds of subterfuge used to deal with taboo issues. The Modess . . . *Because* campaign which ran from 1948 to the 1970s sold sanitary products by concealing the message behind high-class fashion imagery, which included dresses by Dior and photographs by Cecil Beaton. Dandridge, on the other hand, adopted the trappings of middle-class white America but was not able (or willing) to suppress her colour. Thus, while the fan magazines were happy to confirm the excellence of Dandridge's performance, they could not see past her colour, or risk discussing it, as this would have been as taboo and embarrassing as openly discussing menstruation. Consequently, Dandridge was positioned as 'other' and not permitted to extend beyond the roles that Black women had traditionally played. As Bogle notes, fan magazines in the 1950s 'went into the homes of young moviegoers around America, mostly women', and their effectual boycotting of Dandridge was a 'sign that the vast moviegoing public was not really ready for a Black movie star. Or so the industry believed' (Bogle 1998, 313). The sad conclusion is that Dandridge's invisibility in the US fan magazines, as typified by the February 1955 issue of *Photoplay*, was reflected by a lack of quality film offers after *Carmen Jones*, and unhappily after only five further film appearances she prematurely faded away.

Notes

1. A race film was a low-budget film made by a Black filmmaker for Black audiences.
2. A thrush was a female singer with a band, in 1940s American slang.
3. A *Variety* gossip column reported 'Harry Cohn ringsiding at El Rancho Vegas eyeing sepia thrush Dorothy Dandridge for possible pic deal' (Willard 1950, 52).
4. Leslie Caron, Jane Russell, Ann Miller and Deborah Kerr also received the Lady Fair treatment in 1954.
5. David O Selznick's two-hour long 'Light's Diamond Jubilee' (Bogle 1998, 301; Hirsch 2007, 222).
6. Dandridge's coverage in the UK notably included an open articulation about her erotic appeal, such as in reader James Shatwell's letter in *Picturegoer*: 'There are no words to describe *Carmen Jones*. One look from Dorothy Dandridge and I melt' (26). Dandridge was also on the cover of *Der Stern* on 30 October 1955, and *Paris Match* on 30 April 1955.
7. The line 'America's largest selling movie magazine' appears above the title on the cover; in addition, a tagline on the contents page proclaims that the magazine has been 'Favorite of America's moviegoers for over forty years' (2). In her work on fan magazine circulation figures, Polley contests some of the claims made by *Photoplay*. She does however find that in 1955 it was the most popular US fan magazine and had a 25 per cent share of the market (Polley 2019, 74).
8. Dandridge does not in fact appear to be mentioned at all by Parsons in any issue of *Modern Screen*.
9. This was lavishly illustrated with photographs of the star in her Hollywood Hills home, and mirrors the kind of fan magazine feature that Dandridge was denied.
10. See the anonymous review of *Carmen Jones* in *Harrison's Reports* (9 October 1954, 163).

References

Alexander, Karen. 1991. 'Fatal Beauties: Black Women in Hollywood'. In *Stardom: Industry of Desire*, edited by Christine Gledhill, 45–54. London: Routledge.
Anon. 1951. 'Dorothy Dandridge Boasts Added Glamour'. *The Chicago Defender*, 27 January: 21.
Anon. 1951. 'Hollywood's New Glamour Queen'. *Ebony*, April: 48–50, 52.
Anon. 1951. 'Shy No More'. *Life*, 5 November: 65–6, 69–70.
Anon. 1954. 'Hollywood's Newest Love Team'. *Jet*, 30 September: 60–1.
Anon. 1954. Review of *Carmen Jones*. *Harrison's Reports*, 9 October: 163.
Anon. 1954. 'New Films: Carmen Jones'. *Newsweek*, 25 October: 102.
Anon. 1954. Advertisement for *Carmen Jones*. *Boxoffice*, 13 November: 11–13.
Anon. 1955. Advertisement for Nadinola Bleaching Cream. *Ebony*, February: 14.
Anon. 1955. 'Brief Reviews: *Carmen Jones*'. *Photoplay*, February: 12.
Anon. 1955. *Photoplay*, February: front cover.
Anon. 1955. Advertisement for Lustre-Crème shampoo. *Photoplay*, February: 20.
Anon. 1955. Advertisement for Marchand's Golden Hair Wash. *Photoplay*, February: 24.
Anon. 1955. Advertisement for Modess sanitary products. *Photoplay*, February: 30.

Anon. 1955. '*Photoplay* Recommends *Carmen Jones*'. *Photoplay*, February: 31.
Anon. 1955. 'Announcing *Photoplay* Award Winners of 1954–55'. *Photoplay*, March: 62–6, 84.
Anon. 1955. '*Carmen Jones*'. *Picture Show*, 5 March: 8.
Anon. 1955. 'Dorothy Dandridge's Greatest Triumph'. *Ebony*, July: 37–41.
Anon. 1955. 'Do Negroes Have a Future in Hollywood?' *Ebony*, December: 24, 27–30.
Anon. 1959. *Tamango* Campaign Book.
Anon. 1962. 'The Private World of Dorothy Dandridge'. *Ebony*, June: 116–21.
Baldwin, James. [1957] 2017. *Notes of a Native Son*. London: Penguin Books.
Bogle, Donald. 1998. *Dorothy Dandridge: A Biography*. New York: Boulevard Books.
Carroll, Diahann, with Ross Firestone. 1986. *Diahann: The Autobiography of Diahann Carroll*. London: Robson Books.
Cohen, Martin. 1955. 'The Lady is a Go-Getter'. *Photoplay*, February: 44–5, 81–3.
Cripps, Thomas R. 1970. 'The Myth of the Southern Box Office: A Factor in Racial Stereotyping in American Movies, 1920–1940'. In *The Black Experience in America*, edited by James C. Curtis and Lewis L. Gould, 116–44. Austin and London: University of Texas Press.
Crowther, Bosley. 1955. 'The Screen in Review; Doris Day and Sinatra Star at Paramount'. *The New York Times*, 20 January: n.p. <https://www.nytimes.com/1955/01/20/archives/the-screen-in-review-doris-day-and-sinatra-star-at-paramount.html> (last accessed 16 May 2022).
Dyer, Richard. 1997. *White*. London and New York: Routledge.
Dyer, Richard. 1998. *Stars*. New edition with supplementary chapter by Paul McDonald. London: BFI.
Furman, Nelly. 2005. 'Screen Politics: Otto Preminger's *Carmen Jones*'. In *Carmen: From Silent Film to MTV*, edited by Chris Perriam and Ann Davies, 121–3. Amsterdam: Rodopi.
Graves, Janet. 1953. 'Let's Go to the Movies with Janet Graves: *Bright Road*'. *Photoplay*, June: 22.
Henderson, Jessica. 2018. 'Haute Heritage: 6 Vintage Johnson & Johnson Ads Shot by Famous Fashion Photographers'. *Johnson & Johnson*, 5 September: n.p. <https://www.jnj.com/our-heritage/high-fashion-vintage-ads-for-modess-sanitary-napkins> (last accessed 18 October 2021).
Higashi, Sumiko. 2014. *Stars, Fans, and Consumption in the 1950s: Reading Photoplay*. New York: Palgrave Macmillan.
Hinxman, Margaret. 1955. 'Dynamite – yet Hollywood can't hold it'. *Picturegoer*, 1 January: 5.
Hirsch, Foster. 2007. *Otto Preminger: The Man Who Would be King*. New York: Alfred A. Knopf.
Hirsch, Foster. 2010. 'Doris Day and Rock Hudson'. In *Larger Than Life: Movie Stars of the 1950s*, edited by R. Barton Palmer, 147–64. New Brunswick, NJ and London: Rutgers University Press.
Hurl. 1946. 'Million Dollar LA'. *Variety*, 21 August: 57.
Jeffers McDonald, Tamar. 2013. *Doris Day Confidential: Hollywood, Sex and Stardom*. London: I. B. Tauris.

Lanckman, Lies. 2019. 'In Search of Lost Fans: Recovering Fan Magazine Readers, 1910–1950'. In *Star Attractions: Twentieth-Century Movie Magazines and Global Fandom*, edited by Tamar Jeffers McDonald and Lies Lanckman, 45–59. Iowa: University of Iowa Press.

Land. 1959. Review of *Porgy and Bess*. *Variety*, 1 July: 6.

Lucas, Darrell Blaine, and Steuart Henderson Britt. 1950. *Advertising Psychology and Research: An Introductory Book*. New York, London, Toronto: McGraw Hill.

Mask, Mia. 2009. *Divas on Screen: Black Women in American Film*. Urbana and Chicago: University of Illinois Press.

Null, Gary. 1975. *Black Hollywood: The Negro in Motion Pictures*. Secaucus, NJ: Citadel Press.

Orlegard, Anita. 1949. Reader's letter. *Photoplay*, November: 4.

Parsons, Louella. 1954. 'Dorothy Dandridge Stars in a Great New Movie'. *Cosmopolitan*, December: 4.

Parsons, Louella. 1954. 'Louella Parsons in Hollywood'. *Modern Screen*, December: 9–16.

Photoplay. 1955. February.

Polley, Sarah. 2019. 'A Spectrum of Individuals: U.S. Fan Magazine Circulation Figures from 1914–1965'. In *Star Attractions: Twentieth-Century Movie Magazines and Global Fandom*, edited by Tamar Jeffers McDonald and Lies Lanckman, 61–80. Iowa: University of Iowa Press.

Rippy, Marguerite. 2001. 'Commodity, Tragedy, Desire: Female Sexuality and Blackness in the Iconography of Dorothy Dandridge'. In *Classic Hollywood, Classic Whiteness*, edited by Daniel Bernardi, 179–209. Minneapolis and London: University of Minnesota Press.

Shatwell, James. 1955. Reader's letter. *Picturegoer*, 16 April: 26.

Slide, Anthony. 2010. *Inside the Hollywood Fan Magazine: A History of Star Makers, Fabricators and Gossip Mongers*. Jackson: University Press of Mississippi.

Staples, Brent. 2019. 'The Radical Blackness of Ebony Magazine'. *The New York Times*, 11 August: n.p., <https://www.nytimes.com/2019/08/11/opinion/ebony-jet-magazine.html> (last accessed 16 May 2022).

Tambling, Jeremy. 1987. *Opera, Ideology and Film*. New York: St Martin's Press.

Willard, Bill. 1950. 'Chatter: Las Vegas, Nev'. *Variety*, 20 December: 52.

Williams, Esther, with Digby Diehl. 2000. *The Million Dollar Mermaid*. London: Simon & Schuster.

PART TWO

FAN MAGAZINES AND REGULAR CONTENTS

PART TWO INTRODUCTION

It is undeniable that examination of the regular editorial and advertising content of magazines provides vital insight into groups of publications, specific titles, and those who read them. The matter is complex, however, as content has been dubbed 'the trickiest category of all' since '[i]t can refer to the generic type of material published in a typical issue (reporting, reviewing, fiction, poetry, visual art, advertising and so on) or to the topics regularly covered (public life or private lives, local or distant)' (Scholes and Wulfman 2010, 53). Anthony Slide, in *Inside the Hollywood Fan Magazine: A History of Star Makers, Fabricators, and Gossip Mongers*, provides a brief overview of contents in fan magazines from the 1910s, directly segueing into assumptions about their readers:

> There were news stories, articles, and lavish photo spreads on the established stars, the up-and-coming new arrivals on the scene, and the major films in production, as well as reviews [. . .] The emphasis was on glamour, and the magazines were generally directed at a female readership. (2010, 4)

Slide therefore suggests that it is fan magazines' focus on stars and films as 'topics regularly covered' which sets them apart from other publications.

Sumiko Higashi's *Stars, Fans, and Consumption in the 1950s: Reading Photoplay* (2014) narrows Slide's attention from several US fan magazines between the 1910s and the 1980s to the ubiquitous *Photoplay* in the 1950s. Understandably, Higashi offers more detail on the 'generic type of material' than Slide, dedicating chapters to advertisements, beauty tips and fashion, houses, décor and food, advice columns, and contests. Like Slide, Higashi foregrounds glamour and the female reader, most notably in her chapter 'Advertisements for Movie Star Glamour and Romance'. This chapter references women's magazine scholar Janice Winship on the intimacy created by the 'reader identifying with the cover girl and buying products to imitate her look' (2014, 152), before discussing the visual appeal of product advertisements for items such as shampoo, make-up, fragrance and underwear which were sometimes endorsed by stars. While Higashi examines women readers' engagement with fan magazine content in terms of consumption, other fan magazine scholars spotlight the more overtly interactive – and primarily textual – features that Higashi affords less consideration. For example, Adrienne L. McLean (2019) addresses advice columns, in which answers were given to readers' queries in *Photoplay*, and other US fan magazines, from the 1930s to the 1950s. Higashi does not mention fiction or readers' letters, but the former has been the subject of some academic studies (for example McLean 2003) and the latter have been a particularly fruitful area of study across time and space. These include Britain in the interwar years (Stead 2011), the US in the teens (Anselmo Sequeira 2015), the US from the 1920s to the 1950s (Lanckman 2019, 2020) and France in the 1950s (Sellier 2019).

Chapters in this middle section maintain this focus on regular movie magazine contents, but here emphasise and analyse those elements which privilege design: the cover, the contest and comics, as well as the interplay between the imagistic elements and editorial ones. Thus Kelly investigates the appearance of a single – male – star on international covers; Polley looks at regular contents as well as the interplay of advertisements and editorial material in several fan magazine titles. Topp analyses an illustrated weekly story about a French starlet in postwar issues of a French magazine, *Ciné-Miroir* and Jeffers McDonald reads one puzzle competition in terms of its thwarted visuals. These chapters thus all provide insight into general features which were regularly found in these popular publications, as well as the specific ways in which these magazines attempted to engage their readers.

References

Anselmo Sequeira, Diana. 2015. 'Screen-Struck: The Invention of the Movie Girl Fan'. *Cinema Journal* 55 (1): 1–28.

Higashi, Sumiko. 2014. *Stars, Fans, and Consumption in the 1950s: Reading Photoplay*. New York: Palgrave Macmillan.

Lanckman, Lies. 2019. 'In Search of Lost Fans: Recovering Fan Magazine Readers, 1910–1950'. In *Star Attractions: Twentieth-Century Movie Magazines and Global Fandom*, edited by Tamar Jeffers McDonald and Lies Lanckman, 45–59. Iowa: University of Iowa Press.

Lanckman, Lies. 2020. 'Fans, community, and conflict in the pages of "Picture Play", 1920–38'. *Transformative Works and Cultures* 33.

McLean, Adrienne L. 2003. '"New Films in Story Form": Movie Story Magazines and Spectatorship'. *Cinema Journal* 42 (3): 3–26.

McLean, Adrienne L. 2019. '"Give Them a Good Breakfast, Says Nancy Carroll": Fan Magazine Advice Across Time'. In *Star Attractions: Twentieth-Century Movie Magazines and Global Fandom*, edited by Tamar Jeffers McDonald and Lies Lanckman, 11–28. Iowa: University of Iowa Press.

Scholes, Robert, and Clifford Wulfman. 2010. *Modernism in the Magazines: An Introduction*. New Haven and London: Yale University Press.

Sellier, Genevieve. 2019. 'Movie Magazines, Popular Films, and Popular Spectatorship in Postwar France'. In *Star Attractions: Twentieth-Century Movie Magazines and Global Fandom*, edited by Tamar Jeffers McDonald and Lies Lanckman, 81–95. Iowa: Iowa University Press.

Slide, Anthony. 2010. *Inside the Hollywood Fan Magazine: A History of Star Makers, Fabricators and Gossip Mongers*. Jackson: University Press of Mississippi.

Stead, Lisa. 2011. '"So oft to the movies they've been": British Fan Writing and Female Audiences in the Silent Cinema'. *Transformative Works and Cultures* 6.

5. TYRONE POWER: INTERNATIONAL 'COVER BOY'

Gillian Kelly

In *Inside the Hollywood Fan Magazine*, Anthony Slide asserts that during Hollywood's Golden Age, most film fan magazine cover stars were women, because male stars did not sell magazines (2010, 4). Only during the Second World War, he declares, 'male members of the film community' began to appear 'for the first time' on fan magazine covers; even then, however, these images were not dedicated to stars in uniform 'but primarily feature players designated 4F', or unfit for military service, such as Frank Sinatra (2010, 142). As I have demonstrated in my monographs on Robert Taylor (Kelly 2019) and Tyrone Power (Kelly 2021), however, this is not factually accurate: both these actors began appearing regularly as fan magazine cover stars long before this, directly after signing with their respective studios, MGM and 20th Century Fox, in 1934 and 1936.

Taylor and Power were not, of course, the only male cover stars appearing at this time; nonetheless, I consider them particularly useful examples of this phenomenon, because of their similarities in terms of their appearance and audience appeal. Both stars were known especially for their good looks, which were showcased in many brightly lit close-ups within their on-screen work, a mode of presentation often reserved for glamorous female stars. It was only natural, then, that these famously handsome faces would also be displayed on the cover of fan magazines, where they could be expected to provide a strong selling point to the magazines' target audience of mostly young, uneducated, heterosexual women (Allen and Gomery 1985, 24), which also formed the primary audience of their films.

To demonstrate the importance of such cover stars, it is crucial to understand the cover design of film fan magazines at this time. As opposed to modern-day gossip magazines such as the UK's *Heat*, or *Star* in the US, which boast crowded covers awash with unflattering paparazzi shots and shock headlines, fan magazine covers of this earlier era usually consisted of a single image of an individual star or screen couple, either in the form of a photograph or painted image in their likeness. This provided fan magazine covers with a bold, single point of focus, and demonstrates the significance of the chosen cover star. Given that these fan magazines likely had a primarily female readership (Slide 2010, 4), then, a female star on the cover of such publications might be seen as presenting readers with an ideal female face and body which, perhaps, they could try to emulate, whereas a male cover star like Taylor or Power would be put on display as spectacle for the approval of the heterosexual female surveyor, reflecting also how these stars were displayed on screen.

Although, as noted above, Taylor also featured on numerous magazine covers throughout his career, in this chapter I will focus specifically on Power's cover appearances. Power is particularly interesting in this context for multiple reasons. Firstly, as my previous work has demonstrated, his looks were the most significant component of his persona and were crucial in his rapid rise to stardom; across his career he was 'consistently presented to audiences as a highly desirable object of the erotic gaze', both on screen in a variety of genres and off screen in publicity stills and magazine covers (Kelly 2021, 217). In many of his on-screen performances, 'female characters often acted as surrogates for the audience in their appreciation of his good looks', while cinematic techniques such as bright lighting, extreme close-ups and costuming underlined this strategy further (217). Outside of his film appearances, publications like fan magazines played a major part in the construction and development of this image for audiences to consume at their leisure and away from theatres; due to their visibility, cover images were an important part of this element of his stardom.

Secondly, and connected to this, images of Power were consistently present on the covers of global publications, from his first starring role in *Lloyds of London* (King 1936) until after his untimely death in 1958. I therefore wish to designate him here as a true international 'cover boy', a play on words of the more traditional terms 'cover girl' and 'poster boy', which offers a label particularly fitting for Power, both in terms of his international presence and in terms of the focus on his pertinent good looks. In this chapter, I will explore a range of cover images of Power chronologically, which will enable me to trace not only Power's developing career and star persona over time but also, like a visual biography, the developments within his off-screen life.

The Importance of Film Fan Magazines

The first film fan magazine to be published in America was *Motion Picture Story Magazine* in February 1911, closely followed by the now better-known title *Photoplay*, and eventually a plethora of others, including *Modern Screen*, *Movieland*, *Screenland* and *Screen Stars* (Slide 2010, 14). By the start of the 1930s, this number had swelled to roughly twenty-five monthly fan magazines, which presented their readers with an impressive range of contents focused on the world of the movies and their stars. This includes written content – Sennett notes that studios relied greatly on the star-related publicity fan magazines could provide through interviews and articles on performers (1998, 50–1) – but also many images: indeed, the magazines' standalone cover images of beautiful stars speak eloquently for themselves, and even these were carefully constructed.

Many scholars, including Richard Dyer (1979) and Bruce Babington (2001) have argued for the need to explore a star's extra-filmic dimensions, alongside their screen appearances. Around two decades ago, then, Adrienne L. McLean became one of the first scholars to recognise the importance that fan magazines, specifically, hold for studying historical star personas, calling them a rarely examined but 'long-lived and robust ancillary product' of Hollywood's classical era (McLean 2003, 3). Since then, a number of important works have been published both *on* fan magazines and their historical and sociological contexts and *using* fan magazines as resources for historical star and fan studies. These include Anthony Slide's *Inside the Hollywood Fan Magazine: A History of Star Makers, Fabricators, and Gossip Mongers* (2010) and Robert S. Sennett's *Hollywood Hoopla: Creating Stars and Selling Movies in the Golden Age of Hollywood* (1998), but also, more recently, the edited collections *Star Attractions: Twentieth-Century Movie Magazines and Global Fandom* (2019) and *Mapping Movie Magazines: Digitization, Periodicals and Cinema History* (2020), which explore a number of global publications and fandom through a variety of approaches, including several individual star studies. Additionally, Sumiko Higashi's *Stars, Fans, and Consumption in the 1950s: Reading Photoplay* (2014) is concerned with how individual female stars like Debbie Reynolds and Esther Williams were written about and engaged with by fans specifically through the lens of *Photoplay* magazine. Likewise, noteworthy studies employing extra-filmic materials to examine the star images of individual female performers include McLean's pioneering work *Being Rita Hayworth: Labor, Identity and Hollywood* (2004), Tamar Jeffers McDonald's *Doris Day Confidential: Hollywood, Sex and Stardom* (2013) and Ginette Vincendeau's *Brigitte Bardot* (2013).

This chapter builds further on my own research, as referenced above, demonstrating that because fan magazines were published across many years, they can provide a comparatively accurate timeline of the progression of an individual's star image across both geographical and historical contexts. They allow film scholars to decipher when and where a star first began appearing in publications, when the star was covered most frequently, as well as when they ceased to be included in any notable capacity, or, in fact, at all. In this way, the research can establish when and where an individual was most popular, since their off-screen presence in such publications was usually a reasonable reflection of their on-screen manifestations.

This may include frequent appearances at the start of their career, while their home studio was attempting to build a recognisable star persona around them for the public to respond to. Indeed, as Sumiko Higashi notes, the studio publicity departments were 'allied' with leading publications such as *Photoplay* and *Motion Picture*, and this relationship provided the ultimate way for building up stars (2014, 129). Again, cover appearances are important here: since star images were used to sell magazines to fans, the performers featured on the cover formed an extremely important component of these publications, particularly when competing with other magazines of similar content and titles, and such an appearance demonstrated the star's status (and supposed profitability to magazine and studio alike) at the time of publication.

In addition, such images were also crucial in terms of building a star's memorability among fans. Before the age of VHS, DVD and Blu-ray, it was images in fan magazines that allowed historical audiences to maintain continued access to stars beyond film screenings in theatres. For these audiences, then, it was the magazines and not the films that lasted (Jeffers McDonald 2013, 35), and images printed in these magazines were particularly useful for this purpose.

Powerful Images

As noted above, the number of times a star appeared on a magazine cover, featured on a full-page photograph or had an article dedicated to them inside the publication usually reflected their popularity at the time of publication, and also provided details about which stars studios were trying to promote at any given time. Attractive front covers featuring beautiful stars could not only 'encourage regular readers to stay faithful' to that publication, but also meant that 'potential or casual buyers scanning newsstands or newsagent shelves' might choose this publication over its rivals (Kelly 2021, 205). It is also worth mentioning here how many of these magazines are still circulating today on the second-hand market, with publications over eighty years old readily listed for sale on auction sites such as eBay; even now, the price tag of such a magazine is usually dependent on the cover star, largely regardless of the amount of information on the star actually printed within the magazine's pages.

Further demonstrating the importance of cover images, in recent years an increased number of vintage scrapbooks have been seen at auction, likely as their original creators have passed away. While these unique objects each offer a glimpse into an individual's fandom, their commonalities indicate several shared features of this fandom as well. For example, they alert us to the fact that fans of a particular cover star would often detach the front of the magazine from the rest of the publication and paste it into their books for safekeeping and to pore over later. Aside from writing to the performer's home studio for a signed photograph or posting money for a glossy print being sold from a magazine advertisement, this was often the only way that fans could obtain photographs of their favourite stars during Hollywood's classical era.

Moreover, in several of these scrapbooks, such images have been cut around in order to reduce them merely to an image, as a mode of fetishisation, with no surrounding text remaining and even the name of the publication frequently removed. Some of these images were even mounted on pieces of card first to better preserve and make them sturdier. Other fans would place these cover images, and full-page publicity stills, on their walls where they could view them regularly (Jeffers McDonald 2013). This suggests that images of the stars, and not written text about them, was what appeared to interest fans most. Indeed, as Robert S. Sennett has noted, Hollywood was in essence 'an industry [. . .] completely defined by images', with leading stars a major part of this visual appeal.

Likewise, Annette Kuhn, in her aptly titled *The Power of the Image* (1985), discusses a range of culturally dominant images produced for mass audiences, and focuses in this context primarily on various representations of women in mainstream photography. Kuhn focuses particularly on glamour, defining this as a notion applied almost exclusively to women, and notes that glamour images of female stars are especially powerful since they play on the viewer's desire in 'a particularly pristine way: beauty or sexuality is desirable exactly to the extent that it is idealised and unattainable' (1985, 12). I argue here that these discussions of Hollywood glamour portraits, however, are also pertinent when exploring a male performer like Tyrone Power as a cover star. Power, after all, also embodied a particular 'to-be-looked-at-ness', to borrow Laura Mulvey's phrase (1975), with his extraordinary good looks a dominant and persistent feature of his stardom from the beginning of his career until his death at the age of forty-four. In this context, it is worth noting that Power appeared on more magazine covers globally than any other male star of his generation, as archival searches demonstrate; I therefore argue that much like his female counterparts, this male star, too, equally raises 'notable questions of spectatorship and looking' (Kuhn 1985, 9). Indeed, his numerous appearances on magazine covers around the world allowed fans more direct, tangible and inexpensive access to his desirable image outside of his films being shown in movie theatres, and are a key way in which to investigate the developments within this persona, as I shall demonstrate.

Early Years and British Roots

Power was born Tyrone Power III in Cincinnati, Ohio, USA, on 5 May 1914, to British stage actor Tyrone Power II (later known as Tyrone Power Sr) and his wife Patia, an actress and vocal coach. Working with his father on stage during his teenage years, Power first entered films in 1934, but after a few minor bit parts, returned to the stage. Hollywood reclaimed him in 1936, however, when he signed a contract with the newly formed 20th Century Fox, and was almost immediately cast in *Lloyds of London*, which made him a star overnight. Although portraying the film's protagonist and receiving the most screentime, Power was billed fourth after child actor Freddie Bartholomew, who plays Power's character as a child, leading lady Madeleine Carroll and elder actor Sir Guy Standing, demonstrating that he was still at the very beginning of his star trajectory.

Significantly, however, although this was only his first substantial role, Power immediately began appearing on magazine covers across the world, including the British publications *Picture Show* and *Film Pictorial*, with the latter also including a free sixteen-page supplement of the film. Power was the only American performer in the primary cast, the others all being British; nonetheless, his British roots and famous English father may well have been the reasons he was featured extensively in UK publications this early in his career. His namesake great-grandfather, Tyrone Power I (or Tyrone Power the Elder), had also been a popular Irish stage actor, and was the first to perform under the name 'Tyrone Power'. Both his family legacy and his links, through this legacy, to the legitimate stage, therefore, would have added credibility to his star image, particularly in the UK, and perhaps also more respectability than the average American screen actor at this time.

To investigate these covers further, it is important to look at both the historical development of these magazines and their cover designs. *Picture Show*, firstly, was released every Monday and ran from 1919 to 1960, taking over *Film Pictorial* in 1939 and becoming *Picture Show and TV Mirror* in 1959. When the magazine began production in the silent era, early cover designs featured a white background with a strong rectangular border, while all text and images appeared in blue ink. Occasionally featuring one large image (for example, 25 June 1921), most of these early covers were cluttered with images and text: 12 November 1922 features four overlapping images while 2 June 1923 has six. By 1934, however, the covers had become more streamlined and mostly featured one solo image of a screen couple no longer restricted by a border, featuring far less text and coloured in various shades of sepia. For example, the cover for 20 October 1934 features a medium close-up of Carl Brisson and Kitty Carlisle, the latter's elaborate headdress taking up a third of the space and travelling under the publication's name before disappearing off the top of the page. Very little text was used, drawing attention to the bold image and the publication's title.

By the time Power was first featured as a cover star, the magazine had also started incorporating colour on the cover, the name of the publication now in bold black writing across the top. The close-up image of Power with co-star Madeleine Carroll on the 11 September 1937 issue takes up three-quarters of the cover, with the ombre orange background behind the image neatly bleeding into the area with the magazine's, performers' and film's names. Power's historical costuming, featuring an elaborately frilled collared shirt, takes up the centre of the image, his broad frame extending across almost the width of the page as Carroll leans in towards him. As the two smile at each other, Power's long eyelashes and exquisite profile are the main focus of the cover, helping not only to sell the magazine but also to sell the image of this new and highly desirable leading man to readers.

Film Pictorial (which would soon merge with the aforementioned *Picture Show*) was a similar British publication which also featured Power and Carroll on its cover on the same date, 11 September 1937 (Figure 5.1), thus allowing 20th Century Fox further opportunities to sell their new star and his long British lineage to British audiences.

On this cover, Power's name appears first, in the text in the bottom left-hand corner, while the couple are seen in medium close-up in a more serious, romantic pose. Power wears the same costume as on the *Picture Show* cover, and this time appears in a semi-profile pose showing the other side of his face, as if to demonstrate that he photographs well from either side. Again, the image is the central focus of the page, with Power's head effectively disguising some of the magazine's title and demonstrating his dominance and importance on the cover. At this time, *Film Pictorial* used black-and-white images, with a pop of colour added through a range of, sometimes quite elaborate, background designs behind each image. On this occasion, the black-and-white image and white text of the publication's title is accompanied by a background made up of various shades of red, helping draw attention to the stars, with horizontal lines acting almost like neon arrows pointing to Power and Carroll.

Additionally, a band at the top of this cover announces a free sixteen-page souvenir booklet of the film enclosed inside; this featured a full-length image of the couple in an embrace, as co-star George Sanders looks on. As a way of informing readers about this new star, the booklet also features an article called 'Here's Power to You, Tyrone', which begins by asking readers the rhetorical question, 'Does Tyrone Power herald the new cycle of forthright, virile young men in pictures?' before concluding that indeed he does.

By the following year, Power was a full-blown international star, who between 1937 and 1939 appeared on the covers of *Film Weekly*, *Film Pictorial*, *Picturegoer* and *Picture Show* as well as *Screen Pictorial*, Britain's only monthly film publication at this time. On these covers, Power is either dressed in modern tailored suits or in historical costumes for his various film roles, allowing the star and his films to be sold with equal weight. Here, he either

Figure 5.1　Tyrone Power and Madeleine Carroll on the cover of *Film Pictorial*, 11 September 1937.

appeared with a female co-star, such as Loretta Young, Alice Faye or Norma Shearer, or was the sole cover star with his face as the main focus of the cover. This is notable for a performer so early in his career, and also contradicts Slide's belief that male stars were not able to sell magazines.

The story of Power's rapidly developing stardom was similar in the US, although with many more publications available than in the UK, he could reach a wider demographic and be featured on a greater variety of covers. In his early days in Hollywood, the primary focus of the magazines' coverage of Power was his bachelorhood, as well as his potential dating life with co-stars Young, Faye and Sonja Henie, as well as other actresses, such as Ginger Rogers. In fact, rumours about his love life were far more common themes than his film work at this stage, and the magazine covers reflected this; among the covers featuring Power with potential love interests were *Modern Screen* (August 1937) and *Screen Romances* (December 1938) both with Young; *Radio Mirror* (November 1937) with Henie, and again in March 1939 with his *Suez* (Dwan, 1938) co-star, the French actress Annabella, whom he married that same month. In February of that year, he appeared on the *Modern Movies* cover alongside co-star Nancy Kelly in costume for his first Western, *Jesse James* (King 1939), thus displaying a change in direction for his star image but still presenting him as a desirable leading man. Other publications which featured him as a cover star at this time were *True Romances* (October 1936) and *Radio Guide* (November 1937), allowing him to reach a broad audience while his star image was being built up by his studio.

A particularly interesting example from this time period is the cover of *MoviePix* from May 1938 (Figure 5.2), which features Power alongside his *Marie Antoinette* (Van Dyke 1938) co-star, Norma Shearer. Although they featured on many international covers together, what is unusual about this particular candid shot is that Shearer is dressed in full costume for her role as the title character, while Power is dressed in modern, casual clothes including an open-neck shirt and cravat. The actors stand close and smile at each other, suggesting that Power is on set to visit Shearer, while he is not, himself, at work.

Since both the cover and this photograph have a white background, and Shearer, too, is a pale figure with her light skin, white wig and white dress, Power's dark hair, dark eyebrows and thick lashes, along with his dark cravat and suit, make him the dominant element of the cover. What stands out most, however, given the extensive use of black and white, is not only the magazine's title in red, but also the red banner printed across the bottom of the image, reminiscent of police tape on a crime scene, which asks the reader 'Do you think Norma Shearer should re-marry?' Combined with the image, this banner suggests that Power may be the potential husband for the recently widowed Shearer, while a banner above the image reading 'Hollywood's intimate picture magazine' adds fuel to the fire of a completely fabricated story.

Figure 5.2   Tyrone Power and Norma Shearer on the cover of *MoviePix*, May 1938.

In the US during the 1930s, around twenty-five fan magazines were published, with an estimated circulation of between 200,000 and one million; of these, *Photoplay*, *Motion Picture* and *Modern Screen* were among the most popular (Slide 2010, 122), and each featured Power on the cover more than once, as well as in numerous articles within. Echoing the way he was often depicted on screen, *Photoplay*'s December 1938 cover features Power smiling and wearing a tuxedo, with an almost identical image used exactly eight years later for the December 1946 issue. A more serious and sultry Power in a modern suit graced the April 1940 cover. He was *Motion Picture*'s cover star alongside Henie in October 1937 and Faye in July 1939, and alone in January 1938 and October 1946, when he was also the cover star for rival publication *Modern Screen*. He further appeared on the cover of *Modern Screen* alone in December 1947, with Young in August 1937 and with Henie in March 1938. Although the latter shows the pair in costume for their film *Thin Ice*, the cover's tagline refers to Power's off-screen life by asking 'Whom Will Tyrone Power Marry?' Given the accompanying image, the reader is to assume he will marry Henie, and indeed the article of the same name inside mentions her throughout as a rival to actress Janet Gaynor for Power's affections (34–5).

A Married and Military Man

In 1939, however, and much to the dismay of his studio who wished him to remain an available bachelor for his mostly female fanbase, Power married Annabella, and the two were soon presented as a wholesome and happy couple on a range of magazine covers. An example of this is the May 1941 issue of *Movie Life*, which features an image of the couple dressed casually and sitting in their garden, showing Power with one arm around Annabella and the other holding a baby goat. Matching this laid-back approach, within the magazine, the stars are referred to informally as 'Ty' and 'Annie' as if they are close friends of the writers and, by extension, the readers. Images inside also show the pair looking relaxed and smiling as they walk around the grounds, along with images of the interior of their home, including the bedroom.

As the United States joined the Second World War, Power enlisted as a private in the Marine Corps in August 1942 and was off screen for three years as he undertook active war duty, eventually working his way up to the rank of lieutenant. Although absent from Hollywood, however, and therefore not making any new films, he continued to appear both within and on the cover of film fan magazines, only now he was shown in uniform. While Slide asserts that this was not the case for performers on active war duty, in fact Power, Taylor, Clark Gable, James Stewart and Robert Montgomery were just a few of the actors who graced the covers of publications dressed in their authentic military uniforms during this timeframe.

Portraits of Power in uniform standing behind Annabella, his medals on show, were published extensively in magazines across the world, and the US's *Screen Guide* (December 1943) (Figure 5.3), where he is named as 'Lt. Tyrone Power U.S.M.C.', and Britain's *Picturegoer* (22 July 1944) both featured a smiling Power

Figure 5.3   Tyrone Power on the cover of *Screen Guide*, December 1943.

in uniform on their covers despite his current inactivity as an actor. This now allowed 20th Century Fox to sell Power's image as an authentic American war hero still signed to the studio, while shrewdly keeping him relevant in the public's eye in preparation for his hoped-for postwar return to the screen.

Sustained International Appeal

It is also around this time, from approximately 1938 onwards, that Power began appearing regularly on covers outside of the US and UK, as indeed he would do until his death in 1958. The magazines which featured him as a cover star include Austria's *Mein Film* and *Dr Faust*, Brazil's *A Cena Muda*, *Rosalinda*, *Cinemin* and *O Idílio*, Denmark's *Billed Bladet*, Belgium's *De Film*, *Cine Roman* and *Mon Copain*, Sweden's *Filmjournalen*, Chile's *Ecran*, Israel's *Kolnoa*, Argentina's *Cinelandia*, Spain's *Garbo* and *Fotogramas* and *Le Vostre Novelle* and *Avventuroso Film* from Italy. While many of the images involved were examples of typical Hollywood portrait photography of Power with or without a co-star, this last example is unusual in that it featured Power in an almost full-length shot as he sits on a table outside, wearing a suit and open-necked shirt and holding a cigarette, looking casually off to the side. The range of geographical locations and titles given above are in no way exhaustive, but they help demonstrate Power's extended popularity as a cover star throughout his career and across the globe.

Power was also particularly popular in France, Annabella's native country, and mentions of him in French periodicals started to emerge extremely early in his career, at the start of 1937. This began with *Cinémonde* on 11 February, *Le Cinéopse* in June and *Ciné-Miroir* on 29 October, with several mentions in each publication thereafter. Throughout the next twenty years, Power would also feature as a cover star on *Cinémonde* and *Ciné-Miroir* on several occasions, including *Cinémonde* on 31 March 1938 with co-star Alice Faye, and, over a decade later, in a still from *Captain from Castile* (King 1948) alongside Jean Peters on 31 January 1949, showing he had not lost any of his popularity or star appeal even after the war and his divorce from Annabella in 1948. Indeed, he continued appearing on the cover of many other French publications throughout his career, including *Pour Vous*, *CinéVie CinéVogue*, *Noir et Blanc*, *Mon Film* and *Festival*.

Marriage Italian Style: Linda Christian

After Power and Annabella divorced in 1948, the magazines went once more into a frenzy over the star's re-established bachelor status, and saturated the market with stories and images of the newly available Power, much as they had done at the start of his career. This time, however, Power's bachelorhood lasted only briefly, and after a high-profile relationship with actress Lana Turner, he married Mexican actress Linda Christian in January 1949, not long after meeting her in Italy. Indeed, a few months before they wed, Italian publication *Cine Illustrato* featured an image of a seated Power, wearing a houndstooth coat and the words 'Tyrone Power ha annuncaito ufficialmente che sposera Linda Christian' ['Tyrone Power has officially announced that he will marry Linda Christian'] on 15 August 1948.

Power and Annabella had, throughout their marriage, been portrayed by magazines as a wholesome young couple. This can be demonstrated with various examples, including the image of the couple with a baby goat, as well as by other photographs of Power and Annabella at home, usually wearing simple and casual clothing, presenting the pair to readers as a relatable, 'average' young husband and wife. This portrayal became increasingly important after Power joined the military and became 'just another' military man fighting for his country, while Annabella was 'just another' wife waiting at home, sewing her own clothes and doing her best to help the war effort. They were, in the pages of fan magazines, 'just another' couple separated by the war (Kelly 2021, 210), and although Annabella was French, and therefore potentially a somewhat exotic figure to American audiences, she was consistently presented as a cute and petite blonde – albeit one who had been married before, already had a daughter and was seven years older than Power.

Power's second marriage to glamorous, dark-haired Mexican actress Christian, who was nine years younger and known as the 'Anatomic Bomb' for her shapely figure and long legs, on the other hand, was presented as much more sensual, and coverage of this marriage emphasised elements such as high living, parties, designer fashion and expensive jewellery. This was driven particularly by Christian's own star image: although she was the lesser known of the pair, she seems to have taken control of the relationship and was far pushier than the more reserved Power, as images of the two together suggest, and as their oldest daughter, Romina Power, also appears to verify in her 2014 book. Even in photographs where he is casually dressed in an open-necked shirt or sweater, she is perfectly presented with fashionable clothes, coiffured hair, immaculate make-up and elaborate jewellery. In fact, a cover image of *Cine Illustrato* features a 'candid' image of the couple as she picks out a highly decorative bracelet matching the necklace and earrings she is already wearing, as he passively looks on.

Christian's dark beauty and links to Rome meant that she and Power appeared in far many more international publications than Power and Annabella had. They had married in Rome, where they first met, and their wedding attracted the international press because of Power's star status. This too was reflected on magazine covers: indeed, somewhat intrusive-looking photographs taken during the ceremony appeared on the covers of France's *Noir et Blanc* (2 February 1949) (Figure 5.4), and Italy's *Tua* (3 February 1949), the former in black and white and the latter in full colour. Less than three weeks later, *Noir et Blanc* again featured the couple on the cover, this time while on their honeymoon and posing for the camera, and an almost identical image appeared on *Cine Illustrato* (6 March 1949). Both publications also carried similar photographs inside, showing the couple skiing in Austria.

Figure 5.4 Tyrone Power and Linda Christian on the cover of *Noir et Blanc*, 2 February 1949.

In May 1949 several US publications carried the story of their honeymoon, and they featured as *Screenland*'s cover stars that month, using the same image which had appeared on the cover of France's *CinéVie CinéVogue* (9 November 1948) the previous year. Although similar to the cover images with Annabella, in that the couple are seen outside and dressed casually, Annabella tended to wear fairly casual clothing, such as an androgynous trouser suit, while Christian, befitting her more glamorous image, is shown dressed in a feminine, form-fitting strapless sundress, accessorised with a statement necklace. In addition, the two are lying on the grass, her bare shoulders on his chest, again sketching a more sensual image of their marriage.

Cine Illustrato did not just feature Power in images from his private life, however; he had appeared on the cover of the 11 April 1948 issue with co-star Maureen O'Hara in a publicity shot for their adventure film *The Black Swan* (King 1942), a film that had been released six years previously and featured an almost unrecognisable Power as a pirate with a beard and moustache. Rather confusingly, his on-screen/off-screen persona became blurred on the cover of *Cine Illustrato* for 7 May 1950 which featured a photograph of Power and his co-star Cécile Aubrey for *The Black Rose* (Hathaway 1950), while the accompanying text read 'Luna di miele numero due per Tyrone e Linda' ['Honeymoon number two for Tyrone and Linda']. The image is therefore of Aubrey, but the text refers – again – to Christian.

Many other international publications featured Power and Christian in candid shots on their covers; for example, they are seen walking down a street on Italy's *Tempo*, a publication viewed as Italy's version of *Time* magazine, on 21 August 1948. Although both are smiling towards the camera, the shot shows the evolution of magazine covers across Power's career, and indeed evokes the paparazzi-style covers which would become more popular in later years. A similar image was used on the cover of France's *Inter* (21 March 1949) the following year, only this time the walking couple seem unaware of the camera. On 29 January 1949, *Tempo* featured an interesting 'candid' image of the couple and their car. While Power is already behind the wheel, somewhat casually dressed in a lightly coloured raincoat and trilby hat, the highly made-up Christian stands beside the car and is wearing an expensive-looking fur coat, with a spotted headscarf and black gloves. Moreover, while he looks directly forwards in a natural manner from his position in the car, she is looking to the side and slightly over her shoulder in a way that suggests she is posing for the photographer.

Like Power and Annabella in 1948, Power and Christian eventually divorced in 1956, after the birth of their two daughters, but during their marriage Power had become, and subsequently remained, more of an international cover star than ever before. Interestingly, however, neither the gossip columnists nor fans seemed especially surprised when the pair divorced, whereas there had been a sense of genuine shock in the magazines when he and Annabella's marriage had ended; this suggests, perhaps, the perception of this union as a hurried second marriage initially based on physical attraction, as I have suggested elsewhere (Kelly 2019).

Final Stages and Magazine Pages

Power's life and career came full circle in the 1950s when he returned to the stage in the US and the UK, following in the footsteps of his father. At this time, he also appeared on the cover of a number of theatrical publications, such as *Theatre Arts* (March 1955). Additionally, Power remarried after his divorce from Christian, this time to Deborah Ann Minardos, an ex-girlfriend of Elvis Presley. However, on 15 November 1958, just months after the wedding and with a baby on the way, Power died suddenly in Madrid, while filming a scene for *Solomon and Sheba* (Vidor 1959).

Power's untimely death was reported by newspapers and magazines worldwide, making front-page headlines across the globe. Several publications also carried news of the event and published tributes to Power for months afterwards, including three magazine issues all released on 29 November 1958, two weeks after his death, each featuring the late star on the cover. While *Paris Match* used a recent colour photograph of the smiling Power in close-up, the cover of the Italian magazine *Gente* (Figure 5.5) shows him during a break on the set of *Solomon and Sheba*, dressed in costume and looking healthy and happy as he sits smiling with his pregnant wife. The couple also featured on the cover of *Jours de France*, looking more serious but also comfortable and settled as they sit together on a stone bench which looks unnervingly similar to Power's grave. Furthermore, even though he had been replaced by Yul Brynner in *Solomon and Sheba*, a still from a scene Power had already filmed with co-star Gina Lollobrigida appeared on the cover of Danish magazine *Billed Bladet* less than a week after his death, as if indicating a denial or lack of acceptance of what had occurred.

Over the course of the next few months, reports and tributes continued to appear in magazines, including updates covering the birth of Power's only son, future actor Tyrone Power Jr, in January 1959. Despite his popularity as a cover star for many international publications during his life, however, Power's presence in magazines quickly faded after 1959. Unlike some other stars who died early, such as Marilyn Monroe, he only appeared in a handful of publications, and on a handful of covers, during the decades following his death. These include *Film Fan Monthly*, which featured Power and Helen Walker on its cover in March 1968, as well as solo appearances on the covers of *The Movie* in November 1982 and TCM's *Now Playing* in 1992.

Figure 5.5 Tyrone Power and Deborah Ann Minardos on the cover of *Gente*, 29 November 1958.

Conclusion

Throughout their existence, fan magazines were presented as essentially ephemeral materials, expected to be thrown away after they had been read, and yet as McLean has noted, what we now know about them and what 'really makes them important, is that they are still around, saved for decades by fans apparently unwilling to discard their particular obtuse, personal, and indescribable textual pleasures' (2003, 21). During the decades following the heyday of the fan magazine, therefore, fans actively became curators of the very objects which, in many ways, were initially created to manipulate them, and it is thanks to these same fans that academics are now able to study these publications and explore how they represented individual stars.

As this chapter has demonstrated, such preserved magazine issues present us with a historical snapshot of how celebrity culture, fame and stardom functioned at any given time. Additionally, the survival of a vast quantity of such publications, including complete runs of many of these, allows us to trace a star persona like Tyrone Power's through time and across a number of geographical locations, demonstrating his relevance throughout his career. These magazines have allowed me to demonstrate here that Power was indeed an international 'cover boy' in his heyday and that, just as his image sold films to the public, it also helped sell magazines.

A consistent presence on the cover of international publications for two decades, Power appeared alone, with co-stars and with each of his wives in both glamorous publicity stills and in 'candid' shots. During the war, he was a cover star dressed in authentic military uniform, despite not having any new films to be promoted, and for weeks after his death, he continued to appear on the cover of magazines in countries such as France and Italy. As a star known for his extraordinary good looks throughout his life and career, Power is therefore the perfect example of a male star as commodity, able to sell magazines to the target audience merely by appearing on the cover.

References

Allen, Robert, and Douglas Gomery. 1985. *Film History: Theory and Practice*. New York: Knopf.
Anon. 1937. *Film Pictorial*, 11 September: front cover.
Anon. 1937. *Picture Show*, 11 September: front cover.
Anon. 1938. *MoviePix*, May: front cover.
Anon. 1943. *Screen Guide*, December: front cover.
Anon. 1949. *Noir et Blanc*, 2 February: front cover.
Anon. 1958. *Gente*, 29 November: front cover.
Babington, Bruce. 2001. *British Stars and Stardom: From Alma Taylor to Sean Connery*. Manchester: Manchester University Press.

Bilthereyst, Daniel, and Lies Van de Vijver, eds. 2020. *Mapping Movie Magazines: Digitalization, Periodicals and Cinema History*. Cham, Switzerland: Palgrave Macmillan.

Dyer, Richard. 1979. *Stars*. London: BFI.

Higashi, Sumiko. 2014. *Stars, Fans, and Consumption in the 1950s: Reading Photoplay*. New York: Palgrave Macmillan.

Jeffers McDonald, Tamar. 2013. *Doris Day Confidential: Hollywood, Sex and Stardom*. London: I. B. Tauris.

Jeffers McDonald, Tamar, and Lies Lanckman, eds. 2019. *Star Attractions: Twentieth-Century Movie Magazines and Global Fandom*. Iowa: University of Iowa Press.

Kelly, Gillian. 2019. *Robert Taylor: Male Beauty, Masculinity and Stardom in Hollywood*. Jackson, Mississippi: University Press of Mississippi.

Kelly, Gillian. 2021. *Tyrone Power: Gender, Genre and Image in Classical Hollywood Cinema*. Edinburgh: University of Edinburgh Press.

Kuhn, Annette. 1985. *The Power of the Image: Essays on Representation and Sexuality*. London and New York: Routledge.

McLean, Adrienne L. 2003. '"New Films in Story Form": Movie Story Magazines and Spectatorship'. *Cinema Journal* 42 (3): 3–26.

McLean, Adrienne L. 2004. *Being Rita Hayworth: Labor, Identity and Hollywood*. New Brunswick, NJ: Rutgers University Press.

Mulvey, Laura. 1975. 'Visual Pleasure and Narrative Cinema'. *Screen* 16 (3): 6–18.

Power, Romina. 2014. *Searching for my Father, Tyrone Power*. Place not specified: Prime Concepts.

Sennett, Robert S. 1998. *Hollywood Hoopla: Creating Stars and Selling Movies in the Golden Age of Hollywood*. New York: Billboard Books.

Slide, Anthony. 2010. *Inside the Hollywood Fan Magazine: A History of Star Makers, Fabricators and Gossip Mongers*. Jackson: University Press of Mississippi.

Vincendeau, Ginette. 2013. *Brigitte Bardot*. London: Palgrave Macmillan.

6. LEAFING MEN AND LADIES: FAN MAGAZINES AND READING STRATEGIES

Sarah Polley

Between the 1920s and the 1950s, the heyday of fan magazines, *Introduction to Advertising* was published in several editions in the United States. Authored by advertising executives and academics, this industry handbook included advice on the distribution of advertisements and editorial material in magazines. It was recommended that advertisers exploit readers' desire to finish articles. These should terminate among advertisements 'to increase the probability of the advertisement's being read' (Brewster, Palmer and Ingraham 1947, 85). This was considered so commonplace a practice that 'every magazine reader has doubtless learned from his [sic] own experience that it accomplishes this result very effectively' (85). We cannot know whether such reading strategies were followed by those perusing fan magazines. However, analysis of the interaction of advertisements and editorial material in fan magazines is particularly important because these elements are especially entwined. As well as using stars to advertise films, these publications promoted items endorsed by stars, which readers could buy to emulate them. Stars themselves are products, with editorial material not only sating readers' desire for information about stars' lives but contributing to their image. Sumiko Higashi's *Stars, Fans, and Consumption in the 1950s: Reading Photoplay* (2014) provides some useful comment on the relationship between advertisements and editorial material in the ubiquitous US fan magazine. Since structure has rarely been addressed in relation to fan magazines, and there is criticism that scholarship has unjustly focused on *Photoplay* due to its availability (Petersen 13 November 2013, n.p.), this chapter considers the contents and structure of *Photoplay* alongside four other magazine titles. In addition to the August 1955 issue of the little-known *Filmalaya*,[1] I explore the 3 September 1955 issues of the British weeklies *Picturegoer* and *Picture Show* and September 1955 UK and US versions of the monthly *Photoplay*.

Concern with the interplay of advertisements and editorial material has more often been discussed by scholars addressing women's magazines. Since, as Sally Stein comments, women's magazines are 'underwritten by advertisers' (1985, 9), academic work focuses on the address to the increasingly powerful female consumer. Stein's 'The Graphic Ordering of Desire: Modernization of a Middle-Class Magazine 1914–1939' (1985) tackles the structural relation of advertisements to other features in the US women's magazine *Ladies Home Journal* at five-year intervals. Stein determines that while the advertising ratio remains fairly constant at 45 per cent, the editorial material is increasingly pushed to the back of the magazine among advertisements (9). She supplies graphs which effectively convey the structure of six magazine issues. A vertical bar representing each double page is coloured either black (signalling advertisements) or white (editorial), and Stein provides a middle horizontal line standing in for the spine of the magazine to further show material placement. Arrows indicate where material is continued later in the magazine (the strategy promoted by *Introduction to Advertising*).

While I focus on the infrastructure of five different fan magazine titles at a similar date, rather than six issues of one magazine title over time, like Stein I provide graphs. However, my graphs are entirely linear to reflect more closely magazine structure, one bar per page, and material placement on these pages. I do not indicate continuing coverage with arrows, but this is seen by the same colour being used to indicate this. Considering these in conjunction with my detailed written descriptions of all five fan magazines' contents, including page numbers, allows for those reading to reconstruct the magazine issues. Broadening out, I examine the contents of each magazine, remarking on the types of content in relation to a general definition of fan magazines, scholarly interest in interactive elements such as letters, and gender. Focusing then on continuation (that is, the placement of the rest of the article after its initial appearance), which is foregrounded by *Introduction to Advertising*, I comment on the type of material continued in each magazine title and am able to do so alongside analysis of selected advertisements, especially paying attention to gender. By continually shifting between close-ups on specific magazines and contextualising long shots across the sample, this chapter provides an unusual level of detail on fan magazine content and structure, laying foundations for further examinations of how these publications promote stars.

CONTENTS ROUND-UP

Here I take each fan magazine in turn and, after providing a little publication history and other relevant details, give a summary of chronological editorial contents which, unless otherwise stated, deal with US stars and films. British fan magazine weekly *Picture Show* was first published by Amalgamated Press on 3 May 1919, with its final issue appearing on 31 December 1960. From 13 September 1941, two years after combining with *Film Pictorial* (a fellow weekly from the same publisher), it went fortnightly. It returned to weekly frequency on 25 June 1949 and its 3 September 1955 issue ran to sixteen pages and cost threepence. Following the front cover featuring Glenn Ford and Eleanor Parker in *Interrupted Melody*, the editorial contents comprise: Picture Show gossip (3); Alan Ladd photo competition (4); fictionalisation of *Soldier of Fortune* starring Clark Gable and Susan Hayward (5–6, 10, 14); birthday forecasts (astrology, 6); film star birthday book (star birthdays, 6); a portrait of Tab Hunter (7); picture stories (photographs and description of the plot) of *Seven Little Foys* (8) and the UK's *Doctor at Sea* (9); reviews (10); Round the British Studios (UK studio news) (11); The Life Story of Martha Hyer (12); *Picture Show*'s Star Fan Club Column (12); star memorabilia competition (12); previews (13); fashion (14). (Figure 6.1).

Picturegoer, the other weekly magazine in the sample, is, at twenty-eight pages, longer than *Picture Show*. Despite its slightly higher cost (three and a half pence) it had a healthy circulation of 480,000 per issue in 1955 (*The Financial Times*, 18 August 1955, 9). *Picturegoer* was even longer running than its main weekly rival, with Odhams Press publishing it from 11 October 1913 to 23 April 1960 (when it combined with *Date* magazine). It appeared

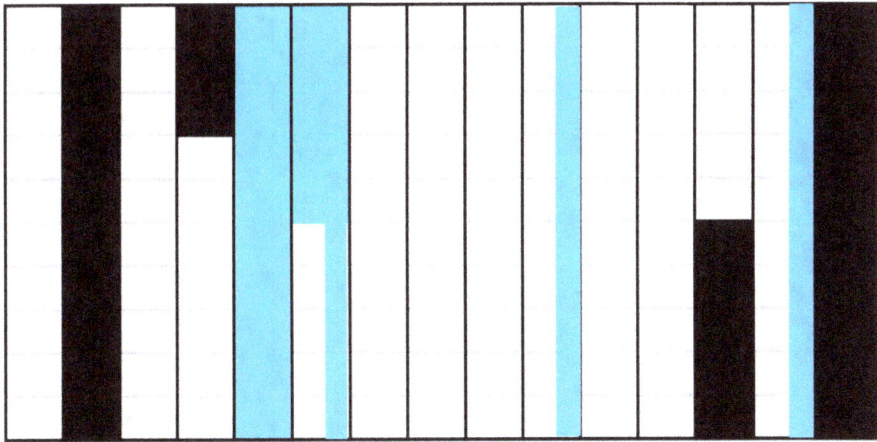

Figure 6.1   Graph of *Picture Show*, 3 September 1955.

under slightly different titles over its run, and after combining with *The Pictures* (another of Odhams weekly publications) in 1914, it went solo and less frequent, as *Picturegoer Monthly*, from January 1921 to May 1931. After this it settled into weekly publication until, like *Picture Show*, it went fortnightly during the Second World War, from 23 August 1941. It returned to weekly frequency on the 2 July 1949, and we are lured into the issue of the 3 September 1955 by a scantily clad Gloria DeHaven on the cover. This is succeeded by readers' letters (3, 5, 26) and its numerous pieces include articles on stars with different nationalities – Broderick Crawford (7–8), British star Vera Day (8), Hungarian-born Eva Bartok (9) – and the Venice film festival (10).[2] The Topsie cartoon strip (10) is followed by articles on British musician Dennis Lotis (11), *Picturegoer*'s photographer (11), DeHaven (11) and Liberace (12–13). After Hollywood gossip (13), articles on Jose Ferrer (14–15), French Jeanmarie (14), British actor Terry-Thomas (16) and British star Michael Wilding (16) ensue. *Picturegoer*'s fictionalisation of *The Seven Year Itch* (17, 25) appears prior to reviews (18–19), and then articles on Irish Stephen Boyd (20) and Disney animation (20). A variety of topics is seen over the next two pages: TV column (21), music coverage (21), 'At Your Service' (answers to showbusiness queries) (22), astrology (22) and mini film reviews (22). (Figure 6.2)

Filmalaya is the first monthly, and the first non-British, magazine in the sample. It has proved difficult to find information on this publication, but the August 1955 issue is the fifth anniversary edition, implying that it began in August 1950. Partial copies seen online range in date from January 1951 to November 1956, suggesting that it continued beyond the August 1955 edition.

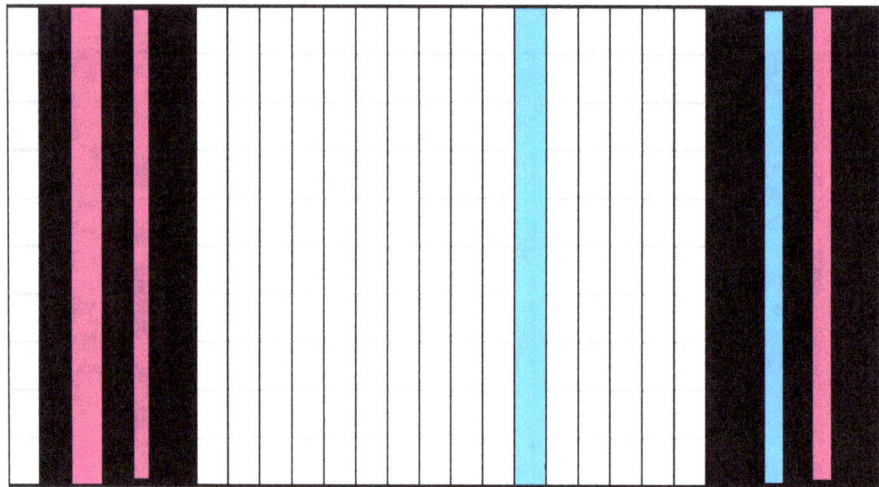

Figure 6.2   Graph of *Picturegoer*, 3 September 1955.

Unlike the British weeklies, *Filmalaya* names editorial staff in addition to the publisher: Cathay Publicity Department (in Singapore). While other members of the workforce are listed in the magazine's back matter (50), Donald Davies' position as editor is foregrounded (3). The 52-page, 40-cent, August 1955 issue is in English, and indeed the cover features British actress Jill Adams, posing in a short-sleeve top and shorts. A table of contents (3) is the first editorial material, with this including Robert Van's Hollywood gossip (4–5, 37) and a fictionalisation of the British film *Moonfleet* (6–7, 22–3, 40–2, 48–9). Articles on *The Seven Year Itch* (8–9, 34–5, 38, 50) and British child star Jon Whiteley (11, 46) are followed by a *Timberjack* picture story (12–13), pictures and text about the Italian *Aida* (14–15) and news from British studio J. A. Rank (16–17). A biography of John Derek (18, 30) is on the same page as an astrology section (18, 46) with behind-the-scenes photographs of *House of Bamboo* (19) opposite. Next, there are double pages on MGM (20–1) and Fox (24–5) studios. After pictures to celebrate the magazine's anniversary (26–7), smaller pieces appear: a portrait of British singer Yana (28), a photo quiz (30–1), joke book (32), an item on female hairstyles (33), articles on Sheree North and Betty Grable (36), Robert Ryan (39), Japanese star Shirley Yamaguchi (43), a popular records page (44) and a portrait of Jarma Lewis (45). Gordon Gow's London gossip (46–7, 50) completes the issue (Figure 6.3).

The monthly British fan magazine *Photoplay* was established at a similar time to *Filmalaya*, in March 1950, by Argus Press. It went through various titles to incorporate new media (television, video) and magazines (fellow Argus publication *Films Illustrated* from February 1982) before its final issue in March 1989. Despite being published by Argus Press, *Photoplay* UK was an offshoot of the important US version, the second fan magazine to be founded. Indeed, the front cover of the 56-page September 1955 issue, featuring model Sue Evans

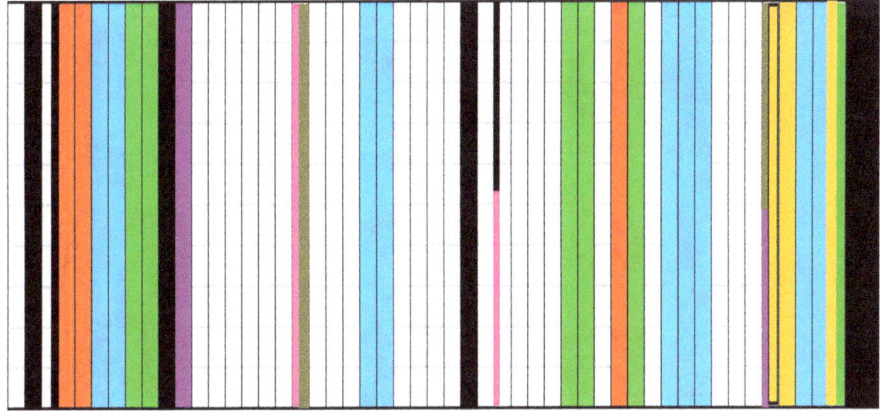

Figure 6.3 Graph of *Filmalaya*, August 1955.

in a swimsuit, proclaims itself 'The world's top film magazine'. Its one shilling and threepence price also makes it far more expensive than the British weeklies.[3] *Photoplay* UK differs from its main competitors by its inclusion of a table of contents (3). After letters (4–5) and Hollywood gossip (6–7), its main features are on stars: James Dean (8–9, 53), Edmond O'Brien (10–11, 50), and Australian actress Mary Parker (13, 48–9). A love triangle between British actor Edmund Purdom, Tyrone Power and Linda Christian appears on the top half of pages 14 and 15, with the lower halves dedicated to Austrian-born actress Mara Lane's injury. Longer articles on stars resume, with pieces on Douglas Fairbanks Jr (17, 47), Rock Hudson (19, 49), Tyrone Power (21, 46) and, after a brief break to a picture spread on *The Seven Year Itch* (22–3), Greta Garbo and Marlene Dietrich (24–5, 47). A feature about music records (26) precedes full-colour portraits of Anne Baxter (27), Montgomery Clift (28) and British star Dirk Bogarde (29), after which an article on Gregory Peck is found (31–3, 44–5). A picture spread concerning the British film *Touch and Go* is placed on the top portions of pages 34 and 35, with the lower listing top films and performances. Following UK gossip (36–9), the magazine returns to star articles on Robert Mitchum (40–1, 54) and Kirk Douglas (42–3). A personality quiz appears on the first two pages of continued matter (the bottom halves of pages 44 and 45), with this succeeded by pieces on Janet Leigh and Tony Curtis (46), Faith Domergue's dinner date with a reader (48–9) and advice on how to hide your – female – figure (50). (Figure 6.4)

The long-running US version of *Photoplay* was published from June 1911 until May/June 1980. The most relevant aspects of its history are that it was taken over by Bernarr Macfadden in 1934 and, prior to the September 1955 issue under consideration here, combined with another Macfadden fan magazine, the decade-long established *Movie Mirror* in January 1941. (For more on this merger

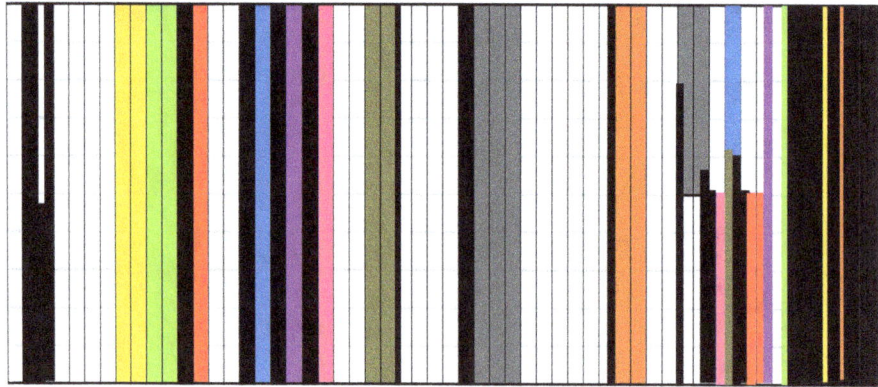

Figure 6.4 Graph of *Photoplay* UK, September 1955.

see Slide 2010, 106–8.) Tony Curtis – topless, and wielding a bow and arrow – cuts a striking figure on the front of *Photoplay* US's 20-cent, 116-page September 1955 issue. Its tagline is more specific than its British counterpart's claim to 'top' status, rightly asserting that it is 'America's Largest Selling Movie Magazine'. In 1955 its US circulation was 1,401,701 per issue (Ayers 1955; also see Polley 2019, 74). It certainly had a large staff, with this listed in far more detail than the other magazines in the sample. It not only named an editor, Ann Higginbotham, but assistant personnel, as well as specific departments: Art, Fashion, and Hollywood (2). Criticism of *Photoplay* bias in scholarship is justified, especially when it is acknowledged that the UK publication *Picturegoer* has a slightly higher issue circulation figure per head of population.[4] It is nonetheless important to include *Photoplay* US among the others in the sample, since its longevity and circulation, the size of its operation, and its offshoots point to its influence.

Unlike the other magazines in the sample, the US magazine does not number its pages from the start since it places more advertisements in its opening pages. Page numbers referenced here are those listed by the magazine. The table of contents (2) is followed by 'Hollywood Whispers' gossip (4), reviews (6, 8, 14), jokes (11), casts of current films (16), 'That's Hollywood For You' gossip (18–19), letters (20, 23), 'Hollywood Party Line' gossip (24), and brief reviews (26–7). *Photoplay* US's own named 'Highlights' begin with a competition (28), a Dean Martin and Jerry Lewis article (30–4, 97), an article on the film *The Private War of Major Benson* (37) and 'Inside Stuff' gossip (38–9, 92–3). A plethora of star, and occasionally film, articles appear in the bulk of the magazine: Russ Tamblyn (40–1, 94–5), Terry Moore (42–3, 106–7), Rock Hudson (44–5, 103–5), Marilyn Monroe (46–7, 111–12), Jack Lemmon (48–51, 108–10), Sheree North (52–3, 98–101), Marlon Brando (54–5), the *Gentlemen Marry Brunettes* film (56–7), British-born Jean Simmons (58–61, 87–9), Tony Curtis (62–3, 84), 'Get These Men' (on various stars' love lives, 64–7, 82) and Gregory Peck (68–70, 90–1). Other features have a female slant: the fashion pages (71–80, 102) and the Becoming Attractions Beauty feature (82). Enmeshed in the back matter is a request to inform the magazine of change of address (88), a survey asking readers about their favourite stories in this issue (92), photo credits (94), 'Needle Novelties' (96) and stars' addresses (110) (Figure 6.5).

Regular Features

In *Inside the Hollywood Fan Magazine*, Anthony Slide notes that early fan magazines concentrated on 'the short story form' (2010, 4). He claims that 'the standard format of the fan magazine was established in the mid 1910s' with this comprising 'news stories, articles, and lavish photo spreads on . . . stars . . . the major films in production, as well as reviews' (4). Slide's focus is

SARAH POLLEY

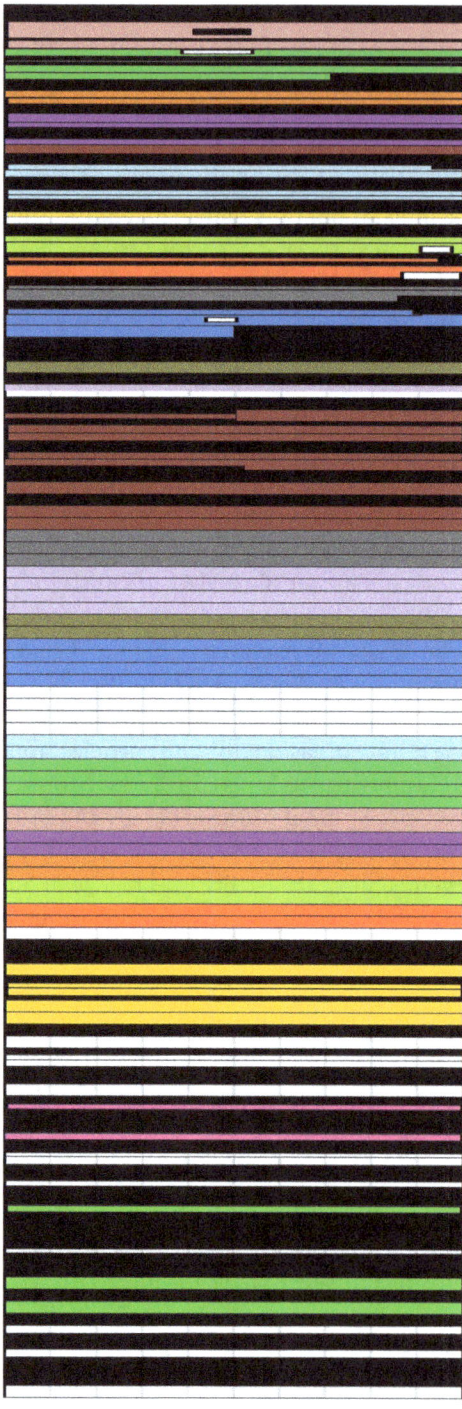

Figure 6.5 Graph of *Photoplay* US, September 1955.

US fan magazines, but other scholars have commented on those from other countries. For example, Jane Bryan and Mark Glancy briefly mention changing contents while surveying British fan magazine *Picturegoer* during times of war (Bryan 2011; Glancy 2011) and Lisa Stead considers *Picturegoer* and fellow British fan magazines in the interwar years (Stead 2017). The contents of early years of US fan magazine *Motion Picture Story Magazine* and *Photoplay* are covered in more detail by Kathryn Fuller's *At the Picture Show: Small Town Audiences and the Creation of Movie Fan Culture* (1996). An article by Sumiko Higashi also addresses early *Photoplay* contents (2017), but her 2014 book on the fan magazine during the 1950s is more pertinent to the period this chapter is discussing. In addition to relating Slide's summary of general contents to the five magazines in the sample, I will reference Higashi's detailed work on *Photoplay* US from 1948 to 1963 (with its chapters on advertisements, beauty and fashion, houses and interior decorating, advice columns, contests and awards) where relevant.

Consistent with Slide, I found that the type of content which appeared in all fan magazines was articles (photographs and text) about stars. Hollywood stars abound in all, though British stars are also seen in *Filmalaya*, the British weeklies *Picture Show* and *Picturegoer*, and occasionally *Photoplay* UK. All the magazines also featured stars in sections on Hollywood gossip (which perhaps comes under Slide's heading of 'news stories'), with *Photoplay* US the only one excluding British gossip. Notably this publication includes four *distinct* Hollywood gossip features: 'Hollywood Whispers', 'That's Hollywood For You', 'Hollywood Party Line', and 'Inside Stuff'. While material quenching readers' desire to find out about stars is often accompanied by photographs, purely visual representations of stars are also present. Lavish full-page portraits and picture spreads occur in most of the magazines, with colour emphasised in both UK and US *Photoplay*. The exception is *Picturegoer*, whose pieces are generally short. Even its unique visual element, a cartoon strip, is brief. By contrast, the film reviews Slide mentions often appear in the sample, but while these are illustrated by photographs, the emphasis is on the text. *Photoplay* UK has only a few lines about the top films and performances but, even more strikingly, these are entirely absent from *Filmalaya*. Conversely, the short stories, which Slide and other scholars (see also McLean 2003; McClain 2009) primarily connect to early magazines, including *Photoplay*, are present in all the non-*Photoplay* magazines in the 1955 sample. Notably, the very long *Photoplay* US is also the only magazine, other than the short *Picture Show*, to lack features on music and/or television.

While Slide's listing of contents includes those which draw on readers' desire for photographs and stories about stars, the desire of readers to interact is at the centre of other scholarship on fan magazines. Following Marsha Orgeron's 2009 article '"You Are Invited to Participate": Interactive Fandom in the Age of the Movie Magazine', several scholars have focused on a specific area – readers' letters – in French (Sellier 2019), UK (Stead 2011) and, more often, US fan magazines (Anselmo 2015; Lanckman 2019, 2020). Most of the magazines in the sample contain letters pages. The short *Picture Show* did not publish letters in the week I have examined, but they are present for the remaining weeks of the month. Letters are missing entirely from *Filmalaya*, which also, as I noted earlier, does not carry film reviews. This, and its lack of any direct film advertisements, suggests a lack of engagement with local film culture. *Photoplay* US, *Picture Show* and *Filmalaya* include another interactive element: competitions. *Filmalaya*'s front cover promotes this one feature, while *Photoplay* UK contains the related matter of a small personality quiz which poses the question 'Are You Sophisticated?' (44–5). In addition to a competition, *Picture Show* also has a unique participatory feature – its Star Fan Club puts readers in touch with each other. Meanwhile, *Picturegoer*'s 'At Your Service' section supplies answers to readers' showbusiness queries. This format evokes *Motion Picture Story Magazine*'s Answer Man from the early days of fan magazines (for more on the Answer Man, see Fuller 1996, 138–42). Notably none of the magazines in the sample includes an advice column, an interactive item which Adrienne L. McLean has written about across various magazine titles over time (2019). Higashi provides some detail about *Photoplay* US's advice column fronted by Claudette Colbert until April 1953, and which returned under the stewardship of Spring Byington for a nine-month stint in 1956 (2014, 207–15). We could perhaps speculate that *Photoplay* US readers themselves called for the return of the column, since the September 1955 issue solicits its readers' opinion about the magazine's contents.

Occasionally academic work on interactive features, most notably Lanckman's work on fan letters (2019, 52), notes that these were also engaged with by men. However, Slide's presumption that fan magazines' 'glamour' means that they are aimed at female readers (2010, 4) is generally accepted. It is certainly the case that some contents in my sample are explicitly aimed at women: the fashion pages in *Photoplay* US stand out here. Rather than including music and television content, this magazine features fashion over an extensive ten pages near its centre. Higashi's work suggests that fashion plays an important part in other issues of the magazine during the decade, though this lessens from 1957 onwards as the magazine increasingly resembles a tabloid (2014, 183). While stars being products blurs the line between advertisements and editorial material, *Photoplay* US's fashion pages are the feature which most mixes these materials across the sample. The black-and-white photographs and illustrations of women's clothing and accessories are marked as editorial material since the feature appears in the table of contents and its pages note that they continue. Nevertheless, prices and brands are mentioned, with readers also directed to a list of stockists at the back of the magazine. These covert advertisements appear alongside overt advertisements, many of which are in full colour (for example, Belgimere sweaters, 73). *Photoplay* US also includes other aspects especially directed at women, for example, its beauty and needlework pages. Some of the other magazines in the sample also engage with women: the fashion page at the very end of *Picture Show*, female hairstyles in *Filmalaya* and *Photoplay* UK's advice on how to obscure the feminine form. *Photoplay* US's direct address to women in its editorial pages is therefore relatively unusual. Its membership of The True Story Women's Group of magazines – a bundle of several of the publisher's magazine titles for advertising purposes (see Polley 2019, 66–7) – is also uncommon. Anticipated readers are indicated by advertisements as well as editorial material, and I turn to this matter in my consideration of continuing coverage next.

Highlights

Before providing details on continuing features which lure readers to advertisements in each magazine, I will briefly consider the matter of tables of contents. For Ellen McCracken, these, along with the front cover and editor's column, form part of a 'relay device' in women's magazines which 'openly send the reader to specific features and indirectly to ads' (1993, 46). Tamar Jeffers McDonald relates this to fan magazines as she traces how Doris Day's 'star trail' leads readers with an interest in the star through these publications (2013, 39–40). Notably the weeklies in the sample, which are shorter than the monthly fan magazines, did not contain tables of contents. Arguably this makes their arrangement of contents (including continuations) more significant because readers are not overtly directed to specific features. There are also differences in the structure of the tables of contents which appear in the monthly fan magazines. *Filmalaya* lists all the contents in the order in which they appear. But it neglects to mention its Jon Whiteley and John Derek articles, as well as its Jarma Lewis portrait, and wrongly states that cartoons occur on the page which is in fact dedicated to popular records. *Photoplay* UK's table of contents groups items into four types: 'picture spreads'; 'colour plates'; 'features'; and 'regular articles' (letters and gossip). Within all these separate sections contents are listed in the order in which they appear. However, the colour plates are the only items entirely grouped together, probably for printing reasons, while the other items in the other groups are well integrated and this alternation provides variety. *Photoplay* US also splits its contents, once more within the groups in the order of their appearance. These comprise: 'Highlights' (mostly star articles), 'stars in full colour' (portraits) and 'special events' (gossip, reviews, cast lists, letters and brief reviews). Both UK and US *Photoplay* emphasise their colour coverage, though the amount of choice given to a reader differs. *Photoplay* US separates out its coverage less, since many of the stars in full colour are photographs accompanying articles about them, and the special events, though listed last, appear before the other materials. The readers' choice in *Photoplay* US is therefore more illusory. Despite seemingly being offered varied places to go, readers are in fact bound to a restricted number of pages with editorial material – possibly due to the proliferation of advertisements.

In the first half of her book on the US version of *Photoplay*, Higashi comments on the matter of continuation; after citing an article about a star, she supplies, in italics, brief notes on the advertisements on the later pages. For example, Higashi describes advertisements which accompanied an article on Esther Williams promoting *'Woodbury Lotion to keep your hand as kissable as your lips' and Richard Hudnut Permanent 'for luxurious, softer, lovelier waves'* (Higashi 2014, 29, Williams article in *Photoplay* November 1948, 35–7, 95–7, advertisements on pages 95 and 96). I will be doing something similar here, as I turn to continuing contents in the fan magazine sample. Weekly *Picture Show*'s only continuing aspect is its fictionalisation of *Soldier of Fortune*. The first of its continuing pages (10) does not occur among or opposite advertisements, but its second (14) terminates opposite a key space for advertising: the inside back cover. This contains the first page of a gender-neutral two-page advertisement for Littlewoods' mail order catalogue which bills itself 'A Personal letter to YOU!' In addition to the fictionalisation being the only feature which continues, its importance to the magazine is indicated by this also being the case for the other weeks of that month (10, 17, 24 September). Furthermore, the fictionalisation is advertised on the front cover using the couple featured in the story for the 17 and 24 September issues.

The 3 September 1955 issue of *Picturegoer* also has a continuing fictionalisation: *The Seven Year Itch*. This begins on page 17, concluding on page 25 among quarter-page advertisements for a woman's product (Scherk Face Lotion) and a neutral product aimed at women on this occasion (Anadin Pain Killers to combat the period pain causing women to feel '"off-colour" for two or three days in every month'). It is opposite the second of a two-page advertisement for Littlewoods catalogues. This is similar to, but different from, the neutral Littlewoods advertisement in *Picture Show* the same week. The first page for both is a typewritten letter extolling the virtues of becoming a Littlewoods agent. While *Picture Show*'s advertisement is not addressed to a specific gender, the *Picturegoer* version describes the letter as a 'magic wand' providing access to items 'which will delight every woman'. It therefore places women's role as consumer centrally. Mirroring the continuation aspect I am analysing here, an instruction at the bottom of both magazines' advertisements encourages the reader to turn the page for the rest of the advertisement. The black-and-white line drawings on the second page of *Picture Show*'s advertisement promote 'EVERYTHING for EVERYBODY'. Meanwhile *Picturegoer*'s advertisement supplies a cartoon strip which expands on the magic wand imagery of the preceding page as it tells 'How the Office Cinderella became THE MOST POPULAR GIRL ON THE STAFF'.

In addition to the fictionalisation, *Picturegoer*'s letters continue, on page 26, among an advertisement for the UK film *Value for Money*.[5] These appear opposite several advertisements on the magazine's inside back cover. Two of these are for women's products (Exquisite Form Bra, Lustre-Crème Shampoo); one uses an illustration of a smiling young woman to promote a foodstuff (Nestlé's Milk Chocolate), and two smaller advertisements are neutrally addressed (Dr Scholl's Zino Pads for feet; *Picturegoer* Salon's 'real photos of the stars'). Both the continuing fiction (and its female-addressed advertisements) and the continuing letters (whose advertisements include gender-neutral ones alongside those aimed at women) seem to be important to *Picturegoer*. However, although the letters continue in all four of *Picturegoer*'s weekly September issues, fiction is only present the first week of the month. *Picturegoer* is nearly twice the length of *Picture Show*, and its advertisement ratio a little higher (30.36% compared to 25%), but because its features are numerous and short comparatively fewer continue.

The monthly *Filmalaya* has approximately triple the number of *Picture Show*'s pages and is twice the length of *Picturegoer*. While it might be thought that its number of continued items would be comparable, perhaps three or four, it is in fact far higher: seven. The majority of these (Hollywood gossip, fictionalisation, Jon Whiteley article, astrology) do not appear among or opposite advertisements. The graph (Figure 6.3) shows that the continuing editorial material (in various colours) is not well integrated with the advertisements (in black). This is partly because *Filmalaya*'s advertisement ratio of 11.54% is less than half that seen in both British weeklies. As noted earlier, *Filmalaya* is missing a few usual fan magazine contents (notably letters, film reviews and film advertisements) and its non-comprehensive and mislabelled table of contents implies a less polished operation. However, its status as a fan magazine is supported by just under half of its aspects, which continue among, and opposite, advertisements (the articles on John Derek, *The Seven Year Itch*, and London gossip), closely paralleling items which I noted as often appearing in such publications. Derek concludes on the same page (30) as a small advertisement for the Vicky Michelle Beauty Parlour in Singapore, especially promoting the safari cut for women: 'LADIES, AT LAST It's Here!' The other items both terminate opposite the inside back cover. This includes a half-page advertisement for 'pure, wholesome & refreshing' Gold Bird Ceylon Tea, and quarter-page ones for the 'best badminton frame' and D. T. Lim's Diabetes Herb Tea (all of which are based in Singapore). None of these is aimed at a specific gender, which is consistent with the Littlewoods advertisement on the inside back cover of *Picture Show* and half of those located in this position in *Picturegoer*.

Several items which are continued in other magazines (notably letters, gossip, reviews) are not afforded the same treatment by *Photoplay* UK. However, the majority of *Photoplay* UK's star articles, an aspect I noted occurred in all fan magazines, continue. At 25.89% *Photoplay* UK's advertisement ratio is more than double that of *Filmalaya*. Comparison of these magazines' graphs (Figure 6.4; cf. Figure 6.3), in conjunction with the more advertisement-heavy graph for *Picturegoer* (Figure 6.2), shows that *Photoplay* UK better integrates continuing editorial material (in various colours) and advertisements (in black). While half of *Filmalaya*'s continuing features on stars were among advertisements (John Derek, but not Jon Whiteley), this is the case for all but one (on Kirk Douglas) in *Photoplay* UK. The continuation of its article on Gregory Peck is placed amid products aimed at women: Devonshire Shoes 'for the girl with a passion for fashion' (44) and Camilatone Tonrinz colour hair rinse (45). Some advertisements' visibility is maximised by different star articles finishing on the same, or opposite, pages. A quarter-page advertisement for Odo-ro-no deodorant (needed by '[e]ven the loveliest girls') is seen on page 46 where the Tyrone Power article ends. The facing page has a large advertisement for Silvikrin women's shampoo, and the conclusions of the articles on Douglas Fairbanks Jr and Greta Garbo/Marlene Dietrich. A neutral advertisement for star photos is on page 48, alongside the closing part of the Mary Parker article, and opposite the completion of the article on Rock Hudson. Such a neutral advertisement is fairly unusual in the magazine. The first page of the female-addressed version of the Littlewoods advertisement is present on page 51, opposite the termination of the Edmond O'Brien article. Littlewoods' second page faces the James Dean article advertised on the cover, which is fittingly surrounded by advertisements for women's products: Tampax, Golden Shadeine hair colour, and Eleanore King's Beauty Secrets from the Stars. Finally, the Mitchum article continuation appears on the last page of editorial material (54). This is in the middle of several small advertisements: some targeted at women – Veet hair removal and Cuticura Soap both have a picture of a woman using the product – and others more neutral (Anadin Pain Killers, Mrs French's Star Lampshades, DDD Antiseptic Skin Balm). This is nonetheless opposite a full-page advertisement for women's skirts (by Gorray), further demonstrating that of the magazines in the sample analysed so far, *Photoplay* UK is most aimed at women.

Photoplay US contains more than double the pages of the other two monthlies. Unsurprisingly, more categories of contents continue: not just the star articles seen in *Photoplay* UK, but gossip, reviews, letters and fashion. Gossip is seen in all the magazines, reviews in most (excepting *Filmalaya*) and letters in several. Notably these non-star article aspects only continue early in the magazine and not among the back matter. Fashion, an aspect given unique emphasis in *Photoplay* US, technically continues later as it lists stockists, among advertisements, on page 102. *Photoplay* US's advertisement ratio of 39.66% is the highest in the sample, and if I were to include the covert advertisements in the fashion pages this would be even nearer the 45% ratio that Stein found in women's magazines (1985, 9). Comparing the amount of non-continuing editorial (in white) in *Photoplay* US's graph (Figure 6.5) to *Photoplay* UK's (Figure 6.4) aptly demonstrates the former's better integration. *Photoplay* US only has one main block of white – double pages on Marlon Brando and *Gentlemen Marry Brunettes*. Furthermore, while *Photoplay* UK's star portraits appear separately, those of *Photoplay* US are part of its star articles, most of which are advertised on its cover.

Due to the greater number of continuing articles, I cannot go into the same detail for *Photoplay* US as for *Photoplay* UK. However, it is significant that, perhaps surprisingly, *Photoplay* US does not maximise advertisement visibility by terminating several articles on the same page. Instead, its longer articles are continued over several pages. This exploits a reader's connection with one star and, in Jeffers McDonald's term, his or her 'star trail' (2013, 39–40). It is also notable that the inside back cover advertisements of both UK and US *Photoplay* are aimed at women. *Photoplay* US has a Breck hair lotion and shampoo advertisement opposite the end of its Marilyn Monroe article. The presence of this grooming product corresponds with Higashi's claim that this occurs in the category comprising the largest group (56%) of advertisements on the front inside, back inside, and back covers from 1948–1963 (2014, 156). This is not the case for most of the continuing pages. Only female products are promoted among and facing the conclusion to the Tony Curtis (84), Jean Simmons (86–9) and Gregory Peck (90–1) articles and the end of Inside Stuff gossip (92–3). But the majority of *Photoplay* US's articles end amid a mix of neutral and woman-aimed advertisements similar to those seen on the last page of *Photoplay* UK's Mitchum article.

Closing Commentary

Fan magazines' treatment of individual stars, such as Monroe, Curtis, Simmons, Peck and Mitchum, and the related matter of star trails, are significant. But it is vital to place any claims about individuality (for example, about the proximity of a star to particular advertisements and types of consumers) in the context of fan magazines' broader design, and that of specific titles. This chapter's analysis of general contents, continuing contents and selected advertisements has shown the variety of design present in five fan magazines from three different countries. Fan magazine content is often presumed to be aimed at women, perhaps partly due to scholarship's bias towards US fan magazines, principally *Photoplay* US. While *Photoplay* US, part of the True Story Women's Group, emphasised women's fashion and contained beauty pages, contents explicitly aimed at women occurred infrequently in the sample.

I have highlighted continuing contents, which the contemporaneous advertising handbook quoted in the introduction argues led readers to advertisements later in magazines. This has demonstrated that two of the magazines in the sample include features which play no, or a smaller, part in *Photoplay* US: fiction in *Picture Show*, and letters (and occasionally fiction) in *Picturegoer*. Furthermore, *Picturegoer*'s UK circulation per head of population being higher than *Photoplay* US's in its home country in 1955 signals that it is as important as the long-running magazine which has been at the heart of much fan magazine scholarship. A focus on star articles seen fleetingly in *Filmalaya* was ramped up in both UK and US *Photoplay*, though the US version also continued other aspects in its back matter, especially gossip and the aforementioned fashion. Unusually, *Filmalaya* placed fewer than half of its continuing features among and opposite advertisements. However, these advertisements' mix of gender address was consistent with the other magazines in the sample. British company Littlewoods was even promoted by two different advertisements, one of which appealed to everyone (*Picture Show*) and the other exclusively to women (*Picturegoer*, *Photoplay* UK).

Concentrating on continuing features does not deal with advertisements appearing outside of this relay device. For example, there were many advertisements aimed at women in *Photoplay* US's fashion section. But this is distinct to the publication, with this magazine's advertisement ratio being the closest to the 45 per cent Stein finds in *Ladies Home Journal* (1985, 9). This further underlines *Photoplay* US's relationship to women's magazines. While this chapter has predominately examined continuing features in five fan magazines from the same date, further detailed work on these issues, as well as the inclusion of additional magazines both in the US and further afield, and at various times, is necessary. This will lead to a fuller understanding of these magazines, and the stars they feature, as objects of desire, as well as providing further insight into the contemporaneous readers who appreciated them.

Notes

1. My grateful thanks to Tamar Jeffers McDonald for sharing this resource with me.
2. The Broderick Crawford article and other magazine features, notably double-page spreads, may be thought of as continuing coverage. However, I am not reflecting this as continuing status in the graphs unless more than one page appears between the coverage, and/or they continue in the magazine back matter. This is because readers would reach them by just glancing at the opposite page, or a usual turning of the page – they are not directed by the continuation of a story.
3. To supply some more recent monetary context, the National Archive's Currency Converter claims that £1 in 1955 was equal to £23.87 in 2017: <https://www.nationalarchives.gov.uk/currency-converter> (last accessed 18 November 2022). According to my calculations, this means that in 2017 *Picture Show* would cost 30p, *Picturegoer* 35p, and *Photoplay* UK £1.49. The online inflation tool Dollar

Time states that $1 would equate to $9.04 in 2017 (<https://www.dollartimes.com/inflation/inflation.php?amount=1&year=1955>). *Photoplay* US would therefore cost $1.81 in 2017 (or approximately £1.47, taking into account 2017 exchange rates on 1 January seen on an online exchange rate site: <https://www.exchangerates.org.uk/USD-GBP-spot-exchange-rates-history-2017.html>).

4. *Photoplay* US's per head figure in 1955 is 0.87% (achieved by dividing the circulation by the population of 161,136,449) and *Picturegoer*'s 0.94% (for a UK population of 51,193,266). The circulations are per issue figures, meaning that *Picturegoer*'s readers are committed weekly compared to *Photoplay* US's monthly frequency. Population figures are from the Macro trends website: <https://www.macrotrends.net/countries/USA/united-states/population and https://www.macrotrends.net/countries/GBR/united-kingdom/population> (last accessed 17 August 2022).

5. The letters also continued earlier in the magazine, but I am not providing analysis of the advertisement for Lifebuoy soap appearing on page 4, since readers would be exposed to this just by leafing through the magazine's pages.

References

Anon. 1955. 'The Prosperous Periodical'. *The Financial Times*, 18 August: 6, 9.
Anon. 1955. Advertisement for Littlewoods. *Picture Show*, 3 September: 15–16.
Anon. 1955. Advertisement for Littlewoods. *Picturegoer*, 3 September: 23–4.
Anon. 1955. Advertisement for Littlewoods. *Photoplay UK*, September: 50–1.
Anselmo, Diana. 2015. 'Screen-Struck: The Invention of the Movie Girl Fan'. *Cinema Journal* 55 (1): 1–28.
Ayer, N. W. and Son. 1955. *American Newspaper Annual and Directory*. N. W. Ayer and Son: Philadelphia.
Brewster, Arthur Judson, Herbert Hall Palmer and Robert G. Ingraham. 1947. *Introduction to Advertising*. New York and London: McGraw-Hill (5th edition, published through 1924–1954).
Bryan, Jane. 2011. '"Shells, Shots and Shrapnel": *Picturegoer* Goes to War'. In *British Silent Cinema and the Great War*, edited by Michael Hammond and Michael Williams, 64–76. London: Palgrave Macmillan.
Filmalaya. 1955. August.
Fuller, Kathryn. 1996. *At the Picture Show: Small Town Audiences and the Invention of Movie Fan Culture*. Washington, DC and London: Smithsonian Institution Press.
Glancy, Mark. 2011. 'Picturegoer: The Fan Magazine and Popular Film Culture in Britain During the Second World War'. *Historical Journal of Film, Radio and Television* 31 (4): 453–78.
Higashi, Sumiko. 2014. *Stars, Fans, and Consumption in the 1950s: Reading Photoplay*. New York: Palgrave Macmillan.
Higashi, Sumiko. 2017. 'Adapting Middlebrow Taste to Sell Stars, Romance, and Consumption: Early Photoplay'. *Feminist Media Histories* 3 (4): 126–61.
Jeffers McDonald, Tamar. 2013. *Doris Day Confidential: Hollywood, Sex and Stardom*. London: I. B. Tauris.

Lanckman, Lies. 2019. 'In Search of Lost Fans: Recovering Fan Magazine Readers, 1910–1950'. In *Star Attractions: Twentieth-Century Movie Magazines and Global Fandom*, edited by Tamar Jeffers McDonald and Lies Lanckman, 45–59. Iowa: University of Iowa Press.

Lanckman, Lies. 2020. 'Fans, community, and conflict in the pages of "Picture Play", 1920–38'. *Transformative Works and Cultures* 33.

McClain, William. 2009. 'Film-Fiction: Fan Magazines, Narrative, and Spectatorship in American Cinema of the 1910s'. *New Review of Film and Television Studies* 7 (4): 377–91.

McCracken, Ellen. 1993. *Decoding Women's Magazines: From Mademoiselle to Ms.* London: Palgrave.

McLean, Adrienne L. 2003. '"New Films in Story Form": Movie Story Magazines and Spectatorship'. *Cinema Journal* 42 (3): 3–26.

McLean, Adrienne L. 2019. '"Give Them a Good Breakfast, Says Nancy Carroll": Fan Magazine Advice Across Time'. In *Star Attractions: Twentieth-Century Movie Magazines and Global Fandom*, edited by Tamar Jeffers McDonald and Lies Lanckman, 11–28. Iowa: University of Iowa Press.

Orgeron, Marsha. 2009. '"You Are Invited to Participate": Interactive Fandom in the Age of the Movie Magazine'. *Journal of Film and Video* 61 (3): 3–23.

Petersen, Anne Helen. 2013. 'The Politics of Fan Magazine Research'. *In Media Res*, 13 November: n.p. <http://mediacommons.org/imr/2013/11/04/politics-fan-magazine-research> (last accessed 16 August 2022)

Polley, Sarah. 2019. 'A Spectrum of Individuals: U.S. Fan Magazine Circulation Figures from 1914–1965'. In *Star Attractions: Twentieth-Century Movie Magazines and Global Fandom*, edited by Tamar Jeffers McDonald and Lies Lanckman, 61–80. Iowa: University of Iowa Press.

Sellier, Genevieve. 2019. 'Movie Magazines, Popular Films, and Popular Spectatorship in Postwar France'. In *Star Attractions: Twentieth-Century Movie Magazines and Global Fandom*, edited by Tamar Jeffers McDonald and Lies Lanckman, 81–95. Iowa: Iowa University Press.

Slide, Anthony. 2010. *Inside the Hollywood Fan Magazine: A History of Star Makers, Fabricators and Gossip Mongers*. Jackson: University Press of Mississippi.

Stead, Lisa. 2011. '"So oft to the movies they've been": British Fan Writing and Female Audiences in the Silent Cinema'. *Transformative Works and Cultures* 6.

Stead, Lisa. 2017. '"Dear Cinema Girls": Girlhood, Picturegoing and the Interwar Film Magazine'. In *Women's Periodicals and Print Culture in Britain, 1918-1939: The Interwar Period*, edited by Catherine Clay, Maria DiCenzo, Barbara Green and Fiona Hackney, 103–20. Edinburgh: Edinburgh University Press.

Stein, Sally. 1985. 'The Graphic Ordering of Desire: Modernization of a Middle-Class Women's Magazine, 1914–1939'. *Heresies: A Feminist Publication on Art and Politics* 18 (3): 7–16.

7. A STAR IS DRAWN: MEDIA HYBRIDITY AND ORDINARY CINEPHILIA IN *LA PASSION DE DORA*

Dominic Topp

In April 1948, readers of the popular French fan magazine *Ciné-Miroir* were introduced to a new starlet, Dora Grey (née Denise Gillard), a 19-year-old fashion model who had been cast in the forthcoming film *Meurtre au music-hall* (*Murder at the Music Hall*), to be shot in the Paris studios of Osiris Films and on location on the Côte d'Azur. Unlike other actresses whose pictures graced the pages of *Ciné-Miroir*, however, Dora Grey never actually existed. Or rather, she was the fictional protagonist of the '*roman en images*' (novel in images) *La Passion de Dora, Starlett audacieuse* (*The Passion of Dora, Audacious Starlet*), a serialised comic written by Gérard Héliotte and illustrated by 'Gal', which ran in the weekly magazine until July 1948. Over the course of fifteen issues, *La Passion de Dora* offered *Ciné-Miroir* readers a genre-bending narrative that combined elements of melodrama, adventure story and gangster film. Week by week, the backstage saga of a young woman's efforts to make it in the movies took twists and turns involving professional and personal rivalries, attempted murder, kidnapping and transvestism, all told in an innovative style mixing images and text.

This chapter investigates *La Passion de Dora* from a number of angles. It first situates it within the context of the movie magazine in which it appeared, comparing and contrasting it with regular features of *Ciné-Miroir* that addressed readers through a combination of words and images. Next, it considers it as an example of the 'drawn novels' that were popular in women's romance magazines in the immediate postwar period. Finally, it discusses *La Passion de Dora* as an informal pedagogical tool that took readers behind the scenes to show them the mechanics of filmmaking and provide a playfully reflexive explication of the promotion and publicity methods by which stars were manufactured and marketed to French audiences, a process in which *Ciné-Miroir* itself is seen to play an active role. In line with recent scholarship on postwar French fan magazines, I suggest that *La Passion de Dora* was an innovative example of media hybridity that contributed to the formation of an 'ordinary cinephilia' among the readers of *Ciné-Miroir*, simultaneously entertaining them and expanding their knowledge of the cinema so as to make them more expert viewers of films and more expert readers of fan magazines.

Framing Dora: *La Passion de Dora* within *Ciné-Miroir*

Before turning to the contents of *La Passion de Dora*, it is useful to frame this *roman en images* within the context of the fan magazine in which it appeared. During the four months of the comic's inclusion in *Ciné-Miroir*, it ran alongside the magazine's regular features relating to the cinema of France and Hollywood. These included articles about the private and professional lives of stars and up-and-coming young performers, reports on films in production, movie reviews, illustrated adaptations of new releases, competitions and a regular column with answers to readers' letters. Although for the majority of the story, Dora is a starlet rather than a star, the quantity of coverage she received in the magazine suggests star treatment. Significantly, Dora and her adventures were trailed a week in advance of the first instalment, with an advertisement announcing her imminent arrival prominently displayed on page 2 of the 13 April 1948 issue. A drawing of the dark-haired Dora looking out at the reader appears next to a text that hints at the rivalry between the ingénue Dora and the established star Marlène Carlys, around which the story will develop:

> A vamp and a starlet clash!
> WHO WILL WIN?
> You'll find out by following each week
> *The Passion of Dora*
> *Audacious Starlet*
> A GREAT NOVEL IN IMAGES
> of a new and engaging formula that will start next week in
> *CINÉ-MIROIR*

From the following week, the comic and its protagonist were allotted considerable space in the magazine, initially filling three pages of each sixteen-page issue. While this was reduced to two pages for later chapters and a single page for the final instalment, over the fifteen issues in which it appeared, *La Passion de*

Dora accounted for 15 per cent of *Ciné-Miroir*'s contents, providing the fictional Dora Grey with more coverage than any of the real-life stars who appeared in the magazine's pages.

The comic's placement within *Ciné-Miroir* is also significant. From the beginning, it appeared at the back of the magazine. While this position might seem to downplay Dora's importance, it was apparently a cause of concern for some readers, who wrote to complain that the starlet's adventures were poaching space from the inside back cover, which was normally dedicated to the letters page. The controversy prompted a short article by the letters editor, 'Jean Caméra', assuring readers that Dora's arrival did not mean his column was going to disappear (1 June 1948, 2). Regardless of this initially rather unenthusiastic reception, the decision to place *La Passion de Dora* where the magazine's most interactive feature was usually located suggests that it was intended to address readers who were especially engaged with stars and their films.

For six of its fifteen weeks (20 April, 27 April, 4 May, 25 May, 1 June, 8 June 1948) the final page of the comic took up *Ciné-Miroir*'s back cover, a privileged position normally dedicated to a portrait photograph, most commonly of a French actress and timed to publicise the release of a new film. Although Dora was not represented in a full-page portrait and, unlike most cover images, was not pictured alone, she was nonetheless afforded a considerable degree of prestige. Additionally, for its first five weeks, *La Passion de Dora* featured on the front of the magazine, with a coverline advertising the *roman en images* appearing alongside that issue's star portrait. For several weeks, then, Dora was effectively wrapped around the magazine, achieving a prominence in text and image that made it likely she would be seen by those perusing the magazine at a newsstand. This bestows something approaching star status on Dora, despite her fictional nature and her lesser rank of starlet.

Notwithstanding some readers' sense of Dora as an outsider invading the magazine format with which they were familiar, certain similarities between *La Passion de Dora* and several regular features of *Ciné-Miroir* may have mitigated the shock of the comic strip's arrival. As a serialised fictional narrative told through a combination of words and images, it resembles the *roman-film* (movie novelisation), which presented the storyline of a current or forthcoming cinema release (mostly from France or Hollywood, but occasionally from Italy or the UK) through a juxtaposition of publicity stills and prose. These made up a significant portion of the magazine, with three appearing in most issues, covering up to six of sixteen pages. Some amounted to little more than a plot synopsis filling a single page, some took the form of a double-page spread, while others were split into chapters and published over several weeks, with at least one such serialisation appearing in each issue.

For example, the 27 April 1948 *Ciné-Miroir* issue, in which the second instalment of *La Passion de Dora* appeared, included three *romans-film*. Pages 4 and 5 were devoted to the first chapter of a novelisation of *Une jeune fille savait* (Lehmann 1948), a comedy released in Paris the previous month, subsequent instalments of which featured in the next six issues. These two pages present the opening scenes of the story through plot description and dialogue, alongside film stills of stars André Luguet, François Périer and Dany Robin. Pages 8 and 9 (the centre spread of the magazine) were devoted to an adaptation of the newly released costume drama *Rocambole* (de Baroncelli 1948), illustrated with stills of stars Pierre Brasseur and Sophie Desmarets (Figure 7.1). And page 11 carried the sixth and final chapter of the Hollywood Western *The Sea of Grass* (Kazan 1947), released in France as *Le Maître de la prairie* in February 1948, with a still of Katharine Hepburn and Spencer Tracy.

Romans-film like these had been a popular feature of French fan magazines since the 1920s, when publications like *Le Film Complet* and *Mon Film* presented an illustrated novelisation of a single film per issue (Crisp 1993, 221). Such adaptations served several functions beyond their role as publicity. While they offered readers an opportunity to familiarise themselves with a new film before seeing it at the cinema, and to re-experience a film after watching it, for those who lived outside Paris and other urban centres, they could be a way to gain access to films that might not play locally for months to come (Sellier

Figure 7. 1 'Rocambole' fiction illustrated with photographs. *Ciné-Miroir*, 27 April 1948. (pp. 8–9)

2019, 84). With several *romans-film* appearing each week in *Ciné-Miroir*, in some cases they would have substituted for a trip to the cinema, even when a film was available to view, with readers engaging with them for their own sake without watching the film on which they were based.

This engagement would have been as much visual as verbal, since *romans-film* in *Ciné-Miroir* were amply illustrated, often with several stills per page. Indeed, images sometimes predominated over words, particularly in double-page spreads. For example, the adaptation of *La Chartreuse de Parme* (Christian-Jaque 1948) in the 1 June 1948 issue condenses the story of this 170-minute film into 121 lines of text, while most of the two-page layout is allotted to six stills, showing the main characters in a variety of narrative situations (8–9). As in other parts of the magazine, stills, accompanied by captions either next to or in the corner of the image, were incorporated into the page design in a dynamic manner, sometimes angled or overlapping one another, sometimes cropped so as to highlight a star against a blank background. With the publication of *La Passion de Dora*, then, readers of *Ciné-Miroir* were invited to enjoy another *roman en images* that told its story by mixing images and words.

One significant difference between *La Passion de Dora* and the *romans-film* with which it shared space is that its story was told through text and drawings rather than text and photographs. However, the magazine did include drawn illustrations on some of its other pages. Caricatures of stars such as François Périer and Gérard Philipe sometimes appeared on the letters page (20 April 1948, 13; 6 July 1948, 12). And the regular column 'La Chronique de Micky' was often accompanied by a cartoon by the comic-book artist René Pellos purporting to show the magazine's pseudonymous female reporter Micky, represented as a stylish young blonde woman, in a situation relating to that week's topic. For example, a column discussing various stars' attitudes toward on-screen kissing is illustrated by a cartoon of Micky looking through a giant magnifying glass at a glamorous couple locked in a passionate embrace (25 May 1948, 5), while one on dancing in Hollywood musicals has an image of Micky and partner at a nightclub, dancing to a Latin American band (20 April 1948, 10). A column in which Micky reports from the Tour de France is spread over an entire page, with three cartoons of Micky encountering cyclists, laid out (along with a title scroll whose shape mimics the snaking cycle route) so as to guide the eye from top left to middle right to bottom left (20 July 1948, 6). Through the illustrations that accompany the weekly chronicle of Micky's adventures behind the scenes of the entertainment industry, the journalist, although supposedly a real person, comes to resemble a comic-book character, and her reports take on a semi-fictitious air. (We will encounter further examples of this blurring of the line between fiction and non-fiction below.) Here again, the pages of *Ciné-Miroir* offered a suitable home for

La Passion de Dora, a comic using words and pictures to recount the story of a young woman's progress through the film industry.

Drawing Dora: *La Passion de Dora* as Drawn Novel

While *La Passion de Dora* fits alongside some of the regular features of *Ciné-Miroir*, it also relates to types of media beyond the fan magazine. As a fictional story told through a combination of words and drawings, it sits within the tradition of the *bande dessinée*, which Laurence Grove defines as 'a French-language mixture of images and written text that together form a narrative' (2010, 16). Although it is hard to assign a point of origin to this form (historians of the *bande dessinée* have traced it back at least as far as the Middle Ages), in its modern version it was firmly established in France and Belgium by the mid-1930s, with the success of characters such as Tintin, whose adventures were initially serialised in newspapers in 1929, and dedicated magazines such as the weekly *Le Journal de Mickey* (first published in 1934), which presented translated versions of imported Walt Disney comic strips alongside locally produced material. However, *La Passion de Dora* was not just another comic strip. To understand why it would have been considered 'new and engaging', as its advertising claimed, it helps to consider *Dora* as an example of the 'drawn novel' (*roman dessinée*). This was a short-lived genre of the *bande dessinée* that was popular in France and Italy for a few years in the immediate postwar period, but quickly faded from view as it was overtaken by the photo novel.

As Jan Baetens explains, the drawn novel was a hybrid media form that innovated by bringing together 'a certain type of storytelling, a certain type of publishing, and a certain type of public' (2017, 71). Appearing in serialised instalments in women's magazines, especially romance publications, rather than in newspapers or specialist comic books, the drawn novel was aimed at female adult readers, a previously untargeted audience for *bandes dessinées*. Narratives were based in melodrama, but mixed with elements of crime fiction, and in this respect can be thought to have been influenced by film genres. Similarly, the drawn novel's visual style shows a cinematic influence through its imitation of black-and-white lighting effects, as well as innovating at the level of page design.

The innovations in the drawn novel that Baetens highlights can be seen in *La Passion de Dora* as its storyline blends aspects of different genres. After Dora's discovery, she begins work on *Meurtre au music-hall*, but the film's star, Marlène, grows jealous of Dora's budding relationship with young male lead Jacques Larsan, who plays her love interest, and plots to eliminate her rival. Marlène first refuses to work with Dora, then plants a compromising letter in her dressing room for Jacques to find, and when these tactics do not succeed, she arranges for the set to be sabotaged so that a piece of scenery falls on Dora as she is filming. Since that plan also fails, Marlène then conspires to have Dora kidnapped when the production goes on location to Cannes. The story's basis in melodrama, with Dora as an innocent victim persecuted by the villainous Marlène, is signalled in the titles of certain instalments, which hark back to the tradition of 19th-century literary serials and their cinematic successors of the 1910s: 'Chapter III: The Mysterious Letter', 'Chapter V: The Tell-Tale Kiss', 'Chapter VII: The Strange Accident'. Dora's role as designated victim within a melodramatic narrative is maintained in the sexual harassment to which she is subjected by the film producer Sokowski, who, after an audition at which he asks her to lift her skirt to show him her legs, repeatedly offers her unwanted invitations to dinner, culminating in a scene in Chapter IV ('Dora Narrowly Escapes') in which he gets her drunk and takes her back to his apartment unconscious. Dora wakes just in time to escape Sokowski's clutches, but this leads him to ally himself with Marlène in her plot to separate Dora and Jacques, which climaxes with Dora's last-minute rescue from an isolated villa by her friends among the film's crew.

As the serial develops, however, influences from other genres become more prominent, some of which are playfully acknowledged within the narrative. In Chapter X, which shows Dora's kidnapping, she muses from her captivity, 'What a fantastical story! I feel like I'm filming an adventure movie . . .' In Chapter XIII, having escaped and held one of her captors at gunpoint, she announces to Jacques, 'You see, I was made for gangster movies!' Such developments move Dora beyond her relatively passive initial role. She stands up for herself against her persecutors, and after Marlène and her accomplices are arrested, forges a successful career in the film business, becoming a star and marrying Jacques. The story concludes with a perfect resolution of the personal and the professional: as the couple fly back from a honeymoon in Venice, Dora announces her plan to dedicate herself entirely to the cinema alongside her husband. The narrative may here be drawing on developments within French cinema during the Occupation, in which a significant number of films presented a reversal of traditional gender roles, with active young female characters taking control of their destiny (Burch and Sellier 2014). This reversal of gender conventions is particularly apparent in the scene of Dora's escape, in which, having been forced to swap clothes with one of her captors to create a diversion, Dora, dressed in male garb, feigns a 'feminine' fainting spell and turns the tables on him, seizing his gun. Genre hybridity is thus intertwined with gender representation, and Dora's somewhat liberated role may have been designed to appeal to female readers in the postwar context.

As with the drawn novels discussed by Baetens, *La Passion de Dora* innovates in its visual style as well as its subject matter and themes. The images are drawn with crayon in a manner that is closer to the wash drawings (*dessin au lavis*) of the *roman dessinée* (Baetens 2017, 72) than the *ligne claire* (clear line) ink drawings of most comics of the period (Grove 2010, 122–3). This allows for a more 'painterly' style and permits lighting effects that follow the conventions for different genres that were developed in classical Hollywood cinema, with dark tonalities used for dramatic sequences while a high-key style is employed for more lighthearted scenes (Keating 2010, 140–51). As with cinematographic practice, lighting is varied from scene to scene to suit changes in narrative mood and balanced within individual scenes to perform multiple functions. For example, Dora is often depicted with the low-contrast 'soft style' lighting associated with romance scenes, and a trace of this remains even in the scenes of her kidnapping, for which some panels involve the harder high-contrast lighting typical of crime scenes, with figures in silhouette or swathed in shadow (Figure 7.2).

While Baetens sees an imitation of Hollywood lighting in the visual style of the drawn novel, these resemblances can just as well be related to the aesthetics of classical French cinema. As Colin Crisp (1993) has established, by the 1940s French cinematographers (drawing on a range of influences, German as well as American) had developed a set of norms for lighting sets and actors that broadly corresponded to the conventions of Hollywood. A hint that 'Gal', *Dora*'s pseudonymous artist, was aware of and perhaps inspired by the lighting of French films is offered in Chapter V, in a scene on the set of *Meurtre au music-hall* in which the clapperboard bears the name 'K. Courant', a reference to the real-life director of photography Curt Courant. Courant was one of several important German cinematographers who moved to France in the 1930s, and is credited by Crisp for bringing an expressionist influence to French lighting in his work on films such as *Le Drame de Shanghaï* (Pabst 1938), *La Bête Humaine* (Renoir 1938) and *De Mayerling à Sarajevo* (Ophuls 1940) (1993, 376–8). That 'Gal' included this reference to Courant as the creator of the images of *Dora*'s fictional film suggests that the chiaroscuro effects found in some scenes were modelled on his work and that of his peers.

Another visual innovation to be found in *La Passion de Dora* is its shift away from the traditional *bande dessinée* page design, which consisted of a series of equally sized rectangular panels arranged in a grid formation of three horizontal panels by four vertical panels (Grove 2010, 27). Baetens highlights 'the richer and more elastic page layout of the drawn novel' (2019, 20), and this can certainly be found in *Dora*, whose pages, in line with the layout of other parts of the magazine, feature much more diverse and dynamic compositions than the standard 3x4 grid. Panels are a variety of shapes and sizes, sometimes overlapping one another, encouraging an interplay between the linear reading invited by conventional page design and a tabular approach, in which readers can notice symmetries and abstract patterns at the global level (see Mikkonen 2017, 36)

A STAR IS DRAWN

Figure 7.2 Film noir lighting in *La Passion de Dora*. *Ciné-Miroir*, 6 July 1948. (p. 14)

147

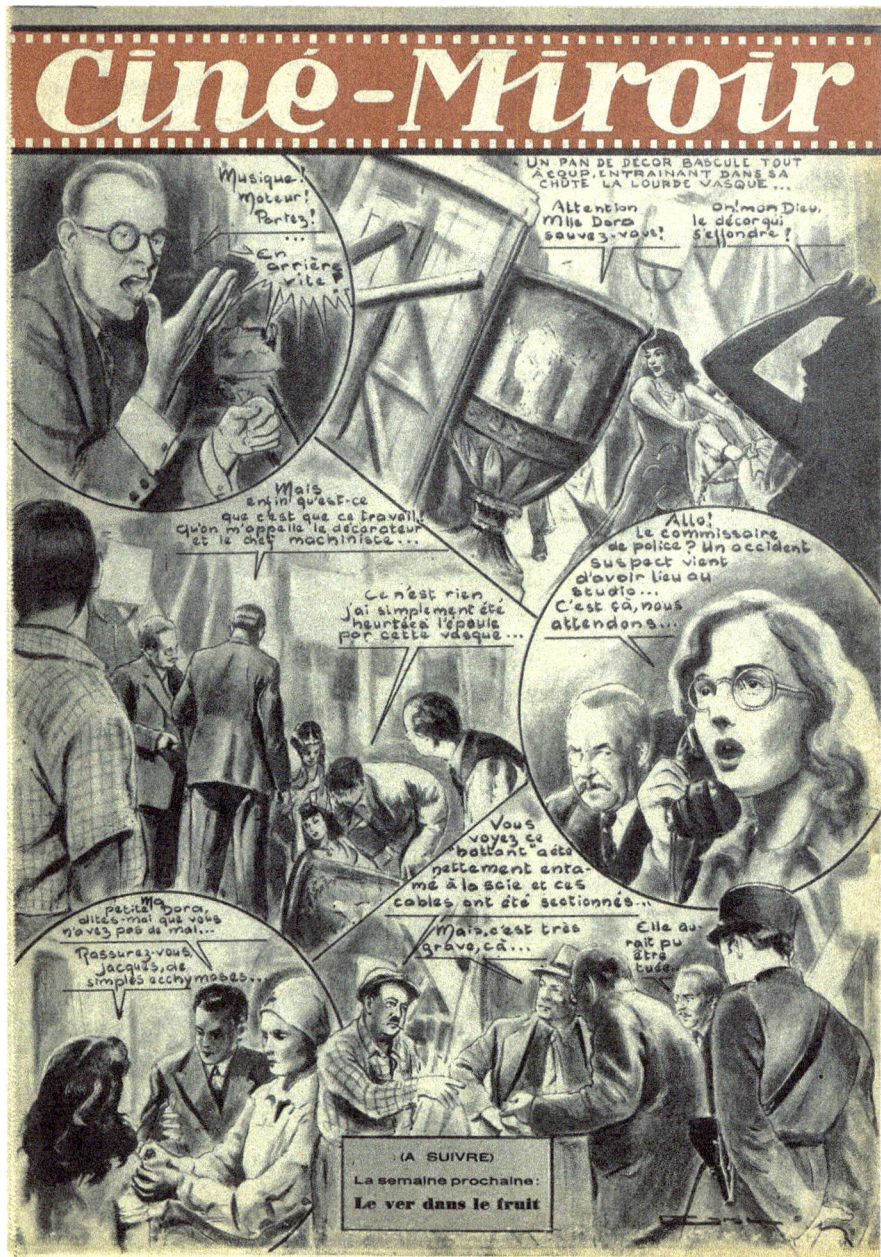

Figure 7.3   Elastic page design in *La Passion de Dora*. *Ciné-Miroir*, 1 June 1948. (p. 16)

(Figure 7.3). This loosening of the structure of the page is combined with several visual techniques that, like the lighting effects discussed above, might derive from the cinema, such as close-ups and inserts of written texts (letters, newspapers, magazines), high and low angles and compositions in depth.

It would be an oversimplification, however, to describe *Dora*'s visual style as straightforwardly cinematic. As Baetens points out, rather than depicting bodies in motion, the still images of the drawn novel often display characters in tableau-like poses, sometimes as a form of erotic spectacle, a tendency in which he detects an imitation of glamour photography – and an appeal to male readers. Examples of this can found in *La Passion de Dora*, with Dora and the other female cast members of *Meurtre au music-hall* presented backstage in their underwear in poses that resemble the style of 'cheesecake' photography. As Baetens argues, this tendency towards static poses, combined with the non-sequentiality of the page design mentioned above, works to deemphasise the linear narrative, and thus produces a temporal structure for readers that 'is definitely not that of watching a movie' (2017, 79). In its interweaving of influences from cinematic storytelling and other forms of popular image culture, then, *La Passion de Dora* stands as an example of the media hybridity that Baetens finds in the drawn novel. Its innovative visual style sets it apart from other *bandes dessinées* as much as its female-centric storyline, and Dora's role as both an object of erotic attention and an active protagonist reflects broader tensions in fan magazines' representation of female performers.

Manufacturing Dora: *La Passion de Dora* as Pedagogical Tool

While the features of *La Passion de Dora* discussed in the previous section align it with drawn novels appearing in romance magazines, the story's setting in the cinema world is specifically designed for the readers of a movie magazine such as *Ciné-Miroir*. And while on one level Dora's adventures in the screen trade are a fictional entertainment offering a 'discourse of pleasure' (Crisp 1993, 216), her story can also be understood to function as an informal pedagogical tool. Through the combination of words and images it takes readers behind the scenes to teach them about some of the procedures that go into the making of a film. Chapter I, for example, shows the events leading to Dora's employment. When Dora is first considered for a role in *Meurtre au music-hall*, the images show the director filming her for a screen test that he then watches back approvingly with the film's producer. After signing her contract, she is instructed to take daily dance lessons to prepare for her role. Later, she visits the studio, where the producer shows her the set. Chapter II presents Dora's first day of shooting. After a panel shows her waking at 6am, we see her at the studio as the make-up artist explains that he will do her make-up every morning,

Figure 7.4 Behind the scenes of a film in *La Passion de Dora*. *Ciné-Miroir*, 11 May 1948. (p. 14)

and the script girl offers to practice her lines with her. Then it is on to her first scene, where the reader is shown the camera and the microphone on its boom, the clapperboard with the number of the scene and the take, and the director calling for silence before they shoot.

In subsequent chapters, the reader is further educated in the technical processes by which a film's sounds and images are produced. We learn that to create a scene of Marlène singing, the song is pre-recorded, and she is then filmed moving her lips in synch to the '*play-back*' (Figure 7.4). As Dora prepares to film a close-up of a kiss between her and Jacques, the director explains (to her and to us) that they have to position their feet on the marks on the floor, and the camera crew is illustrated measuring the distance from her face to the camera to ensure that she will be in focus. Later, as the actors go on location in Cannes, the revelation of 'trade secrets' continues. As they prepare a shot in which Dora's and Jacques's characters take a ride in a horse-drawn carriage, a high angle framing discloses that they are sitting, with no horse in sight, in a cutaway section of carriage that is towed behind a car with the camera in it. Meanwhile, a passer-by explains to her friend that when the shot appears on the screen, 'you'll believe they're riding in a real carriage'.

In these scenes, the characters, settings and events of the fictional narrative serve as a reason to take readers onto a movie set and show them what goes on there. Dora's ingénue status provides a realistic motivation for demonstrating how a film is made, and she functions as a focalising presence through which this information can be channelled. It is rare that the comic's narration overtly addresses the reader through what Thierry Groensteen terms an 'extra-diegetic reciter' (2013, 88) – a verbal intervention in the form of a caption. Instead, most of the information we receive about the technical processes of filmmaking is communicated either through dialogue between characters or through purely visual means. Thus, we can learn about the work involved in a way that feels effortless and entertaining rather than instructive. This sort of technical information on how films are made rarely appears in other parts of *Ciné-Miroir*, but we find examples of it in other magazines of the period, such as *Ciné-Monde*, whose on-set reports sometimes focus on, and include images of, the technical processes by which the finished film is achieved. Like their Hollywood counterparts (see Topp 2020), French fan magazines saw no contradiction between promoting stars and the films they appeared in and educating their readers as to how the screen stories they enjoyed at the cinema were constructed.

In addition to informing readers of filmmaking techniques, *La Passion de Dora* also teaches them how films, and specifically their stars, are promoted and publicised, a process in which fan magazines and other media texts play an important role. Foundational star studies scholar Richard Dyer usefully proposes the notion of the star image as separate from the real person of the star. Dyer considers that this is conveyed to audiences not just through films, but also through promotion (for example, posters, public appearances), publicity (for example, interviews, gossip columns) and criticism and commentaries (Dyer 1979, 68–72). Several of the mechanisms of promotion and publicity are highlighted over the course of Dora's story. When the model Denise Gillard is put under contract to Osiris Films, the company changes her name to the more international-sounding 'Dora Grey'. This recalls French actresses of the period such as Dora Doll (née Dorothea Feinberg) and Viviane Romance (née Pauline Ortmans), whose names were changed to make them more appealing to audiences. Later, Dora's image appears on a poster announcing her as 'tomorrow's great star' presented by Osiris Films, alongside a newsstand selling fan magazines with her photograph on the cover. (In fact, this publicity has been planted by the film's producer, in league with the jealous Marlène, as a ruse to make Jacques jealous.) When Dora is kidnapped, a newsboy sells the latest special edition with the story of her mysterious disappearance. And at the story's conclusion, Dora's rise to stardom is shown, appropriately, through a montage of promotional events at which she appears: a car show, a beauty contest, and a series of radio broadcasts she does with Jacques. Self-reflexively, *Ciné-Miroir* itself appears as a mode of promotion, carrying news of Dora in a section called '*Du Studio à la ville*' (From the Studio to the Town), which presented news about stars and their projects. She and Jacques are then voted cinema's 'Ideal Couple', apparently by the readers of a magazine such as *Ciné-Miroir*, which ran monthly competitions in which readers could choose their favourite male and female stars (Figure 7.5). Dora is drawn being interviewed about her plans by a reporter from another publication, *Ciné-Journal*, and after her marriage to Jacques, a radio reporter is at Orly airport to cover their departure on honeymoon.

Once again, then, the story's fictional narrative informs readers about real practices in the cinema world – this time, the role of film studios and a variety of media outlets in manufacturing and marketing stars such as Dora. The relationship between items about stars that appear in the media and the studios that often plant them there for promotional purposes is hinted at when, as Marlène slaps Jacques in a fit of jealousy over his relationship with Dora, the film's cameraman secretly records the scene and then passes the images to a reporter he is friends with, so that the story is carried in the next day's newspaper.

As noted above, *Ciné-Miroir* itself appears within the story world as one of the channels through which Dora is promoted. The explication of the media's role in promoting stars takes an even more intertextual turn when, in order to publicise *Meurtre au music-hall*, the film's producer organises a reception for the press, at which Dora is introduced to *Ciné-Miroir*'s pseudonymous columnist 'Micky', discussed above. A charmed Dora declares that she often reads Micky's

Figure 7.5   *Ciné-Miroir* appears in itself: *La Passion de Dora*, *Ciné-Miroir*, 20 July 1948. (p. 15)

column, and two days later an article appears in the magazine reporting that while Dora's and Marlène's characters fight in the film, 'in real life they're the best of friends', a claim the reader knows to be untrue. Furthermore, Micky's appearance as a character promoting Dora within the fictional story world is balanced by the 'real' Micky's promotion of Dora's adventures within her actual weekly column. At the end of a story entitled 'Ici on fabrique des "pin-ups"...' (This is where pin-ups are made...), focusing on the photographer Lucien Lorelle, who took publicity photographs of many of the leading French stars, Micky offers a plug for *La Passion de Dora*, which was then in its third week in the magazine:

> Are you reading our new illustrated novel *La Passion de Dora*? I find it fascinating and I'm sure I'm the reader who's most impatient to know what will happen next... And I can tell you: it often happens like that in the cinema world. (4 May 1948, 6)

The appearance of a *Ciné-Miroir* journalist within the fictional story of Dora Grey[1] highlights the blurring of the boundary between fiction and reality that is a recurring theme of *La Passion de Dora*. On various occasions there is confusion as to whether events within the story are real or 'just' cinema. When Marlène leaves the door of her dressing room open so that Dora can see her and Jacques kissing, another actress comments that 'it doesn't seem like a movie kiss'. The tables are turned when Dora and Jacques are instructed by the director to do multiple takes of their kissing scene, which leads Marlène to get jealous, as she suspects they are not just performing for the camera. Soon afterwards, the time comes to film the fight scene between Dora's and Marlène's characters, and one of the technicians suggests that they are actually feeling the emotions they have to portray. After Dora has been kidnapped, the pilot of the boat that took her is able to identify the voice on the phone that gave him his instructions when he is played a clip of one of Marlène's accomplices performing in a film. When Dora's colleagues arrive at the crooks' hideaway to look for her, one of them comments on how exciting it all is, exclaiming, 'You'd think we were at the cinema!' Finally, once Dora has been rescued and returned to Paris, a producer from another company offers her the starring role in a new film inspired by her adventures entitled *Une Starlett a disparu* (*A Starlet Vanishes*). This sort of slippage between fiction and reality is of course common in films about filmmaking, but we can also link it back to the representation of the media's role in developing a star's persona and selling it to the public. With the story playfully foregrounding the way in which fan magazines, including *Ciné-Miroir* itself, distort reality to present a fictionalised version of the stars they write stories about, the reader is invited to view the rest of the magazine through this lens, and to enjoy its contents with a healthy dose of scepticism.

Conclusion

Until quite recently, the study of post-World War Two French cinemagoing was restricted to the activities and aesthetic judgements of spectators associated with the tradition of cinephilia promoted by such consecrated publications as *Cahiers du cinéma* (for example de Baecque 2003). In the last decade, however, a number of French cinema scholars have shifted their attention to the reception by ordinary spectators of a wide variety of films, stars and genres in the postwar period (for example Chedaleux and Leventopoulos 2019; Le Gras and Sellier 2015; Sellier 2019). This has involved new attention to previously overlooked historical sources, including popular movie magazines aimed at predominantly female fans, rather than the more highbrow journals that were the domain of male intellectuals. Complementing this approach, Laurent Jullier and Jean-Marc Leveratto have advocated for an enlarged vision of cinephilia that takes into consideration not just the '*discours savant*' (erudite discourse) of self-styled experts, but also the '*cinephilie ordinaire*' (ordinary cinephilia) of popular audiences (2010, 3).

This chapter has explored *La Passion de Dora* as one small example of how this ordinary cinephilia was cultivated within the pages of a postwar French fan magazine. In highlighting *Dora*'s media hybridity, I have shown that, in both its genre influences and its visual design, it draws on various forms of popular media culture (both within fan magazines and beyond), many of them based around a creative interaction between images and text. Considering it as an example of the 'new and engaging' format of the drawn novel that appeared in women's magazines in the immediate postwar period helps emphasise the degree to which *Dora* addressed a female public at the level of both its story and its style.

There is a long tradition – at times promoted by the kind of highbrow cinephilia that seeks to distinguish itself from 'mere' movie fandom – that claims that popular film audiences, traditionally gendered as female, are somehow deceived into thinking that what they see on the screen is real. Similarly, it is sometimes presumed that readers of popular fan magazines (similarly gendered) unquestionably accept the stories that appear within them as true and believe that they can gain direct access to the lives of performers through the words and images the magazines present. My analysis of *La Passion de Dora* suggests that the readers of *Ciné-Miroir*, and by extension other French fan magazines, were more sophisticated than this. They could engage with and enjoy the words and images they consumed on multiple levels, and apply this multilevel understanding to the films they watched. In particular, they could appreciate the creative blending of reality and unreality that produced the stars they looked at and read about in their favourite magazines, understanding that they were as manufactured as the fictional Dora Grey. As the (real? fictional?) columnist Micky explains, 'it often happens like that in the cinema world'.

ACKNOWLEDGEMENT

Many thanks to Sarah Polley for her help and suggestions.

NOTE

1. As mentioned earlier, it should be noted that Micky refused to reveal her true identity to her readers, leaving it open to conjecture as to whether she actually did correspond to the image presented of her as a glamorous insider.

REFERENCES

Anon. 1948. Advertisement for *La Passion de Dora*. *Ciné-Miroir*, 13 April: 2.
Anon. 1948. 'Une jeune fille savait'. *Ciné-Miroir*, 27 April: 4–5.
Anon. 1948. 'Rocambole'. *Ciné-Miroir*, 27 April: 8–9.
Anon. 1948. 'Le Maître de la prairie'. *Ciné-Miroir*, 27 April: 11.
Anon. 1948. 'La Chartreuse de Parme'. *Ciné-Miroir*, 1 June: 8–9.
Baetens, Jan. 2017. 'The *Roman Dessinée*: a Little-Known Genre'. In *Bande Dessinée: Thinking Outside the Boxes*, edited by Laurence Groves and Michael Syrotinski, 65–83. New Haven, CT: Yale University Press.
Baetens, Jan. 2019. *The Film Photonovel: A Cultural History of Forgotten Adaptations*. Austin: University of Texas Press.
Burch, Noel, and Geneviève Sellier. 2014. *The Battle of the Sexes in French Cinema, 1930–1956*. Translated by Peter Graham. Durham, NC: Duke University Press.
'Caméra, Jean'. 1948. 'Jean Caméra vous parle . . .'. *Ciné-Miroir*, 1 June: 2.
Chedaleux, Delphine, and Melisande Leventopoulos, eds. 2019. *Cinéphilies plurielles dans la France des années 1940–1950: Sortir, lire, rêver, collectionner*. Paris, France: L'Harmattan.
Crisp, Colin. 1993. *The Classic French Cinema, 1930–1960*. Bloomington: Indiana University Press.
de Baecque, Antoine. 2003. *La cinéphilie. Invention d'un regard, histoire d'une culture, 1944–1968*. Paris: Fayard.
Dyer, Richard. 1979. *Stars*. London: BFI.
Groensteen, Thierry. 2013. *Comics and Narration*. Translated by Ann Miller. Jackson: University of Mississippi Press.
Grove, Laurence. 2010. *Comics in French: The European Bande Dessinée in Context*. Oxford: Berghahn Books.
Héliotte, Gérard, and Gal. 1948. *La Passion de Dora, starlett audacieuse*. *Ciné-Miroir*, 20 April: 14–16.
Héliotte, Gérard, and Gal. 1948. *La Passion de Dora, starlett audacieuse*. *Ciné-Miroir*, 27 April: 14–16.
Héliotte, Gérard, and Gal. 1948. *La Passion de Dora, starlett audacieuse*. *Ciné-Miroir*, 4 May: 14–16.
Héliotte, Gérard, and Gal. 1948. *La Passion de Dora, starlett audacieuse*. *Ciné-Miroir*, 11 May: 13–15.

Héliotte, Gérard, and Gal. 1948. *La Passion de Dora, starlett audacieuse*. *Ciné-Miroir*, 18 May: 13–15.
Héliotte, Gérard, and Gal. 1948. *La Passion de Dora, starlett audacieuse*. *Ciné-Miroir*, 25 May: 15–16.
Héliotte, Gérard, and Gal. 1948. *La Passion de Dora, starlett audacieuse*. *Ciné-Miroir*, 1 June: 14–16.
Héliotte, Gérard, and Gal. 1948. *La Passion de Dora, starlett audacieuse*. *Ciné-Miroir*, 8 June: 14–16.
Héliotte, Gérard, and Gal. 1948. *La Passion de Dora, starlett audacieuse*. *Ciné-Miroir*, 15 June: 14–15.
Héliotte, Gérard, and Gal. 1948. *La Passion de Dora, starlett audacieuse*. *Ciné-Miroir*, 22 June: 14–15.
Héliotte, Gérard, and Gal. 1948. *La Passion de Dora, starlett audacieuse*. *Ciné-Miroir*, 29 June: 14–15.
Héliotte, Gérard, and Gal. 1948. *La Passion de Dora, starlett audacieuse*. *Ciné-Miroir*, 6 July: 14–15.
Héliotte, Gérard, and Gal. 1948. *La Passion de Dora, starlett audacieuse*. *Ciné-Miroir*, 13 July: 14–15.
Héliotte, Gérard, and Gal. 1948. *La Passion de Dora, starlett audacieuse*. *Ciné-Miroir*, 20 July: 14–15.
Héliotte, Gérard, and Gal. 1948. *La Passion de Dora, starlett audacieuse*. *Ciné-Miroir*, 27 July: 15.
Jullier, Laurent, and Jean-Marc Leveratto. 2010. *Cinéphiles et cinéphilies: Une histoire de la qualité cinématographique*. Paris: Armand Colin.
Keating, Patrick. 2010. *Hollywood Lighting from the Silent Era to Film Noir*. New York: Columbia University Press.
Le Gras, Gwenaelle, and Genevieve Sellier, eds. 2015. *Cinémas et cinéphilies populaires dans la France d'après-guerre 1945–1958*. Paris: Nouveau Monde.
'Micky'. 1948. 'Sambas et Rumbas'. *Ciné-Miroir*, 20 April: 10.
'Micky'. 1948. 'Ici on fabrique des "pin-ups". . .'. *Ciné-Miroir*, 4 May: 6.
'Micky'. 1948. 'Le Baiser le point rose'. *Ciné-Miroir*, 25 May: 5.
'Micky'. 1948. 'Quand je faisais le tour'. *Ciné-Miroir*, 20 July: 6.
Mikkonen, Kai. 2017. *The Narratology of Comic Art*. New York: Routledge.
Sellier, Geneviève. 2019. 'Movie Magazines, Popular Films, and Popular Spectatorship in Postwar France'. In *Star Attractions: Twentieth-Century Movie Magazines and Global Fandom*, edited by Tamar Jeffers McDonald and Lies Lanckman, 81–95. Iowa: Iowa University Press.
Topp, Dominic. 2020. '"How's Your Sense of Direction?" Studying Audiences' Perception of Classical Hollywood Directors, 1934–1943'. In *Mapping Movie Magazines: Digitization, Periodicals and Cinema History*, edited by Daniel Biltereyst and Lies Van de Vijver, 257–78. London: Palgrave Macmillan.

8. WIELDING THE SCISSORS: INDUSTRY POLITICS AND PLAY IN MOVIE MAGAZINES, 1933–1934

Tamar Jeffers McDonald

In 1937, American publisher Albert Griffith-Grey attempted to launch a new movie magazine. Introducing his new publication into an already crowded market,[1] Griffith-Grey justified his venture by explaining that this was to be not just a new publication, but a new *type* of publication entirely: a movie magazine *not* designed for movie fans. Instead, his proposed publication would have 'contents directed to the discriminating class', as *Film Daily* noted (20 July 1936, 2).

Attempting to inaugurate a new kind of publication, Griffith-Grey seemed to have made assumptions about the gender of the usual readers of regular movie magazines:

> CINEMA ARTS is a quality movie magazine (*cinemagazine* to you). It will attempt to do for the Cinema what FORTUNE has done for Industry and ESQUIRE for Men.
> [. . .]
> One thing we guarantee: You won't have to hide CINEMA ARTS under your arm when you meet a friend. Most likely, the friend will have one too . . . (*LIFE*, 7 June 1937, 5)

With its comparisons to male-oriented business and lifestyle magazines, and its promotion in 'serious' lifestyle magazine and trade journals,[2] *Cinema Arts* set out to capture a serious-minded cultural readership. Larger, more high-minded, and more expensive than its rivals on newsstands, *Cinema Arts* lasted for just three issues.

While much could be made of the circumstances surrounding *Cinema Arts*' launch and sinking, including the misogynistic presumptions about its readership, I take Griffith-Grey's slight against the seriousness of the then contemporary movie fan magazines as a point of departure for this chapter, since my aim is to dispute the inevitable triviality of these publications. In doing this I will consciously delve into a particular recurring element of movie magazines, the prize competition for readers, which ostensibly bears out all Griffith-Grey's implicit snobbery, especially since, in the contest I will consider, the top prize was a one-week trip to Hollywood, and the runners-up awards included a refrigerator, a radio, and ten Max Factor make-up sets, all rewards likely to be coveted most by female readers.

The competition was run in the December 1933 and January 1934 issues of *Modern Screen* to tie in with the imminent release of a new MGM film, *Dancing Lady* (Leonard 1933), starring Joan Crawford, who would be the lucky top prize winner's hostess in Hollywood. To win the competition, *Modern Screen* readers had to complete two tasks; one, writing a description of Crawford in 'ten words or less', was a common-enough requirement of magazine contests. It may have been intended as a tie-breaker, since the successful entry was not deemed important enough to publish alongside the name of the victor and runners-up in April 1934 (8), or in a subsequent issue, in July, when there was an article purporting to be by the winner, Jean Kraft, about her experiences in Hollywood ('Happy Contest Winner', *Modern Screen*, July 1934).

If the tie-breaker, then, was a make-weight, this emphasises the importance of the other part of the competition, which was a little more unusual. MGM had supplied the magazine with eight stills from *Dancing Lady* which had been cut into odd shapes before they were reproduced within *Modern Screen* (Figure 8.1): the reader needed to cut out all these irregular tesserae from the magazine and put the images together again. Altogether, four of these 'cut-ups' appeared in the December issue and another four in January 1934: all eight reconstituted pictures had to be sent in with the description to complete the entry.

This element of the competition is interesting for several reasons. Obviously, it acted as a spur to magazine readers to buy *both* issues of the publication, since they needed to secure, cut out and reconstitute all eight pictures. The competition also inevitably encouraged readers to see the film. The intact images were not published in the magazine, so while it is very difficult to complete these tiny puzzles *with* knowledge of the scenes from which they come, it would be nigh-impossible without. And the contest was strategically timed to appear in the issues of the magazine that would coincide with the film's release window.

Dancing Lady went into movie theatres on 24 November 1933, when the December issue of *Modern Screen* would have been on newsstands, and the film would still have been being exhibited in many parts of the country when the January issue came out in December, in time for Christmas. Since readers

Figure 8.1   Joan Crawford contest. *Modern Screen*, December 1933. (pp. 40–1)

of the magazine were being encouraged to see the film in order to stand a good chance of completing the puzzles, *Modern Screen*'s contest was thus promoting the film, the stars, especially Crawford, and itself, as both December and January issues had to be purchased to complete a single competition entry.

In the month the *Dancing Lady* contest began, December 1933, there were at least twenty other monthly titles available on American newsstands, with others published weekly, fortnightly and quarterly. All contained the same basic diet of movie news, gossip, recipes, fashion items, readers' letters, reviews, contests, adverts, and all had the identical central topic: stars. But *Modern Screen* was then the bestselling movie title, with 556,421 issues sold each month that year, as official figures indicate (*The Hollywood Reporter*, 25 May 1933, 6; Polley 2019, 73). Furthermore, from May through November that year, the magazine included on its own covers the proud boast that it had the 'Largest Guaranteed Circulation of Any Screen Magazine'. Although this legend did not appear on the December issue, it was back in January 1934, and then appeared, with a variety of wordings, intermittently into 1941. It is thus easy to speculate why MGM would have been interested in working with *Modern Screen* for this competition, rather than one of its rivals. Besides the sales bounce that the magazine might derive from carrying the Crawford contest, however, I suggest there was another reason that the magazine's editors might have agreed to take on the running of the puzzle feature.

For there seems to me to be something rather radical in the disarticulation done to the stars through the 'cut-ups', and to Crawford in particular. Cutting pictures out of movie magazines was not a new occupation, as archived scrapbooks attest, and competitions with cut-ups needing reassembling had been running since the teens in movie magazines. But in this competition the participant was encouraged not to cut *around* Crawford's outline but *across* her face, separating one eye from the other in some instances, her head from body in others. Co-stars Clark Gable and Franchot Tone, who were also included in the images, suffered similar slashes, but Crawford appeared in every picture, maximising the impact of slicing her. Although the aim of the competition was to reconstruct the performers' famous faces, restoring their physical integrity, the damage remained: while the competition text contained the jocular command that readers should 'put the pictures together again, like Humpty-Dumpty' (*Modern Screen*, December 1933, 40), the lines of cutting inevitably remain visible (Figure 8.2).

For an indication that this puzzle was trickier and more perverse than usual, we can compare cut-ups from similar contests. *Photoplay* began holding what became an annual cut puzzle contest in 1923, pairing stars' faces with rhymes to provide clues to their identities. Although the performers' faces were sectioned, the cuts were always three clean laterals dividing forehead and eyes, nose and

Figure 8.2 Reconstituting Joan Crawford and Clark Gable from the Joan Crawford contest.

cheeks, and mouth and chin. Similarly, *Screenland*'s 1931 contest, which ran for four months, featured stars' shadows, the aim here being to cut out these slightly amorphous but whole shapes and place them over the photographic originals found elsewhere in the magazine (*Screenland*, July 1931, 35–7). And earlier in 1933, *Photoplay*'s July issue carried 'Movie Muddles' (32–3), which required cutting stars' pictures into ribbons along straight lines. In levels of difficulty, then, the *Modern Screen* contest far outdid its competitors.

This chapter takes the magazine's emphasis on the *wielding of scissors* and juxtaposes it against the particular moment of the film's wider industrial background, suggesting that there is more at work in the 'thrilling contest' than just an opportunity to promote a newly released film and its main star. By examining the historical and filmic contexts and the specific issue of this movie magazine as material object together, I hope to reveal that although movie magazines have often been dismissed as puerile publications, they could actually deal with serious political topics, perhaps with particular effectiveness since covert messages would be uncovered during play.

Stars and Cut Puzzles

Magazine use of competitions to boost reader interest and thus circulation was, of course, neither new to the 1930s nor limited to movie magazines. Stephanie Rains notes that '[m]agazine competitions were a central feature of popular culture in the late nineteenth and early twentieth centuries' (Rains 2015, 138), continuing:

> the point of these competitions for the magazines was to boost circulation by making the competitions – especially those with very valuable prizes – a source of publicity and interest among readers. That increased readership not only created direct extra revenue through sales, but also increased the magazine's appeal to advertisers, who were often the real source of profit for publications, especially those which appealed to the mass market and had a low cover price. (Rains 2015, 140)

This has a clear resonance with *Modern Screen*'s promotion of a competition for *Dancing Lady*; not only was its studio, MGM, one that regularly advertised its films in the magazine, including in the December 1933 issue, which carried an advertisement for *Comin' Round The Mountain* (*Modern Screen*, December 1933, 5), but also Max Factor, which had donated ten make-up kits as joint 5th prizes, was a contributor to its advertising revenue on a monthly basis. The cosmetics company also paid for ads mentioning Crawford – 'MGM star in "Dancing Lady"' – in other contemporaneous movie magazines, such as *Screenland* (October 1933, 49) and *Photoplay* (October 1933, 95), while MGM returned the compliment by including a lightly veiled tribute to Max Factor in the name of a beauty company shown in the film's climactic musical number.[3]

Writing specifically about competitions using favourite performers, Michael Cowan points to the prevalence of contests revolving around the image of the star in movie magazines from France and Germany in the 1920s:

> The cropped-eye game was perhaps the most familiar form these puzzles took [. . .] In other variables, readers were asked to identify stars with parts of their faces blotted out or transformed, star profiles shown in silhouette, stars reduced to their noses, childhood pictures of stars, or star photographs that had been cut apart and jumbled in a kind of photographic jigsaw puzzle. (Cowan 2015, 5)

What all these puzzle competitions clearly have in common is the play with the image of the star: whether to be recognised by a single feature, unmasked from a disguised form or cut up and put together again, *stars* remain the constant shared constituent, and, as Cowan continues, the constant shared *aim* is for readers to recognise them:

> Though they ranged from the simple to the highly complex, nearly all of these puzzles operated on the same basic principle, challenging readers to identify well-known performers and scenes from recent films they ought to have seen. (Cowan 2015, 5)

Rains discusses a similar example of a cut puzzle earlier, in an Irish story magazine from 1908, where:

> They published cartoons of body parts such as heads, torsos and limbs, and readers were invited to cut out these cartoons and assemble them into whole drawings of people, each with the correct limbs and heads. These reassembled cartoons were then to be pasted onto a piece of card and submitted to the magazine [. . .] This competition was not unique in requiring competitors to cut out shapes and reassemble them in order to enter. (Rains 2015, 143)

It is fascinating that this example uses cartoon drawings of people, rather than photographs, and predates the genesis of stardom as it is understood to have developed in cinema (see deCordova 2001), indicating that part of the appeal for puzzlers, beyond the chance of winning a prize, was the satisfaction of 'restoring the integrity' of the image, as Cowan notes about the French and German magazine contests (Cowan 2015, 12). Cowan also points to the simultaneity of these competitions within the 1920s European magazines, the rise of photographic star portraits, and the development of montage in film (12). While the magazines and their competitions he and Rains examine are both geographically and chronologically removed from the *Modern Screen* contest, the fundamental element of the puzzle challenge they discuss remains the same: the objective was to reconstruct the unity of the cut-up image. As this chapter will demonstrate, my contention is that *Modern Screen*'s intention with its star cut puzzle was, intriguingly, to frustrate this reconstruction.

I also find montage, which Cowan invokes alongside the work of Dada collagists (Cowan 2015, 12), provocative in investigating *Dancing Lady*; while by the early 1930s in Hollywood montage would not have seemed such an innovative filmic technique as in the context of European cinema a decade earlier, I justify this investigation since there is a short montage sequence in *Dancing Lady* itself. Approximately one-minute long, it occurs about a quarter of an hour into the film. To put this section in context, a short synopsis of the narrative is useful.

Aspiring dancer Janie Barlow (Joan Crawford) works in a burlesque house stripping, the only dancing work she can get. Wealthy Tod Newton (Franchot Tone) is in the audience when the theatre is raided by the police and the dancers taken to night court. Tod pays Janie's $30 fine, but she rejects his advances, prioritising her career. She chases famous Broadway producer Patch Gallagher (Clark Gable) around Manhattan for an interview. Tod secretly arranges to fund Patch's new show, *Dancing Lady*, if Janie can be in the chorus, but soon Patch promotes her on her own merits. Janie continues to refuse Tod, who withdraws the show's backing. With no show to star in, Janie leaves New York with Tod, unaware that Patch has decide to finance *Dancing Lady* himself. Returning just before the premiere, Janie meets Patch, and Tod's ruse is revealed. Janie convinces Patch to put her back in the show, and makes it a huge success. Rejecting Tod for the final time, she tells Patch she's free, and they embrace.

The montage in *Dancing Lady* occurs when Janie is trying to meet Patch and trails him all over town. In the course of its minute's duration, the montage most frequently shows the pair's feet: Gable's retreating, Crawford's pursuing (Figure 8.3). It also shifts focus between their feet, their full figures, and their faces, as he tries to evade her, and she relentlessly attempts to catch him.

Figure 8.3 Screenshots from *Dancing Lady* (1933).

While this emphasis on body segments – feet, faces – is not novel or unique to the film, its parallel within the cut puzzle sections is noticeable: within the puzzle pieces, eyes are separated from heads, hands from arms, feet from legs. It is conspicuous, and apt, that top-billed star Crawford has her face reproduced in each of the eight stills that have been cut up to form the puzzle pieces. Her large eyes feature prominently on four occasions, her mouth twice; in a move that would have raised a laugh contemporaneously, Gable, who was renowned and mocked for having large ears,[4] has those particular features reproduced as the most evident within a sliver of photograph on three occasions. By comparison, bits of the features of Franchot Tone and Ted Healy are dissected with no attempt to render them recognisable. Feet and hands, hair and shoulders all appear within the puzzle pieces too.

Moreover, not just the human face and body, but the entire filmic *mise en scène* is disassembled in these puzzles, with elements of the background, including other characters, cut into bizarre shapes. Significantly, the lozenge- and wedge-shapes, while very much present in the art deco style then appearing in architecture, decorative ware, and personal and domestic items, are also to be found within the film. Lucy Fischer has discussed the use of art deco within cinema of the late 1920s and early 1930s, and suggests a particularly fruitful association with the movie musical (Fischer 2003, 137–47). While she discusses the Busby Berkeley routines that 'resonate with extreme abstraction and mark a complete break with diegetic logic and space' (137), the same can be seen in *Dancing Lady*'s final spectacular musical number, 'The Rhythm of the Day'. Here, just as the highlighting of anatomised body parts in the puzzle finds its corollary in *Dancing Lady*, the deco shapes are also prominent. Progressing from a narrative in a futuristic cityscape, which, if bizarre, is still a narrative, the show's chorines move into a nowhere space to appear – and disappear and reappear – in a kaleidoscopic fan that both reflects and rotates: their bodies first prone, then supine, then curled into near-foetal shapes, they almost resemble Eadweard Muybridge's series of photographs analysing bodily movements, and seem nearly as naked as those famous images of subjects running and jumping. The back cover of the pressbook produced by MGM for the film features images from this sequence – which it calls 'the Mirrors of Venus' – but, again, these are cut into odd shapes. Interestingly, however, while the images have clearly been cut out from their backgrounds, they do not mar the faces of the featured stars and extras.

While, then, certain moments within the narrative of *Dancing Lady*, such as the montage and the Mirrors of Venus scene, may have prompted the cutting up of the film stills into odd-shaped portions that foreground anatomised body parts, I would sound a note of caution here. It might be tempting to conclude that the inspiration behind the *Modern Screen* cut puzzle contest was the technique of montage in general and the aforementioned comic chase sequence in *Dancing Lady* in particular, but drawing conclusions about what inspired specific elements of magazine contents must always be done with caution. Although the film content might have influenced the constitution of the cut puzzle contest, for the competition to be 'quoting' the film, the person/s in charge of setting the contest would have had to have seen *Dancing Lady*. We need to factor magazine lead times into this calculation: the puzzle pages would have been compiled from stills given to the magazine probably two to three months in advance of the film's premiere. With the contest, therefore, created before the film was released, a specific referencing of the montage scene *might* be directly behind its use of the disarticulated stars, but there could be alternative influences too.

One such would be existing promotional practices within contemporaneous publications: as noted above, periodical advertising regularly made use of the cut-up female body. For example, in December 1933, the same month that the first part of the *Dancing Lady* contest appeared in *Modern Screen*, the *Ladies Home Journal*, one of the top-selling women's monthlies,[5] featured ads showing atomised hands four times, and feet twice. Similarly, the movie magazines also regularly featured paid advertising material which zoned in on parts of facial features or bodies. Indeed, when the January 1934 issue of *Modern Screen* reprinted the December pictures, it arranged the selections alongside two adverts that featured isolated feet, a page after another emphasising atomised hands. Women magazine readers, in particular, then, would be used to seeing a similar disarticulation of the female body in advertising displayed in publications aimed at them.

It should be acknowledged, however, that although the single feet with shapely ankles (109) or hands benefitting from softening hand cream (86) were highlighted in *Modern Screen* without the rest of the human body being allowed to dissipate the impact of the isolated feature – rather like a close-up in a movie, focusing the viewer's attention on a significant item – they were always shown whole and entire in themselves. Hands might be separated from arms, but they were not then themselves subject to further dissection. To find another impetus behind the more destructive cutting done to the stills in the *Dancing Lady* competition, the next part of this chapter widens its perspective, to examine the environment in which the film and competition appeared.

DANCING LADY'S WIDER CONTEXT

James Warner Bellah's novel *Dancing Lady* was published in instalments in *The Saturday Evening Post*, from April–June 1932, then as a book by Farrar and Rinehart later in the year. The novel told the story of a daughter of the tenements, a born dancer who 'stepped and stamped her way through the night clubs and the burlesque wheel to Broadway glory',[6] attracting various men along the way, but for the film treatment, these seamier elements were largely purged, apart from the beginning that sees Janie working, and then arrested, at the burlesque house. The film was in production late June through early October 1933 and released on 24 November that year.

At the same time that the movie was going into production, late June, the pages of the movie trade papers were reporting the increasing influence being exerted in Hollywood by Will Hays, former Postmaster General and current President of the Motion Picture Producers and Distributors of America. Hays had been responsible for introducing an industry Code of Conduct in 1930 which was intended to prevent salacious material reaching the supposedly impressionable public, but although the Code existed, it had no teeth: it could request a studio to cut scenes or lines of dialogue, but had no powers to enforce its suggestions – *yet*. But throughout the early 1930s, and building to a climax in 1933 and 1934, proponents and opponents of this potential censorship debated the merits of strengthening the Code. Religious groups from a variety of faiths came together to agree that Hollywood movies were too titillating, and that Hays's Code needed greater powers to curb their excesses. And gradually industry insiders began to debate whether it would be better to firm up the Code, mainly because it was a method of control organised from within Hollywood, rather than one exerted by exterior forces, such as the government.

Perhaps unsurprisingly, the *Motion Picture Herald* maintained the most positive outlook about the potential changes, since its editor, Martin Quigley, had helped draw up the original code; thus his publication presented the looming changes in factual terms, reporting on meetings and personnel (*Motion Picture Herald*, 17 June 1933, 11, 14). By contrast, a survey of the front pages of *The Hollywood Reporter* from May 1934 onwards reveals dual narratives: the intensification of the movement to clean up the movies, and editor Billy Wilkerson's growing awareness of the serious impact the proposed changes could have on the industry. The story of Hollywood's gradual submission to the Hays Office was played out on the pages of this trade daily. On 31 May, 'Catholics On Warpath' (1, 3) relayed that all Catholic bishops in the US had been instructed to write to the exhibitors in their dioceses, 'demanding [a] rigid ban on filth' (1), an injunction taken very seriously at least by the Cardinal of Philadelphia: *The Hollywood Reporter* relayed on 9 June that 'Cardinal Bans All Pix', noting that the prelate was urging 'All Catholics To Stay Away From All Picture Theatres' (1).

While the publication advised against capitulation for some days, by 18 June, the editorial column 'Tradeviews' approved the plan, developing among the studios, that the best way to protect Hollywood content was for studios to clean it up themselves, in order 'to give the reformers nothing to reform' (Pope 1934, 1).

While *Dancing Lady* was in production, then, the specific industry environment was one in which the 'war on dirt' (*The Hollywood Reporter*, 19 June 1934, 1) and concomitant moves to increase the power of Hays and the Code were being publicly debated. With this environment as its backdrop, the puzzle contest in *Modern Screen* might possess, I suggest, a particular significance. Against this particular setting, it seems possible to me that the concept of 'cutting', in relation to film, might have overtones of censorship, as much as or more than montage or editing. And, since cutting the studio-provided stills did not require the contest-setter to have seen *Dancing Lady*, the question about lead times is not as problematic, as it is with the montage-influence suggestion.

Instead, reading the puzzle in light of debates about *censors*' scissors, any frustration readers might feel over their reluctance to cut up Crawford, and annoyance at not being able to stick her famous face back together again invisibly, could be intended to colour those same readers' views of the censorship discussions. For, like the trade papers, which might perhaps be relied upon to deliberate industry questions, the movie magazines were also very open in foregrounding the looming threat of interference with film content, despite those contemporary assumptions that theirs was a fluffier and more superficial worldview. Throughout 1933 and into 1934, movie magazines including *Movie Classic*, *Picture Play*, *Motion Picture* and *New Movie Magazine*[7] debated whether there was any need for firmer strictures, usually concluding that there would be other, better, ways to control content than the one Hays represented.

Modern Screen significantly fought this fight also, refusing to give up even after the Production Code Administration formally came into being in June 1934 and, with it, the Seal of Approval all movies needed in order to be exhibited after 1 July. That very month's magazine contained an article exploring favourite scenes from recent films that would not have been permitted under the Code. The major image from this piece, 'Here's What The Censors Took Out', was a pair of scissors, juxtaposed against film stills. (Figure 8.4)

The author, James B. M. Fisher, attempted to show that local state cuts had made nonsense of various scenes, while appealing to the reader directly: 'Do you agree that such scenes are harmful to the morals of American youth?' (Fisher July 1934, 43). By contrasting the different cuts made to the same films by censor boards in different states, the article set out to undermine the concept of censorship entirely, mocking the squeamishness of those who removed dialogue or, in one case, a painting of a nude, without understanding that performance can be more suggestive. Fisher concludes his article by comparing cuts to the Mae West film *I'm No Angel* (Ruggles 1933):

> When examined with the magnifying glass of reason then, censorship seems to make no sense at all. It is like some strange vulture that nibbles haphazardly at its prey and then levies a privilege tax on the mutilated,

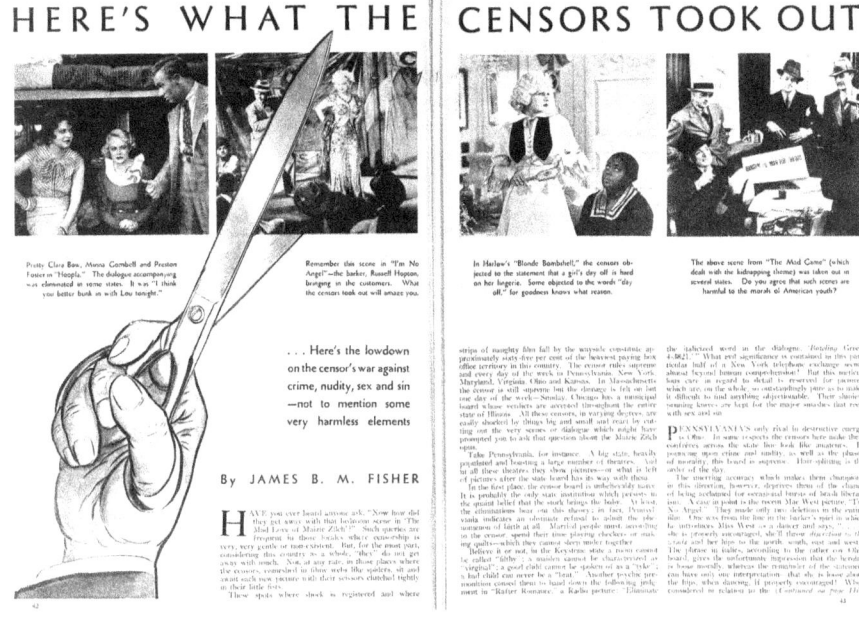

Figure 8.4   Article 'Here's what the Censors Took Out'. *Modern Screen*, July 1934. (pp. 42–3)

half dead remains. Its standards, its rules are negligible; one state chokes on what another swallows with the greatest ease. (Fisher July 1934, 112)

Even in September, when films were already being cut in line with Code constraints, the magazine persisted with both its call to action and its now-familiar imagery, juxtaposing scissors and film strip, as a glowering man prepared to make cuts, under the banner 'Let's Fight For Our Movies . . .!' (Ramsey 1934, 26–7). (Figure 8.5)

That this was an important issue to the *Modern Screen* editorial team is underlined by the use of the same words on the front cover; in his article, journalist Walter Ramsey again addresses the reader directly, listing recent popular films such as *Queen Christina* (Mamoulian 1933) *Riptide* (Goulding 1934) and *Twentieth Century* (Hawks 1934), noting that 'The Box Office proves these films entertained you. Yet, if the censors ruled, you might not have been permitted to see them!' (Ramsey 1934, 26–7), and prophesying organised censorship would mean nothing less than 'Oblivion for pictures!' (27).

While publishing lead times again impact here, with the editors putting their issues to bed three months or so before the date shown on the cover, and thus this September number being assembled around the time the Code was being

Figure 8.5 Article 'Let's Fight for Our Movies!' *Modern Screen*, September 1934. (pp. 26–7)

ratified, it does still indicate that the magazine staff had faith that no major change would happen so fast – or perhaps at all. And they continued to debate the topic in October; the conclusion of Ramsey's piece contains a trailer for an article in the following month's issue:

> WHAT THE NATION'S BIGWIGS THINK OF THE CURRENT WAR ON PICTURES
>
> Read what prominent clergyman and national personalities have to say about this censorship fuss in the October issue of MODERN SCREEN. (September 1934, 78)

Even in the December issue, which must have been sent to print after the Code was confirmed, one editorial response to a reader's letter against bowdlerisation reads cheerily, 'don't be too alarmed, my dears, we have a feeling that this "censorship crusade" won't last much longer' (115).

Just as the practice of cutting up star bodies in montage finds its correlation in a moment from *Dancing Lady*, so too does the idea of censorship. Various scenes from the film were represented in the stills chosen to be cut up and reassembled by readers. While the point of using the two-shots of Crawford and Gable, and Crawford and Tone, seems to me to be to cause frustration at the impossibility of reconstructing the famous faces perfectly, be one's scissors never so sharp, with others the act of cutting can also be seen to bear a deeper symbolic weight.

In the first of these the image comes from an extended scene which uses all of Crawford's star power to condemn those who would criticise her character – literally, within the movie, to censor her.

Arrested in a raid on the International Burlesque house, Janie ends up attending night court wearing little more than a blanket, thanks to the inflexibility of the policeman, who will not let her dress before hauling her away. Janie then encounters the stuffy judge who, unimpressed by her explanation for dancing, sentences her to a $30 fine or 30 days in jail.

Throughout the arrest and court scenes Janie's lively indignation at being handled so inflexibly by these male representatives of the Law is overlain with Crawford's star wattage as she confronts bit-part players in roles written to suggest their stupidity and hypocrisy. Janie's need to dance is censored by the state powers, applying rigid rules in which they do not believe. It is easy to read Crawford as Janie standing in for Crawford as Crawford, as *star*, censored by an inflexible Code.

That the courtroom scene is represented in those stills chosen for the contest seems significant, since it underlines the act of censorship within the narrative; while at this distance it is of course impossible to verify, the suggestion that this might be the intention of the competition compiler is supported by a further moment of suppression. Despite the fact that the toothless 1930 version of the Production Code did not have the weight to impose cuts on films – the very reason the moral crusaders were escalating their efforts across 1933 – censors could still demand them and hope that studios would comply. As files on *Dancing Lady* held in the Library of the Academy of Motion Picture Arts and Sciences in Los Angeles indicate, there were three pieces of correspondence concerning a joke involving one of the three Stooges, which James Wingate, then head of the Studio Relations Committee (forerunner of the PCA) requested be removed from the script before it was filmed: '. . . we believe you should eliminate this interpolated gag with the jigsaw puzzle of Hitler, as offensive to the German nation' (Wingate 1933a). Indicating how much leeway studios had before the strengthening of the Code the following year, the next version of the script countered 'The HITLER jig-saw business – IN' (Anon 10 June 1933), and it seems to have been filmed, as a further letter (Wingate 1933b) again requested its removal. A piece in *Variety*'s 'Inside Stuff' gossip column, however, confirmed the cut was eventually made:

> A Hitler gag was cut out of 'Dancing Lady' by Metro. Jerry Howard [. . .] of Ted Healy's stooges, is shown working on a jigsaw puzzle all through the picture until finally supplying the missing piece. He jumps

up registering a sick expression, exclaiming, 'I've been working on this for five weeks and look what I finally got, Hitler!' To which Healy replies, 'What did you expect, Santa Claus?'

The Santa tag is in plus the business, but Hitler is out (5 December 1933, 51)

Again, the scene is captured in a still used in the cut puzzle. It is interesting to wonder whether *Modern Screen* readers attempting to join up the pieces of the puzzle would have been aided by seeing the lobby cards that referred to it, although it is likely the entire scene was cut before the film's premiere on 24 November 1933.[8] What does seem provocative, however, is the fact that the gag concerned both puzzles and identity obscured by missing pieces, and was used in a contest concerned with both ideas.

Conclusion

Although perhaps because of their ubiquity as well as their gossipy tone, and the resultant legacy of being worthless objects (cf. *Cinema Arts*), movie magazines have only just begun to participate in the rehabilitation being granted material objects by the New Cinema History. As this chapter has shown, however, research into these popular periodicals can reveal not only contemporaneous assumptions about stars, fans, readers and consumers, but the fact that the editorial teams in the movie fan publications both had and conveyed views on important topics such as industry censorship.

In 1933 and 1934, as the Code debate reached its high point, *Modern Screen* sought to influence its readers' views on the potential imposition of stricter censorship through overt discussion in serious articles but also, I have suggested, via more tacit means. In the cut puzzle contest we can see reader participation in considering the ramifications of *cutting* being encouraged through symbolic play; by then experiencing frustration with the damage done to Crawford and her co-stars readers might feel, vicariously and in anticipation, the annoyance that would ensue if censorship were allowed to ruin the appearances of favourite stars.

This neatly returns us to Albert Griffith-Grey's assumptions about the gender of the movie magazine reader. In (tacitly) addressing a *man* who would not be ashamed to be seen by a friend carrying *Cinema Arts*, the publisher implied that the inevitable reader of the other numerous and popular magazines already on the market was a woman. He was not alone in this guess; cultural critic Clifton Fadiman, writing about movie magazines in *Stage* in 1937, hazarded that the readership of these publications was 'probably ninety per cent women' (Fadiman 1937, 53). Ten years later screenwriter Gordon Kahn put his guess even more succinctly: 'this product was no more designed for men than was the sidesaddle' (Kahn 1947, 98).

Probably, then, although the magazines did expect to have male readers too, their primary address was to women, as can be seen in both article focus and advertising. Unlike Fadiman, Kahn and *Cinema Arts*' Griffith-Grey, however, the movie magazine editors seemed to perceive no clash in including content on stars' love lives, new diets and the latest fashion notes alongside articles on important industry matters. In this they can be seen to be less patronising of their readers, treating them as active participants engaging in debates about important political issues. It was not only censors who wielded scissors, but also women magazine readers, women who had learned through their needlework or scrapbook maintenance to ply them adroitly.

While it is problematic to read intentionality from results, especially at this historical remove, I posit that the *Dancing Lady* contest provided an excellent opportunity for the editors of *Modern Screen*. They seem to have been already exercised about the potential of increasing censorship, and had sought through their articles and judicious curating of letters' pages to present their views.

The editors might then have recognised in *Dancing Lady* an excellent opportunity to recruit their readers to their own oppositional view of the Code by other means. With its general narrative well known from publication in a highly popular magazine the year before, *Dancing Lady* could be seen to provide a likely opportunity to make play out of politics, even if this were just through the removal of extra characters or the toning down of incidents, as did happen with the adaptation. Beyond this, however, its own diegetic critiques of inflexible rule enforcement made the film version even more suitable to the task.

The most suggestive fact, to me, indicating the conscious use of the contest to make an anti-censorship point is the very oddness of the shapes printed by the magazine. The film stills for the competition would have been supplied whole by MGM, then dissected and *then* printed; therefore, in order to participate in the contest, the reader had to repeat the slashes, having no choice but to cut Crawford up, employing scissors to slice across her face. This emblematic violence, along with the impossibility of seamlessly joining the images together again, seems clearly put to use as a metaphor for the damage that would be done to movies if the Code were fortified. Thus, wielding their scissors in emulation of the censor, even the readers of a popular low-cultural product such as *Modern Screen* could participate through play in industry debate.

NOTES

1. Consulting <www.moviemags.com>, a database of periodicals concerning film, I count at least thirty-five titles being published in 1937, ranging from (and mostly) fan magazines, through trades, smut titles such as *Film Fun* and *Movie Humor*, to hobby and intellectual fare including *Movie Makers* and *American Cinematographer*.

2. Trade journals were daily or weekly publications intended for film industry insiders, such as *Variety*, *The Film Daily* and *The Hollywood Reporter*. Griffith-Grey also advertised *Cinema Arts* in intellectual hobby mag *International Photographer* and, as referenced here, in premiere photo-journal *LIFE*.
3. The 'Rhythm of the Day' number at the end of *Dancing Lady* features representations of beauty shops, including one called MAXWELL (cf. Max Factor), another dubbed RODY, in a similar font to Coty, and a 'Beauty Repair Shop'.
4. See, for example, *Screenland*, February 1932, 10; *Modern Screen*, October 1932, 112 ('those ears of his are fascinating, don't you think?') and *Modern Screen*, April 1933, 80–1, as well as animated cartoons *Hollywood Picnic* (Columbia 1937) and *Hollywood Steps Out* (Warner Bros 1941).
5. David E. Sumner provides the information that in 1930 the *Ladies Home Journal* was reaching nearly 2.5 million sales per month (Sumner 2010: 77).
6. The quotation is from the dust jacket of *Dancing Lady*, published in 1934 by Farrar and Rinehart.
7. 'Censorship means goodbye to Garbo, Dietrich and Me – Anna Sten', *Movie Classic*, October 1934: 28–9, 69, 71; 'The Clean-Up Earthquake', Edwin Schallert, *Picture Play*, October 1934: 12–13, 58, 65; 'Hollywood Taboos', Eric Ergenbright, *New Movie*, October 1934: 46–7, 79, 80, 81 and 'The Decency Drive –Does it have the support of American women?', *New Movie*, October 1934: 50–1, 82; 'Are the Movies Guilty? Cecil B. De Mille speaks for the defense!', Jack Grant, *Motion Picture*, September 1934: 30–1, 84–5.
8. The details about *Dancing Lady* given on the American Film Institute website suggest that this scene was not shown at the premiere in 1934, but has been shown in a print aired on television: '. . .the scene was resurrected when an uncut film positive was sourced for prints in a 1950s television release'. AFI catalogue entry for *Dancing Lady* (1933): <https://catalog.afi.com/Film/3436-DANCING-LADY?sid=62579e87-e921–467f-bff7-ab7f43c5acd8&sr=9.867183&cp=1&pos=0> (last accessed 18 November 2022).

References

Anon. 1931. 'Star Shadow Contest'. *Screenland*, July: 35–7.
Anon. 1933. 'Big Fan Magazine Drop'. *The Hollywood Reporter*, 25 May: 1, 6.
Anon. 1933. Internal memo on *Dancing Lady*. 10 June. PCA file collection on *Dancing Lady*, Margaret Herrick Library, Academy of Motion Picture Arts and Sciences.
Anon. 1933. 'Industry sets up Code machinery . . .'. *Motion Picture Herald*, 17 June: 11, 14.
Anon. 1933. 'Movie Muddles'. *Photoplay,* July: 32–3.
Anon. 1933. Max Factor advert for Joan Crawford, 'MGM star in "Dancing Lady"'. *Screenland*, October: 49, and *Photoplay*, October: 95.
Anon. 1933. Advert for *Comin' Round the Mountain*. *Modern Screen*, December: 5.
Anon. 1933. Joan Crawford Contest. *Modern Screen*, December: 40–3.
Anon. 1933. 'Inside Stuff'. *Variety*, 5 December: 51.
Anon. 1934. Joan Crawford Contest. *Modern Screen*, January: 43–5, 96–7.
Anon. 1934. 'Catholics on Warpath'. *The Hollywood Reporter*, 31 May: 1, 3.

Anon. 1934. 'Cardinal Bans All Pix'. *The Hollywood Reporter,* 9 June: 1.
Anon. 1934. 'Jewish Conference Joins War on Dirt'. *The Hollywood Reporter*, 19 June: 1.
Anon. 1934. 'The Decency Drive –Does it have the support of American women?' *New Movie*, October: 50–51, 82.
Anon. 1934. 'Between You and Me'. Editorial response to letter by 'P.B. Buchans, Newfoundland'. *Modern Screen*, December: 6, 115.
Anon. 1936. 'New Class Movie Magazine'. *Film Daily*, 20 July: 2.
Anon. 1937. Advertisement for *Cinema Arts*. *LIFE*, 7 June: 5.
Cowan, Michael. 2015. 'Learning to Love the Movies: Puzzles, Participation and Cinephilia in Interwar European Movie Magazines'. *Film History* 27 (4): 1–45.
deCordova, Richard. 2001. *Picture Personalities: The Emergence of the Star System in America*. Urbana: University of Illinois Press.
Ergenbright, Eric. 1934. 'Hollywood Taboos'. *New Movie*, October: 46–7, 79, 80–1.
Fadiman, Clifton. 1937. 'The Narcissi'. *Stage* 17 (10): 52–3.
Fischer, Lucy. 2003. *Designing Women: Cinema, Art Deco, and the Female Form*. New York: Columbia University Press.
Fisher, James B. 1934. 'Here's What the Censors Took Out'. *Modern Screen*, July: 42–3, 110–13.
Grant, Jack. 1934. 'Are the Movies Guilty? Cecil B. De Mille speaks for the defense!' *Motion Picture*, September: 30–1, 84–5.
Kahn, Gordon. 1947. 'The Gospel According to Hollywood'. *Atlantic Monthly* 179 (5): 98–102.
'Kraft, Jean'. 1934. 'Happy Contest Winner'. *Modern Screen*, July: 62–3, 95–7.
Leonard, Robert Z. (Director). 1933. *Dancing Lady* [Motion Picture]. USA: MGM.
Polley, Sarah. 2019. 'A Spectrum of Individuals: U.S. Fan Magazine Circulation Figures from 1914–1965'. In *Star Attractions: Twentieth-Century Movie Magazines and Global Fandom*, edited by Tamar Jeffers McDonald and Lies Lanckman, 61–80. Iowa: University of Iowa Press.
Pope, Frank. 1934. 'Tradeviews'. *The Hollywood Reporter*, 18 June: 1.
Rains, Stephanie. 2015. 'Going in for Competitions: Active Readers and Magazine Culture, 1900–1910'. *Media History* 21 (2): 138–49.
Ramsey, Walter. 1934. 'Let's Fight For Our Movies . . .!' *Modern Screen*, September: 26–7, 76, 78.
Schallert, Edwin. 1934. 'The Clean-Up Earthquake'. *Picture Play*, October: 12–13, 58, 65.
'Sten, Anna'. 1934. 'Censorship means Goodbye to Garbo, Dietrich and Me'. *Movie Classic*, October: 28–9, 69, 71.
Sumner, David E. 2010. *The Magazine Century, American Magazines Since 1900*. New York: Peter Lang.
Warner Bellah, James. 1932. *Dancing Lady*. New York: Farrar and Rinehart.
Wingate, James. 1933a. Letter to Eddie Mannix, 7 June. PCA file collection on *Dancing Lady*, Margaret Herrick Library, Academy of Motion Picture Arts and Sciences.
Wingate, James. 1933b. Letter to Eddie Mannix, 17 November. PCA file collection on *Dancing Lady*, Margaret Herrick Library, Academy of Motion Picture Arts and Sciences.

PART THREE

FAN MAGAZINES AND RELATED PUBLICATIONS

PART THREE INTRODUCTION

While the previous sections of this book focused exclusively on fan magazines, albeit occasionally referencing women's magazines, this portion casts the net wider. It encompasses other non-fan film publications to complicate general notions about what a fan or movie magazine might be.

In the last two decades, the New Cinema History turn in film studies has placed centrally film historians Robert Allen and Douglas Gomery's brief thoughts on the importance of 'non-filmic evidence' such as trade publications and studio records (1985, 38–42). Fan magazines also belong to the 'non-filmic evidence' category, but those in the field of New Cinema History have addressed film coverage in general interest local and national newspapers (Abel 2015, 2019; Moore 2011, 2019). Martin Loiperdinger (2019) considers newspapers alongside trade magazines – publications which carried production news, box office reports and advice on exhibiting films. Even though these were aimed at a relatively small readership that invariably had a financial interest in the film industry, trade publications are often seen as reliable or impartial, where fan magazines might not be. Eric Hoyt (2014), co-founder of the Media History Digital Library (MHDL), has written of the scholarly bias towards one particular long-running and influential entertainment trade paper, *Variety* (1905 – current). Certainly, several studies have used *Variety* as their main source (for instance Hoyt et al. 2015; Thissen and Eisenstein Baker 2020). However, others have focused on alternative trade publications (for example Whitehead, Pelletier and Moore on *Canadian Moving Picture*

Digest 2020). Academic work using non-*Variety* trade magazines is only likely to increase as the MHDL continues to digitize diverse titles, including *Moving Picture World*, *Motion Picture News*, *Film Daily* and *The Hollywood Reporter*, alongside other material, such as pressbooks for specific films[1] and fan magazines.

Occasionally scholars have placed fan and trade magazines in closer dialogue with one another. Tamar Jeffers McDonald notes that while many trade magazines – especially *Variety* – treated fan magazines with scorn (2016, 31), in June 1933 the daily US trade paper *The Hollywood Reporter* considered them a positive ally in promoting the film industry (30). Its 'Reviewing the Fan Mags' feature surveyed 145 fan magazine issues in terms of their content until mid-1934 when it described them as a 'growing evil' which needed cleaning up (30). The relationship between trade and fan magazines was therefore complex and changeable. They served diverse readerships (fans vs professionals) and functions (enjoyment vs business), which meant that they were distributed at different frequencies – often daily rather than the movie magazine's usual monthly appearance – and contained distinct content.

Apart from sometimes carrying advertisements which might later appear in fan magazines, or complement those which did, trade publications generally eschewed the visual splendour of their higher circulating counterparts. In fact, in format and frequency, trade magazines arguably bear a closer relationship to the text-heavy black-and-white newspapers, which as well as news and opinion, included some film-related content.

Chapters in this section thus consider fan magazines directly within wider contexts of publication. Kumar reverses the single magazine perspective found earlier in this volume to examine several trade magazines and their campaigns to advertise one sole film, the 1933 Universal horror, *The Invisible Man*, investigating the particular challenges this film caused for advertising predicated on the visible. Voss examines actor training manuals in comparison to British and US fan magazines and newspapers, in considering attempts to understand the skills-based training of actresses in the 1920s – and perhaps to undermine it. The emphasis throughout this edited collection on the professionally published publication – movie magazines as products of the publishing industry – is overturned in the chapter by Wright and Smith, who examine British fan publications assembled by stars, their family members or their fans themselves, while the international focus found in the volume is maintained in the final two chapters. Peirano and Bossay present audience research in relation to the Chilean fan magazine *Ecran*, while in her chapter, Lanckman explores a Yiddish-language film magazine published in Warsaw from 1936–1938, *Film-Nayes*, with particular emphasis on how the publication handled complex feelings about Jewish stars in Hollywood.

Thus, in addition to providing commentary on non-Anglophone publications, these contributions offer detailed analysis of related publications and different contexts, teasing out similarities and differences between how, and for whom, fan magazines and non-fan magazines designed desire.

NOTE

1. Earlier examples of those dealing with pressbooks include Miller 1994 and Klinger 1994.

REFERENCES

Abel, Richard. 2015. *Menus for Movieland. Newspapers and the Emergence of American Film Culture 1913–1916*. Oakland: University of California Press.

Abel, Richard. 2019. 'Reading Newspapers and Writing American Silent Cinema History'. In *The Routledge Companion to New Cinema History*, edited by Daniel Biltereyst, Richard Maltby and Philippe Meers, 68–82. Abingdon and New York: Routledge.

Allen, Robert, and Douglas Gomery. 1985. *Film History: Theory and Practice*. New York: Knopf.

Hoyt, Eric. 2014. 'Lenses for Lantern: Data Mining, Visualization, and Excavating Film History's Neglected Sources'. *Film History* 26 (2): 146–68.

Hoyt, Eric, Derek Long, Anthony Tran and Kit Hughes. 2015. '*Variety*'s Transformations: Digitizing and Analyzing a Canonical Trade Paper'. *Film History* 27 (4): 76–105.

Jeffers McDonald, Tamar. 2016. 'Reviewing "Reviewing the Fan Mags"'. *Film History* 28 (4): 29–57.

Klinger, Barbara. 1994. *Melodrama and Meaning: History, Culture, and the Films of Douglas Sirk*. Bloomington: Indiana University Press.

Loiperdinger, Martin. 2019. 'Early Film Stars in Trade Journals and Newspapers: Data-Based Research on Global Distribution and Local Exhibition'. In *The Routledge Companion to New Cinema History*, edited by Daniel Biltereyst, Richard Maltby and Philippe Meers, 138–46. Abingdon and New York: Routledge.

Miller, Mark S. 1994. 'Helping Exhibitors: Pressbooks at Warner Bros. in the Late 1930s'. *Film History* 6 (2): 188–96.

Moore, Paul. S. 2011. 'Newspapers as Archives of the Regional Mass Market for Movies'. In *Explorations in New Cinema History: Approaches and Case Studies*, edited by Richard Maltby, Daniel Biltereyst and Philippe Meers, 263–79. Malden, MA: Wiley-Blackwell.

Moore, Paul. S. 2019. '"It Pays to Plan'em!": The Newspaper Movie Directory and the Paternal Logic of Mass Consumption'. In *The Routledge Companion to New Cinema History*, edited by Daniel Biltereyst, Richard Maltby and Philippe Meers, 365–77. Abingdon and New York: Routledge.

Thissen, Judith and Paula Eisenstein Baker. 2020. 'Who Knew? Using Digital Trade Papers to Explore Ethnic Programming in American Picture Palaces'. In *Mapping*

Movie Magazines: Digitization, Periodicals and Cinema History, edited by Daniel Biltereyst and Lies van de Vijver, 39–55. London: Palgrave Macmillan.

Whitehead, Jessica L., Louis Pelletier and Paul S. Moore. 2020. '"The Girl Friend in Canada": Ray Lewis and Canadian Moving Picture Digest (1915–1957)'. In *Mapping Movie Magazines: Digitization, Periodicals and Cinema History*, edited by Daniel Biltereyst and Lies van de Vijver, 127–52. London: Palgrave Macmillan.

9. UNIVERSAL HORROR AND *UNIVERSAL WEEKLY*: THE VISIBLE INVISIBILITY OF THE INVISIBLE MAN

Rahul Kumar

Film magazines have played a significant role in constituting the history of film culture in the twentieth century and have been crucial in the enhancement of the audiences' affective engagement with cinema. As demonstrated by the existing scholarship[1] as well as the other chapters in this edited collection, stars have been a highly visible part of these movie magazines, including the film ads that appear in them. The association of the audiences with the stars is dependent on the latter's clarity and discernability, that is, they must be 'seen'. But how do movie magazines engage with the representation of a star/character whose defining characteristic is invisibility? In this chapter, I look at the figure of the Invisible Man, the protagonist in Universal's 1933 monster film *The Invisible Man* (Whale), as it appeared in the pages of Universal's house organ *Universal Weekly*. Since the publicity machinery in the 1930s was dependent on the print medium, inevitably predicated on the visible, I look at the ways in which Universal publicity executives negotiated the problems encountered while trying to advertise a film that had a central character who was invisible.

THE INVISIBLE MAN: A VISIBLY DIFFERENT HORROR

A simple keyword search on Project Arclight[2] throws up a very interesting set of statistics. The resulting graph shows that during the period 1930–1936, there is a gradual spike in the usage of the word 'horror' in the printed paratextual literature on American popular cinema. The word 'monster' also follows a similar pattern and increases during this period. It is not just a coincidence that

Universal Studios had a very successful run of a series of horror films that started with *Dracula* (Browning 1931) and ended with *Dracula's Daughter* (Hillyer 1936). Although Universal was not in the league of the 'Big Five' studios, its success during the 1930s was due to its veritable monopoly on the horror film market. A careful examination of film magazines and journals during the period 1930–1936 shows that popular print was replete with images of monsters such as Dracula, Frankenstein's Monster, the Mummy and others.

The Invisible Man was based on the H. G. Wells novel, published in 1897, which cemented the author's place as a pioneer in the modern science fiction genre. The film offered a faithful adaptation of the original novel with only minor variations: Dr Jack Griffin (Claude Rains) is a scientist who works as Dr Cranley's (Henry Travers) apprentice and is engaged to his daughter Flora Cranley (Gloria Stuart). While researching a new drug, Griffin stumbles on a potion that can make him invisible. One of the side-effects of the drug is insanity. Thinking of his invisibility as a superpower, Jack plans to rule the world and goes on a violent rampage that leads to the death of several people. The police struggle to hunt him down, unable to see their target, while Dr Cranley and Jack's former partner (William Harrigan) try to devise a plan to capture him.

While Universal staff could draw on their experience of making three very successful monster films by the time *The Invisible Man* went into production – *Dracula*; *Frankenstein* (Whale 1931); *The Mummy* (Freund 1932) – the three central characters had in common a well-defined corporeal appearance that existed in the physical world. The corporeality of the Invisible Man, on the other hand, existed beyond the boundaries of the physical world. Similarly, while the earlier films had their monsters sculpted primarily by the studio's make-up department, *The Invisible Man* was shaped by the studio's special-effects department. Scholars such as Jeffrey Cohen (1996) and Noël Carroll (1990) have written about the corporeality of a monster and their ideas are useful for exploring the invisible form and corporeality of the Invisible Man as distinct from other Universal monsters. I argue that this monster's body was incoherent with the expectations of the dominant filmmaking traditions of Hollywood. Therefore, its representation also defied any easy categorisation.[3]

Cohen analyses the monster as a reflection of culturally specific anxieties and desires, as mechanisms of social control and as potential sites of resistance to oppressive paradigms. Carroll's understanding of the monster's physicality comes through the concepts of fusion ('the compounding of ordinarily disjoint or conflicting categories in an integral, spatio-temporally unified individual') (1990, 44) and fission ('the contradictory elements are, so to speak, distributed over *different*, though metaphysically related, identities') (46). Carroll's concepts are applicable to monsters such as Frankenstein's Monster, the Mummy and Dracula, whose corporeality exists in the physical world.

But for a monster such as the Invisible Man, a category is needed that either exists at the threshold of fusion and fission, or beyond it. Cohen's theses are more applicable in this latter case. He posits that one possible way to classify the monster would be a system that allows mixed responses such as difference in sameness, and repulsion in attraction (1996, 7). While the corporeality of the Invisible Man is invisible, his representation on film is about visualising his invisibility. Therefore, his corporeality can be understood in terms of the mixed system that Cohen talks about – visible invisibility or invisible visibility. Universal's publicity department latched on to the visible invisibility of this figure and overtly made the problem of representing this invisibility its publicity theme, especially in the advertisements that appeared in its in-house movie magazine *Universal Weekly*.

Universal Weekly was Universal's 'house organ', a magazine that came out of the studio itself. Studio house organs were primarily the outlets through which the studios relayed information regarding upcoming releases to their exhibitors as well as the general readership. *Universal Weekly* had a successful run during the silent era with studio head Carl Laemmle Sr in charge of the publication. Due to the Great Depression, in the summer of 1930 the studio ceased the weekly's publication to cut costs, but publication resumed by autumn 1932, when the success of *Dracula* and *Frankenstein* had helped the studio revive its fortunes. It was primarily in the pages of *Universal Weekly* and Universal press books that the pre-release ads for *The Invisible Man* first appeared, which were then used as a blueprint by the exhibitors to further advertise it. A two-page achromatic spread in the 9 September 1933 issue of *Universal Weekly* carried multiple ad campaign ideas for the film, with both text and images attempting to arouse interest in the forthcoming film (4–5) (Figure 9.1).

The images for these ad campaign ideas looked visually distinct from the film posters, which were characterised by resplendent and riotous colours. The colour posters for *The Invisible Man* were quite dense and cluttered in terms of content, and one could see a lot of action happening there. The posters showed the major characters from the film, as well as the crowd of panicked villagers and the policemen running around while the figure of Griffin, the Invisible Man, looms large. These posters showed the figure of the Invisible Man in his physical configuration with his bandaged head, dark goggles and trench coat. The conception of this monster manifested very differently in the *Universal Weekly* ad campaigns that focused fundamentally on the two characters from the film: Griffin and his love interest Flora. The campaign images seen in Figure 9.1 mobilised an aesthetic of minimalism, framing Jack and Flora in relation to one another through the use of silhouettes and lights and shadows. The elimination of every other character from these images in favour of the couple is a signifier of the idea of fear/desire that I will return to later in this chapter.

Figure 9.1 Advertisements for *The Invisible Man* (1933). *Universal Weekly*, 9 September 1933. (pp. 4–5)

These *Universal Weekly* ad campaigns can be read as illustrating Tzvetan Todorov's (1975) ideas about ghosts, specifically that the uncertainty a ghost or a spectral figure engenders manifests in the multiplication of the degree of the fantastic and in turn creates its terrifying presence. This hesitation is felt by the characters in the text (cinematic or literary) as well as the recipient of the text (viewer/reader). The film advertisements used the concept of hesitation/uncertainty while depicting the corporeality of the invisible monster. Multiple images in Figure 9.1 show Flora Cranley's scared-looking face within the shadowy outline of Griffin's head. The uncertainty about the physicality of the Invisible Man here is something that is experienced on multiple levels: Flora as Griffin's fiancée is not able to identify him because of his invisibility, and experiences terror; the same terror is communicated via the cinematic text to the viewer; and finally, this terror gets transmitted to the readers of the *Motion Picture Herald* and other magazines in which this particular advertisement was printed.

Wells's novel was published two years after the discovery of X-rays in 1895 by Wilhelm Röntgen. This new technology brought discourses related to contemporary photographic media and human mortality into the public sphere. By opening the human body up to the penetrating gaze of the X-ray machine, its interiority and exteriority were collapsed into one, signalling a liquidation of the physicality and in turn gesturing towards invisibility. Akira Lippit suggests that, with X-rays, the flesh is subjected to transgression and the interiority of the body is brought to the surface, indicating a premonition of the future and of death (2013, 260). Allen Grove in his essay on X-rays and photography argues that the X-ray photographs were basically the images of humans who had 'taken off their flesh to pose in their bones' (1997, 162). The images represented a kind of clairvoyance as they predicted what the person would look like when long dead since fleshless skeletons and bare bones were synonymous with death and decomposition (162).

Another source of useful imagery for advertising *The Invisible Man* was spirit photography, which was popular during the late nineteenth century. Tom Gunning writes that spirit photography's portrayal of ghosts drew upon a visual experience that did not conform to the normalised conditions of sight and recognition (2013, 213). In such photographs, the spectral figure was represented as something that was out of focus, had a semi-transparent physicality, and was dissolving into shrouds of gauze (213). Spirit photography represented a certain realm of existence which opened up the possibilities for representing a ghost, a spirit or a phantom, things that subjected normal human vision into a mode of crisis (216). Similarly, the images draw on what Lippit terms 'avisuality' – an optical quality that leaves traces but nevertheless stays predominantly invisible to the eye (2005, 32). Thus, throughout the print advertising images for the Invisible Man, technology associated with mortality is used by the marketeers at Universal, appropriately, in sketching their new monstrous character.

The possibilities of capturing the Invisible Man in magazine advertisements drew upon all these visual conventions. Some of the images bear an uncanny resemblance to the early photographic plates and X-ray scans. Figure 9.2 shows an advertisement, arranged as a double-page spread, from the 12 August 1933 issue of *Universal Weekly* (8–9). The text directly addresses the reader, asking 'How would YOU draw or illustrate The Invisible Man?' The advert copy openly acknowledges the problem that the new character poses for representation, but notes that while the film can rely on special effects to 'show' the monster, 'the same method won't work in silent pen and ink' (9). Six drawings are then shown to illustrate how some of the Universal art directors have suggested making visible the invisible. Several of the images in Figure 9.2 indicate obliteration and formlessness, characteristics associated with mortality.

While all the suggestions play with the black-and-white format of the magazine's image reproduction, casting the Invisible Man in shadow or obscuring his face in some way, those by Fred Kulz and Gene Schwalm could especially pass as X-ray plates. Lorne Braddock offers a rebus, an image made of words arranged in the shape of a human skull (even though it has eyebrows and ears), which the negative, white, space of the advert around the word serves to delineate. Universal's publicity team can here be seen turning to X-rays and other similar methods evocative of ambiguity and the uncanny to capture the invisible corporeality of the monster for advertising in print media.

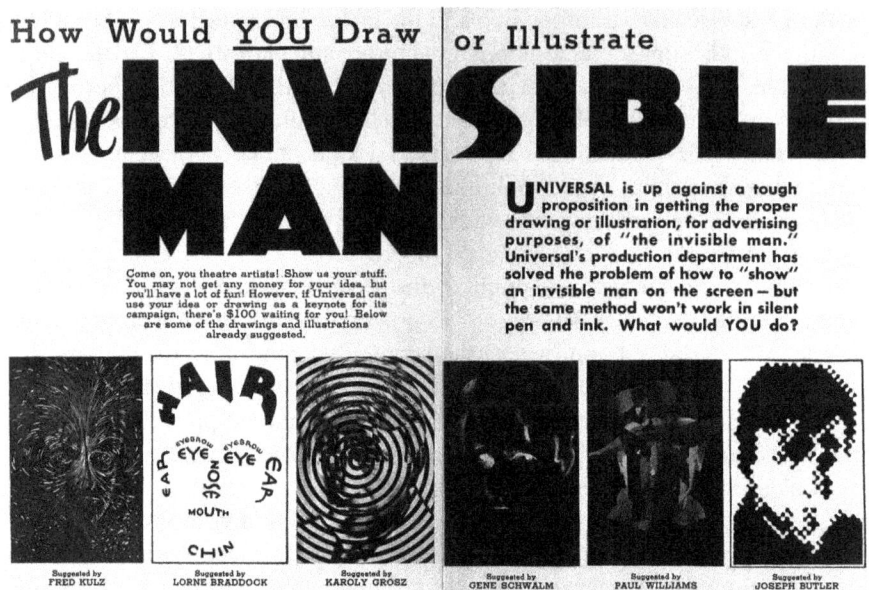

Figure 9.2 'How Would You Draw or Illustrate the Invisible Man?' *Universal Weekly*, 12 August 1933. (pp. 8–9)

UNIVERSAL ADVERTISING AND *THE INVISIBLE MAN* ADS

David Bordwell, Janet Staiger and Kristin Thompson have argued that by the 1930s certain industrial mechanisms had started emerging that facilitated standardisation, one of them being advertising practices (1985, see especially 97–102, 129). Advertising was important because it put both exhibitors and audiences in touch with the kind of pleasure that was to be expected from a film. The print culture sphere (house organs, newspapers, magazines, press books, and so on) was one of the most important outlets of film publicity by the time Universal started producing its series of horror films in 1931. From the 1920s, the studios had started to employ publicity and marketing teams for creating and producing publicity materials such as press books and house organs, which were intended to encourage film exhibitors in the full exploitation of each film being advertised. These print materials would carry information about the film and its production, such as plot synopses, cast details, background information and all the necessary logistical particulars, such as the availability of publicity posters or other promotional aids, including lobby cards and life-sized cardboard cut-outs of characters from the film, which could be ordered and erected in the foyers of the film theatres. House organs and press books were also used to promote competitions and quizzes, as well as providing suggested text and campaign ideas for local newspapers and for exploitation events the exhibitors could adopt.

One of the ways in which the studios advertised their films was through the use of superlatives. For example, *The Invisible Man* was advertised as being superior not just to the horror films that came before, but also to the earlier monsters. This apparent superiority was a major selling point for the studio, which is underlined by an ad in *Universal Weekly* that proclaimed:

> Warning! Don't compare me with 'Frankenstein!' He was a sap! Don't compare me with 'Dracula!' He was a sissy! Don't compare me with anybody that ever was, or ever will be, for there never was before nor ever will be again anybody like me. You'll find out why when you catch me (if you can). (18 November 1933, 16–17)

Philip Ball argues that invisibility engenders fright, 'the fright of *not* seeing what we should' (2015, 172). It leads to the 'paranoid fear of being the prey, the object of voyeuristic malice' (172). A disembodied voice hints at the supernatural and causes feelings of fear and revulsion because of the dissolution of the physical body into thin air. The aim of the aforementioned advertisement was to underscore invisibility as the most dominant power of a monster and highlight the fright that it could generate. Dracula and Frankenstein were termed sissies because of their visible corporealities, which could not produce as much terror as the Invisible Man. The image of the Invisible Man in the advertisement also looked like something out of a nineteenth-century spirit photography catalogue where the spirit was portrayed as an out-of-focus foggy/smoky spectral figure that hovered between partial visibility and complete invisibility. Paul Williams's suggestion in Figure 9.2 also corresponds to the likeness of a spirit photograph which Tom Gunning says yielded an 'eerie image of the encounter of two ontologically separate worlds' (2013, 213). Gunning suggests that the way in which spirit photography played with human vision was that it transformed the human body into the similitude of a phantom but did not remove it from our vision. It simply furnished the image with an unreal appearance (213). This certainly seemed to be the case for Universal, so that in its characterisation of the Invisible Man, *Universal Weekly* tried to render its invisible physicality by harking back to an older media form.

Anthony Slide (2010) also highlights the importance of print materials like fan magazines as crucial to film advertising. He mentions that although the advertisements in fan magazines helped the studios to sell tickets and increase profits, fan magazines could be unpredictable regarding their writings about a certain film, and therefore, the studios wanted tighter control over their publicity outlets. This is where paid advertisements in fan or trade magazines, or having a house organ such as *Universal Weekly*, would become important. Richard

Abel has specifically examined house organs and their purpose in the context of film promotion and exhibition. He asserts that they functioned as an 'extra-added attraction, luring moviegoers to attend specific film theatres, whether downtown palace cinemas or neighbourhood venues' (Abel 2015, 155). The pages in *Universal Weekly* frequently carried the news of elaborate ballyhoos and attractions at the exhibition venues to draw the audiences. While the studio would have less control over the publicity for these films in smaller exhibition markets such as Wisconsin or Iowa, places such as Philadelphia or New York were big money-makers, and the studio publicity heads would have both a larger stake and tighter control over this. In fact, the publicity department for Universal during the 1930s employed a series of stunts and theatrics to attract the audiences to the theatre. For example, the premiere of *The Mummy* (1932) in New York was an important occasion for Universal, and the publicity was carried on accordingly. RKO's Mayfair movie theatre in Times Square carried above the marquee huge cut-outs of Boris Karloff's head, which had colourful lighting and flashing eye sockets. The theatre lobby was embellished with painted enlargements of characters and scenes from the film. But the primary attraction was a full-sized mummy that RKO borrowed from Universal Home Office Exploitation Department. Using two-way microphones, it was turned into a talking mummy, and this led to people thronging the Mayfair and causing traffic jams in Times Square. Such stunts could, it was suggested, be emulated on a more modest scale at local theatres. The publicity department at Universal could advise exhibitors on how to install the microphones with the help of local radio dealers and suggested enlisting local art schools to prepare a mummy. All this information occupied a significant space in the pages of *Universal Weekly*.

When nothing new or unique in the films was worth promoting, the advertisers would highlight related material such as the high cost of spectacles, stars and filmmakers as evidence of the films' value. And while highlighting the stars, it would invariably be their faces that were emphasised, even if the star was not yet a big one.

The face was an inseparable part of an actor's corporeality in the film as well as outside of it in the realm of advertising. Christine Gledhill notes that star personae are constructed in a way whereby the stars connect to their audiences primarily through their bodies, and the mechanical reproduction of the images of their bodies, especially the face, helps establish this connection in a more intimate manner (1991, 210). Colin McArthur, whom Gledhill references, argues that the stars are constituted by certain meanings offered to the audiences through 'qualities that are almost entirely physical' (211), the face being a significant part of this physicality. Therefore, one of the most important parts of the association that forms between the star and the audience is the face of the star.

Star Claude Rains' face was missing in *The Invisible Man*, due to the needs of the plot. Therefore, Universal turned to the filmmaker James Whale as evidence of the film's value. Carl Laemmle Sr, the President of Universal Studios, in a rhetorical open letter, heaped praise on Whale, saying that the director was a filmmaker of unusual calibre who had achieved the impossible by filming a man who was invisible and was able to make the viewers see the invisibility of the Invisible Man (Laemmle 11 November 1933, 2–3). The studio was, therefore, invested in the idea of visible invisibility of the Invisible Man which was about making the viewers visualise the invisibility of this monster on the film screen. The invisibility factor of a monster and its representation was novel in the 1930s and the distinctness of the corporeality of the Invisible Man was emphasised by the studio repeatedly.

The Invisible Man ads in *Universal Weekly* were markedly different from the ads for films from genres other than horror. A double-page spread for the musical *Moonlight and Pretzels* (Freund 1933) in the same issue of *Universal Weekly* as Figure 9.2 showed the full-body image of the star Mary Brian in her elaborate dancing costume (12 August 1933, 16–17). The image also showed other dancers in the background laid out in a Busby Berkeley like pattern. Another advert, for the comedy film *Ladies Must Love* (Dupont 1933), only displayed the faces of the four leading women (12–13). Unlike the drawings and hand-painted images of Claude Rains as the Invisible Man, the images for 'normal' films were photographs edited together to make a collage for a double-page spread. These ads were characterised by the significant display of the physicality of the actors, and the readers could clearly see their faces. The stylised faces with embellished hairstyles acted as points of identification of these stars by the target audience. The representation of the stars in these ads, therefore, conforms to the discourses of stardom that privilege the face of the star above other components of the printed advertisements.

The Invisible Man was obviously a horror film and not advertised in the same manner as a musical or a comedy by Universal. The departure from the regular norms of advertising was also due to the fact that the campaign was about making the invisible visible, which was a challenging task, especially in print. It was possible to achieve invisibility with the cinematic frame through the use of special effects, as the copy shown in Figure 9.2 overtly acknowledges, but how to explore and display the dimensions of invisibility in print was a question that was not easy to answer.

Since the earlier Universal monsters' corporeality existed in the physical world, representing them in print was easier. *Universal Weekly* ads for *Frankenstein*, *Dracula* and *The Mummy* laid out the still images of the monsters' bodies to be seen by readers. While the question of representation of the Invisible Man was 'resolved' on film – the Figure 9.2 copy sees Universal boast that its production department had 'solved the problem of how to "show" an invisible man on the screen' – its representation in print was still open-ended and the studio turned this problem into a bonus by using it as a marketing gimmick.

Advertising campaigns by Hollywood studios were often excessive, and Universal's campaigns for *The Invisible Man* were no different. Right before the release of the film, Universal requested exhibitors in a very straightforward way to publicise it. The 'Showmanship' column of *Universal Weekly* proclaimed:

> When you play H.G. Wells' 'Invisible Man' you should use strong punchy words to intrigue interest in this fantastic sensation. TELL YOUR PUBLIC enough in the ads to make them hot-foot it to your box office to see this indescribable – astonishing screen novelty! SELL your pictures with red-hot lines in real ADVERTISEMENTS. Leave the super-dignified announcements to the banks. You're in the picture business and if you want to do real banking as a result of your efforts you should sell your shows with real ADVERTISING! (2 December 1933, 27)

Many theatre managers seem to have resorted to elaborate and quirky acts to mount the publicity campaign for *The Invisible Man*, working on the campaign premise of playing up the amorphous nature of the invisible monster's bodily materiality. While *Universal Weekly* had an obvious incentive in printing many such reported incidents about their film, accounts of 'ballyhoo' – promotional activities designed to generate interest – for *The Invisible Man* can be found in other contemporaneous publications. For example, *The Philadelphia Exhibitor* (15 December 1933, 17) presents the information that a theatre manager in Atlantic City hired a man to play the invisible monster. He was 'dressed in a black coat, with a black hood and white eye covering and mouth', and walked up and down Atlantic Avenue, generating such a large crowd that police had to be called. Whether this account is accurate or not, the point here is that publications were relaying the information that Universal wanted disseminated: that the new monster would draw crowds – in any movie theatre showing it.

Other publicity gags for the film utilised various electrical and mechanical devices to signal the absent presence of the monster, such as a tele-autograph installation at Roxy Theatre in New York, which wrote messages from the Invisible Man, or an installation at Warner Theatre in Pittsburgh where putting one's hand over a crystal ball would make a fan revolve, a bell ring or a door open. All these were being promoted as done by the Invisible Man. In the context of these publicity theatrics from Universal, the ad campaign in Figure 9.2 did not offer an actual competition to readers of *Universal Weekly*, but was just another outlet for the publicity executives to try to heighten awareness of the film.

As noted, most of these film advertisements were black-and-white prints, spread across two adjacent pages of the magazines. Kostoula Margariti et al. argue that the 'monochrome, white space, linked with the minimalist movement in architecture, is also applicable in advertising' and that '[w]hite space is considered to be a conspicuous, non-pictorial, visual trope that foregrounds absence rather than presence' (2017, 4). This is something that comes across quite distinctly in these film advertisements. One of the publicity advertisements was composed entirely of text, full of excerpts from various film critics and Hollywood trade papers about the uniqueness and the achievement of the film. In terms of images, all that existed was a puff of smoke that barely covered a fifth of the entire space of the advertisement. Another teaser advertisement (Figure 9.3) shows nothing but two black squares with a pair of cat's eyes in the first; the corresponding text proclaims that it is the picture of 'an unusually black coloured man chasing a very black cat through an utterly dark room at midnight' (*Universal Weekly*, 4 November 1933, 20–1). The second, entirely black, square alleges it 'shows' the Invisible Man himself. This ad was another gimmick through which Universal tried to solve the problem of the Invisible Man's representation in print. The ad's declaration that this was the best they could have done without a movie camera sought to generate curiosity among movie theatre owners, as well as provide an example of how to market

Figure 9.3 Advertisement for *The Invisible Man* (1933). *Universal Weekly*, 4 November 1933. (pp. 20–1)

such an unusual subject to the public, drawing them into the theatre to witness the impossible: the manifesting of a formless monster on screen.

Since the ad campaigns for *The Invisible Man* were different from the regular Hollywood ad campaigns, unable to trade on the familiar faces of the film's stars, they focused a significant part of the ads, instead posing questions that dealt with the corporeality of the Invisible Man and the problem of resolving the conundrum of this corporeality in print as well as the screen: 'How does the screen "show" an invisible man – in action? COME AND SEE!' (Figure 9.1). The publicity executives resorted to a form of advertising that titillated with questions, instead of faces. While these questions kept the physicality of the invisible monster a puzzle to deal with, they also became the theme that defined Universal's ad campaign for their latest monster film.

Fear and Desire

The publicity campaigns for Universal's monster films from the 1930s seem to be based on the premise of Cohen's idea that the fear of the monster is a kind of desire. The simultaneous fear and lure of the monster were at the core of these advertisements. Cohen says that while the primary response to the monster is fear and repulsion, the creature also elicits the emotion of attraction, and this binary of attraction and repulsion accounts for the cultural popularity of a monster (1996, 17). The monster familiarises us with the 'simple and fleeting joys of being frightened, or frightening – to the experience of mortality and corporality' (17). Figure 9.4 is an advertisement for another very popular Universal horror film from the 1930s cycle – *Werewolf of London* (Walker 1935) (*Universal Weekly*, 20 April 1935, frontmatter). The right panel of the advertisement shows four iterations of the same image at each corner, with a message from 'The Management' inscribed in between 'To all hysterical women'. The reproduced image is that of a woman with the Werewolf lurking in the background. The woman's face bears an ambiguous expression, that seems a curious mixture of fear and attraction; attracted, wanting to attract, she seems both desirous of being unnoticed and simultaneously of being seen. The message from 'The Management' underscores this emotion of repulsion mixed with attraction.

Cohen says that the reason people watch the monsters of horror films is because of this unconscious knowledge that the space of the theatre and the horrific images on screen exist in unreality and are only fleeting (1996, 17). The monster exists in an in-between space of ambiguity, the primal space between fear and attraction. This became even truer for a monster like the Invisible Man not only because the very concept of such a man existed in an interstitial space, but also because even his corporeality negotiated multiple binaries. As noted before, several of the posters for the movie shown in Figure 9.1 frame the image

UNIVERSAL HORROR AND *UNIVERSAL WEEKLY*

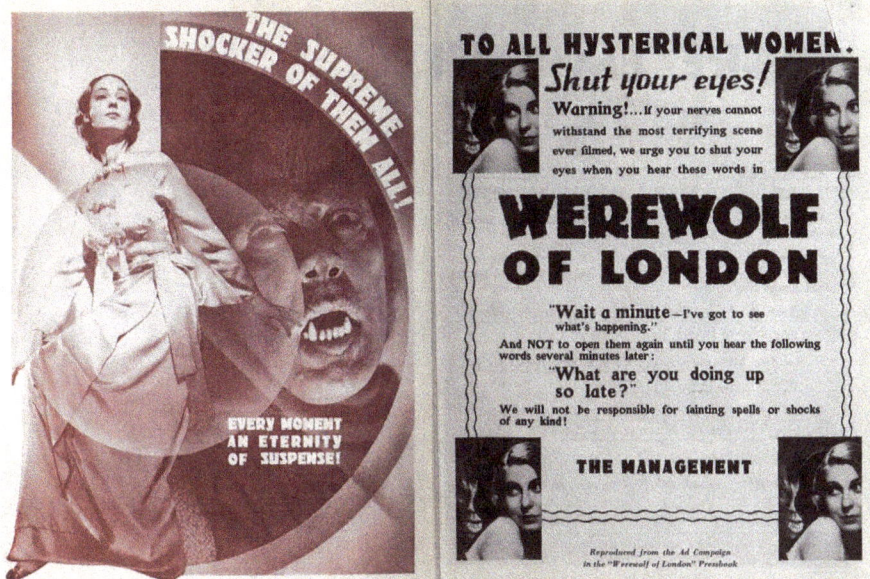

Figure 9.4 Advertisement for *Werewolf of London* (1935). *Universal Weekly*, 20 April 1935. (frontmatter)

of Gloria Stuart within an outlined profile of the Invisible Man, showing the starlet with her hand clasped to her chin and expressing an emotion of fear and bewilderment. These images stand in stark contrast to the cover image of Stuart in the same issue of *Universal Weekly*, which captures her reclining on a cushion, her full face shown at a 90-degree angle, looking calmly into the eyes of the reader. The cover looks like any other fan magazine from the 1930s, presenting the star in a glamour shot, and while the tagline underneath does link the image directly to the film – 'Gloria Stuart: The Beauty Who Fell in Love with THE INVISIBLE MAN' – the usual slippage where an actor's name is substituted for the character she plays underlines her actual identity as beautiful star. In reality, Stuart's character does not have much screen time in the film, and the romantic angle in the plot is firmly secondary to the spectacle of invisibility, but she nevertheless occupies a prominent position in the ads. Not only does this make the film conform to the usual Hollywood template of a leading character and their romantic opposite, but here the use of Stuart's face compensates for the lack of the Invisible Man's.

While the use of Stuart's image in the Figure 9.1 ads further underlines the fear/attraction binary, and underlines the contrast of physical existence versus formlessness, the use of her face elsewhere reinforces her emerging star status, the film's potential romance narrative *and* her co-star's unusual lack of facial

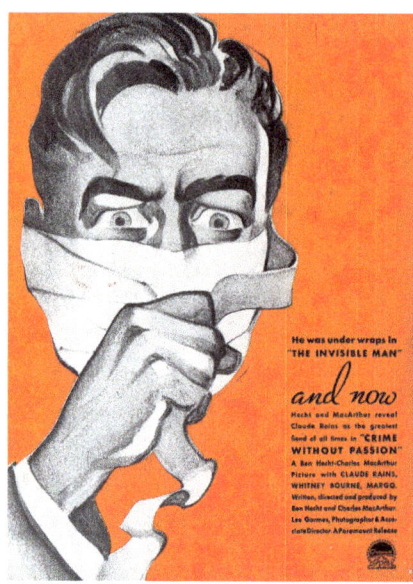

Figure 9.5 Advertisement for *Crime Without Passion* (1934). *Motion Picture Herald*, 25 August 1934. (back cover)

prominence in the marketing. This latter fact was so marked, in fact, that advertising continued to play on Claude Rains's star invisibility, even when the film was not from Universal. An advertisement (Figure 9.5) for Paramount's *Crime Without Passion* (MacArthur, Hecht 1934) published in *Motion Picture Herald* ten months after the debut of *The Invisible Man* prominently displays the face of Claude Rains emerging from his Griffin character's bandages, while the accompanying text asserts 'He was under wraps in "The Invisible Man" and now Hecht and MacArthur reveal Claude Rains as the greatest fiend of all times in "Crime Without Passion"' (*Motion Picture Herald*, 25 August 1934, back cover). Notably, this image has absolutely no correlation with the plot of the film. Paramount's publicity department took inspiration from the bandaged-face image of Rains from *The Invisible Man* and produced an image that would attract the publication's audience of movie theatre owners, since the memory of the Invisible Man iconography would still be fresh in their minds.

Conclusion

This chapter has looked at various entries in the publicity campaign for *The Invisible Man* in *Universal Weekly*, revealing that this campaign was largely built around overtly acknowledging the difficulty of representing this formless monster on screen and in print. Jeffrey Cohen has posited that some monsters radically undermine our usual binary thinking because they cannot be categorised easily, and we are forced to rethink the boundaries and concepts of normality (1996, 6). Universal's obsession with the form of the Invisible Man can be understood along similar lines. The earlier Universal monsters like Dracula, Frankenstein's Monster and the Mummy had a well-defined physical appearance, unlike the Invisible Man. The notion of the new monster's corporeality existing outside the boundaries of the physical world defied not only the familiar ways of conceptualising and categorising a monster, but also the ways of showing one. Thus, a running thread in the chapter has been the difficulty of representing the Invisible Man in print, and the explicit play about the difficulty of bestowing visibility on a formless and invisible entity. While this was a case study of a specific film and a specific genre, situating *The Invisible Man* within the general Hollywood context, in which film marketing relies on stars and their faces, allows us to think more flexibly about the ways in which the layout and design of movie magazines – beyond the fan magazine and into the trade journal – create the desire to consume the movie and its stars, even when the main star is defined by invisibility and formlessness.

Notes

1. For example, Williams 2013; Jeffers McDonald and Lanckman 2019; Wickham 2010; Abrahamson 1996; Bandhauer and Royer 2015; deCordova 2001; Desjardins 2002; Hoyt 2022; McLean 2004.
2. Project Arclight is a database search tool that searches the nearly 2-million-page collection of the Media History Digital Library and graphs the results. The Media History Digital Library is a non-profit initiative dedicated to digitising historic books and magazines about film and broadcasting.
3. Cohen's essay has been very influential in the field of monster theory and 'art horror' since it was first published in 1996. In terms of its broader framework, the essay resembles Robin Wood's 'An Introduction to the American Horror Film' (1979), where rooted in Freudian concept of psychoanalysis and repression, Wood formulates the cinematic monster as it exists in the form of the 'other'. Likewise, using the Foucauldian methodology of archaeology of ideas, Cohen's writing clearly sets the parameters for what constitutes a monster and what its larger socio-cultural purpose is.

References

Abel, Richard. 2015. 'House Organs and the Detroit Weekly Film News in the 1910s'. *Film History* 27 (3): 137–59.

Abrahamson, David. 1996. *Magazine-Made America: The Cultural Transformation of the Postwar Periodical*. Cresskill, NJ: Hampton Press.

Anon. 1933. Advertisement for *The Invisible Man*. *Universal Weekly*, 12 August: 8–9.
Anon. 1933. Advertisement for *Ladies Must Love*. *Universal Weekly*, 12 August: 12–13.
Anon. 1933. Advertisement for *Moonlight and Pretzels*. *Universal Weekly*, 12 August: 16–17.
Anon. 1933. *Universal Weekly*. 9 September: front cover.
Anon. 1933. Advertisement for *The Invisible Man*. *Universal Weekly*, 9 September: 4–5.
Anon. 1933. Advertisement for *The Invisible Man*. *Universal Weekly*, 18 November: 16–17.
Anon. 1933. 'Announcing Title is Not Enough: Real Ads Should Carry Play-up Phrases'. *Universal Weekly*, 2 December: 27.
Anon. 1933. *The Philadelphia Exhibitor*, 15 December: 17.
Anon. 1934. Advertisement for *Crime Without Passion*. *Motion Picture Herald*, 25 August: back cover.
Anon. 1935. Advertisement for *Werewolf of London*. *Universal Weekly*, 20 April: frontmatter.
Ball, Philip. 2015. *Invisible: The Dangerous Allure of the Unseen*. Chicago: The University of Chicago Press.
Bandhauer, Andrea, and Michelle Royer, eds. 2015. *Stars in World Cinema: Screen Icons and Star Systems Across Cultures*. London: I. B. Tauris.
Bordwell, David, Janet Staiger and Kristin Thompson. 1985. *The Classical Hollywood Cinema: Film Style & Mode of Production to 1960*. New York: Columbia University Press.
Carroll, Noël. 1990. *The Philosophy of Horror or Paradoxes of the Heart*. New York and London: Routledge.
Cohen, Jeffrey. 1996. 'Monster Culture (Seven Theses)'. In *Monster Theory: Reading Culture*, edited by Jeffrey Cohen, 3–25. Minneapolis: University of Minnesota Press.
deCordova, Richard. 2001. *Picture Personalities: The Emergence of the Star System in America*. Urbana: University of Illinois Press.
Desjardins, Mary. 2002. 'Maureen O'Hara's Confidential Life: Recycling Stars Through Gossip and Moral Biography'. In *Small Screens, Big Ideas: Television in the 1950s*, edited by Janet Thumim, 118–30. London: I. B. Tauris.
Gledhill, Christine. 1991. 'Signs of Melodrama'. In *Stardom: Industry of Desire*, edited by Christine Gledhill, 207–29. London and New York: Routledge.
Grove, Allen W. 1997. 'Röntgen's Ghosts: Photography, X-Rays, and the Victorian Imagination'. *Literature and Medicine* 16 (2): 141–73.
Gunning, Tom. 2013. 'To Scan a Ghost: The Ontology of a Mediated Vision'. In *The Spectralities Reader: Ghosts and Hauntings in Contemporary Cultural Theory*, edited by Maria del Pilar Blanco and Esther Peeren, 207–44. London: Bloomsbury.
Hoyt, Eric. 2022. *Ink-Stained Hollywood: The Triumph of American Cinema's Trade Press*. Berkeley: University of California Press.
Jeffers McDonald, Tamar, and Lies Lanckman, eds. 2019. *Star Attractions: Twentieth-Century Movie Magazines and Global Fandom*. Iowa: University of Iowa Press.
Laemmle Sr, Carl. 1933. Open Letter to James Whale. *Universal Weekly*, 11 November: 2–3.
Lippit, Akira Mizuta. 2005. *Atomic Light (Shadow Optics)*. Minneapolis: University of Minnesota Press.

Lippit, Akira Mizuta. 2013. 'From Modes of Avisuality: Psychoanalysis – X-ray – Cinema'. In *The Spectralities Reader: Ghosts and Hauntings in Contemporary Cultural Theory*, edited by Maria del Pilar Blanco and Esther Peeren, 257–78. London: Bloomsbury.

McLean, Adrienne L. 2004. *Being Rita Hayworth: Labor, Identity and Hollywood*. New Brunswick, NJ: Rutgers University Press.

Margariti, Kostoula, Christina Boutsouki, Leonidas Hatzithomas and Yorgos Zotos. 2017. 'A Typology of Minimalism in Advertising'. In *Advances in Advertising Research VIII: Challenges in an Age of Dis-Engagement*, edited by Vesna Zabkar and Martin Eisend, 1–15. No Place Specified: Springer.

Slide, Anthony. 2010. *Inside the Hollywood Fan Magazine: A History of Star Makers, Fabricators and Gossip Mongers*. Jackson: University Press of Mississippi.

Todorov, Tzvetan. 1975. *The Fantastic: A Structural Approach to a Literary Genre*. Translated by Richard Howard. Ithaca, NY: Cornell University Press.

Wickham, Phil. 2010. 'Scrapbooks, Soap Dishes and Screen Dreams: Ephemera, Everyday Life and Cinema History'. *New Review of Film and Television Studies* 8 (3): 315–30.

Williams, Michael. 2013. *Film Stardom, Myth and Classicism: The Rise of Hollywood's Gods*. Basingstoke: Palgrave Macmillan.

Wood, Robin. [1979] 2020. 'An Introduction to the American Horror Film'. In *The Monster Theory Reader*, edited by Jeffrey Andrew Weinstock, 108–35. Minneapolis: Minnesota University Press.

10. A PERFORMANCE STUDIES PERSPECTIVE ON FAN MAGAZINE IMAGES AND SILENT FILM ACTING

Jennifer Voss

In her autobiography *Silent Star* (1968), American silent and early sound film actress Colleen Moore reminisces about her earliest experiences and aspirations of learning to act for the screen. She writes

> I read one time in *Photoplay* magazine that Norma Talmadge had said an actress must be able to weep spontaneously, so I thought the sooner I learned to cry, the better off I'd be. (Moore 1968, 12)

This story of fan magazine engagement is one echoed by many actresses. Clara Bow reportedly spent her weekends 'surrounded by movie magazines . . . fantasizing about how someday she would appear in them' (Stenn 2000, 13). Similarly, Norma Shearer was said to have been an 'avid reader of movie magazines' from a young age, devouring 'the Cinderella stories of girls who were picture stars . . . [imagining] herself in their place' (Ramsey 1931, 111). As such, we might connect them to the 'movie struck' or 'screen struck girls' written about by Shelley Stamp (2000) and Diana Anselmo Sequeira (2015), as well as those addressed by American fan magazines in the early teens (Fuller 1996). However, Moore's particular reference to the magazine's emphasis on developing screen acting skills, especially the practice of crying, challenges the pejorative framing of young women engaging with movie fandom as purely 'vapid' consumers. Throughout her autobiography, Moore frequently references the ways in which she trained herself and worked hard to continue improving her skills, by observing, and taking advice from other actresses – particularly in relation to emotional expression. Indeed, her memoir returns to the matter of crying, asking 'I could cry now whenever I had to, but what about technique?' (1968, 27).

This chapter incorporates a performance studies perspective with fan magazine analysis to explore how fan magazines readers, such as Moore, were presented with visually engaging and instructional texts through which they could learn about their favourite stars, while simultaneously developing a knowledge of screen acting styles and appreciation of specific performances. It is possible to identify a feedback loop whereby fan magazines were teaching aspiring (and even established) performers how to perform. I begin by outlining some of the central skills and techniques utilised within silent film performance, especially the focus on posing and crying. Problematic essentialist discourses tend to downplay the screen craft and labour in discussing women's performances, particularly in relation to emotive displays. However, these skills were at the fore of the training manuals which were sources encouraging and supporting self-guided actor training. Chris O'Rourke (2014, 2017) has commented on the proliferation of these in Britain in the 1910s and 1920s. I build on and extend O'Rourke's work by offering a close analysis of the similarities within the layout and design of selected pages of acting training manuals and fan magazines. For the latter, this is most evident in the long-running 'Expressions of . . .' series in the British fan magazine *Picture Show* which focused on a different star performing expressions each week from 1919 to 1925.

After discussing similarities between selected training manual and fan magazine pages, this chapter considers one such star – Colleen Moore – in detail. Moore was the subject of *Picture Show*'s 'Expressions of . . .' series in July 1922, and since the publication earlier boasted of having Moore among its star readership, as evidenced by a 'candid' image of her perusing the 28 August 1920 issue of the magazine (3), it might even be inferred that she learned from earlier editions of the feature. Moore was an important star of the 1920s; Mary Desjardins, in her consideration of the 'new woman' and female stardom in the 1920s, designates Moore as one actress who was 'frequently listed in exhibitor polls of the time as [one of the] top audience favourites' (2010, 109). Desjardins emphasises the significance of Moore's embodiment of the flapper trope, noting her 'expressing her liberation from tradition . . .[via] an androgyny that included bobbed hair and clothing that allowed for free movement . . . and experimentation with sexual freedoms' (2010, 121). Within the writing of film historians and Star Studies scholars, analyses of Moore's career are thus predominantly bound up with the significance of her flapper persona (Basinger 2000; Negra 2001; Ross 2010). There has been little focus, however, on Moore's training and what this reveals about the complex requirements of silent film acting. In this chapter I especially draw attention to Moore's earlier, more melodramatic, career, by focusing on the way contemporaneous fan magazine articles about her privileged her highly expressive performance style in presenting and discussing her performances of emotion. The increased availability of ephemeral archival materials such as fan magazines means that it is still possible to offer detailed interrogations of silent film performance, despite the loss of so many silent films. Analysis of Moore's appearance in a clipping then teases out some of the specific purposes of fan magazines, before I also move to comment on these publications' regular downplaying of actresses' skills, while the view of Moore as a flapper was becoming fixed in the public's imagination.

SILENT FILM ACTING AND INFORMAL MODES OF ACTOR TRAINING

Ben Brewster and Lea Jacobs's *Theatre to Cinema: Stage Pictorialism and the Early Feature Film* (1997) offers a detailed exploration of the development of silent film acting in relation to its shared heritage with stage melodrama. Highlighting the prevalence of pictorial acting styles across centuries of stage performance, they discuss how 'actors were enjoined to study statues and paintings, and to practice poses', and also noted the 'consistent use of illustrative drawings in manuals on acting and oratory' (Brewster and Jacobs 1997, 85). Indeed, as evidenced in the work of scholars of early silent film such as Roberta Pearson (1992), the significance of sequences of gesture and poses deriving from the theatrical melodrama was foundational to early screen performance. Addressing this idea of sequences of performed expression in relation to emotional expression, Christine Gledhill has written on the once-prevalent practice of '[registering] melodrama's primary emotions' (2003, 64). 'Registering emotions' is a practice that reflected contemporaneous ideas that acting is reliant on learnable, and repeatable, manifestations of emotions. Such emotions were also gendered. There was an expectation, for example, that for a woman to succeed in film acting, she must perfect her ability to cry on cue. As such, a number of prominent silent film stars have been historically framed specifically in relation to this highly praised ability. Stars such as Mary Pickford, Moore, Bow, as well as Lillian Gish, are often written about in terms of their overtly emotive performances, with Bow being described as 'an emotional machine' (Stenn 2000, 37). Yet, while the codification of women crying on screen has historically been framed pejoratively by some critics, with melodramatic displays of emotion being denigrated for being excessive or 'too much' (Grodal 1997, 253), it is important to recognise the training, both formal and informal, that goes into creating such dynamic displays.

Informal training, as proposed by performance studies scholar Richard Schechner, includes practices through which 'the novice acquires skills over time by absorbing what is going on' (2006, 228), and is a term used within this chapter to refer to a variety of performance processes undertaken by actresses outside of, or in combination with, formal or institutional acting or performance training. Informal performance processes, either emotional or physical responses to on-set direction, or self-directed exercises, are methods of performer training frequently documented by actresses. Due to the lack of established film acting schools in the early 1920s, actors and actresses who were successful in securing a much-coveted studio contract would have had to draw upon a range of previously learned skills to inform and develop their screen acting craft. Others would have learned to act for the screen through watching and mimicking performances seen in the movies, or through watching and mimicking stars, while performing on set as an extra. Examples of instruction and guidance encouraging aspiring screen stars to participate in these methods of self-training, and to draw upon their alternative performance experience in order to do so, were prevalent both within fan magazines and within dedicated acting training manuals.

Technique and Training: Self-Guided Practice and Actor Training Manuals

As O'Rourke's *Acting for the Silent Screen: Film Actors and Aspiration Between the Wars* suggests, 'the idea that acting could be rehearsed at home, discreetly or furtively, was a common one in the 1920s' (2017, 43). Exploring the great number of acting training manuals that emerged in the 1910s, particularly in Britain, O'Rourke writes that these texts were aimed at aspiring film stars, and 'combined practical advice about seeking employment, acquiring costumes and "making-up" for the screen with more thoughtful discussions about the art of film performance' (50). Jean Bernique's *Motion Picture Acting for Professionals and Amateurs* (1916), an actor training manual which includes '191 posed photos of motion picture stars showing 499 different expressions of emotion' (1916, cover matter), illustrates this prevalence of a focus on the manifestation of emotional expression in early modes of screen acting. Bernique's reference to the idea of '"made to-order" expressions' being key to silent film performance (22) highlights the dominance of repeatable, identifiable depictions of emotion as tools in actor training manuals. It also suggests how similar depictions of emotions in fan magazines might equally be utilised by aspiring performers.

There were also manuals which appeared under the names of stars. In a 1920 manual credited to actress Mary Pickford, advice on various techniques for crowd work, characterisation, as well as hair and make-up, is interspersed with images of character studies. One page within the manual shows four close-up images of Pickford's face. The four portrait pictures are presented in a two-by-two format below the title 'Some Remarkable Mary Pickford Expressions and Make-Up' with a caption below each image identifying the character type and what they represent. The labels identify the four stills as depicting 'happiness', 'severity', 'pity', as well as a character study showcasing make-up to represent 'dirt' (1920, 16). The images are positioned as archetypes to be learned and imitated by readers. On the following page, Pickford outlines a number of exercises which echo the technique of 'registering emotions', instructing readers to 'find out exactly the emotions to be portrayed in the part, and practice them as you would practice at the piano' (17). Referring to depictions of 'sorrow, anger, anticipation, fear, joy, surprise', Pickford advises aspiring performers to 'discover which is your weak point [and] then keep hammering away at it until it is your strongest' and to 'express it in your face on every possible occasion' (18). In a later chapter, Pickford returns to the importance of understanding the relationship between the action of the film and the emotions a performer is expected to portray, stating that performers should 'always remember that the camera records every action', and that it is 'necessary for a player to have constant control over her emotions' (22). As such, Pickford's manual illustrates both the necessity of emotional expression in screen acting and how this ought to be applied in a professional setting.

The ideas proffered within Pickford's acting manual clearly reflect the dominant discourses on silent film acting that were also disseminated within fan magazines in the 1910s and 1920s. For example, in a March 1918 *Picture Play* article 'How to Act', American stage and screen actress Violet Mersereau (allegedly)[1] writes:

> the modern use of the 'close-up', which reveals the actor's every thought, eliminates the distance between you and your audience, which exists in every playhouse. Your lonely face is all by itself on a twenty-foot screen ... That is why the screen actress must learn to weep real tears, and that is why every movement of her body should be expressive ... She can't put tears in her voice, so she has to put them in her eyes. (Mersereau, March 1918, 70)

Here the focus on the epitome of emotional expression being the ability to produce tears is a technique evidently considered foundational for women's screen acting at the time. The article therefore provides contemporaneous evidence within fan magazines which highlights an emphasis on women crying within silent film acting, as illustrated by the *Photoplay* piece on Norma Talmadge that Moore refers to in her autobiography. Some of the content offered within training manuals of the 1910s and 1920s was therefore also seen in fan magazines, albeit in altered forms, and next I turn to specific design and layout similarities and differences in these sources.

Magazines as a Site of Mimicry

Lisa Stead has written about British interwar fan magazines, including *Picture Show*. She describes how some of these especially engaged young women through their participatory structure, explaining how readers' letters debated and deconstructed star images in a virtual community (Stead 2017, 106). However, another important interactive feature can be discerned. In addition to his focus on actor training manuals, O'Rourke's work addresses particular growing trends within British fan magazines which focused on discussions of film technique and the dissection of images displaying close-ups of film star expressions (2017, 60). Accompanying his consideration of these 'star appreciation' articles, which embraced stars performing in both Britain and America, O'Rourke includes an image of a 16 April 1921 *Picture Show* magazine article titled 'The Expressions of Geraldine Farrar' (Figure 10.1).

O'Rourke mainly uses this image for illustrative purposes, and he does not look at this important series in depth, nor provide analysis of the images which include stars performing expressions. Positioned among short stories, advertisements and discussions of the latest films, 'The Expressions of . . .' feature sits comfortably alongside the other image-dominated pages of the magazine. However, while the portraits of film stars presented throughout the magazine may appear similar in their focus on the close-up and stills of film performance, it is the concentration of images of a single star, with the text directly drawing readers' attention to the performer's expression, which sets these articles apart.

The series began on 10 May 1919, with a feature entitled 'Mae Marsh – Some of Her "Thousand Expressions"' (Figure 10.2). The article offers an overview of the American actress's early life, her career, as well as her marriage and hobbies, with a portrait of Marsh in the lower-right quarter of the page, and a row of five small close-up images of her displaying various facial expressions bordering the top of the text. In terms of composition, the images can be seen as drawing on the influences in Victorian narrative painting, whereby the 'emotional impact of the "painting is judged by the expressions on the depicted figures" faces, and on the variety and contrast of emotions represented and evoked' (Fletcher 2009, 462). Much like the individual captions below the portraits presented in Pickford's manual, the images of Marsh feature text below, relating to the emotions being portrayed. The captions read 'I AM quiet sometimes – I like nice things said to me – I have my sad times too – I don't believe ALL I hear – Oh! Oh! Oh!' (*Picture Show*, 10 May 1919, 13). As the series developed, the focus on the small close-up images presenting stars' dynamic expressions increased, with each image starting to feature a more explicit caption identifying and naming the emotion or character on display, and 'The Expressions of . . .' swiftly became the standard title for each article.

The distinct formatting of this feature clearly lends itself to further interrogation in order to unpack the interesting points of connection between magazines and instructional acting texts. Returning to the 'The Expressions

Figure 10.1 'Mae Marsh – Some of her "Thousand" Expressions'. *Picture Show*, 10 May 1919. (p. 13)

Figure 10.2 'The Expressions of Geraldine Farrar'. *Picture Show*, 16 April 1921. (p. 9)

of . . .' feature on American opera star and silent film actress Geraldine Farrar, the 16 April 1921 article follows the standard formatting of the series. The centralised text is accompanied by a three-quarter height body-length bordered portrait of Farrar in the bottom right corner – the same placement as for Marsh. On this occasion, however, the small close-up images of Farrar frame the left, bottom, and right of the piece rather than only appearing at the top. Each of these eight images captures a still of Farrar performing a distinct facial expression, each demonstration of feeling an exemplar of a character study rooted in the displays of emotion. Providing more explicit descriptions than the Marsh feature, the stills of Farrar are presented with a caption offering a title for each individual emotion being displayed, thus inviting an even more direct comparison with the Pickford manual, and demonstrating further how the feature developed. The captions describe Farrar as being thoughtful, delighted, pensive, demure, conveying grief, fear, embodying a coquette, and more generally 'her smile'. Indeed, throughout the series, words such as 'pensive', 'fear', as well as those associated with grief and sadness, were frequently included in the captions of female stars. Contrastingly, while the male actors were also shown in states of deep thought and pensiveness, they were often framed as displaying emotions such as anger, suspicion, determination, and being 'ready for a fight' (see 21 May 1921, 7; 16 July 1921, 7; 17 December 1921, 9), clearly highlighting the different expectations of emotional expressions for men and women, with the association of women and states of sadness perpetuated within the series. The text of the Farrar article comments on her most recent film and stage roles as well as her marriage, but also offers skills and tips: on how to dress for different character roles and how to appear taller on screen. Read in conjunction, the images and part of the text resemble a 'how-to' guide not unlike the published actor training manual, though the fan magazine also provided readers with personal information about the chosen star, as well as setting these personal details within the context of advertisements showing the star, other star articles, and indeed the wider environment of stardom per se.

The series lasted until 1925, and over its six-year span featured approximately 300 stars, both men and women, based in both Britain and the US, including high-profile actors such as Mary Pickford, Lillian and Dorothy Gish, and Rudolph Valentino. The section always appeared in the early portion of the magazine, enabling recurring readers to locate the feature easily. Its presence in *Picture Show* from the magazine's inception and throughout most of the silent era points to its significance, and further evidences the editors' belief, perhaps borne out by letters they received, about the popularity of magazine articles which provide informative, and even instructional, images for readers who dreamt of becoming stars. While the focus in actor training manuals and fan magazines is on learning and replicating a set of identifiable emotions, in practice nuances exist between the performances of different stars.

Colleen Moore in *Picture Show*

As noted in the introduction, Moore's autobiography referenced her reading of American fan magazines, while she was also apparently among the 'famous readers' of the British publication *Picture Show* – according to *Picture Show* itself (28 August 1920, 3). Moore's readership is important in terms of unpicking the feedback loop at play, but it is also necessary to home in on how her performances were presented in fan magazines, to garner a sense of how her performance skills were framed. By 1921, magazine coverage is focusing on her overt expressiveness, mirroring 'The Expressions of . . .' series. This is seen in an issue of 26 November 1921. In an article titled 'Colleen Moore: The Film Star with The Expressive Eyes', the story of her career in Hollywood is interspersed with a combination of large (one full-figure unframed shot on the right-hand side) and small stills of Moore displaying various expressions (Figure 10.3). Unlike 'The Expressions of . . .' feature, the images are less uniform in size, presented in both circle as well as square frames, and spread across the page. Only the small image at the top right-hand corner has a one-word caption – 'sorrow'. However, the majority of the images are still focused on Moore's face, demonstrating a variety of emotional states. The article reads that, '[a]s you will see by the photographs on this page, Colleen has a wonderful power of expression. Various emotions flit across her little face with lightning-like rapidity' (*Picture Show*, 26 November 1921, 7). Through these combinations of images and text, Moore is framed not only as an actress capable of producing clearly identifiable emotional expression, but as someone whose performative persona and success as a silent film actress are built around this coveted ability. Furthermore, the focus on Moore's face as the foundation of her performance style within film magazines offers a pertinent insight into the way in which her body is compartmentalised for the consumption of her particular star image.

Moore's eyes are also seen as a key element of her star persona in the 4 March 1922 *Picture Show* article, 'Colleen Moore as Impersonator'. The article reports on an alleged incident in which Moore entertained her co-stars on set 'with her impersonations of other film stars', performing as Douglas Fairbanks's 'dashing D'Artagnan' and '[growing] pathetic' as Lillian Gish (4 March 1922, 21). Referring to Moore as a 'born mimic', the article offers parallels with Moore's particular approach to her own informal training processes of mimicking other screen stars, both on set and from magazines. The latter section of the piece shifts the focus specifically to Moore's eyes, with the writer suggesting that they are central to Moore's 'fascinating charm', adding

Figure 10.3 'Colleen Moore – The Film Star with the Expressive Eyes'. *Picture Show*, 26 November 1921. (p. 7)

that a poet once tried to write an ode to Moore's 'eyes of blue that thrill you through', but had to stop when he realised that one was blue, and one was brown (4 March 1922, 21).

Moore's appearance in 'The Expressions of . . .' series in *Picture Show* on 1 July 1922 also references this mystery bard's attempted poem. In this feature, the writer asserts that the unknown poet had 'seldom seen lovelier, more living orbs' (1 July 1922, 7), reinforcing the positioning of Moore as an energetic and highly expressive performer. In terms of the composition of the piece, images of Moore follow the distinct formatting of the 'The Expressions of . . .' feature with the row of five uniform images detailing a different emotional expression appearing at the bottom of the page, with captions below, and a larger full-length image of Moore, in this instance in the centre. In this example, there is also a smaller picture of Moore in each of the top corners of the page (Figure 10.4). In the image captioned 'startled', Moore is shown facing the camera, her eyes wide, her brows lowered, with her mouth open. For 'grief', Moore looks into the distance, the lighting capturing the glint of tears in her eyes, brows raised in the middle, with her lips pressed together. Yet, while the emotions and expressions ascribed to the stills – startled, grief, suspicious, enquiry – prove to be similar to those given to the images of Farrar, and indeed many of the women within 'The Expressions of . . .' series, the repetition of the reference to Moore's thrilling, living eyes once again reinforces the idea of Moore as an actress whose talent in emotional expression was perceived to be rooted in those features. Moreover, while the previous examples present Moore in a way that encourages the reader to focus on her overtly emotive performance style, 'The Expressions of . . .' feature is much more explicit in its intention.

However, some of the article's text foregrounds a fact briefly mentioned in the 'Expressive Eyes' article – Moore's 'fortunate meeting' with director D. W. Griffith. Two sentences about Moore travelling to California two days after telling Griffith of her ambition to act are expanded to two paragraphs. These supposedly directly quote Moore about the opportunities Griffith afforded her, downplaying much of her own carefully executed performance ability. The dominance of language describing Moore's performances as unintentional, attributing them to an 'elusive quality known as temperament' (1 July 1922, 7), further undermines the skill and labour involved in Moore's screen acting style. The visual demonstration of range and skill, whether overtly animated or subtle, is discussed in a manner suggesting that Moore's performances transcend training, into truthful expression, as through what she is portraying are uncensored glimpses of her natural self, rather than a deliberate framing of mediated stills. While this might be thought to query the significance of fan magazines as sites of training, their readership would likely have consisted of

Picture Show, July 1st, 1922.

THE EXPRESSIONS OF COLLEEN MOORE

A BELIEF IN FATE
How Colleen Moore Achieved Her Ambition

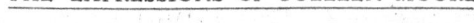

Her happy smile.

Out for revenge.

IF that elusive quality known as temperament counts for anything in cinema acting, then Colleen Moore was born to be a star. She has a grandmother in Kilkenny and another in Edinburgh, and everybody knows that when it comes to temperament you can't beat the Celt.

Colleen does not remember when she first began to act. As a very little girl she was always playing at acting with an audience of one, herself, seen in the big mirror of her mother's bedroom. When she was nine she got all the kiddies in the neighbourhood together and formed a company, with herself as stage manager and star. They gave weekly performances, and Colleen relates how they took buttons at the box office when their patrons had run out of money.

In a recent interview Colleen says:

"I suppose it must have been those early shows that filled me with a burning ambition to be an actress, but I received no encouragement at home. My parents had determined I was to be a musician, and I was trained for a concert pianist. I fought hard for the stage, but the family was too strong, and at the age of fifteen I had given up all hope of rivalling Sarah Bernhardt.

A Fortunate Meeting.

"IN 1916 I graduated from the Detroit Conservatory of Music and went home for a fortnight's holiday, prior to going to Europe to finish my musical education, but right here Fate stepped in and made me what I am to-day, or, at least, put me on the road to a screen career.

"Mother and I went to visit some relatives in Chicago, and one evening at a dinner party we met W. D. Griffith. You can imagine how awed I was in the presence of the great man, for, young as I was, I had heard much about W. D.

"We were introduced, and when I spoke to him all the pent-up aspirations for the life of an actress burst into flood.

"I remember how hard I tried to make an impression on Mr. Griffith, but, looking back on that meeting, I have to smile. He must have thought I was a silly kid.

A Chance.

"THERE was I, a girl of fifteen, trying to talk like a woman of the work world. Fortunately for me, Mr. Griffith did not take me at the valuation I was trying to put on myself. He must have seen that I was not so silly as my talk, for later in the evening he came across to where mother and I were sitting and asked me if I would like to be a cinema actress.

"Naturally, I said it was the one ambition of my young life, but mother was not at all enthusiastic. She told Mr. Griffith that I was much too young to be an actress, and she doubted very much whether I had any talent in that direction.

"'Oh, I think we might make something of her,' said Mr. Griffith kindly. 'Anyway, let me know to-morrow.'

"I have done some pleading in my time, but never did I try to persuade mother against her wish as I did that night. Eventually I managed to convince her that it would do no harm for me to try one picture. Then we had to convince father by wire. That took some time, but we did it, for by this time mother was as enthusiastic as I was. Mother went with me to Los Angeles.

Her Screen Career.

"MY first picture was 'The Bad Boy.' Bobby Harron played in it. I was the *ingénue*. I remained with Mr. Griffith for a year, so I suppose he must have seen something in me. After that I went to Selig, where I got my first real big parts, playing the featured rôles in 'Little Orphan Annie' and 'The Hoosier Romance.'

"Since then I have played with Charles Ray in 'The Busher' and 'The Knock-out Blow.'

"Good luck was right by my side when I was chosen to play in Marshall Neilan's productions for a year. Perhaps you will remember me in 'Dinty' and 'The Lotus Eater.'

"Anyway, if you have seen me, you will have formed your own impression of me, and I will leave it at that."

He Gave It Up.

IT is said that once a bard tried to write a poem to Colleen Moore. The logical lead, thought the poet, would be her eyes. He had seldom seen lovelier, more living orbs. So he began, "Oh, eyes of blue that thrill you through,"—and then he looked at her again. Surely he had been mistaken, Miss Moore's eyes were not blue, but brown. So he made another start, "Brown eyes that seem a poet's dream——"

And then he gave it up—which was just as well, as it would have been a poor poem, anyway, because he discovered, to his dismay, that Colleen's eyes were neither brown nor blue—that is, *one* was blue and one was *brown*—and what's a poet to do in a case like that?

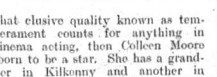

COLLEEN MOORE.

If you want to write to her, address your letter—
COLLEEN MOORE,
c/o "Picture Show,"
Fleetway House,
Farringdon Street,
London, E.C.4.
(*Mention* PICTURE SHOW *to ensure an early reply.*)

Suspicious.   Startled.   Grief.   Enquiry.   Her profile.

Figure 10.4   'The Expressions of Colleen Moore'. *Picture Show*, 1 July 1922. (p. 7) both those who wished to access such acting advice and those who dreamt of fame without effort.

COLLEEN MOORE IN NEWSPAPERS

Having considered how Moore was presented in selected fan magazines during her silent film career, and the distinct design features which supported this representation, it is also interesting to consider the similarities and differences in how she was presented in newspaper publications. Unlike fan magazines, these had less investment in supporting the film industry and its building of stars. Within Moore's scrapbooks, held at the Margaret Herrick Library in Los Angeles, there is a wide variety of publications that has been collected together and which gives a detailed picture of how both her screen acting style and prominent flapper persona were presented within the popular press. These pieces reveal a complex relationship between the detailed examination of Moore's effective performances of emotion and a simultaneous undermining of Moore's expertise as an actress. For example, a clipping taken from the 31 August 1924 edition of the *Los Angeles Examiner* suggests that certain actresses were actually unable to contain or control their natural, truthful, deepest emotions on screen (Figure 10.5). The article implies that, while Moore may be attempting to perform in a style that is

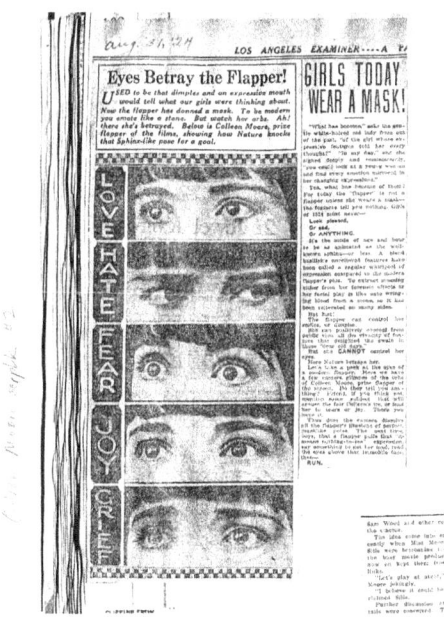

Figure 10.5   *Los Angeles Examiner* newspaper clipping, 31 August 1924.

representative of the carefree, sexually liberated flapper she was most known for, and that audiences would have expected to see, she is in fact being 'betrayed' by her natural emotions. The clipping reads:

> Eyes Betray The Flapper!
> To be modern, you emote like a stone. But watch her orbs. Ah! there she's betrayed. Below is Colleen Moore, prize flapper of the films, showing how Nature knocks that sphinx-like pose for a goal (*Los Angeles Examiner*, 31 August 1924)

Below the text, there is a series of close-up images of Moore's eyes, shown to be depicting Love, Hate, Fear, Joy and Grief. Unlike the row of images in 'The Expressions of . . .' series, the images here are presented in a vertical row, in a style similar to a film strip, with the title of the emotion presented in large letters down the side of the pictures. In terms of the expressions themselves, love is represented as a soft gaze, seemingly focused towards the subject; hate is depicted with furrowed brows, with eyes in opposition to love, fixed away from the subject; fear is demonstrated by wide eyes and raised eyebrows, with the face slightly tilted upwards; joy shows smiling cheeks pushing up the lower eyelids, with softly raised brows; and lastly, grief is shown with brows raised at the centre, eyes angled upwards, with tears welling, reflecting the light. This focus on Moore's expressive performed emotion, as well as the reference to her flapper image, can be read as way of reinforcing the persona Moore was creating throughout her silent film performances. Yet, there is a noticeable difference in the prioritisation of Moore's flapper image in this piece, compared to the focus on performance style offered in the fan magazines. This may be attributed to Moore's appearance in *Flaming Youth* (Dillon 1923) securing her position as an archetypal flapper, so that by 1924 there was a much heavier focus of her typing than evidenced in the earlier fan magazine examples. Nevertheless, the framing of Moore's eyes within this clipping, and the annotations ascribed to them, once again demonstrates a strong parallel with the dominant discourses surrounding screen acting training throughout the 1910s and 1920s, particularly regarding the 'registration of melodrama's primary emotions' (Gledhill 2003, 64). This breaking down and compartmentalisation of particular emotional expression, and the consideration of the impact this might have on viewers, is clearly in line with magazine trends evidenced in the previous examples of Farrar and Moore.

However, what is particularly notable about the newspaper example is the way in which it demonstrates an erasure of Moore's labour and screen craft. The accompanying text to the images of Moore's 'expressive' orbs demonstrates this apparent dichotomy between training and truth. It reads:

> The flapper can control her smiles, or dimples. She can positively conceal from public view all the vivacity of feature that delighted the swain in those dear old days. But she CANNOT control her eyes. Here Nature betrays her ... the camera dissolve[s] all the flappers' illusions of perfect masklike poise. The next time, boys, that a flapper pulls that "it means nothing to me" expression, say something to get her mad, read the eyes above that immobile face then – RUN (*Los Angeles Examiner*, 31 August 1924)

In this extract, Moore is written about as though her striking performances are unintentional. However, despite the language used in the piece, what the images themselves reveal is Moore's skill in performing clearly deliberate and cultivated performances of emotion. In relation to Moore's particular star image, this clipping offers a pertinent example through which it is possible to identify and begin to articulate her unique performance style and understand how she was presented for audiences to consume.

An earlier fan magazine piece helps us to tease out the negotiations noted above between showing Moore acting (posing) and simultaneously denying the skill of this performance, as ways of instilling desire in readers, both for those who wish to train and those who want immediate fame. The July 1917 *Photo-Play Journal* asked,

> Is there an ideal screen face? By this is meant a face which registers the varying human emotions accurately and so impressively that little is left to the imagination.
>
> [. . .]
>
> Such faces as these are extremely rare, and when found are very carefully utilized. Of course a screen actor or actress who has personality in large quantities can be taught by the director to properly register emotions and prove equal to big moments, but, without personality shining through, there is always the evidence of the trained performer. (*Photo-Play Journal*, July 1917, 25)

In this article, skill, training and technique have been overshadowed or undermined by the prioritisation and praise of a perceived natural talent, temperament or personality. The understanding is that, while an actress ought to train in registering emotions, having an 'ideal screen face' means that this training comes secondary to the actress's perceived personality. However, this framing of training and skill as things which must be kept hidden means that examples of highly skilled screen acting end up being framed as evidence of talent: in effect, the labour of training is erased.

Conclusion

The examples within this chapter have revealed a unique use for fan magazines within both performance and film historiography. Examining how stars' faces and bodies are compartmentalised, positioned and captioned within magazines not only helps to support the analysis of an actress's on-screen performances, but is key to understanding dominant performance training practices and processes. *Picture Show*'s 'Expressions of . . .' series provides an invaluable look into how these ideas were disseminated within the popular press, as well as how they developed throughout the silent period. The layout of this feature directly mirrors the formatting of certain actor training manuals that were disseminated during the silent period: presenting clearly labelled images offering informative visual examples of a range of physical manifestations of emotional expression. This feature appeared weekly in the British fan magazine for over six years, recognisable to readers through its consistent design, and easily findable by usually being located in the same place.

I have highlighted how it is possible to garner a deeper understanding of the unique cyclical process of screen acting training in the silent period, and the role of fan magazines within this. This is ably demonstrated by Colleen Moore's autobiographical reminiscences of reading American fan magazines to gain skills in her youth, with the connection to *Picture Show* made clear as Moore was claimed to be a reader in 1920, two years prior to being featured in its 'Expressions of . . .' series.

Looking in detail at Moore, this chapter has demonstrated the different ways in which fan magazines and newspapers contribute to the framing and undermining of skill within screen acting. Superficially the images discussed bear relation to those appearing in acting training manuals. However, in addition to fan magazines serving as potential sites of training for those desiring to be stars, they would inevitably also have been read by those dreaming of fame for themselves, and who were happy to consume information about their favourites' performance exercises as well as images of those favourites themselves. In this way, the magazine articles on actor training would act as lures for the reader, their images providing yet another consumable within the publications, alongside advertisements for products including films, stars and the movies themselves.

Interestingly, as noted, while the images devoted to Moore indicate her skill at adapting her expressions to convey emotion, the texts continually downplay her talent. This is seen even more clearly in the dismissive language of the newspaper clipping, which had less of a stake in supporting the film industry and its building of stars. Despite this occasionally trivialising text, however, the images aid us by offering key evidence of the attention Moore paid to certain aspects of her body, especially the framing of her face. This suggests that by exploring screen acting alongside magazine representations of a star's image, it is possible to begin bridging the gap in writings which have failed to consider the intricacies of certain performance styles and idiosyncrasies of different performers.

Returning to the example of Moore's 'betraying eyes', it might therefore be useful to identify the lens through which this representation is being constructed, in order to reframe how her performances of emotional expression are presented and written about. The embodiment of sexual liberation and excess, the flapper is an image Moore would have consumed in the cinema, through other women's representations on set, as well as in the carefully constructed formatting of magazines. Yet, as highlighted in the clippings, throughout various performances Moore is perceived to be representing this persona in a way that does not necessarily conform to the flapper trope. Moore is positioned as offering something different through the expression in her eyes. But her performances are neither unruly nor unintentional. From joy to grief, the stills demonstrate Moore's ability to perform a complex layering of emotion, drawing on a combination of skilfully employed performance techniques, developed throughout her career as a film actress. Moreover, concentrating on the performances of stars such as Moore, it is possible to build effectively upon the wealth of feminist Star Studies scholarship undertaken by academics such as Desjardins, Basinger, Negra and Ross, which acknowledges the importance of these developing representations of women during the silent era and of incorporating a performance-centric perspective within feminist film historiography.

Note

1. I acknowledge that articles allegedly penned by actors were often, in fact, written by staff on the magazine or newspaper in which a piece appeared, or by those within a studio's marketing department. At this distance it is highly unlikely we will ever know for sure.

References

Anon. 1917. 'In the Case of Personality Versus Beauty, the Former Wins'. *Photo-Play Journal*, July: 25, 49.
Anon. 1919. 'Mae Marsh – Some of Her "Thousand Expressions"'. *Picture Show*, 10 May: 13.
Anon. 1920. 'Famous Readers of the *Picture Show*, no. 33 – Colleen Moore'. *Picture Show*, 28 August: 3.
Anon. 1921. 'The Expressions of Geraldine Farrar'. *Picture Show*, 16 April: 9.
Anon. 1921. 'The Expressions of George Walsh'. *Picture Show*, 21 May: 7.
Anon. 1921. 'The Expressions of Harry Houdini'. *Picture Show*, 16 July: 7.
Anon. 1921. 'Colleen Moore – The Film Star with Expressive Eyes'. *Picture Show*, 26 November: 7.
Anon. 1921. 'The Expressions of Earle Williams'. *Picture Show*, 17 December: 9.
Anon. 1922. 'Colleen Moore as Impersonator'. *Picture Show*, 4 March: 21.
Anon. 1922. 'The Expressions of Colleen Moore'. *Picture Show*, 1 July: 7.

Anon. 1924. *Los Angeles Examiner*. [Magazine Clipping dated 31 August 1924]. Scrapbook no 2., *Colleen Moore Scrapbooks, 1921–1936*, File ID 71424681, Los Angeles, CA: Margaret Herrick Library.
Anselmo Sequeira, Diana. 2015. 'Screen-Struck: The Invention of the Movie Girl Fan'. *Cinema Journal* 55 (1): 1–28.
Basinger, Jeanine. 2000. *Silent Stars*. Hanover, NH: Wesleyan University Press.
Bernique, Jean. 1916. *Motion Picture Acting for Professionals and Amateurs*. Chicago, IL: Producers Service Company.
Brewster, Ben, and Lea Jacobs. 1997. *Theatre to Cinema: Stage Pictorialism and the Early Feature Film*. Oxford: Oxford University Press.
Desjardins, Mary. 2010. 'An appetite for living: Gloria Swanson, Colleen Moore, and Clara Bow'. In *Idols of Modernity: Film Stars of the 1920s*, edited by Patrice Petro, 108–36. New Brunswick, NJ and London: Rutgers University Press.
Fletcher, Pamela. 2009. '"To Wipe a Manly Tear": The Aesthetics of Emotion in Victorian Narrative Painting'. *Victorian Studies* 52 (3): 457–69.
Fuller, Kathryn. 1996. *At the Picture Show: Small Town Audiences and the Invention of Movie Fan Culture*. Washington and London: Smithsonian Institution Press.
Gledhill, Christine. 2003. *Reframing British Cinema 1918–1928: Between Restraint and Passion*. London: BFI.
Grodal, Torben. 1997. *Moving Pictures: A New Theory of Film Genres, Feelings, and Cognition*. Oxford: Clarendon Press.
'Mersereau, Violet'. 1918. 'How to Act'. *Picture Play*, March: 69–74.
Moore, Colleen. 1968. *Silent Star*. Garden City, NY: Doubleday.
Negra, Diane. 2001. *Off-white Hollywood: American Culture and Ethnic Female Stardom*. London and New York: Routledge.
O'Rourke, Chris. 2014. '"On the First Rung of the Ladder of Fame": Would-Be Cinema Stars in Silent-Era Britain'. *Film History: An International Journal* 26 (3): 84–105.
O'Rourke, Chris. 2017. *Acting for the Silent Screen: Film Actors and Aspiration Between the Wars*. London: Bloomsbury Publishing.
Pearson, Roberta. 1992. *Eloquent Gestures*. Berkeley: University of California Press.
Pickford, Mary. 1920. *Cinema Acting as a Profession: How to Act for the Screen*. London: The Standard Art Book Co.
Ramsey, Walter. 1931. 'The True Story of Norma Shearer'. *Modern Screen*, August: 43, 111.
Ross, Sara. 2010. 'Screening the Modern Girl: Intermediality in the Adaptation of *Flaming Youth*'. *Modernism/Modernity* 17 (2): 271–90.
Schechner, Richard. 2006. *Performance Studies: An Introduction*. 2nd edition. New York and London: Routledge.
Stamp, Shelley. 2000. *Movie-Struck Girls: Women and Motion Picture Culture after the Nickelodeon*. Princeton, NJ: Princeton University Press.
Stead, Lisa. 2017. '"Dear Cinema Girls": Girlhood, Picturegoing and the Interwar Film Magazine'. In *Women's Periodicals and Print Culture in Britain, 1918–1939: The Interwar Period*, edited by Catherine Clay, Maria DiCenzo, Barbara Green and Fiona Hackney, 103–20. Edinburgh: Edinburgh University Press.
Stenn, David. 2000. *Clara Bow: Runnin' Wild*. New York: Cooper Square Press.

11. CONTEXT, CONTENT AND FORM IN 1940S BRITISH FILM STAR FAN CLUB PUBLICATIONS

Ellen Wright and Phyll Smith

'I was very disappointed', says Jean Kent, in the July/August 1949 issue of her fan club magazine, 'to miss the Film Garden Party, and I'm afraid some of you must have been disappointed too. I had been looking forward to meeting our Club Members there'. This is one of many 'I'm sorry's, 'I hope we can's' and 'I'll see you when's' that pepper these magazines, which are not only couched in the friendly but formal vernacular of correspondence and appointment-making, but which also form a regular dialogue between stars and fans, and fans and stars, within their pages. In this discourse with her filmgoing fans, the fact that Kent was derailed from the said appointment by last-minute filming responsibilities is secondary to the primary relationship she has with her followers, which is conducted not through the public screen but through the personal missives of the club. This edition of the section 'Jean's Letter to You' ends with 'I must toddle off and post this to the printers', underlining the imperative of catching the post, which ended so much correspondence of the pre-digital age.

This column, and Kent's club more broadly, are indicative of a distinctive film star fan club culture that emerged in Britain in the mid-to-late 1940s. This was a culture in which the fan club functioned as a form of social life both real and imaginary, including appointments with the stars both figurative and literal, which can be traced through the magazines which formed the organs of these clubs (Figure 11.1). Just as the design, form and function of these magazines shaped their central star's image and fandom, so the material, social and economic conditions of their production shaped the content

Figure 11.1 Scale in centimetres. A comparative view of several issues of *The International Jean Kent Fan Club Magazine*.

and physical formats of this unique collection of studio-sanctioned bulletins. Reciprocally, the design of these fan- or star-produced magazines provided new and distinctive opportunities for agency on the part of stars and fans alike, including for Rank studio actors such as Jean Kent, Patricia Roc, Anne Crawford and Richard Attenborough.

Despite their ephemeral status, especially given the poor quality of the paper they were printed on, the miniature sizing of many of the issues, and the period of austerity in which they were produced and distributed, these resources warrant consideration because they provide us with valuable historic examples of visible and 'invisible' star and fan labour and personal brand-building in a socio-industrial context decades before social media celebrity culture. (For further work in this area, see Lueck 2015; Marshall 2010; Marwick 2013) In doing so, they enable us to elucidate the British postwar film star system (in as much as there was one), and to investigate the lives and complex, differentiated culture of British postwar film fans, while, most importantly in the context of this book, also demonstrating how socio-cultural, industrial and economic factors shaped form and convention, providing a means of placing these stars, fans, organisations and this labour into their historical context.

As we have outlined elsewhere (Wright and Smith 2021), these fan clubs were established in response to an assumption, held by the British film industry and its stars themselves, that they were following a successful American model of stardom. This is a model that Edgar Morin ([1957] 1960) suggested was typical of European/US star promotion practices in the mid-1950s, whereby fan clubs were regularly employed as a means of facilitating the desire/worship of literal screen gods/goddesses. This notion forms a useful metaphor for fan devotion and the star economy, but is also one based upon a model rarely used in the US fan and industry press itself, and which was more the invention of studio press offices than reflective of the typical behaviour of US studios, stars or clubs. Here, then, we draw upon Morin's work, not as a methodological exemplar, but to highlight what we believe was the impact of his assumptions regarding US clubs.

This includes the influence these assumptions had on subsequent academic work, perhaps most notably Richard Dyer's *Stars* (1979, 9), which builds upon some of the 'givens' around film stars and their fan clubs found in Morin's 1950s desire/devotion model. While Dyer is indebted to Morin's model of an economy of stardom, he disregards some of the metaphoric structures that support his thesis (see 1979, 21, 51–2), though many of these have resonance for/with models of structuring fan desire and the affective purpose of DIY fan offerings, or the personalised or handmade labour/intervention of the stars. At the same time, Dyer accepts many of the elements presented as 'factual' which without much evidence have become received truths as a result, and which misplace the role of the fan club magazine entirely (1979, 68). Placing these (mis)conceptions in relation to a handful of British film stars of that time, alongside their fan followings, exposes where the mechanisms of fan desire and star agency which Morin claimed the fan club performed were mere myths or exceptions, and where they aligned with a temporary reality.

Through the example of these magazines, we will, in this chapter, not only consider the form and function, social and industrial contexts of the British film star fan club publication, but also highlight the interconnected relationship between star fans, star capital and the stars themselves. In this way, we will examine the labour involved in these publications, much of which was undertaken by the stars themselves with a view to increasing their value in the star marketplace, or what we refer to here and in previous work as their star capital.[1]

The Rise of the Film Star Fan Club and the Fan Club Bulletin

While the types of publications we discuss here were part of a uniquely British and 1940s trend, and can therefore be dated exactly, it is more difficult to pin down when and where fan clubs first became a phenomenon, and which models influenced their development. However, moments at which the British industry identified these clubs as potentially large enough to be economically important are easier to find. The UK *Kine Year Book*, for example, included a 'fan club' section in its 1939 edition, and by the decade's end these clubs were so popular that studios ignored them at their cost. As *The Year's Work in the Film, 1949* sniffily observed, they charged:

> about four shillings a year for the privilege of receiving a photograph and regular printed gossip from the favourite star. Nearly all stars have such clubs, and the average membership is about 4,000. But that for Jean Kent, started four years ago, now has 25,000 members, and the International Jean Kent Fan Club Magazine thus has a circulation which begins to rival that of serious journals such as [current affairs magazine] the *Spectator*. (Rotha and Manvell 1949, 64)

The precarious materiality of these items – particularly the diminutive size, low resolution and poor archival qualities of the UK magazines – is therefore certainly not indicative of a lowly nature beyond their physical formats. Indeed, Alan Jenkins, (1977, 117) notes that 'Fan clubs became big business (Jean Kent's was the first, and, with more than twenty-five thousand members, the biggest)'. Nonetheless, these publications have, until recently, largely escaped academic interest, despite the fascinating historic counterpoint they provide to the Internet and social media as examples of the most current media of their times, used synergistically for star/fan interaction and for the building of a coherent, appealing and saleable media personality. Indeed, such publications were items of personal import and the result of considerable labour, which exemplified a source of capital for fans as well as stars – a source of economic capital, sometimes real, sometimes presumed, but certainly also of social capital for both, and of a kind of symbolic capital on which both star and fan could trade.

While the economically and industrially marginal nature of these publications differentiates their design 'professionalism' within the larger field of British magazine production, the socio-industrial conditions of the time tempered this, and their 'homemade' design factors dovetailed both with a culture of make-do-and-mend and austerity, and with a DIY 'personal touch' which the Rank studios in particular encouraged and certain stars and their fan clubs sought to foster.

THE FUNCTION OF FILM STAR FAN CLUB MAGAZINES

> Fan clubs are the chapels in which particular passions are raised to a frenzy. The idol periodically comes to sanctify her club, revealing to it new aspects of her private-public life, of her cinematic activities. She answers the questions that are fired at her, she sings, dances, organises some collective excursion... The clubs' resources, like those of churches, are expended in part on charitable works, in part on the propagation of the faith. (Morin [1957] 1960, 72)

In terms of Rank's impetus for encouraging their stars to establish fan clubs and produce regular bulletins, Sarah Street notes that the postwar 'Rank Publicity Department was bombarded with requests for photographs of stars and for guest appearances', (1997, 134) which fan clubs were expected to be able to respond to. As an example, the *British Film and Television Year Book: 1949–1950* observed that 'the Patricia Roc and Margaret Lockwood fan clubs are run by the J. Arthur Rank Organisation... [and] handle more than 30,000 fan letters a week', while 'top ranking stars [responded to] four or five hundred of these letters weekly'. Similarly, the Anne Crawford fan club, and its bulletin, it was claimed, were created as a method of getting fans to sift and respond to her fan mail at a time when the war meant a shortage of clerical staff, while 'keeping the letters under [Crawford's] control' and marshalling the resources and opinions of 'these postal partisans who wield such influence in shaping the policies of the studios' (Alexander 1950, 71).

Regarding the stars' own motivations for producing these publications, Morin's work offers several pertinent observations. Firstly, he defines the promotional trappings of stardom, or more specifically of media celebrity, which emerged in the period of industrial consolidation of the American studio system.

These include the star photograph, the fan club, the movie magazine and the fan letter, all of which are features of the star system, which he defines as the period of commodification of the star as an economic unit, above and beyond their individual performances. In doing this, Morin suggests a series of functions that fan clubs offer for stars and their studios, but does so with little evidence; his arguments here appear based upon a couple of examples and largely depend upon supposed truths unhesitatingly received largely from the press and the Hollywood studios themselves. He then defines these functions according to his overall divine metaphor where stars are '*[w]orshipped* as heroes, *divinized*, the stars are more than objects of admiration. They are also subjects of a *cult*. A *religion* in embryo has formed around them' (our emphasis) ([1957] 1960, 71). Here, divinity is a transaction as part of an economy of followers and prayers; the stars are discussed as gods and goddesses, fandom as a religious cult with the fan club as the chapel, the place where believers commune, while the fan club magazine institutionalises this adoration of the fan ([1957] 1960, 75). The star then becomes a 'worshipped' product within a broader film economy, and engagement with them and with other fans becomes a form of social currency.

Most importantly, throughout his book, Morin unhesitatingly discusses fandom, engagement and devotion as indexes of a star's success, and of their accumulating value within the larger star economy. To extend his religious metaphor further, just as a god needs believers, so a star needs fans. It is not surprising, then, that following this US model, the British studios expected that 'British would-be stars . . . [would] *behave* like stars. They toured the country, attended beauty contests, film premieres and civic events and created an aura of British stardom which was popular with the public' (Street 1997, 134), all with a view to generating a following.

While it is not incorrect to say that in the star economy, fans can be equated with relevance and relevance can be equated with increased value, Morin overlooks here the considerable additional, uncredited, labour required on the part of the star and, where they delegated, their family, friends and fans, which nurtured and then managed that considerable evidence of fandom and success. In this sense, while Dyer (1979, 102–3) sees 'Morin's gods-to-mortals shift in the stars as an aspect of the cinema's embourgeoisement', it comes ironically at the cost of the star's own labour and trade – a process of (hidden) de-embourgeoisement.

In the British industry, at least, the glamorous aura of celebrity and cultural significance surrounding a star, far from being natural and effortless (as audiences were encouraged to assume), or being furnished and funded by specialist departments at the studios, was in fact built on concealed star (and fan) labour. In addition to this, as Rank consolidated British production and distribution, it effectively developed a monopoly; this meant that performers who did not successfully fulfil this obligation to 'behave like stars' threatened their prospects of future work. Just as today's neoliberal celebrity subject is compelled to undertake relentless work on their 'selves' and develop a brand identity, to differentiate themselves within the celebrity marketplace, so was the British film star expected to perform very similar labour, some eight decades previously.

This star labour was also significant in terms of providing an incentive for fans to engage with, and even help produce, fan bulletins, and the analogy of the archaeologist finding the fingerprints of the potter in the slip of an ancient pot is a pertinent one here. After all, such a revelation of the process of (home-made/handmade) production adds to the effect of being close to the producer, who in many of these cases was the object of the fans' affections themselves. As Samantha Barbas's work on US film fans demonstrates, clubs were 'formed [by fans] not only to boost' a favoured performer, but also often 'to provide a closer contact with the star than is possible through ordinary channels of newspaper and magazine publicity' (2001, 124).

Barbas also highlights the studios' reflexive use of fans and fan club persuasions when developing subsequent 'product' (be that films or stars), as well as the attempted use of the perceived power of fan clubs in these instances by the stars themselves, in order to achieve greater agency in their career choices, as well as the further development of their star image and financial value (2001, 124). Demonstrating this, Jean Kent repeatedly used her magazine to urge fans to nominate her for the annual *Daily Mail* Film Award and thus raise her profile:

> The voting for the Daily Mail Film Award takes place this month, I don't know who you intend to vote for but – let me whisper it – I should love you to vote for me. So please tell your family! Tell your friends! Tell the world!!! (February 1949, 2)

while Anne Crawford observed to her fans that:

> The publication of this souvenir book gives me an opportunity which I have long wanted of publicly expressing my sincere thanks to the many thousands who have written me such wonderful letters. Screen artistes like myself have not the advantages enjoyed by actors and actresses who, by audience reaction, are able to alter each performance at will. Therefore, the letters which you write are of invaluable assistance; they not only enable me to judge whether or not you liked my performance in a particular picture, but also provide a reliable guide as to current trends of cinema audiences. (November/December 1947, 4)

The actions of US film stars and their fan clubs, as evidenced through their publications, while admittedly subject to broader contextual factors, were nevertheless deliberate, intentional and self-conscious but they were no more straightforward than they were under the control of the studios. In the case of the British industry, its stars and their fan clubs, this lack of a straightforward relationship is even more apparent.

The Bigger Picture of Magazine Design

If we consider these broader contextual factors, there are two further sets of relations governing the design of the 1940s film star fan club magazines (see Figure 11.2 for further examples) that also warrant discussion. Firstly, the way in which industrial context regulated the form of the magazine (their design and materiality), and, secondly, the way in which the magazines' resulting forms regulated their content. Roughly these equate to Karl Marx's notion that 'the nature of individuals [their economy and intercourse] prevail only when the material conditions determining their production allow' (Marx and Engels [1846] 1974, 42–3) so that 'new relations of production never appear before the material conditions of their existence have matured' ([1859] 1968, 182) and so 'the mode of production of material life conditions the social, political and intellectual life' (181). This can also be reframed in terms of Pierre Bourdieu's notion of cultural distinction, the habitus – whereby the contextual habitat shapes the behavioural habit (2019, 122).

Conditions for fan clubs and their magazines had been fairly similar in Britain and the US in the 1930s, with the one key difference: while British clubs were split between US and native stars, in the US, predominantly Hollywood stars had active clubs. Many of these 'clubs' had no magazines, newsletters or regular organ, but either offered little more than the opportunity to buy a badge or membership to denote one's fandom, or were essentially single-interest pen pal lists, with larger clubs allowing those with multiple members in a town or city to meet up in local clubs or chapters. However, as noted above, publications did exist for some clubs even at this earlier time.

During the 1940s, another major difference between the context in which US and British fan clubs and their magazines operated surfaced, and this was connected to industrial conditions such as wartime paper rationing. This significantly affected social practices linked to the British magazine sector, including readers' expectations of what magazines might look and feel like. A series of increasingly strict Control of Paper orders reduced UK publishers' supplies of paper (by weight) by 40 per cent in early 1940, with further restrictions as the war continued. While large-circulation magazines with powerful corporate owners had an economy of scale and could leverage their wealth, influence and market share to acquire more paper than others, moving their paper allocation between titles in their stables, smaller independent publishers and niche, specialist titles in larger houses had to adopt different strategies to survive, while

CONTEXT, CONTENT AND FORM

Figure 11.2   Scale in centimetres. A comparative view of several other fan club magazines, devoted to stars Richard Attenborough, Patricia Roc, Michael Rennie and John Mills.

the reduced supply based on a precedent model effectively blocked new producers from entering the market at all. As a result, firstly, paper became thinner across almost all publications, while the percentage of recycled paper used increased, and so the quality of the paper decreased. British 'War Economy Paper' tore easily, discoloured quickly, and became friable, brittle and foxed. Bindings of paperbacks (their wrappers rapidly becoming more like paper than card) quickly became unstable with the degrading of the paper substrate against glued bindings, and as animal glues became expensive, metal staple bindings, using the cheapest steels, rusted quickly in the oxidising acid-bleached paper. For magazines, with the expectation of ephemerality, these pressures and problems were doubly significant.

At the beginning of the Second World War, British publishers began preparing for restrictions by culling fading or unreliable titles (such as *Boy's Cinema*), and merging competing titles into single, stronger ones (such as Amalgamated Press's *Film Pictorial* and *Picture Show*, and Odham's *Picturegoer* and *Film Weekly*), and as restrictions increased, the number of pages per issue decreased, with paper saved from shrunken unprofitable magazines allowing the 'big' titles to retain the same page format with reduced pagination. Small-circulation publications, on the other hand, commonly became physically smaller, not just in page numbers but paper size too (*Labour Monthly*, for example, shrank from 68 pages at 9.5x6.5cm to 20 pages at 5.5x4cm). Across all of these titles, a cramped style of tiny print became the norm.

By the end of the war, those wishing to start magazines, such as fan clubs – even before issues of distribution and sales – had to seek permission from the Board of Trade to begin a new title and then needed to find a supply of paper from an independent printer with paper supply capacity. Once established, they had to maintain that paper supply, which in the independent sector might go to a higher bidder from month to month, and any increase in circulation might require renegotiations of contracts or the requisitioning of a new printer with greater supplies (making occasional or one-off publications more viable than serials). These kinds of supply issues were directly referred to by Jean Kent in June 1947:

> First of all, I would like to know how the magazines are arriving. That is, are they in good condition when they reach you; if they are we shall be able to continue to send them out like this indefinitely, as the anxiety of getting envelopes is an awful strain, also my staff say they can get prepared much earlier, so that when the mag. arrives it can be sent out quicker.
>
> The wrapping is done by the printer and the labels by us, so all we have to do is stick them on. This takes us about five days, but the postman calls every day and takes away about 5,000 until we have finished. Last month – I mean April month – it took nearly three weeks to get

them all out, as they came in only as fast as the printer could get the paper, and you all know just how short paper has been since the fuel cut. However, we hope things will brighten up soon. (2)

At the same time, these publications had a readership whose expectations had been systematically eroded over the war period, whose focus was likely more on content than presentation, who did not experience a pocket-sized magazine with just a few pages as anything out of the ordinary, and who would have been appreciative of any small concession to quality – photographs, colour, glossy stock – amid the late 1940s austerity. Indeed, the May/June 1949 issue of Patricia Roc's club magazine pleaded with readers to help justify the size of their publication by increasing the membership and demonstrating demand:

> HELP your friends to join the Patricia Roc International Fan Club. HELP to keep our magazine the biggest film star magazine in the country . . . We want to keep it this size but can only do so with your help. HELP TO KEEP OUR MAGAZINE TWELVE PAGES EVERY ISSUE. (Emphasis in original) (1949, 11)

The discourse in these publications reveals a tension, then, between the available resources and the desire to produce something as professionally as possible, as befits an 'official' publication, but without the benefit of experienced staff or the economies of industrial scale. In the US, fan club magazines were mimeographed as standard and required hand-drawn images which contributed to a DIY feel that was distinctly 'unofficial'. However, in the UK, a diminutive but print-set magazine, produced amid a context of make-do-and-mend and the war effort, made the homemade and homely nature of the British magazines chime with the zeitgeist, and where the means of production and the labour inherent in it were visible, this allowed for a sense of closeness and sympathetic process of mediating and resisting austerity alongside the star and fellow club members. Through the design constraints and contingency of austerity, and the common experiences of deprivation and make-do-and-mend, 1940s fan club magazines reproduced the same desire bond which Teal Triggs identifies in punk fanzine communities in the 1970s in a 'graphic language' of resistance. This is 'a visual system incorporating not only image-based symbols but also a typographic language' (Triggs 2006, 73). Additionally, the 'way in which graphic language is depicted will add value to its intended meaning' (73).

However, as immediate austerity receded and with the gradual easing and then removal of most paper control restrictions in 1949, large publishing corporations quickly took advantage of their economies of scale to make those accepted wartime standards seem redundant, cheap and unprofessional. What we witness during this short window, then, is a distinctively dynamic decade of ancillary film industry production in which the economic conditions were ideal for the British film star fan club magazines not only to flourish but to compete effectively with larger publishers.

Magazine Function Dictates Form

As we have discussed elsewhere (Smith and Wright 2020), just like in the US, British stars did find ways of negotiating how much the club would impinge upon their time, drawing boundaries for their involvement and the intrusion into their personal lives. This meant that the aforementioned sense of closeness evoked within these fan club magazines often involved the fan running the club as much as it did the star. Nonetheless, the purposeful outsourcing of promotional labour to stars by the British studios in the 1940s created a specific and complicated context, within which some stars sought strategies of intrusion limitation, but others balanced this with the benefits of controlling their own image, and of being able to gauge and mobilise public opinion in the limited sense of their membership.

Obviously, the limitations on the star's time also dictated a magazine's form and content, and given that most British stars produced or were party to the production of a large quantity of the additional content in their club publications, the result was an association between content and star that was sometimes tangential and far from glitzy or juicy. For example, the March/April 1949 edition of Richard Attenborough's club magazine features a spectacularly unrevelatory interview with his housekeeper (Williams 1949, 4), while Kent's fans are treated to stories of travel sickness (July/August 1949, 5) and the purchase of a new sow she named Diana, with an 'annoying habit of getting out of her sty' (November/December 1949, 5).

In US clubs, on the other hand, star input was often limited to a single letter from the central star, while the club president formed a locus of attention and admiration as intermediary between the star and the fan, second only to the star themselves. These magazines had the president and their travails on behalf of the club at hand to fall back on when copy was thin, with this president also representing an 'ordinary' figure to whom readers could relate. Despite the greater star labour involved in the British context, a variation on the US technique was also occasionally employed in Britain: Anne Crawford turned to her secretary Marie, who ultimately became the dominant personality of Crawford's club publication; Jean Kent enlisted the help of 'Honorary Member' Sybil Bailey as her membership secretary when that roster became unmanageable; and Richard Attenborough observed that:

> to help deal with the mountains of fan mail, I'd persuaded Arthur Goodbourne, a school friend from Leicester, to act as my secretary . . . It was

Arthur who founded the Richard Attenborough Fan Club and produced its quarterly magazine which, at one time, had over 1,500 subscribers. (2008, 148)

Elsewhere, Kent's husband, Yusef, frequently helped her with magazine content and, when Kent was ill with acute appendicitis, her mother stepped into the breach mid-edition:

> I hope you will forgive me for not writing my 'Candid Column' and 'Jean looks back' but I just cannot concentrate; this morning when I felt one of my attacks coming on, I took the tablets the doctor gave me to try and carry on, but they knocked me out instead. So here I am in bed, waiting for the doctor to come and put me right, I hope ... the letter broke off here and this is Jean's mother trying to fill in the gap. (August 1947, 2)

Nonetheless, despite these occasional contributions by others connected to the central star, question-and-answer articles and correspondence columns such as 'My Dear Pat' in *The Patricia Roc International Fan Club Magazine* or 'Between You and Me' and 'Replies to Members' in the *International Jean Kent Fan Club Magazine* filled ample space while offering fans the chance, seemingly, to converse directly with their idol, while general updates such as 'A Message from Anne' and 'A Glimpse into Anne's Diary' in the *Anne Crawford Bulletin*, Patricia Roc's 'Letter from Pat' and 'Dear friends', or Jean Kent's 'Jean's Letter to You' and 'Kent's Candid Column' offered tantalisingly intimate insights into the star's personal and professional life. Again, these often were domestic, homely and commonplace, including notes on gardening (Kent May/June 1950, 5), cooking (Kent March 1949, 8–9), beauty regimens (Roc October 1948, 6), or homemaking (Kent March 1947, 3), as well as the 'chores' of being a star (Roc May/June 1949, 7), or of magazine production.[2]

This provided both a sense of familiarity with the star and made a virtue of the mundanity of some of the star's contributions, in terms of what might now be labelled 'relatability' – a framing perhaps more suited to some stars than others.[3] In this sense, the stars' fan club magazines were, essentially, the star's zines, and the fan club organisation a demonstrable 'family firm' / 'cottage industry', with the star putting both their family and cottage, as well as their work on behalf of the fan, very much on show. There is a symbiosis of industrial conditions causing necessary limitations, and a type of personal contact which, charming at any time, was perhaps particularly embraced in this austere postwar setting.

After all, even when publications were coordinated by or mediated through a professional secretary (as was the case for Crawford and Attenborough), the likelihood of these individuals also being an experienced editor, copy setter or layout designer was limited and, as such, publications still retained their amateurish appearance, as well as their emphasis on an appeal of equals, in the stories of overcoming hardships and restrictions to get the magazine out. What was then important for British stars running their own clubs was a particular, context-specific definition of professionalism that kept them competitive with other small magazines of the period, even when they didn't have the advantages of other established publishers.

One of the markers of this professionalism was continuity. As one of the first and longest-running of this period, Kent's fan club magazine went through various travails, discussed within the magazine itself; this included its struggles to maintain a consistent size and colour, but also the shortages involved, frequently mentioned by Kent and other stars to their readers, as well as the tedium and stress of magazine organisation. Some editions were deliberately 'double' issues (annually at Christmas, allowing time off and avoiding confusion with Christmas post), twice the regular page size and with an increased number of pages, presented as a 'bonus' to readers rather than a time- or stress-saving measure for the producer. The booklet sizes also varied on other occasions, however, for example as paper stock shifted and Kent was forced to chop and change between different printers.

The magazines had a simple visual house style, with single colour printing – blue on white and a two-colour outer cover of red and blue – and, for the first few years, a design virtue was made of economic necessity, with each cover featuring a monochrome photograph in blue, with red livery. However, 1947 paper shortages led to a scramble for print stock, and resulted in one issue being printed on orange, while another issue came in a variety of stocks including cream and pink. In late 1948, a jazzier colour cover format was introduced as these processes became available and cheaper once again (though not stretching to separation printing for colour photography – just the decorative illusion of colour), before being reined in again in 1949, initially for a cheaper, revamped two-colour cover, and in 1950 returning to black and white. At this time, the magazine also began publishing a double issue every two months rather than monthly, in order to compete with the retooled magazine industry while remaining economically viable.

The design of other magazines follows strikingly similar patterns. Michael Rennie's club magazine has the same small booklet formation and similar glossy stock as Kent's, periodically sharing the same printers (clearly stars followed each other's example when reliable suppliers were found). Anne Crawford's publication also began with similar glossy paper stock but switched in 1947 for the more readily available and cheaper black-and-white newsprint, allowing a larger page size. Similarly, John Mills's club magazine *Footlights* had a glossy cover, with newsprint interior. Meanwhile, later arrivals, such as Richard

Attenborough's and Patricia Roc's magazines, were printed at larger size but on thinner matte stock, but with fine (usually black and one colour) printing. Attenborough's magazine developed a house style through a cover design palette of only grey cover photographs with blue tooling and backgrounds and monochrome interior.

Despite Dyer's (1979, 68) assertion that (primarily American) fan club publications '[were] largely controlled by the studios', control – and function – of the British clubs was in the hands of the stars themselves. While the clubs and their magazines were encouraged and to some extent supported by Rank, Gainsborough or the star's agent, on a practical level, it was the star and their household who took charge, and the agency they exerted through them, as well as the communities they forged and the uses to which they sought to put that fandom and its energy and desires, are reflected in the designs of these magazines. In the absence of studio writers and compositors, fans, too, were able to channel content and influence design according to their own desires and needs.

The End of an Era

However, just as this window of material conditions opened to allow this fandom to flourish and these magazines to be produced, it closed again just as quickly. With the easing of austerity and the end of legislated paper control restrictions in 1949, mainstream magazines reverted back to larger sizes, featuring more pages and more colour printing, with any available paper going to the highest and most powerful bidder, rather than following an equitable distribution according to need. In these various races – of adapting to changing industry standards and reader expectations, of having the economies of scale to barter for resource, and of remaining financially viable at a larger scale – both physically and circulation-wise, British film star fan club bulletins were left behind by the established cinema papers and the many new entrants to the market, and those clubs with larger circulations were likely over-exposed financially by those circulation requirements when it came to increased overheads.

This loss was compounded by Rank's withdrawal of its support, such as it was, in terms of secretarial and organisational assistance, publicity materials and motivation. While Rank was in its integrating, monopolising ascendancy, it had pushed stars to take on their own publicity, applying pressure through models such as its Charm School[4] and keeping a roster of players who had to vie for key roles – but with the government's failure to support the film industry directly, Rank found itself financially over-extended and over-exposed in a ruthless market. Production reduced drastically, studios were mothballed, the

Charm School and star promotion departments were closed, contract players let go, and those who could retreated to the US for regular work. In 1952, Rank's biographer, Alan Wood, described the failure of protectionism and state support as 'Socialism by halves' (261), and in her final fan club magazine Kent was equally as blunt:

> It is sad to hear of film productions being postponed and studios closing down, and so many skilled technicians being out of work. I don't think the cinema audience quite realise how the film business is being crushed by taxation ... It is killing the British film industry and it is really a wonder that it has survived at all. Last year the Entertainment Tax took £38,000,000 from the British cinemas. That would have given plenty of employment to the staffs at all the studios and made quite a lot of good pictures too. Fans often ask: 'why are the stars deserting us and going to Hollywood, and why are they leaving films and going on the stage?' Well, perhaps this is a little explanation. The stars are not really leaving films – it is the films leaving them. (May/June 1950, 2)

In conclusion, the UK fan clubs emerged at a specific time when conditions enabled them to compete. At this time, they were a distinct and peculiar expression of both star/fan interaction and of star control of their image and career, allowing the stars to utilise the perceived economic value of their fans' symbolic capital to accumulate agency, while being, in part, supported by their studios. This phenomenon would reappear in a slightly different form in the 1990s when fan clubs organised by promotional agencies became the de rigueur tool for pop stars and their record labels who would seek to mobilise their fanbase at key times to 'boost' their records and appearances to motivate a wider public attention (other examples of stars, studios and labels looking to harness an economic value of fandom surely exist periodically everywhere). The 1940s fan clubs and their magazines form a bridge between these examples and the US fan club 'fanzines' of the 1930–1950s.

However, as much as the UK fan club magazines borrowed and adapted forms their producers believed existed in the US, they also managed to innovate and thrive, achieving traction and agency for stars and genuine communities for fans, with a tangible connection to their patrons, in ways which the American clubs may have frequently affected but in reality did not achieve. Despite their ephemerality, these unique British publications were by no means a poor man's version of the Hollywood model; both bounded and liberated by different constraints in the UK context, in terms of quality and professionalism, star content and contact, circulation and scope, they exceeded the imagined model they aspired to, if only for a while.

Notes

1. Here, where we discuss star capital, we borrow both from Karl Marx's notion of capital, or the accumulated wealth or value embodied in the means of production or that is potentially available, with which surplus value can be generated, as well as from Pierre Bourdieu's notions of cultural and social capital, namely what Beverley Skeggs (1997, 16) succinctly terms as a form of power that 'enables bodies to move in social space' and exists in various embodied forms. Based on these principles, we want to draw attention to how a small handful of British stars developed their worth or value in the broader star economy through sustained engagement with and development of their fan clubs using fan club bulletins.
2. For example, in the July 1946 edition of her magazine, Kent reflects that establishing and running a fan club magazine 'was not easy. There were difficulties and shortage of all supplies, paper, photos, envelopes, boards, and particularly printing . . . twice the printing has been lost or mislaid on the railway' (7).
3. As Geoffrey Macnab (1993, 100) notes, stars such as Roc were 'sold' to British audiences as unique and yet still inherently 'ordinary' due to the austere and moralising media context of their home market.
4. Established in 1945, the Rank Charm School was essentially an apprenticeship scheme for promising stars where they were taught to act on stage and screen, but also taught the hidden labour of promotional work, to develop and maintain their public persona, thereby building their social capital within the industry and press, and their star capital with fans. As well as frequent personal appearances, establishing and maintaining a fan club either oneself, or in collaboration with an enthusiastic fan, friend or family member, was one of the tools these stars were strongly encouraged to employ in order to succeed. See Bruce Babington (2001, 11).

References

Alexander, Norah. 1950. 'Frustrated, Lonely and Peculiar'. In *Diversion: 22 Authors on the Lively Arts*, edited by John Sutro. London: Parrish: 70–7.
Attenborough, Richard, and Diana Hawkins. 2008. *Entirely Up to You Darling*. London: Hutchinson.
Babington, Bruce. 2001. *British Stars and Stardom: From Alma Taylor to Sean Connery*. Manchester: Manchester University Press.
Barbas, Samantha. 2001. *Movie Crazy: Fans, Stars and the Cult of Celebrity*. London: Palgrave Macmillan.
Bourdieu, Pierre. 2019. *Habitus and Field: Lectures at the College de France 1982–3*. Cambridge: Polity Press.
Crawford, Anne. 1947. *Anne Crawford Souvenir Booklet*, November/December: 4.
Dyer, Richard. 1979. *Stars*. London: BFI.
Jenkins, Alan. 1977. *The Forties*. London: Heinemann.
Kent, Jean. 1946. *International Jean Kent Fan Club Magazine*, July: 7.
Kent, Jean. 1947. 'Kent's Candid Column'. *International Jean Kent Fan Club Magazine*, March: 3.

Kent, Jean. 1947. 'Jean's Letter to You'. *Jean Kent International Fan Club Magazine*, June: 2.
Kent, Jean. 1947. 'Jean's Letter to You'. *Jean Kent International Fan Club Magazine*, August: 2.
Kent, Jean. 1949. 'Jean's Letter to You'. *The International Jean Kent Fan Club Magazine*, February: 2.
Kent, Jean. 1949. 'Jean Tells you Some of Her Favourite Dishes'. *International Jean Kent Fan Club Magazine*, March: 8–9.
Kent, Jean. 1949. 'Kent's Candid Column'. *The International Jean Kent Fan Club Magazine*, July/August: 5.
Kent, Jean. 1949. 'Kent's Candid Column'. *The International Jean Kent Fan Club Magazine*, November/December: 5.
Kent, Jean. 1950. 'Jean's Letter to You'. *Jean Kent International Fan Club Magazine*, May/June: 2.
Kent, Jean. 1950. 'Kent's Candid Column'. *The International Jean Kent Fan Club Magazine*, May/June: 5.
Lueck, Jennifer Anette. 2015. 'Friend-Zone with Benefits: The Parasocial Advertising of Kim Kardashian'. *Journal of Marketing Communications* 21 (2): 91–109.
Macnab, Geoffrey. 1993. *J. Arthur Rank and the British Film Industry*. London: Routledge.
Marshall, P. David. 2010. 'The Promotion and Presentation of the Self: Celebrity as Marker of Presentational Media'. *Celebrity Studies* 1 (1): 35–48.
Marwick, Alice. 2013. *Status Update: Celebrity, Publicity, and Branding in the Social Media Age*. New Haven, CT: Yale University Press.
Marx, Karl. [1859] 1968. 'Preface to *A Contribution to the Critique of Political Economy*'. In *Marx–Engels Selected Works*. London: Lawrence and Wishart.
Marx, Karl, and Friedrich Engels. [1846] 1974. *The German Ideology*. London: Lawrence and Wishart.
Morin, Edgar. [1957] 1960. *The Stars*. New York; London: Grove Press/John Calder.
Roc, Patricia. 1948. 'Best Face Forward: Pat Writes About Her Beauty Routine'. *The Patricia Roc International Fan Club Magazine*, October: 6.
Roc, Patricia. 1949. 'It's Not All Glamour'. *The Patricia Roc International Fan Club Magazine*, May/June: 7.
Roc, Patricia. 1949. 'Special Announcement'. *The Patricia Roc International Fan Club Magazine*, May/June: 11.
Rotha, Paul, and Roger Manvell. 1949. *The Year's Work in the Film 1949*. London: Longmans, Green and Co.
Skeggs, Beverley. 1997. *Formations of Class and Gender: Becoming Respectable*. London: Sage.
Smith, Phyll, and Ellen Wright. 2020. *Star Products, Star Capital, Fan Markets: Examining 1940s British film star and fan labour through fan club publications* [paper presentation]. Stardom and the Archive conference, Exeter.
Street, Sarah. 1997. *British National Cinema*. London: Routledge.
Triggs, Teal. 2006. 'Scissors and Glue: Punk Fanzines and the Creation of a DIY Aesthetic'. *Journal of Design History* 19 (3): 69–83.

Williams, M. 1949. 'Housekeeper's Choice'. *International Richard Attenborough Fan Club Magazine*, March/April: 4.
Wood, Alan. 1952. *Mr. Rank: A Study of J. Arthur Rank and British Films*. London: Hodder and Stoughton.
Wright, Ellen, and Phyll Smith. 2021. 'Star Products, Star Capital, Fan Markets: Examining 1940s British Film Stardom through Fan Club Publications'. *Celebrity Studies* 12 (3): 423–43.

12. THE MISSING PIECE: IMAGINARY AUDIENCES IN THE *ECRAN* FAN MAGAZINE OF THE 1940S

María Paz Peirano and Claudia Bossay

> Perhaps the most interesting thing about this kind of film is not on the screen, but in the reaction of the public who, moved by what they see on the screen, intervene, as a kind of protagonist, clapping, shouting for or against, without standing still for a moment.
>
> (*Ecran*, 10 December 1940, 10–11)[1]

This chapter analyses some of the imaginary constructions of local audiences which can be identified in Chilean fan magazines of the 1940s, focusing on the case of *Ecran*,[2] the main specialised film fan magazine of the period.[3] It derives from a broader ongoing research project which investigates historical cinemagoing practices in the city of Santiago, looking to map movie theatres and film experiences from the past.[4] Following the film consumption and reception focus present in much of 'new cinema history', which examines cinema as a site of social and cultural exchange (Maltby, Bilttereyst and Meers 2011), this research aims to reconstruct audiences' experiences and to situate them as part of local cinema history, understanding this as a social history of film cultures that goes beyond films themselves. This point of view aims to reposition audiences within film studies, as empirical research can assist us in contesting the idea of a single universal 'spectator', and can allow us to discuss the specificities of local audiences in greater detail.

We will therefore refer here to different audiences formed in relation to the circulation of texts, images and objects produced by the mediatisation of culture (Warner 2002) in Chile. We will consider being part of the audience as a condition, 'a mode of existence of subjects' (Mata 2001, 187) within their social context. During the 1940s, both the cinema and print media industries[5] were part of the same media ecology, in which film fan magazines mediated audiences' film experiences. We are interested therefore in analysing how such fan magazines can reveal some characteristics of historical audiences, either directly, by giving space to their voices and/or describing audience behaviour, or indirectly, by targeting particular articles at an implicit audience that went to the movies and read the magazines. In this sense, we assume that audiences are

> among other things [. . .], an idea shared by journalists, editors, screenwriters and other individuals and groups who are in the process of developing a cultural product that will eventually find its way to particular receivers. (Mihelj 2015, 22)

Thus, we not only focus on explicit descriptions of movie attendance but also on the implicit ideas about the audience that can be traced in film magazines, looking at both their written texts and visual design. These aspects allow us to think about the complexity of 'imaginary' audiences, as represented in printed media.

Fan magazines construct imagined audiences through their articles, reports, photographs and other engagement strategies. Their design and rhetoric express different perceptions of and attitudes towards cinemagoing, telling us something about how societies viewed their audiences (Bourdon 2015, 13), and unveiling some aspects of local film consumption. Magazines reveal, as Mihelj (2015) suggests, historical ideas about cinemagoers, and show how these notions relate to the broader context in which they were produced. Their pages expand our knowledge of cinemagoing, understood as a situated practice that has developed specific forms of film culture in different socio-historical contexts (Ravazzoli 2016).

The focus on film magazines also allows us to better understand a missing piece of Chilean film history, since film audiences have rarely been a subject of study in this national context. There are only limited sources that refer to historical cinemagoing, and it is only recently that Latin American audiences have been studied in depth (see, for example, Domínguez and Rosas 2021; Gil 2015; Kelly and Sasiain 2018; Kriger 2018; Lozano, Meers and Biltereyst 2016; Rosas 2017). The historiography of Chilean cinema has also only recently examined in detail the formation of Chilean film culture in the first half of the twentieth century (Bongers et al. 2011; Bossay 2014; Gatica 2011, 2016; Iturriaga 2015, 2018; Mouesca 1997; Santa Cruz 2004, 2005; Sasiain et al. 2021). For all these authors, the examination of audiences has remained rather elusive, for there are few sources that refer to them directly, and even then, references tend to be hidden amid magazines' reports on Hollywood, film stars and industry news, which are still the main source available to investigate past film cultures in Chile.

The case of *Ecran* allows us to observe film audiences through the eyes of the print media. In this chapter, we will analyse the magazine's strategies to engage with its readers, looking at direct references, such as editors' descriptions, impressions expressed in screening reports and photographs, as well as other forms of reader participation, including letters, rankings and local contests. By comparing diverse forms of engagement and magazine narratives, we aim to analyse *Ecran*'s image of local audiences. In doing so, we will demonstrate that there are two imagined audiences that interact in the magazine: on the one hand, a desirable audience that reflects the social distinction and even glamour apparent in certain cinemagoing practices, and on the other, a rather undisciplined audience that escapes social control and conveys the contradictions of the cinemagoing experience.

Seeing the Audience through *Ecran*

At the beginning of the twentieth century, magazines and periodicals emerged as one of the most popular forms of media in Chile. During the country's modernisation process in the first half of the century, magazines were considered fashionable and progressive, helping to articulate and expand the modern imagination of Chilean audiences (Ossandón and Santa Cruz 2005, 34). Particularly from the 1910s onwards, such publications became popular among an emergent readership of the middle and working classes,[6] attracted by the combination of text and image that contributed to the communication of popular messages within both literate and illiterate audiences.[7]

Ecran belonged to one of the largest publishing companies of the period, *Editorial Zig-Zag*, and first appeared in April 1930, amid the expansion of local mass media and the increase in movie attendance by the Chilean urban middle classes (Iturriaga 2015). By the 1940s, under the editorship of journalist María Romero, it had become the main Chilean publication specialising in cinema.[8] At this time, the magazine was particularly successful among the emergent middle and working classes, a readership that likely grew as a response to the expansion of cinema as one of the main forms of urban entertainment in Chile.

Primarily, *Ecran* offered this readership an insider's view of the American film industry, describing Hollywood productions, the studio environment, and the stars' everyday lives, and working in this way as a bridge between Hollywood and Chile.[9] As Mouesca (1997, 62) has suggested, the magazine embodied 'the spirit of Hollywood's golden era, [becoming] its loyal interpreter, ambassador and spokesperson'. Through its articles and its large pictures of beautiful film stars, *Ecran* displayed aspirational images of elegance and style, while also presenting Hollywood as a sign of modernity and branding cinema as a horizon of novelty and progress. The depiction of Hollywood's film stars, their houses and private lives provided a glimpse of a sophisticated modern lifestyle, which represented some of the economic, social and cultural aspirations of the local readership, particularly the emergent middle class (Peirano 2020, 246). Underlining this, on most pages, reports on Hollywood were surrounded by advertisements, often directed at women, which existed in dialogue with the magazine's other contents, such as references to Hollywood film stars. Particularly beauty and fashion ads reinforced readers' aspirations, promising that these would become achievable through consumption of the advertised products. Some ads even emphasised the possibility of 'doing-it-yourself' with the guidance of industry experts (Figure 12.1), putting the desired lifestyle even more clearly within reach.

Among these numerous pieces focusing on Hollywood gossip and dreams of stardom, then, local audiences also emerge from *Ecran*'s pages. They appear indirectly in items such as advertisements, as the implicit target of the magazine's marketing efforts, but are also referred to directly elsewhere in the magazine,

Figure 12.1 'You can use the same makeup as Irene Dunne!' Max Factor Hollywood make-up advertisement. Note that it includes both the image of the star and a coupon to cut out and send back to Max Factor Studios to learn which colour make-up from the stars best suits your complexion. *Ecran*, 6 February 1940. (p. 29)

providing us with some clear glimpses of local cinemagoers. Indeed, from time to time, the magazine provides general descriptions of 'the audience', often judging its character and measuring its qualities. For example, during the Second World War, *Ecran* lamented that the local audience was the 'direct victim' of the film shortage, expressing that 'it is not soothing for the audience of these lands, *which has a reputation for being demanding* and for possessing, to a high degree, *an up-to-date spirit*' (*Ecran*, 17 November 1942, 3). Here, the magazine suggested that the Chilean public was 'in love with *modernisms*' and that it had made 'a lot of progress' since the early days of cinema (*Ecran*, 12 January 1943, 27).

This characterisation is coherent with the overall emphasis on the audience's aspiration to be, or become, 'modern', with the magazine often implying that audiences could learn about cinema and about being modern by educating themselves. Readers were considered active subjects in this learning process, and were invited to be part of film culture through different engagement strategies, such as games, contests and polls. These games occupied a small part of the magazine – less than a page per issue – but nonetheless opened up some space for reader participation (Figure 12.2). By including these elements, *Ecran* positioned itself as providing a 'mixture of play and pedagogy' that framed 'the kinds of film knowledge worthy of cultivating and [allowed readers] to see themselves as part of a community of "film friends" with its shared rituals and protocols' (Cowan 2015, 12, 19). Such games consisted of a form of ludic discipline, aimed at 'civilising' audiences by organising film knowledge and providing the space for the actualisation of local film culture. This educative and playful attitude shows an image

Figure 12.2   Example of a game that also teaches readers about film culture. 'Puzzle cinematográfico', *Ecran*, 30 January 1940. (p. 18)

of the audience as, on the one hand, active and entitled to have an opinion but, on the other, also a mass in need of guidance and discipline.

Most of the time, *Ecran* refers to 'the public' as a single voice with a particular opinion, which was channelled by the magazine through their critical assessments of films premiered in the movie theatres of the city centre. In these, *Ecran* reported on film reception, highlighting the impact of film productions on local audiences. In the 'Control de estrenos' ('Premieres' Reviews') section, for example, we can find feelings and opinions attributed to the public such as 'the audience comes out disappointed, and rightfully so. Enough of old movies with exaggerated propaganda!' (*Ecran*, 18 September 1940, 10–11). Despite this tendency to unify cinemagoers into a single audience, *Ecran* nonetheless also reveals some of their complex diversity and offers some distinctions when referring to film spectators. Regarding their relationship with Chilean cinema, for example, it mentions that 'for the audience [. . .] the appraisal of national films, their actors and those who make them is contradictory, heterogeneous and has absolutely personal and impartial phases' (*Ecran*, 10 November 1942, 3).

One of the clearest distinctions made by the magazine is that between a cultured and a non-cultured audience, with the latter depicted as going to the cinema purely for entertainment:

> Surely this film will be much discussed by the critics, but regarding the audience, the opinion will be almost unanimous [. . .] And that is a necessary condition *for the gentleman who buys his ticket to kill time for an hour* and comes out satisfied. (*Ecran*, 15 June 1943, 10)

By the 1940s, *Ecran* did appear to assume that contemporary cinemagoers were to some extent used to complex films, having learnt about them by watching films, reading the press, film magazines and film criticism, but nonetheless appeared convinced that some audiences still needed further guidance. Sometimes, the magazine explicitly suggested that even at this point, the public as a whole lacked the proper knowledge and expertise to fully understand cinema. When the magazine ran a competition for 'The Best of Chilean Cinema' of 1942, for example, readers were invited to vote for some categories but not others, with the magazine stating that 'given that technical analysis would be too complicated for the public, we have decided that this aspect will be in charge of an ad hoc jury [. . .] Thus, the public will vote for the actors, film director and the composer' (*Ecran*, 15 December 1942, 20). Here and elsewhere, *Ecran* refers to and makes a distinction between two types of audiences: a progressive and cultured minority (*la minoría cultivada*), who appreciate the cinema's art and complexity, and a mass audience (*el grueso público*), who only seek entertainment.

The scope of this distinction, however, is not always clear. As demonstrated above, the magazine frequently shows some ambivalence about the audience's legitimate authority to fully appreciate cinema, with the main audience often regarded as naive and uncritical, easy to seduce and manipulate:

> They go to the cinema because they do. If they're told the film is a comedy, they laugh, they paid for it and they can't afford to waste their money [... but] is this a good indication of how cultured people are? (*Ecran*, 11 March 1947, 19)

On the other hand, however, *Ecran* also frequently suggests that all audiences are entitled to their legitimate opinion, even referring to them as the 'supreme judge' (*Ecran*, 10 November 1942, 13) and the 'supreme chief' (*Ecran*, 26 January 1943, 3). Occasionally, we can read how that 'masa espectadora' (mass of spectators) was tired of being exposed to bad and naive films, implying a higher level of sophistication even among non-cultured audiences. Reflecting on the editorial team's own work as film critics, we can read that *'the audience always knows better than us.* It's senseless to claim that the person that pays for a seat needs to read the press or listen to the radio to know if they have or haven't liked what they've seen' (*Ecran*, 12 January 1943, 27).

These conflicting ideas about audiences are linked to other representations of cinemagoers in *Ecran*, related to social class and cultural disposition, which reflect these distinctions. The desire to educate and discipline local audiences in the name of progress appears in different features of the magazine, including letters from its readers. The next two sections will examine some of these ideas, related to both desirable and undisciplined audiences.

Desirable Audiences

Ecran's promotion of cinema and of modern ways of life involved engaging audiences in specific cinemagoing practices, thereby inviting readers to share and participate in the experience of modernity. As López has suggested, Latin American film magazines specifically emphasised 'a national self-confidence that its own modernity was "in progress"' (2000, 52), connecting their readers with the global experience of the modern world. In the previous section, we have seen that *Ecran* evoked the experience of modernity and reflected audiences' aspiration to be modern, highlighting cultural distinctions related to film reception, and assuming different tastes and cultural capital from the main audience and the more 'cultured' one. This difference implied a class distinction, related to the acquisition of cultural capital through a learning process facilitated by the magazine.

The class connotation, linked to access to better education, is reinforced also by *Ecran*'s descriptions of actual cinemagoers seen in some of Santiago's movie theatres at the time. The magazine frequently covered local film premieres and published photographs of venues in which, from time to time, one can see the faces of the audience, check out their outfits, read about them and imagine the environment captured by the photographers. Most such mentions are of theatres within the city centre, including first-, second- and third-run cinemas attended by people from different parts of the city.[10] In this context, *Ecran* tended to focus on the more elegant cinemas of the city centre, where film premieres took place, and references to these theatres could include descriptions and pictures of stylish audience members:

> It was very pleasant for us to attend last Tuesday's screening at the Victoria Theatre, since, in addition to the pleasure of seeing a good movie, we were able to enjoy the attractive show offered by the distinguished and *chic* audience that had gathered in this downtown theatre. (*Ecran*, 2 January 1940, 21)

The magazine hence gave particular attention to audiences attending these film premieres or special events, and often included pictures of high-class cinemagoers in the foyer:

> In front of the ticket office, a large and motley audience gathers [. . .] All of the ladies, or most of them, are wearing fur coats [. . .] hats for all tastes [. . .] and sparkling jewellery. (Munizaga Ibarren, 7 May 1940, 24)

Most of these descriptions were included in a section called 'Cine y Gran Mundo' (Cinema and the Great World), which covered fashion, high society and cinema. The very title of the section clearly expressed the modern cosmopolitan aspiration embedded in these cinemagoing practices, framing theatre audiences as 'part of the world' and showing them practising a form of cosmopolitan citizenship by participating in a film premiere. The section could take up one or two whole pages (Figures 12.3, 12.4 and 12.5), and its page composition privileged particularly the images of audience members. Here, several pictures are arranged side by side at the top, accompanied by a short caption at the bottom; these photographs generally show beautiful and well-dressed women, whose high-society names are carefully listed in the captions. The text therefore served to reinforce the images, describing who attended the premiere, but also emphasising the ladies' fashion style, through which they appeared to display their social and symbolic capital at local theatres. By that time, city centre cinemas were important places for social encounters at which one could 'see and be seen', and *Ecran* helped to communicate this form of social performance:

> Thus, the Real [Theatre], at its last premiere, saw in its foyer a group of female figures, [. . . including] Luz Barros Vial, who wore a charming gown of thick pale pink silk with a white leaf print. (*Ecran*, 30 January 1940, 15)

Arguably, this section was also designed as an invitation for readers to be part of the event, or at least to experience it through *Ecran*'s mediation.

Figure 12.3 'Inside the Teatro Real'. *Ecran*, 16 January 1940. (pp. 14–15)

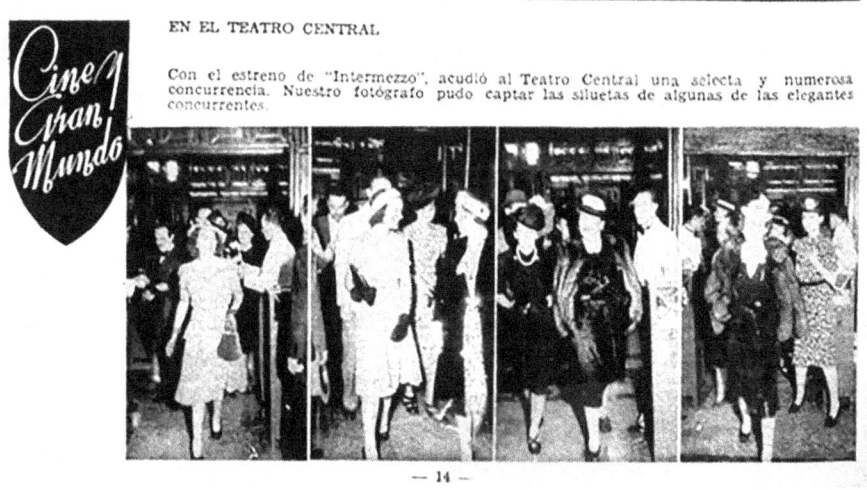

Figure 12.4 'The premiere of *Intermezzo* was attended by a select and numerous audience at the Central Theatre. Our photographer was able to capture the silhouettes of some of the elegant attendees'. 'Día de estreno en el Central'. *Ecran*, 19 March 1940. (p. 14)

Figure 12.5 'En el teatro Real' and 'Notas sociales'. *Ecran*, 16 January 1940. (pp. 14–15)

The references to these aspirational audiences allow us to understand a sense of commonality among cinemagoers, as well as the way in which cinemas became places of more prestigious cultural consumption than in previous decades (Iturriaga 2015). As Bourdon (2015) suggests, cinema audiences seemed prepared to be watched and considered, but also judged, generating a sense of distinction in conformity to the social rules of Chilean society. In 1941, *Ecran* described these 'premiere days', and noted that:

> the people who attend the theatres on those days are not going to see the film, they are not interested in the plot, and they do not care about the charms of the 'star'. They attend simply out of obligation, to meet somewhere, to find friends and to criticize women's outfits. (*Ecran*, 22 April 1941, 4)

Despite this interest in elegant audiences and the aspirational images built around them, however, these upper-class cinemagoers do not constitute the only (or the most relevant) desirable type of audience. Indeed, *Ecran* seems to have sided more with middle-class cinemagoers, that is, less aristocratic audiences, with less money, but who were considered more 'cultured'. These audiences were, according to the magazine, more interested in films themselves, and therefore displayed the 'proper' behaviour at the cinema. *Ecran* valued fashion, but negatively assessed an exaggerated display that, while it was desirable in the foyer, was not so acceptable inside the theatre. A good example is the issue of women's hats, with some articles explicitly mocking this phenomenon, evidencing the extent of the hat problem at cinemas. One report describes a film screening preceded by an announcement through the theatre's speakers: 'We ask the ladies in attendance to be kind enough to take off their hats'. After this, according to *Ecran*, the main show was not the 'film and animated film programs', but the audience's reaction to this public announcement when, 'in broad daylight, among the curious looks of the attendees, the ladies begin to take off their hats. They do it with reluctance, almost with indignation' (*Ecran*, 8 July 1941, 4). Another article comments:

> We don't know where the ladies get those tremendous hats they wear in theatres. They are not hats from the store; they do not appear in any shop windows. They are never seen on the streets. But it is enough that one enters a movie theatre to be blinded by a veritable jungle of hats. (*Ecran*, 25 February 1941, 4)

The above examples show how the magazine constructed ideal forms of spectatorship. Through these, *Ecran* expressed aspirational models for movie attendance, underlining the symbolic and social value of cinemagoing. In addition, it provided visual and socio-cultural guidelines for how audiences should look and behave, highlighting potential social conflicts at cinemas. Commenting on deviations from the norms served not only as gossip for entertainment (which was probably good for selling issues), but also as a way of reinforcing compliance with social standards. *Ecran*'s corrective and authoritative tone assumed a disciplinary purpose in this context, as a way of contributing to appropriate audience modernisation. We will see that several complaints about inappropriate behaviour reinforced this aspirational stance.

Undisciplined Audiences

By the 1940s, cinemagoing had become an extremely popular form of entertainment among the emergent and expanding urban middle classes. At this time, the increasing size of audiences led to the building of fifteen new movie theatres within the city centre, where Santiago's showbusiness and nightlife were concentrated:

> Theatrical entrepreneurs are beginning to worry about the immense queues that form on Saturdays and Sundays in front of cinema ticket offices, and the hundreds of people who wander around the theatre without having obtained tickets after long hours of waiting. The concern of businessmen translates into the construction and opening of several cinemas in the city centre. (*Ecran*, 1 April 1947, 2)

By the 1940s, cinema had long stopped being a form of lower-class entertainment, and audiences from all social classes increasingly filled theatres, even if they would not necessarily attend the same venues, at the same time, or in the same way. Because of this, the middle classes attempted to distance themselves from the lower classes by adhering to a set of norms of good behaviour that reflected their greater education and cultural capital, even while they, too, were avid filmgoers. We can infer some of these rules from *Ecran*'s description of audiences and from the voices of its readers. Indeed, within its pages, *Ecran* made space for audiences to comment on their experiences, with 'respectful' viewers often complaining about the awful condition of older and 'popular' movie theatres, which were perceived as an aftertaste of the old days of cinemagoing. As the importance of 'quality cinema' increased, the more 'cultured' audiences demanded, for example, better technical conditions in film projection and more comfortable theatres, as seen in these two viewer comments:

> This is the most uncomfortable theatre in the capital. Every time I go to that theatre, I leave indignant because [. . .] in addition to not being able to see the film, the heat in it is unbearable. (*Ecran*, 22 February 1944, 25)

> The seats, for example, are not far enough apart, and as the public is coming in every moment to occupy the empty seats, wherever they are, stomping proliferates. There aren't adequate facilities to renew the air, and less sensitive noses can notice that there are times when the atmosphere

is already unbreathable. Nor has special material been provided to muffle the noise of footsteps, and not infrequently the sound effects of the projected film are lost, drowned out by the sounds of the footsteps of those entering and leaving. (*Ecran*, 15 February 1944, 3)

We have seen that *Ecran* normally focused on audience theatre attendance within the city centre. Indeed, the magazine hardly mentioned other more frequent forms of cinemagoing, except when including this type of complaint or supporting the construction of new theatres further away from the centre. Nonetheless, both rich and poor neighbourhoods did have their own film theatres, either small ones for the benefit of the immediate neighbourhood or large ones that hosted people from different areas. The latter were meeting places for people from different social classes, and their behaviour would denote their class. The disorder and deviation from the norms that took place in these cinemas tended to be seen as a lower-class issue, and it was only occasionally mentioned in the magazine:

> We do not believe in rudeness, in the repetition of almanac jokes, in vulgarity to make the public laugh [. . .] Cantinflas, both in this film and in others, always displays the same repetition of violent and vulgar situations, which are intended to please *only the gallery audience*. (*Ecran*, 22 December 1942, 11)

'La galería' ('the gallery') housed the cheaper gallery seats where poorer cinemagoers would be located. The word became a synonym for popular audiences, identified with both simple tastes and undisciplined behaviour.

The expansion of cinema seemed to mean the pacification of popular audiences and the further development of aspirations of good conduct, and therefore also a greater need for social distinction inside the theatres. This does not mean that this behaviour was always correct or 'that audiences were ever really immobilized following the institutionalisation of modern movie theatres' (Cowan 2015, 16), but it did mean that public behaviour needed to be controlled and directed for filmgoers to perform the role of respectable audiences. Yet, popular audiences and their supposedly 'disordered' behaviour were still a feature of theatres, even respectable ones; *Ecran* condemned:

> the disorder that occurs in theatres, cinemas, etc., from the moment the performance begins until about twenty minutes after it begins. [. . . and] the outrage that the arrival of those 'late' to the shows [causes] [. . .]. This audience, not very fond of expressing culture, many out of ignorance, and others because it is more 'chic' to be late for the show, believe they have a broad right to demand that those who arrived in good time

get up from their seats or have to let them pass so that they can reach their seats. We also have those who, once they reach those seats, turn back, because they got the wrong row, repeating this annoyance and starting all over again in the new row [...] How much longer, gentlemen, *will the disciplined audience have to endure so much abuse, so much lack of culture*, so much annoyance? (*Ecran*, 26 October 1943, 3)

The above call for council and official intervention shows how audiences behaved at local cinemas, as well as what was expected of them. It also demonstrates that, apparently, certain readers wrote to the magazine feeling that it was a space that could mediate for achieving that control. The wish for a more disciplined audience expressed above indicates what some cinemagoers considered proper behaviour inside cinemas, and how they also made the distinction between cultured and uncultured audiences. This and similar complaints by *Ecran*'s readers also reveal the desire for social control of fellow cinemagoers and the conflicts embedded in collective viewing. *Ecran* went along with this desire and actively promoted it, even designing a special section for audience voices that promoted their participation. For example, *Pilatunadas* was a small section accommodating one or two letters from readers and was framed as a space where 'Readers give their opinion' and '*Ecran* washes its hands', implying that the magazine did not impose its own ideas on the readers and was not responsible for them. This section was, however, an invitation not only for interaction but also for social disciplining, which fit very well with *Ecran*'s educational role and its wish for modernisation.

Conclusions

In this chapter, we have investigated several ways in which *Ecran* referred to local audiences and built an image of Chilean cinemagoers of the 1940s. The magazine articulated this image through its engagement with broader ideas of culture and progress, which reveal the aspirations to modernisation of some sectors of Chilean society, particularly the magazine's middle-class readers. *Ecran* was in a privileged position to reconstruct and popularise cosmopolitan and upper-middle-class imaginaries linked to the film industry, building a cultural space for some cinemagoers' ideas and desires. The appearance of actual audiences in the magazine can be contrasted with these ideal social images, which *Ecran* communicated through advertising, photographs, Hollywood reports, articles and games. The magazine installed expectations of civilisation, modernity and social class that did not always correspond to the idea of the Chilean audiences encoded in its pages. Exploring these contradictions provides valuable information about the behaviour of local cinemagoers, but over and above this, about the media strategies and negotiations which responded to these spectators. Thus, *Ecran*'s images of the audience tell us more about the desirable traits of Chilean cinemagoers than about their actual practices and diversity.

Since *Ecran* also assumed an active role of its readers, sometimes we can read the views of audience members themselves within its pages. By reading their letters to the magazine, and therefore their complaints, suggestions and opinions, it is possible to access, indirectly, empirical evidence about their character and practices, as well as the conflicts that both troubled and upheld their social positioning at the time. Their ideas on the need to discipline audiences seem to be in line with the tone of the magazine, and to reinforce the imagined authority with which *Ecran* positioned itself. We can assume that *Ecran*'s representations of local audiences added to cinemagoers' actual experiences and contributed not only to a sense of a common 'lived experience' but also affected, like other texts 'from above', 'how audiences view[ed] themselves' (Butsch 2000, 2) and how they wished to behave to distinguish themselves from other viewers, especially in terms of class and levels of education.

The research results presented in this chapter suggest the extent to which film magazines can help us understand audiences and cinemagoing experiences. We can see how distinctions in modern cinema culture were beginning to take shape in this period, including those between popular films and more complex ones, and between mainstream audiences and 'cultured' ones. In addition, film magazines can shed light on a missing piece of local film histories – that of local readers and cinemagoers – especially considering the absence of data about historical audiences in smaller countries like Chile. Magazines' texts and images, as well as the way in which these contents were presented, reveal the experiences, ideas and aspirations prevalent at the time, helping us understand situated cinemagoing in different parts of the world.

Acknowledgements

This publication is funded by the National Research and Development Agency of Chile (ANID) FONDECYT 1211594. The authors wish to thank the research assistant Eduardo Pizarro for his work with the database and archival materials that helped us write this chapter.

Notes

1. All quotations from *Ecran* are in Spanish in the original, translated by the authors. All emphases are ours.
2. Available at <http://www.memoriachilena.gob.cl> (last accessed 18 November 2022).
3. Although there were around 34 other magazines referring to cinema in existence together with *Ecran*, it was not only the most enduring one (1930–1969), but arguably

the one with most social impact. Most of the other publications existed for brief periods of time, and some of them do not even have copies preserved in the archives.
4. A map of the theatres is available at <www.salasybutacas.cl>, derived from the project 'Cartelera histórica. Estudio de exhibición y recepción de cines en Santiago entre 1918–1969', funded by PAI 79170064, FONDECYT.
5. Radio was also an important part of this, but due to the lack of broadcast archives we cannot incorporate this aspect into our research.
6. The first magazine specialised in film that is archived in the National Library Archive is *El Cinematógrafo* (aka *El Punta Arenas*), printed in Magallanes, the southernmost region of Chile, in 1909.
7. The national literacy rate during the 1920s was around 50% (García-Huidobro and Escobar 2012, 22).
8. *Ecran* also had some sections for radio and theatre, but cinema was its main focus during this period.
9. For a more detailed history of *Ecran* magazine and its relationship to Hollywood, see Mouesca (1997) and Peirano (2020).
10. During the 1940s, *Ecran* mentioned forty-eight theatres, all within the city centre.

References

Anon. 1940. *Ecran*, 2 January: 21.
Anon. 1940. 'En el teatro Real and Notas sociales'. Cine y Gran Mundo section. *Ecran*, 16 January: 14–15.
Anon. 1940. 'Día de estreno en el Real'. *Ecran*, 30 January: 15.
Anon. 1940. 'Puzzle cinematográfico'. *Ecran*, 30 January: 18.
Anon. 1940. 'Concurso de artistas sin cara'. *Ecran*, 30 January: 27.
Anon. 1940. Max Factor Hollywood make-up advertisement. *Ecran*, 6 February: 29.
Anon. 1940. 'Día de estreno en el Central'. Cine y Gran Mundo section. *Ecran*, 19 March: 14.
Anon. 1940. 'Control de estrenos'. *Ecran*, 18 September: 10–11.
Anon. 1940. 'Control de estrenos'. *Ecran*, 10 December: 10–11.
Anon. 1941. 'Sombreros de señora'. *Ecran*, 25 February: 4.
Anon. 1941. 'Días de estreno'. *Ecran*, 22 April: 4.
Anon. 1941. 'La Butaca nº 13'. *Ecran*, 8 July: 4.
Anon. 1942. 'Lo mejor de 1942'. *Ecran*, 10 November: 3.
Anon. 1942. 'Josephine Baker no ha muerto'. *Ecran*, 10 November: 13.
Anon. 1942. '¿No hay películas?' *Ecran*, 17 November: 3.
Anon. 1942. '¿Cuál será la mejor película chilena de 1942? ¿Quiénes son los mejores intérpretes y quién el mejor director?' *Ecran*, 15 December: 20.
Anon. 1942. 'El gendarme desconocido'. *Ecran*, 22 December: 11.
Anon. 1943. 'A veces se ha de ser malo para ser bueno'. *Ecran*, 12 January: 27.
Anon. 1943. '¿Dónde ir esta noche?' *Ecran*, 12 January: 27.
Anon. 1943. 'Los incapaces se están defendiendo'. *Ecran*, 26 January: 3.
Anon. 1943. 'Vidas marcadas'. *Ecran*, 15 June: 10.
Anon. 1943. '¡Hasta cuándo, señores alcaldes!' *Ecran*, 26 October: 3.

Anon. 1944. 'El culto de la incomodidad'. *Ecran*, 15 February: 3.
Anon. 1944. 'Sus cuellos tienen maltrato en ese incómodo teatro'. *Ecran*, 22 February: 25.
Anon. 1947. 'Santiago, ciudad sin espectáculos'. *Ecran*, 11 March: 19.
Anon. 1947. 'Paquete de noticias'. *Ecran*, 1 April: 2.
Bongers, Wolfgang, María Jose Torrealba and Ximena Vergara eds. 2011. *Archivos I Letrados. Escritos sobre cine en Chile (1908–1940)*. Santiago, Chile: Cuarto Propio.
Bossay, Claudia. 2014. 'Lo clásico en la periferia: Las influencias de Hollywood en la producción de cine nacional en la década de 1940'. Available at: *cinechile.cl*. <https://cinechile.cl/lo-clasico-en-la-periferia-las-influencias-de-hollywood-en-la-produccion-de-cine-nacional-en-la-decada-de-1940> (last accessed 18 November 2022).
Bourdon, Jerome. 2015. 'Detextualizing: How to Write the History of Audiences'. *European Journal of Communication* 30 (1): 7–21.
Butsch, Richard. 2000. *The Making of American Audiences*. Cambridge: Cambridge University Press.
Cowan, Michael. 2015. 'Learning to Love the Movies: Puzzles, Participation and Cinephilia in Interwar European Movie Magazines'. *Film History* 27 (4): 1–45.
Domínguez, Juan Carlos, and Ana Rosas. 2021. *Públicos Iberoamericanos del Cine Mexicano de la Época de Oro*. PROCINECDMX, México.
García-Huidobro, Cecilia, and Paula Escobar. 2012. *Una historia de las revistas chilenas*. Santiago, Chile: Publicaciones Universidad Diego Portales.
Gatica, Camila. 2011. 'Al sur de la frontera: Historias de cowboys en Chile. Recepción y apropiación del cine western Hollywood en los locos años 20'. *Revista de Humanidades* 23: 91–118.
Gatica, Camila. 2016. '"Cuéntate una de vaqueros" El cine western en las salas nacionales, 1935–1945'. *Palimpsesto* 6 (9): 28–46.
Gil, Cecilia. 2015. *El mercado del deseo: Tango, cine y cultura de masas en la Argentina de los '30*. Buenos Aires: Teseo.
Iturriaga, Jorge. 2015. *La masificación del cine en Chile, 1907–1932. La conflictiva construcción de una cultura plebeya*. Santiago, Chile: Lom.
Iturriaga, Jorge. 2018. 'Salas de cine en Santiago de Chile: teatros, 'barracones' y coliseos, 1896–1940'. *Apuntes. Revista de Estudios sobre Patrimonio Cultural* 31 (1): 24–37.
Kelly, Alejandro, and Sonia Sasiain. 2018. Aproximaciones digitales a la reconstrucción de la historia de los públicos cinematográficos de Buenos Aires. Tercer Congreso de la Asociación Argentina de Humanidades Digitales. La Cultura de los Datos. Asociación Argentina de Humanidades Digitales, Rosario.
Kriger, Clara. 2018. *Imágenes y públicos del cine argentino clásico*. Tandil: Universidad Nacional del Centro de la Provincia de Buenos Aires.
López, Ana M. 2000. 'Early Cinema and Modernity in Latin America'. *Cinema Journal* 40 (1): 48–78.
Lozano Jose Carlos, Philippe Meers and Daniel Biltereyst. 2016. 'La experiencia social histórica de asistencia al cine en Monterrey, Nuevo León, México durante las décadas de los 1930 a los 1960'. *Palabra Clave* 19 (3): 691–720.
Maltby, Richard, Daniel Biltereyst and Philippe Meers eds. 2011. *Explorations in New Cinema History: Approaches and Case Studies*. Malden, MA: Wiley-Blackwell.

Mata, Maria C. 2001. 'Interrogaciones sobre el público'. In *Comunicación, campo y objeto de estudio*, edited by Maria Vassallo de Lopes and Raul Fuentes, 183–99. México: InstitutoTecnológico y de Estudios Superiores de Occidente (ITESO).

Mihelj, Sabina. 2015. 'Audience History as a History of Ideas: Towards a Transnational History'. *European Journal of Communication* 30 (1): 22–35.

Mouesca, Jacqueline. 1997. *El cine en Chile. Crónica en Tres Tiempos*. Santiago, Chile: Editorial Planeta/Universidad Nacional Andrés Bello.

Munizaga Ibarren, M. 1940. 'Tarde de estreno'. *Ecran*, 7 May: 24.

Ossandón, Carlos, and Eduardo Santa Cruz eds. 2005. *El Estallido de las Formas. Chile en los albores de la 'Cultura de Masas'*. Santiago, Chile: Lom/Arcis.

Peirano, María Paz. 2020. 'Hollywood Imaginaries at the End of the World: *Ecran* and the Construction of the International Industry from the Periphery'. In *Mapping Movie Magazines: Digitization, Periodicals and Cinema History*, edited by Daniel Biltereyst and Lies van de Vijver, 237–55. Cham, Switzerland: Palgrave Macmillan.

Ravazzoli, Elisa. 2016. 'Cinemagoing as Spatially Contextualised Cultural and Social Practice'. *Alphaville: Journal of Film and Screen Media* 11: 33–44.

Rosas, Ana. 2017. *Ir al cine: antropología de los públicos, la ciudad y las pantallas*. Barcelona, Spain: Gedisa.

Santa Cruz, Eduardo. 2004. 'Cultura de masas y espacio público en Chile: las revistas de cine (1910–1930)'. *Comunicación y Medios* 15: 139–55.

Santa Cruz, Eduardo. 2005. 'Las revistas de cine (1910–1920)'. In *El Estallido de las Formas. Chile en los albores de la 'Cultura de Masas'*, edited by Carlos Ossandón and Eduardo Santa Cruz, 213–45. Santiago, Chile: Lom/Arcis.

Sasiain, Sonia, Cecilia Gil Mariño, Claudia Bossay and María Paz Peirano. 2021. 'Memoria y cartografías afectivas del entretenimiento. Experiencias comparadas entre la ciudad de Buenos Aires y Santiago'. *Imagofagia* 24: 407–34. <http://asaeca.org/imagofagia/index.php/imagofagia/article/view/831> (last accessed 18 November 2022).

Warner, Michael. 2002. 'Publics and counterpublics'. *Public Culture* 14 (1): 49–90.

13. THE SILVER SCREEN AND THE GOLDEN LAND: HOLLYWOOD AND 'HERENESS' IN THE PAGES OF *FILM-NAYES* (1936–1938)

Lies Lanckman

On 21 and 28 February 1934, the Yiddish-language, Polish newspaper *Vokhnshrift far Literatur, Kunst un Kultur* (*Weekly for Literature, Art and Culture*) published two articles entitled 'In di Fabrik fun Lebedike Shotns' – or 'In the Factory of Living Shadows'. Both articles essentially presented to readers a series of observations connected to the cinema industry, accompanied by a series of photographs and sketches of mostly Hollywood stars and personalities. The opening section of the first article was entitled 'On the Extras Market'; I wish to draw attention to it here as it taps usefully into a number of the topics this chapter will focus on.

Indeed, in just a few paragraphs, the author of the piece sketches a picture, almost filmic in its vivid description, of a number of young, Polish-Jewish youths, whose 'mania' for particular Hollywood stars has led them down the path of working as underpaid extras in the Polish film industry. They are now gathered together in impoverished surroundings, where the author finds them: the dark-haired young men who fancy themselves the second Rudolph Valentino or Ramon Novarro, the fair-haired girl who strives to be a Greta Garbo at all costs. Throughout this brief piece, their poverty is emphasised, as is the ultimate pointlessness of their ambitions – the girl may, the author notes, have Garbo's hair and Garbo's figure, but she definitely has not her talent!

The piece is therefore not an idealised narrative of an easy road to stardom – but at the same time, and perhaps surprisingly, it is also not a cautionary tale. It does not strive to reveal, to such would-be Valentinos and (perhaps especially!) Garbos, the abuses and misery to which they might fall victim, and to steer them onto a more prudent path. Instead, its author states his confidence that the girl who fancies herself a second Garbo will, no doubt, yet awaken from her Greta-mania and will find more productive work in time; but in the meantime, she's 'roguishly' smoking a cigarette, just like her idol, and – it is implied – is having a rather fun time (6).

The piece is therefore not really a condemnation of the lives of extras in 1930s Poland, but instead provides a fairly nuanced commentary on a number of broader topics: the lives of young, assimilated Jewish people within the Second Polish Republic, their interest in and connection to Hollywood and its stars, as well as the way in which ephemera such as movie magazines – an issue of which one particular extra, fast asleep, is described as 'clutching' in his hand – helped shape this interest. Indeed, building upon the interest in cinema culture already on display within these two articles, their author, the art critic Maks Geler, would soon create his own Yiddish-language fan magazine. This magazine, *Film-Nayes* (*Film News*), would be published for the first time in October 1936, two years after the *Vokhnshrift* articles, and it is this magazine which I wish to investigate further in this chapter.

Fan magazines have, in recent years and in part thanks to the impressive digitisation efforts by the Media History Digital Library, been recognised as a useful resource by an increasing number of film historians. Such magazines, described by Anthony Slide as 'film- and entertainment-related periodical[s] aimed at a general fan' (2010, 11), can be used to investigate a range of topics including stardom and fandom in Hollywood and beyond. Indeed, magazines such as *Photoplay*, *Motion Picture* and *Picture Play* continue to be studied in a range of contexts, and have not yet surrendered the last of their secrets to eager investigators. At the same time, digitisation has also made lesser-known publications accessible to the wider public. In the case of *Film-Nayes*, a Yiddish-language periodical originally published in Warsaw from 1936–1938, the magazine is now available in fully digitised format thanks to the efforts of the National Libraries of Poland and Israel, although it has not previously been discussed in a film-historical, or any other, scholarly context.

While magazines such as *Film-Nayes* were not read by *Photoplay*'s millions, they nonetheless fulfilled an important role within their own contexts and allow us as historians to understand the world of their readers better. In this chapter, I will look at the magazine firstly, therefore, to bring both it and the vision of its creator to the broader attention of film history as a discipline, and thereby to cast a light on a hitherto largely unexplored film-historical context. Secondly, and more specifically, I aim to investigate this magazine particularly in the context of cross-cultural exchange which was a key characteristic of the increasingly global film industry of the 1930s, but which also characterised the lives of assimilated Jews living as members of an ethnic minority group in Poland at this time. I will demonstrate how this emphasis on the cross-cultural is apparent

257

within the contents of the magazine over the course of the year and a half of its existence, but also within certain aspects of the design of the magazine.

YIDDISHLAND AND ITS PRESS

To fully understand the context which produced *Film-Nayes*, we must, firstly, introduce both its language – Yiddish – and the Polish, Yiddish-language press of which it formed a part.

Yiddish is a European language which is part of the Western Germanic language family; as such, it is closely related to other such languages like German, Dutch and Flemish, but is nonetheless heavily influenced also by Hebrew, from which it takes its alphabet, as well as by several Slavic languages. It originated in Central Europe approximately one thousand years ago, as the spoken language of Ashkenazi Jews, and became known among them as the 'mame-loshn', the 'mother-tongue'. It has since been used for a wide range of purposes, becoming the source language for a rich cultural, musical, intellectual and literary tradition, including also, in the early twentieth century, a number of films such as *Yidl Mitn Fidl* (Green 1936) and *Mir Kumen On* (Ford 1936), both made in Poland.

The language experienced a major crisis when an estimated five million Yiddish speakers were murdered in the Holocaust between 1939 and 1945, particularly in Central and Eastern Europe (Jacobs 2005, 3), with an additional number of speakers lost through processes of immigration and subsequent assimilation, particularly in the context of the United States. Nonetheless, the language survived and is currently spoken by at least half a million people, including Haredi Jews as well as many non-Orthodox enthusiasts (YIVO Institute for Jewish Research 2014, 1–2), with publications such as the *Jewish Daily Forward*, or *Forverts*, continuing to publish in Yiddish to this day.

Indeed, *Forverts*, which was first published in 1896, is arguably the most recognised historical Yiddish publication, becoming known as the 'voice of the Jewish immigrant' in the United States in the early twentieth century. These immigrants, however, largely hailed from Eastern Europe, where a diverse press also flourished in the late nineteenth and early twentieth centuries. This includes the first recorded Yiddish periodical, which was *Kol-mevaser* (Hebrew for *The Heralding Voice*), a Yiddish supplement to the Hebrew weekly *Hamelits* (*The Advocate*) published in Odessa by Aleksander Tsederboym in 1862; upon its widespread success, it was followed by other magazines and newspapers, such as the *Yidishes folksblat* (*Jewish People's Newspaper*, 1881–1890), *Der Yid* (*The Jew*, 1899–1902), and *Der fraynd* (*The Friend*, 1903–1913), all published within the then Russian empire (Cohen 2008, 149–52; Portnoy 2017, 7).

As Poland gained its independence from this empire in 1919, and became the Second Polish Republic, Yiddish newspapers published within its borders proliferated. The popular newspapers *Haynt* (*Today*, 1906–1939) and *Der Moment* (*The Moment*, 1910–1939) both boasted circulations of over 100,000 by this time, and many other newspapers and periodicals, with various political and cultural emphases, were created and published during the 1920s and 1930s (Greenbaum n. d., n.p.).

Film-Nayes and its Editor

This same time period was also, more widely, the heyday of the film fan magazine; in the United States, fan magazines such as *Motion Picture Story Magazine* and *Photoplay* had been published since 1911, and others, both within that country and globally, proliferated during the 1920s and 1930s. In Poland, too, Polish-language film magazines such as *Kino dla Wszystkich* (*Cinema for Everyone*), which was published under various similar titles from 1925 to 1939, followed in this tradition, as did Yiddish-language magazines such as *Film-Nayes*, which was published for the first time in October 1936.

The magazine's editor was the aforementioned Maks Geler, as is noted at the bottom of each final page; the very rare mention of any other writers, as well as the limited page count of each issue, leads us to believe that he was likely its main, and sometimes sole, contributor. Geler was a Warsaw-based writer, translator and critic with a particular interest in art, theatre and film; non-professional biographical information about him is, however, fairly scarce. The most accessible source on both his life and work is his entry in the *Leksikon fun der nayer yidisher literatur* (*Lexicon of New Yiddish Literature*), which was published by the Congress for Jewish Culture in eight volumes between 1956 and 1981 (Cohen and Clarke April 2016, n.p.). Here, we can learn that Geler was likely born in 1900; we cannot, however, be certain when he died, although it is likely that he perished in the Holocaust. The last trace of him is a brief mention in Jonas Turkov's memoir *Azoy Iz Es Geven* (*That's How It Was*), which lists him among the Jewish writers and artists imprisoned alongside Turkov in the Warsaw Ghetto (309–10). Just like hundreds of thousands of others, Geler likely died in the ghetto or was deported from there and subsequently murdered.

Nonetheless, traces of Geler and his work remain in the now-digitised prewar Yiddish press, and his contributions to a number of magazines at this time demonstrate the trajectory that would lead him to *Film-Nayes*. During the 1920s, he contributed to newspapers such as *Haynt* and magazines such as the highly respected *Literarishe Bleter* (*Literary Pages*), the leading Polish literary publication in Yiddish, with articles on Ukrainian literature (Geler 8 August 1924) and on particular theatrical performances (Geler 12 March 1926). Additional mentions of his name highlight his lectures on art and his guided tours of particular art exhibitions, including at the Zachęta National Gallery of Art (*Unzer Ekspres*, 16 August 1929).

During the 1930s, then, his work included numerous contributions to the *Vokhnshrift far Literatur, Kunst un Kultur*, which provided me with the opening example of this chapter. Here, it is worth noting that this publication was in fact a weekly supplement to the Bundist, that is, Jewish-socialist, newspaper *Folkstsaytung (The People's Newspaper)*; Geler initially contributed mainly pieces on art exhibitions and individual artists, but also, at this stage, occasionally wrote about film. In 1931, this included a piece on filmic representations of the First World War (Geler 28 August 1931), and on 21 and 28 February 1934, the pieces entitled 'In der Fabrik fun Lebndike Shotns', which, apart from the segment on Polish-Jewish extras, also covered, for example, the impact of the advent of talking pictures. Geler's interest in film therefore becomes particularly apparent at this early stage, with the drawings accompanying the article reminding the reader of a similar playfulness also demonstrated by dedicated fan magazines.

Two years after the publication of this article, then, in October 1936, Geler used this interest in film and art criticism to publish the first issue of *Film-Nayes*. In total, he would produce twelve issues between October 1936 and May 1938; these would be published on a roughly monthly basis, with some months skipped altogether (as the continuous issue numbering indicates). These issues appeared in October 1936, January–April 1937, July 1937, September 1937–January 1938 and May 1938; of these twelve issues, eleven are available via the Historical Jewish Press website of the National Library of Israel, with only the April 1937 issue marked as missing. In the next part of this chapter, I will take an initial look at one of these individual issues, to demonstrate the types of content covered by Geler in his fan magazine.

An Issue Analysis of *Film-Nayes*

As the magazine was only published for eighteen months, its basic layout and composition did not evolve greatly over the course of its lifespan; for this reason, the first issue, published in October 1936, can give us a useful glimpse at the magazine as it existed throughout its run. Like all others, this issue counted twelve pages overall, and unlike film fan magazines in the United States and indeed similar magazines published in Polish at this time (such as the aforementioned Polish film magazine *Kino dla Wszystkich*), *Film-Nayes* did not have a traditional cover. Instead, its front page presented the magazine masthead, and then immediately followed up with regular content. (This varied somewhat over the course of the next few issues, with those dated March and October 1937 and January and May 1938 sporting more traditional covers, featuring a single image.)

The contents covered within *Film-Nayes*'s twelve pages can be divided into seven categories: coverage of a single film, articles on film more broadly, interviews, photo sections, and three different kinds of film advertisements, for Hollywood film, for Polish-language film and for Yiddish-language film. Of these, the sections taking up the most space in this first issue include coverage of a single film (2.375 pages), photo or illustration sections (2.625 pages) and ads for Hollywood films (2.83 pages), which together account for well over half of the magazine's twelve pages. Particularly the significant dominance of Hollywood ads – over ads for Yiddish or Polish films – is interesting and demonstrates the hegemony of Hollywood even in this Polish-Jewish magazine published in a non-majority language. Indeed, both the first article on the cover page – a review of the Fox film *Under Two Flags* (Lloyd 1936) – and the piece of content dominating page 3, the page immediately facing a reader turning the cover page, which is a Polish-language, almost full-page ad for the RKO film *Mary of Scotland* (Ford 1936), are Hollywood focused.

Yiddish-language film does also have a significant presence within this first issue, which features a half-page ad for Polish-American coproduction *Yidl Mitn Fidl*, as well as a full-page ad for the Polish film *Di Freylekhe Kabtsonim* (*The Jolly Paupers*, Jeannot and Turkow 1937). Overall, almost half of the magazine is taken up by advertisements for particular films, demonstrating its focus on promoting new cinematic material. Underlining this promotional emphasis, then, the articles published on single films also focus quite heavily on the above two Yiddish-language productions, with an illustrated article focusing especially on Joseph Green as the creator of *Yidl Mitn Fidl*, and another two-page article focusing on various people involved with the production of *Di Freylekhe Kabtsonim*, including its screenwriter, director, composer, actors, etc.

It is in the visual sections, however, that the focus on Hollywood and its stars again becomes clearer. Indeed, the issue's centrefold is a two-page 'Photo-Reportage' focusing particularly on Paramount stars; somewhere between an advertisement and a photo section, it features portraits of individual stars and performers such as Joan Bennett, Sylvia Sidney and Gladys Swarthout, alongside photographed scenes from films such as *The Princess Comes Across* (Howard 1936) and *The General Died At Dawn* (Milestone 1936). The section is framed with borders reminiscent of a stylised film strip. Finally, then, the last page of the magazine is again largely devoted to the coverage of Hollywood stars through visual means: the top section of this page features a number of small photographs of stars such as Errol Flynn, whereas the bottom section is entitled 'Film People in the Mirror of Caricature' and features drawings of Max Reinhardt, Kay Francis and Al Jolson (Figure 13.1). At the bottom of this final page, we can also find the name of the magazine's editor and publisher, its administrative address, as well as the name and address of its printer.

The first issue, therefore, already demonstrates the ways in which this magazine, like many European magazines but in truth largely unlike the big American fan magazines, balanced coverage of multiple different film contexts;

Figure 13.1 Caricatures of famous Hollywoodians in the October 1936 issue of *Film-Nayes*. (p. 12)

while magazines such as *Photoplay* and *Motion Picture* in the United States primarily focused on Hollywood, European magazines such as the French *Mon Ciné*, the British *Picturegoer* and indeed the Polish *Kino dla Wszystkich* focused both on their 'home' industries and, often to a large extent, on Hollywood. This is no different for *Film-Nayes*.

At the same time, however, *Film-Nayes* occupied a space of greater complexity even than these other European magazines; as a Yiddish-language periodical published in Poland, it existed, in a number of ways, between two worlds. It existed, after all, between the Hollywood and European film industries, but also, crucially, between the Yiddish and Polish cultural universes, which its readers, too, would jointly have inhabited. In the remainder of this chapter, I will investigate how this distinction, particularly relevant on the eve of the Shoah, permeated the pages of *Film-Nayes*, in terms of content but also, interestingly, in terms of design and layout.

CONTENT: JEWISH EMIGRATION AND THE FILM INDUSTRY

This double perspective, in terms of the magazine's contents, is demonstrated firstly through a focus on the Jewish background of particular stars and indeed movie executives, which becomes particularly apparent from the second issue onwards.

An example is Sylvia Sidney; this American star was featured, as I noted above, in the photography section in the middle of the first issue, which praised her 'allure and charm' as well as her successful films (6). In the second issue (dated January 1937), however, the reader is provided with further information, introducing her, in a brief article on her return to work after a trip to London, as 'a Jewish girl', whose family 'comes from the region of Grodno' (11). Grodno was then a Polish city and a major centre of Polish-Jewish life; Sidney is here presented, therefore, as the American offspring of people not unlike the potential readers of *Film-Nayes*.

This same emphasis on Hollywood personalities as Jewish immigrants to the United States appears also in the issue's cover article, which focuses on the twenty-fifth anniversary of the career of Adolph Zukor, co-founder of Paramount Pictures and a major Hollywood magnate. As opposed to Sidney, who was American-born, Zukor is described here as a Jewish immigrant from Hungary, who grew up in a religious family in a shtetl and who was destined to become a shokhet, or ritual butcher. Zukor instead became caught up in what Geler here calls the 'emigration psychosis' of the time and ended up moving to America, where, after a brief career as a salesman in furs, he entered the nascent movie industry (1).

While these observations on Sidney and Zukor are presented as miscellaneous facts, certain stories of European-Jewish actors, however, take on a darker hue; these stories, such as those on Erich Pommer and Franciska Gaal, combine a description of the Jewish origins of these movie personalities with an explanation of how the political situation within 1930s Europe has impacted their career trajectories.

In the case of German-Jewish film producer Pommer, *Film-Nayes* describes how he was, according to the title of the article, 'Once in Germany – Now in London'. Before the 'Hitler-upheaval', this article notes, Pommer was a crucial figure within the German film industry, instrumental in the development of the UFA film studio and in the production of films such as *Metropolis* (Lang 1927) and *Der Blaue Engel* (von Sternberg 1930), as well as in the training of now famous directors like Fritz Lang and F. W. Murnau. After Hitler came to power, however, Pommer had to cease his work because he was Jewish, and, alongside many other producers, directors and actors, left Germany. He briefly worked in Hollywood and France but has now, Geler notes, settled in London, invited there by British film director Alexander Korda (6).

Similarly, an article on Gaal, a Hungarian-Jewish actress then about to embark for Hollywood, also notes her Jewish origins in Budapest, connecting these to a rags-to-riches narrative, including insufficient food as a child and a miraculous discovery by a theatrical impresario, worthy of American fan magazine fare. Here, we see a classic Dyerian representation of stardom, with a twin focus on hard work and good luck (Dyer 1979, 42). At the same time, however, this article again goes beyond generic star representation and also delves into some of the realities of Jewish life in Europe in the late 1930s, when it notes that Gaal previously worked mostly in Germany but has now, as a Jewish girl, been forced to leave the country due to the rise of the Nazis (4).

Interestingly, the magazine's engagement with the rapidly escalating political situation in Nazi Germany also entered its discourse about another, this time non-Jewish, star; this was the German-born Hollywood star Marlene Dietrich, who was mentioned periodically throughout the magazine's run. She is mentioned for the first time, again, in this same second issue, which describes her as a star who 'has German origins' (8), but is featured most prominently in the November 1937 issue, where a large article on the magazine's second page notes that she 'rejected the invitation to come to Germany' (2).

The star, the magazine explains, is the most famous German actress in Hollywood, and has suffered heavy criticism from Hitler's supporters in her homeland, including in the Nazi newspaper *Der Stürmer* (*The Stormer*), for her associations with Jewish artistic circles. Hitler, therefore, personally tried to convince her to return to Germany and to reject 'Jewish Hollywood'; Dietrich's response to this has been to acquire American, rather than German, citizenship. The article speculates that Dietrich's close relationship with Jewish director Josef von Sternberg may have played an important role, or that the German push for war has scandalised the actress, who lost her father in the Great War (2). The next time *Film-Nayes* mentions Dietrich, in January 1938, it describes her simply as 'the American film actress', without any mention of Germany (12).

Nonetheless, and as Geler's reference to 'emigration psychosis' in the Zukor article in the January 1937 issue already suggests, the magazine's relationship with Hollywood was not a straightforward one, or indeed even a straightforwardly positive one. This leading film industry, so prominently featured on its pages, was not, after all, simply described as a golden opportunity for Jewish-European, or for non-Jewish but anti-Nazi, actors. While Geler recognises the role it has played in giving opportunities to such people, he also fundamentally espouses the view that immigration to the United States is draining European cultural life, and that this is essentially a problem.

After all, this same second issue of *Film-Nayes* also mentioned the star Elisabeth Bergner, highlighting again Bergner's Jewish background: she was born in Drohobych, which was in Poland at this time (though it was in Austria-Hungary when Bergner was born in 1897, and it is in Ukraine today), and came from a Chasidic family in Galicia. Bergner, too, was a star who had left the German movie industry to escape Nazi antisemitism, but she was now working not in the United States, but in the United Kingdom. Geler therefore praises particularly Bergner's Europeanness, describing her work as imbued with 'culture and taste', as if to set her apart, as a Galician actress working in Britain, from her counterparts who went to Hollywood. This is underlined further in Geler's description of her latest film, *As You Like It* (Czinner 1936), which he erroneously claims was made in Hollywood: even though it was in fact a British film, the author takes the opportunity to remind his readers that 'America steals all the best actors from Europe, that's an old rule' (2).

This thread of discourse, as well, is woven through the next few issues, both as a general problem and in connection to particular European stars making the move to Hollywood. In the March 1937 issue, for example, the very first article the magazine published was entitled 'Hollywood "kidnaps" the best Europeans', and focused particularly on a number of Jewish and non-Jewish film personnel who had moved to Hollywood, including the Russian-Jewish director Anatole Litvak and the French actress Simone Simon. The article uses strong language in explaining this process, referring to it as a 'theft' or 'kidnapping' and to the European émigrés as Hollywood's 'catch' (2).

This thread is continued in other items, for example, in a further article on Franciska Gaal in Hollywood, in the October 1937 issue of *Film-Nayes*. This article announces Gaal's first Hollywood film with some excitement, but also describes, again, the process whereby as soon as a European actor or actress becomes famous, along comes Hollywood with its 'fat checkbook'. This has happened, the article reminds its readers, to Greta Garbo and Marlene Dietrich, to French stars Simone Simon and Danielle Darrieux, and it is now happening to Gaal, who, like these others, has been caught in Hollywood's 'golden net' (8). In this sense, Geler's terminology echoes the wider reference to the United States as the 'goldene medine' or 'goldn land' (both mean 'golden land') in Yiddish-language texts; just like this term, which echoed in some sense the concept of the American dream, but which was also frequently used ironically and negatively (Slobin 1982, 157), Geler's descriptions reveal a double feeling towards both the United States and towards Hollywood.

While Geler undoubtedly loves Hollywood film and sees its great potential, he also displays a fundamental ambiguity towards the global dominance of this industry; he recognises that especially as Jewish life in Europe becomes harder due to the rise of Nazism, it offers certain opportunities to European-Jewish actors, but also expresses concerns about the drain caused in this way to European cultural life. Indeed, his views here align closely with the concept of 'doikayt', or 'hereness', which was one of the central ideas espoused by the Jewish Labour Bund, an important Yiddishist and socialist organisation, at this time. The ideology of 'doikayt' posited that Jews should focus on tackling the challenges facing them in the countries in which they lived, rather than espousing either Zionism – a 'thereness' which longed for a return to an ancestral homeland – or indeed immigration more broadly (Rabinovitch 2012, 106).

Here, again, Geler's work for *Vokhnshrift far Literatur, Kunst un Kultur* becomes significant; as I noted above, this was a supplement to the *Folkstsaytung (People's Newspaper)* which was the daily newspaper published by the Jewish Labour Bund in Poland. It is likely, therefore, that Geler shared at least in part this political ideology, and brought it to bear, in *Film-Nayes*, on his views on immigration in the context of the US film industry. In the aforementioned articles, he essentially espouses the view that Jewish actors should negotiate their complex position within 1930s Europe, despite its potential pitfalls, rather than leave for Hollywood.

Design: Yiddish Film Fandom Between Two Worlds

Interestingly, however, this complex position and its accompanying sense of ambiguity, of negotiation between two or more worlds, can also be found within the design of this Yiddish magazine, and not solely within its contents. Here, it is important to reflect again, firstly, upon the language in which the magazine is written, and more specifically on the most obvious characteristic of its alphabet. Yiddish is, after all, written using the Hebrew alphabet, and is therefore read from right to left, unlike Polish, English and all other European languages. This necessarily impacted the way in which this magazine, and indeed most other Yiddish-language magazines, opened and would be leafed through, and therefore also how particular pages within this magazine were designed.

Although the magazine can only currently be accessed through digitised PDFs, which do not allow the reader to experience the 'leafing through' motion that would be apparent if one were to hold a physical copy, several items within the magazine nonetheless demonstrate the editorial assumption that the reader's eyes would move from right to left, rather than from left to right, in moving through the pages. This can be seen in a broad sense through the way in which the magazine often favours its left-hand pages over its right-hand pages, as these, leafed through from right to left, would be exposed before the right-hand pages and would therefore gain additional visibility (Lucas and Britt 1950, 232–3). We can see, for example, that *Film-Nayes* frequently uses its first left-hand page to print large, full-page advertisements of films it will discuss elsewhere within the same issue, such as *Mary of Scotland* in the first issue.

Another, more specific, example of such design choices can be found in the issue dated November 1937 where page 4 (Figure 13.2) offers the reader six distinct items of film news, presented in a roughly symmetrical layout. The central article, presented in a T-shape, is 'a letter from London' and focuses on the success of *Victoria the Great* (Wilcox 1937), while the two articles below it deal with a Polish and a French film respectively, and the image at the bottom is a still from a Hollywood film. These items can be consumed in any order. The two articles alongside the image, however, clearly demonstrate the reading direction associated with this page. The brief article on the right, entitled '1000 km on dance-wheels!', talks about how Fred Astaire and Ginger Rogers practised dancing on roller skates in *Shall We Dance* (Sandrich 1937). The brief article on the left, however, is entitled 'Fred Astaire Again', and deals with a scene from the same film in which Astaire sings a song aboard an ocean liner. The use of 'again' in the title here is an indication of the page's presumed

פילם

"די קעניגין וויקטאריע"
דער גרעסטער פילם אין איצטיקן סעזאן
א בריוו פון לאנדאן

בעת איך שרייב אייך דעמדאזיקן בריוו ווערט שוין "די קעניגין וויקטאריע" מן הסתם געוויזן אין פוילן. דאס שטערט מיר אבער נישט צוצוגעבן איינייקע כאראקטע• ריסטישע באמערקונגען, וועלכע וועלן זיכער פאראינטערעסירן אייערע חשובע לעזער.

זייט וויים, אז "די קעניגין וויקטאריע" ווערט שוין זייט 2 חדשים געוויזן אין לאנ• דאן מיט אן אויסערגעוויינלעכן דערפאלג. און קיין וווּנדער נישט: דאס איז בלי גוזמא דער שענסטער און גרעסטער פילם אין איצטיקן סעזאן. אלץ: דער סצענאר, די אויפפאסונג, די רעזשי פון הערבערט ווילי• קאנס, דאס אוּמפאַרגעסלעכע שפילן פון די שויםפילער אנאַ ניגל און וואַלבריק, די אויסשטאטונג – שטייען אויף דער העכסטער מדרגה.

די דערלויבנעיש צו רעאליזירן דעם פילם האט מען נאך גרויסע שוועריקייטן באקומען פון דער ענגלישער רעגירונג. די דערלויב• נעיש האט אבער אריוסגערוקט אסף באא"• רענישן פון היסטאריש-קונסטלערישן כאַראַק• טער. דער רעזשיסער האט זיך צו די גענומטע רעדענען מיט יערע קלייניקיים אפילו: די קרינונג-סצענע פון דער יונגעטשקער קעניגין וויקטאריע, דאן די סצענע פון איר באריומטן יובילעי – דאס זענען אמתע פערל. אלע מומן אנגערעכנט, אז דאס איז פאקטיש דער גרעסטער פילם. וועלכן מהאט ביז איצט געשאפן אין ענגלאנד. דער אינהאלט פון פילם איז געוואַרן אויסגעארבעטס אזוי ארום די צושויער אין דער גארער וועלט.

ס באווּנדערן ליוב פארזיכערן דער קונסט• לערישער ליסטער וויאַמס. אונטער ווטעגע ליסטונג עס זענעג געשאפן געווארן דאס פרעכטיקע דעקארציעס. אין וועלכע עס איז איבערגעגעבן די שטימונג און אימפעט• כמות דער גייסט און כאראקטער פון יענע היסטארישער עפאכע.

עס וועט אבסאלוט נישט זיין איבער•

געטריבן, ווען איך וועל באַהויפטן, אז אַלץ באַשטייליקטע שוישפיעלער שפילן דאָ, ווי אמת'ע סטארס. איבריגנס, דער פילם ווערט שוין געוווגן אויך ביי אייך פויליל, און אייערע חשובע לעזער וועלן נאָר קאָנען ב.שטעטיקן מיינע רייד.

מ. וואַלם.

דער פילם
"די מארסיליעזע"

די גאַנצע וועלט אינטערעסירט זיך מיט א פילם "די מאַרסילעזע", וועלכער ווערט איצט געשאפן אין פראַנקרייך. דעם• אזיקן אינטערעסאנטן פילם רעזשיסירט פרעד רענואר, איינער פון די סיב• טיקסטע רעזשיסערן און היינטיקן פראנקרייך. ער האט באקומען אויף דער אינטערנאצאניאלער פילם אויסשטעלונג אין וענעדיג אן אויסצייכנונג פאר זיין פילם "די גרויסע איליוזיע", וועלכער האט געמאכט א שטארקן רושם. דער דערפאלגרייכער פילם "די מארסיליעזע" ווערט צוגעגרייט מיט דער גרעסטער פיעטעט און מיט דער קונסט• לערישער ערנסט;ייט. וועלכע כאראקטעריזירן דעם רעזשיסער פיער רענואר. עס דארף ווערן באמערקט. אז דעם פילם "די מאר• סיליעזע" שאפט עס איינגנטלעך דאס גאַנצע פראַנצויישע פאָלק. וואָס האָט זיך בא• שטייערט לטובת דער יונגערציצע פון דער פראנצויישער מלוכה. און זיין זאַל אויסן• שאַם פון די היסטארישע קאמפן פאר פריי• הייט אין גערעטיקייט.

נאך א מאל
דער אסטער

אין איינער פון די סצענעס אין נייעסטן פילם "מיר וועלן א טאנץ טון!" מיט פרעד אסטער און דושינדושער ראדוישערס אין די הויפטראלן. זינגט פרעד אסטער אויף דער שיף בעת א נעפל. די דאָזיקע סטימונג• פילם סצענע האט פארשאפן דעם רעזשיסער אסכן עגמת-נפש. ביז ענדלעך איז געקומטן א ספעציאליסט פון מאנכן נעפלאן. ער האט באלד קאנסטרואירט א נעפל פון צעשטויב• טער נאפט-ראסע, וועלכע האם יענער טרעף. דער אימיטירט א נעפל, וואס האט אבער גישט גערייצט דעם האלז פון דעם סטענצער.

דושינדושערס ראלארסקי/ילט. נעטער אין פון מאן ודדי. ויסגא, א אסטער

דער אולאנער
פון יוזעף פאניאטארוסקי

דער היסטארישער אנעגדאָטע האט אנגע• הויבן דעראַרבערן פאר זיך וואס אמאל מער ארם אין פוילן. דערהדאזיקער ניער ושאַן אַנטלעכעט גרויםע פילם-מעגלעכקייטן. דאס איז נישט קיין היסטאַרישער פילם, וועלכער איז איצט אזוי פאר זיך שוואך און איבער• געלאדן. און נישט קיין קאסטיום-פילם. וועלכער ליינט דעם שווער פונקט גישט אויפן מעטוש. נאָר אויפן קאסטיום און דעקאָראטיון רעקוויזיט. די היסטארישע אנעגדאטע דאקעגן שטעלט זיך אויף א גע• שיכטלעכן פאקט, וועלכן זי באארבעט אבער ווי גיהערט, פלעכט ארין אן אינטערע• סאַנטע אקציע פון דראַמטישן אדער קא• מעדיש-כאראקטער.

אזא מין פילם וועט זיין "דער אולאנער" פון יוזעף פאניאטאווסקי" וועלכן עס רעאליזירט די פילם-נעז. "Warszawskie Tow. Filmowe"; די הויפטראלן שפילן: יאדוויגא סמאסארסקא. בראנצעויוּטש. וויטאָלד קאנטי. שעלאנסקי. אהרוֹית א. א. רעזשי פירט קאנראד טאם. אויסאמעם פון איגיט. גניאדאווסקי. דער אויסקער פילם וועט זיך באהייזן אין קינא "קאפיטאל".

1000 קילאמעטער אויף
טאנך-רעדלעך

אין זייער נייעסטן פילם "מיר וועלן א טאנץ טון!" דעמאנסטרירט דאס וועלט• בארימטע טעַנצער פאָרעלפרעד אסטער און דושינדושער ראדשערס א טאנץ אויף רעד• לעך. בכדי דאָזיקן צו דערגרייכן האבן זיי ויאָק.לאנג אדורכגענעטרט די שוערסטע פרוון און רעפטיצעיס. לוים אן אויסרעכנונג האבן זיי יעדן טאָג אדורכגעמאכט אויף די רעדלעך א 200 קילאמעטער. דאס מאכט אויס דער גאנצער צייט שפיל פאָרן אויפגאָאַ• אפאַרטס א 1000 קילאַמעטער. דערדאַזיקער טאַנץ איז אבער דער אינטערעסאַנטעסטער און אריגנעלסטער טאנץ אין פילם אין אלגעמיין.

Figure 13.2 *Film-Nayes*, November 1937. (p. 4)

reading order, in which readers would read the different articles presented here from top to bottom and from right to left.

However, while this different orientation sets apart *Film-Nayes* from other film magazines published in languages such as Polish or English, demonstrating its clear links to a particular minority culture, the situation is actually more complex than this. While the magazine is, after all, written almost exclusively in Yiddish, it also includes a number of Polish words and phrases, particularly in its advertising context, as the magazine would most likely have been read by assimilated Polish Jews, who inhabited both worlds at once. (Additionally, occasional English words, especially in the context of particular movie titles, appear.)

The magazine therefore relies mostly on the conventions associated with design in a right-to-left language, but also, crucially, relies on the fact that its natural audience consists of bi-directional readers (Norouzi 24 January 2018, n.p.), who are able to read the magazine's main right-to-left language, Yiddish, but also the left-to-right language, Polish, most commonly spoken in the country where it is published.

This assumption of bi-directional and bilingual reading skills, and the ability to follow the accompanying intricate reading patterns, is already demonstrated by the masthead of the very first *Film-Nayes* issue from October 1936; indeed, this masthead (Figure 13.3) featured Yiddish, Polish, as well as some Yiddish transliteration in the Latin alphabet. The magazine's title is conveyed at the centre of the masthead, in Yiddish, with a smaller-print transliteration ('Film-Najes') and Polish translation ('Nowiny Filmowe' or 'Movie News') printed above the title. Further information conveyed in Yiddish alone, underneath the title, includes the magazine's price (20 groszy) and its promise of '14 pages with illustrations'. Its publication place (Warsaw) and date (October 1936) are conveyed in both Yiddish and Polish, also underneath the title. Interestingly, some information is

Figure 13.3 *Film-Nayes* masthead, October 1936. (p. 1)

added in Polish alone, above the title. This includes the word 'Jednodniówka', which indicates that this first issue was meant to be a standalone, one-off film publication, as is also demonstrated by the absence of an issue number; from the second issue onwards, this word would be replaced by the issue numbers. Additionally, at the very top of the front page, we find the Polish announcement 'Wysłano bezpłatnie do kin i biur filmowych w kraju', or 'Sent free of charge to cinemas and film offices in the country'. In order to take in this masthead fully, therefore, readers needed to be bilingual, as well as bi-alphabetic, inhabiting the Polish and Polish-Jewish worlds at once.

An advertisement for American company 20th Century Fox (Figure 13.4) in this same first issue demonstrates this as well, as its design demonstrates both the fundamental right-to-left orientation of the magazine and the central assumption that those reading *Film-Nayes* could read both Latin and Hebrew script.

This is demonstrated here through the magazine's deployment of a Z-pattern within the layout of the advertisement; this is a common strategy used within both historical and contemporary advertising, in which the reader's eyes are pulled along a path in the shape of one or more Z-shapes, with the final, and most crucial, piece of information found at the end of the Z (as demonstrated for example in Lucas and Britt 1950, 256) (Figure 13.5). Since *Film-Nayes* uses the right-to-left Hebrew alphabet, then, it uses a series of mirrored Z-patterns, as can be seen illustrated in Figure 13.5. Here, this pattern, combined with the assumption of bi-alphabetism, is utilised to guide the reader's gaze most effectively.

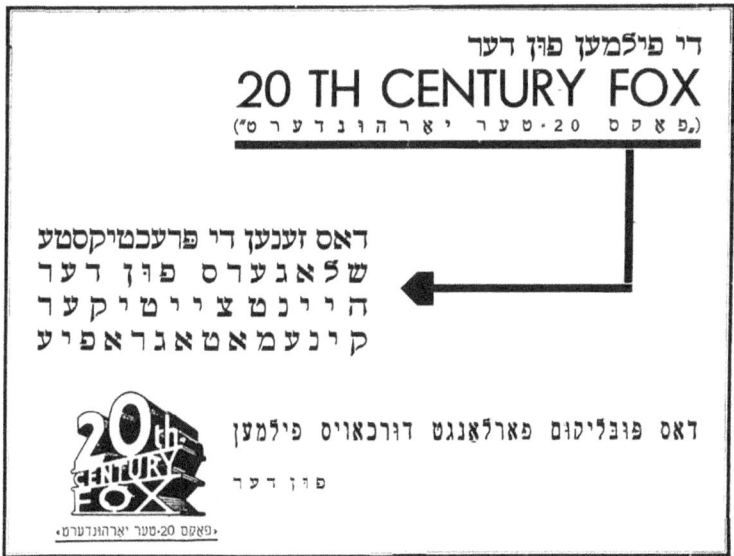

Figure 13.4   Advertisement for 20th Century Fox. *Film-Nayes*, October 1936. (p. 4)

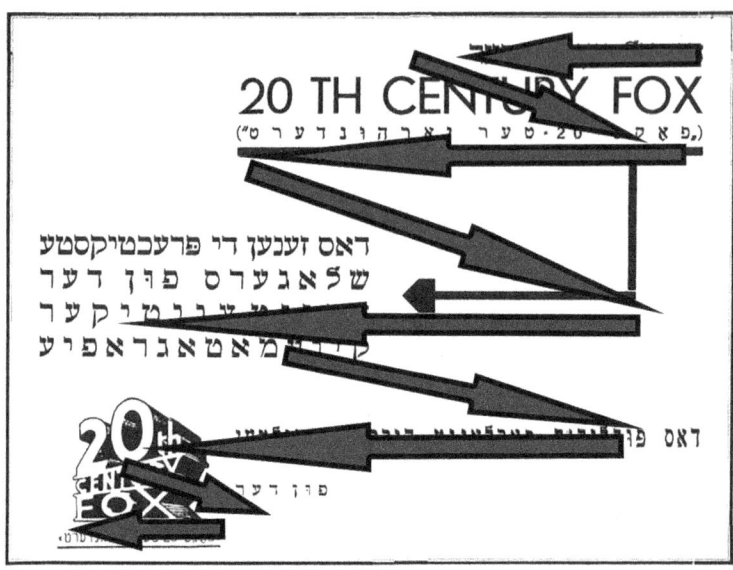

Figure 13.5   Suggested reading direction within the 20th Century Fox advertisement.

The reading direction of this ad runs therefore from the top right corner to the lower left corner: readers are first presented (in the top right corner) with text which reads:

The films of	(in Yiddish, right-to-left)
20TH CENTURY FOX	(in English, left-to-right)
('20th century Fox')	(in Yiddish, right-to-left)

This text therefore uses the bi-directional reading skills of the magazine's readers to form a first reverse-Z; next, then, the reader is taken through the use of a down-then-left arrow to another block of Yiddish text, which reads 'These are the most beautiful successes of contemporary cinematography'. Finally, a section at the bottom presents the reader first with two lines of right-to-left Yiddish text which read 'The audience longs for the films / from the', followed, on the left, by the classic 20th Century Fox logo (read left-to-right) with its Yiddish translation (read right-to-left) printed in tiny letters below. In this way, the ad uses four overlapping reversed Z-patterns to direct the Yiddish reader's gaze from right to left and from top to bottom, to finish up where the company logo, and its Yiddish translation, can be found.

Here, a classic advertising technique is used, and is not only adapted for a right-to-left reading orientation, but also taps directly into the ability of the magazine's readers to manage several reading orientations at once, with the second stroke of both the first and fourth reverse-Z consisting of English-language words. In this way, through its design, the ad reminds readers that they exist at the intersection of multiple worlds. As film lovers, the design here reminds them, they exist between Hollywood and Europe, but as Jews, they also exist between Poland and Yiddishland. In this way, the ambiguous in-between-ness of their position in society is emphasised in *Film-Nayes* through both content *and* design.

Conclusion

Within seven years of the publication of the final *Film-Nayes* issue, in May 1938, its editor, much of its hypothetical readership, and indeed the entire cultural universe which produced it, would be gone. The Shoah – designated in Yiddish with the word 'khurbn', meaning 'destruction' – changed the face of Jewish life, in Europe as elsewhere, forever, and the work to recover traces of that which existed before these years of genocide is, in a very real sense, both ongoing and forever incomplete.

The Yiddish press, though, insofar as it survived this onslaught, can help us with this work. Indeed, in investigating *Film-Nayes*, we can find traces of the specific characteristics of the world that produced it not only in its contents, but also in the design choices its editor made. Each of these spheres – content and design – mirrors a number of aspects of the reality in which its author and readers lived, and emphasises particularly this reality's fundamental in-betweenness, in which assimilated Jews in Poland were expected to inhabit multiple worlds with equal dexterity.

This was expressed in terms of content through the magazine's coverage of the frightening rise of Nazism, but also its fundamental ambiguity towards the global dominance of Hollywood and of the United States, which was rooted in Geler's belief in Europeanness and, likely, in the Bundist concept of 'doikayt', or hereness. At the same time, and demonstrating the importance of magazine design, the visual aspects exhibited by *Film-Nayes* also underline this particular, double reality, as they reflect the right-to-left orientation of the Hebrew (and therefore Yiddish) alphabet, but also, crucially, the positioning of its audience as bi-directional readers, capable of existing in the Yiddish and Polish worlds at the same time.

In casting a light on the faded pages of *Film-Nayes*, therefore, this chapter has attempted to show how a film fan magazine, so often derided as a frivolous medium dedicated to a popular, and therefore unserious, artform, can help us recover a group of fans who no longer exist, not through the natural passage of time – as is the case with the fan magazine readers of America's past – but also through the ravages of genocide. The world in which these fans lived can still speak to us today, through both the pages of this magazine and through the pixels of its digitised likeness. In the words of the Yiddish *Partizaner Lid*, a song of hope and resistance written in the midst of the Holocaust which would take the lives of Maks Geler and many of his readers, these magazine issues tell us that even after eighty years, 'mir zaynen do' – 'we are here'.

REFERENCES

Anon. 1929. 'Kultur-Komisye baym Druker-Fereyn'. *Unzer Ekspres*, 16 August: 14.

Cohen, Madeleine, and Clarke, Diana. 2016. '"Eight Volumes in Dour Maroon": Josh Fogel on Translating the Leksikon'. *In Geveb: A Journal of Yiddish Studies*. April. <https://ingeveb.org/blog/eight-volumes-in-dour-maroon-josh-fogel-on-translating-the-leksikon> (last accessed 19 August 2022).

Cohen, Nathan. 2008. 'The Yiddish Press and Yiddish Literature: A Fertile but Complex Relationship'. *Modern Judaism* 28 (2): 149–72.

Congress for Jewish Culture. 1956. *Leksikon fun der nayer yidisher literatur*. New York: Marstin Press, Inc.

Dyer, Richard. 1979. *Stars*. London: BFI.

Geler, Maks. 1924. 'Ukrainishe Literatur'. *Literarishe Bleter*, 8 August: 4.

Geler, Maks. 1926. 'Der "Dibuk" in der "Habimah"'. *Folk un Land*, 12 March: 8–10.

Geler, Maks. 1931. 'Di Velt-Milkhome in Kino'. *Vokhnshrift far Literatur, Kunst un Kultur*, 28 August: 4.

Geler, Maks. 1934. 'In di Fabrik fun Lebedike Shotns'. *Vokhnshrift far Literatur, Kunst un Kultur*, 21 February: 6–7.

Geler, Maks. 1934. 'In di Fabrik fun Lebedike Shotns'. *Vokhnshrift far Literatur, Kunst un Kultur*, 28 February: 6–7.

Geler, Maks. 1936. *Film-Nayes*, October: 1.

Geler, Maks. 1936. 'Di filmen fun der 20th Century Fox'. *Film-Nayes*, October: 4.

Geler, Maks. 1936. 'Foto-Reportazh fun der Film-Gezelshaft "Paramount"'. *Film-Nayes*, October: 6–7.

Geler, Maks. 1937. 'A yontif in der Film-Velt'. *Film-Nayes*, January: 1.

Geler, Maks. 1937. 'Elisabeth Bergner in a nayer role'. *Film-Nayes*, January: 2.

Geler, Maks. 1937. 'Di yidishe shoyshpilerin Franciska Gaal'. *Film-Nayes*, January: 4.

Geler, Maks. 1937. 'Amol in Deytshland, atsind in London'. *Film-Nayes*, January: 6.

Geler, Maks. 1937. '"Alah's Gartn", an internatsionaler film'. *Film-Nayes*, January: 8.

Geler, Maks. 1937. 'Sylvia Sidney nemt zikh tsurik tsu der arbet'. *Film-Nayes*, January: 11.

Geler, Maks. 1937. 'Hollywood "farkhapt" di beste eyropeyer'. *Film-Nayes*, March: 2.

Geler, Maks. 1937. 'Franciska Gaal in ir ershtn amerikaner film'. *Film-Nayes*, October: 8.

Geler, Maks. 1937. 'Marlene Dietrich varft op di aynladung'. *Film-Nayes*, November: 2.

Geler, Maks. 1937. *Film-Nayes*, November: 4.

Geler, Maks. 1938. 'Di barimte amerikaner film-shoyshpilerin Marlene Dietrich'. *Film-Nayes*, January: 12.

Greenbaum, Avraham. n. d. 'Newspapers and Periodicals'. *The YIVO Encyclopedia of Jews in Eastern Europe*. <https://yivoencyclopedia.org/article.aspx/Newspapers_and_Periodicals> (last accessed 19 August 2022).

Jacobs, Neil G. 2005. *Yiddish: A Linguistic Introduction*. Cambridge: Cambridge University Press.

Lucas, Darrell Blaine, and Steuart Henderson Britt. 1950. *Advertising Psychology and Research: An Introductory Book*. New York, London, Toronto: McGraw Hill.
Norouzi, Kian. 2018. 'What is the Corner of Death?' *Neuronsinc.com*. 24 January. <https://www.neuronsinc.com/insights/what-is-the-corner-of-death> (last accessed 19 August 2022).
Portnoy, Eddy. 2017. *Bad Rabbi: And Other Strange but True Stories from the Yiddish Press*. Redwood City, CA: Stanford University Press.
Rabinovitch, Simon. 2012. *Jews and Diaspora Nationalism*. Lebanon, NH: Brandeis University Press.
Slide, Anthony. 2010. *Inside the Hollywood Fan Magazine: A History of Star Makers, Fabricators and Gossip Mongers*. Jackson: University Press of Mississippi.
Slobin, Mark. 1982. *Tenement Songs: The Popular Music of the Jewish Immigrants*. Urbana: University of Illinois Press.
YIVO Institute for Jewish Research. 2014. 'Basic Facts about Yiddish'. New York: YIVO.

INDEX

Note: 'n' indicates note

Acting manuals, 201, 203–5, 208, 216
Advertising, 2–4, 7–8, 14, 73, 85–6, 91, 121–2, 131, 133–6, 140, 144
Alexander, Karen, 76–7
Amazing Mr Williams, The, 51–2
American Dream, The, 62, 64, 265
American fan magazines *see Modern Screen*, *Motion Picture*, *Motion Picture Story Magazine*, *Movie Classic*, *Movie Life*, *Movie Mirror*, *MoviePix*, *Photoplay US*, *Screen Guide*, *Screenland*
Americanisation, 6, 28, 32, 49
Annabella, 109, 111, 113–14, 116–17
As You Desire Me, 3–4
Attenborough, Richard, 221, 227, 230, 233
Austerity, 38, 41, 221, 223, 229, 231, 233

Babington, Bruce, 103, 235n
Baldwin, James, 78, 91

Barthelmess, Richard, 20, 23–7, 29, 31–3
Beegan, Gerry, 39, 47, 55
Belafonte, Harry, 67–8, 78, 83, 88
Blondell, Joan, 51, 52
Blondeness, 7, 76, 84
Bogle, Donald, 75, 83, 91, 92n
Bossay, Claudia, 239
Bourdieu, Pierre, 226, 235
Bourdon, Jerome, 239, 247
Brando, Marlon, 59, 61–3, 65–9, 73, 127, 135
Bright Road, 77–8, 82
British fan magazines *see Film Pictorial*, *Film Weekly*, *Photoplay UK*, *Picture Show*, *Picturegoer*
British imperialism, 19–20, 24, 26, 28–9
Britt, Steuart Henderson, 85–6, 266, 269
Broken Blossoms, 20, 24, 27–33
Bryan, Jane, 13, 129

274

Buley, E. C., 31–2
Burrows, Jon, 18–19, 29–31

Cantor, Eddie, 51, 53
Carmen Jones, 68, 75–9, 82–5, 87–91, 92n
Carroll, Diahann, 87–8
Carroll, Madeleine, 106–8
Censorship, 18, 168–73
Chile, 180, 238–53
Chilean fan magazines *see Ecran*
Christian, Linda, 66, 113–17, 126
Cine Illustrato, 113–14, 116
Ciné-Miroir, 98, 113, 139–44, 147–55
Cinema Arts, 158–9, 172–3
Cinémonde, 113, 151
Cinephilia, 140, 155
Class, 14, 27–8, 43, 51, 55, 73, 88, 91, 158, 240–1, 244–5, 248–9, 250–2
Cohen, Jeffrey, 184–5, 194, 197, 197n
Comic strip, 98, 139–56
Corwin, Jane, 61, 67–9
Cosmopolitan, 75, 79, 83
Cowan, Michael, 163–4, 242, 250
Crawford, Anne, 221, 223, 225, 230–2
Crawford, Joan, 159–62, 164–5, 168, 170–3
Curtis, Tony, 126–7, 135

Dancing Lady, 159–60, 162, 164, 166–173
Dandridge, Dorothy, 75–9, 82–91, 92n
Day, Doris, 45, 79–84, 131
Derek, John, 125, 131, 133–4
Desjardins, Mary, 201, 217
Dietrich, Marlene, 126, 134, 264, 265
Dootson, Kirsty, 45, 47, 56n
Dracula, 184–5, 189, 191, 197
Dyer, Richard, 24, 84, 90, 103, 151–2, 221, 224, 233, 263

Ebony, 75–9, 84, 87–8, 90
Ecran, 113, 180, 238–53
Egyptian, The, 65–6, 73
Emotional expression, 200–17
Escapism, 38–9
Esquire, 75, 79, 158

Fan magazine
 advice columns, 98, 130
 circulation, 37, 92n, 110, 123, 127, 136, 137n, 160, 162, 222, 226, 228, 233–4, 259
 competitions, 98, 130, 140, 152, 159–66, 188, 243
 covers, 39–41, 79–80, 82–4, 98, 101–2, 104–19
 fashion pages, 86, 91, 130–1, 134–6, 241, 245, 248
 fiction, 3–4, 98, 129, 132–3, 136, 139–56
 film reviews, 45, 82–3, 129, 134, 261
 gossip, 129, 134, 136, 160, 171–2, 222, 241, 273
 readers' letters, 17, 38, 51, 54–5, 84, 86–7, 92n, 98, 130, 133–4, 136, 141, 170, 173, 205, 251–2
 structure, 3–4, 6–7, 13, 39, 121–2, 132, 133–6, 149, 205
 tables of contents, 4, 131
Farrar, Geraldine, 206, 208, 211, 214
Femininity, 3, 6, 18, 29–30, 38, 42, 43–4, 49, 55, 69, 73, 90–1
Film-Nayes, 180, 257–71
Film noir, 59, 147
Film Pictorial, 106, 107, 108, 123, 228
Film Weekly, 37, 107, 228
Filmalaya, 122, 124–5, 129–31, 133–4, 136
Flapper, 201–2, 213–15, 217
Frankenstein, 184–5, 189, 191, 197

INDEX

French fan magazines *see Ciné-Miroir, Cinémonde, Noir et Blanc*
Fuller, Kathryn, 129–30, 200

Gaal, Franciska, 263, 265
Gable, Clark, 49, 51, 53, 111, 123, 161, 164–5, 170
Gaines, Jane, 42, 44
'Gal', 139, 146
Gangster film, 139, 145
Garbo, Greta, 3–4, 9n, 126, 134, 256–7, 265
Geler, Maks, 257, 259–60, 263–5, 271–2
Gender, 2–7, 14, 19, 23, 28, 32, 37–9, 41–51, 54–5, 59, 72–3, 76, 86, 91, 97–8, 101–2, 105, 109, 111, 130–1, 132–6, 145
Gente, 117–18
Gish, Lillian, 20, 23–7, 29, 31–3, 202, 208–9
Glamour, 14, 18, 27, 37–9, 41–5, 47, 49, 55, 83, 97–8, 105, 130, 149, 195, 240
Glancy, Mark, 13, 21, 27, 32, 37–9, 41, 49, 54–5, 59, 70, 129
Gledhill, Christine, 18–19, 21, 24, 190, 202, 214
Gone with the Wind, 45, 49
Grant, Cary, 38, 48–9
Griffith, D. W., 20, 211
Griffith-Grey, Albert, 158–9, 172–3
Gunning, Tom, 187, 189

Hallelujah, 78, 87
Hatch, Kristen, 29–30
Higashi, Sumiko, 1–4, 6, 9n, 87, 97–8, 103–4, 121, 129–30, 132, 135
Hirsch, Foster, 82, 92n
Holocaust, 258, 259, 262, 271–2
Hopper, Hedda, 70, 84
Horne, Lena, 83, 87

Horror, 183–4, 188–9, 191, 194
Hudson, Rock, 59, 63–7, 73, 126–7, 134

Informal actor training, 202–3, 209
Italian fan magazines *see Cine Ilustrato, Gente*

Jeffers McDonald, Tamar, 13, 39, 45, 59, 60, 68, 82, 103–5, 131, 135
Jet, 75, 78
Jewish assimilation in Poland, 257–8, 268, 271
Jewish emigration before the Holocaust, 262–4

Kelly, Gillian, 101–2, 104, 114, 117
Kent, Jean, 219–22, 225, 228, 230–2, 234
Kipling, Rudyard, 24, 32
Kuhn, Annette, 18, 105

Ladies Home Journal, 4, 122, 136, 166
Laemmle, Carl Sr., 185, 191
Lanckman, Lies, 17, 39, 51, 54, 59, 84, 98, 130
Latin America, 238–53
Leigh, Vivien, 38, 47, 49–50, 55
Liberace, 70, 124
Life magazine, 75, 77, 79, 158
Lloyds of London, 102, 106
Lucas, Darrell Blaine, 85–6, 266, 269

Malaysian fan magazines *see Filmalaya*
Manning, Ray, 63–4, 68
Marchetti, Gina, 27, 32
Marx, Karl, 226, 235
Masculinity, 6, 7, 29–30, 51, 60, 63, 67, 69–70, 73
Mask, Mia, 76, 88
Mass Observation, 38, 54

Materiality, 17–18, 21, 24, 105, 222, 226
Mature, Victor, 58–61, 62–3, 64, 68–73, 74n
Max Factor, 41, 43, 45–7, 49, 159, 162, 241
McCracken, Ellen, 13, 131
McLean, Adrienne L., 98, 103, 119, 129, 130
Media History Digital Library, 32, 74n, 179–80, 197n, 257
Media hybridity, 140, 149, 155
Melodrama, 139, 144–5, 201–2, 214
MGM, 41, 45, 65–6, 77, 101, 125, 159–60, 162, 165, 171, 173
Mitchum, Robert, 126, 134–5
Modern Screen, 39, 69–70, 75, 83, 92n, 103, 109–11, 159–70, 172–3
Monroe, Marilyn, 76, 117, 127, 135
Montage, 164–6, 168, 170
Moore, Colleen, 200–4, 209–17
Morin, Edgar, 221–4
Motion Picture, 4–5, 39, 75, 83, 104, 110–11, 168, 257, 262
Motion Picture Story Magazine, 1, 103, 129–30, 259
Movie Classic, 4
Movie Life, 111
Movie Mirror, 3–4, 126
MoviePix, 109–10
Mummy, The, 184, 190–1, 197

National identity, 2, 6, 14, 49
New Cinema History, 172, 179, 238
Newspapers, 2, 28, 31, 60, 82, 87, 144, 152, 179–80, 188–9, 213–15, 256, 258–9, 260, 264–5
Noir et Blanc, 113–15

O'Rourke, Chris, 201, 203, 205
On the Waterfront, 67, 68
Orgeron, Marsha, 17–18, 51, 129–30
Orientalism, 24, 27, 29, 31

Paramount, 60, 196, 261, 263
Parsons, Louella, 69–70, 79, 83, 92n
Passion de Dora, La/Passion of Dora, The, 7, 139–41, 143–54, 155
Paz Peirano, Maria, 239, 241
Peck, Gregory, 126–7, 134–5
Performance Studies, 8, 201–3
Performance, 18, 77, 91, 168, 200–17, 225
Photoplay UK, 122, 125–7, 129, 130–1, 134–6
Photoplay US, 6–7, 13–14, 39, 58–68, 70–3, 75–6, 79–91, 92n, 97–8, 103–4, 110–11, 121–2, 125–32, 134–5, 136, 137n, 161–2, 200, 204, 257, 259, 262
Pickford, Mary, 202–5, 208
Picture Show, 6, 8, 14, 18–19, 20–7, 32–3, 37, 79, 88–9, 106–7, 122–4, 129–33, 136, 201, 204–13, 216, 228
Picturegoer, 6, 13–14, 37–46, 47–55, 56n, 79, 88, 92n, 107, 111, 122–4, 127, 129–30, 132–6, 137n, 228, 262
Poland, 257, 258, 259, 262, 271
Polish fan magazines *see Film-Nayes*
Polley, Sarah, 92n, 160
Porgy and Bess, 77, 90
Postwar France, 143–54
Power, Tyrone, 66, 101–2, 105–6, 107–19, 126, 134
Preminger, Otto, 75, 77–9, 83–4, 91
Production Code, 89–90, 167–73
Purdom, Edmund, 59, 63, 65–7, 73, 126

Race, 2, 6–7, 14, 19–20, 24, 26–32, 45, 47, 54–5, 68, 75–8, 83–91, 92n
Rains, Claude, 184, 191, 196
Rains, Stephanie, 162–3
Rank Studio, 125, 221, 223–4, 233–4, 235n

INDEX

Reading direction, 268, 270–2
Restraint, 18–19, 24, 28–30, 31–3
Reynolds, Debbie, 66, 103
Robe, The, 59, 60
Roc, Patricia, 223, 229, 231, 235n
Roman-film, 141–3
Russell, Rosalind, 38, 44–7, 49, 55

Samson and Delilah, 59–60
Sanders, Lise Shapiro, 18, 28
Saturday Evening Post, The, 68–9, 166
Scholes, Robert, 14, 97
Schroeder, Carl, 69–70
Screen Guide, 111–12
Screenland, 103, 116, 162
Second World War, 37–9, 41–5, 47–9, 54–5, 70, 101, 111–12, 114
Segregation, 76, 87–8
Sennett, Robert S., 103, 105
Sexuality, 19, 23–4, 27–33, 51, 55, 64, 67, 69–70, 73, 76, 78–9, 83, 105
Shearer, Norma, 44–5, 109–10, 200
Sidney, Sylvia, 261–3
Silent film acting, 200–17
Sinatra, Frank, 82, 101
Slide, Anthony, 59, 83–4, 97–8, 101–3, 109, 110–11, 127, 129–30, 189, 257
Smith, Phyll, and Ellen Wright, 230
Spirit photography, 187, 189
Stacey, Jackie, 38, 54
Star economy, 221, 224, 235
Stead, Lisa, 17–19, 28–9, 38, 43, 47, 49, 54–5, 98, 129–30, 204–5

Stein, Sally, 7, 13, 17, 23, 122, 135–6
Stoler, Ann Laura, 19, 28, 29
Stuart, Gloria, 184, 195
Student Prince, The, 65, 66
Sullavan, Margaret, 39–41

Talmadge, Norma, 23, 200, 204
Taylor, Robert, 101–2, 111
Tone, Franchot, 161, 165
Topp, Dominic, 151
Touch, 4, 6, 17–24, 32–3
Turner, Lana, 69, 113
20th Century Fox, 77–9, 83–4, 88, 101, 106–7, 112, 125, 261, 269–70

Universal Weekly, 183–97

Variety, 77, 171–2, 179–80

Warner Bros, 79, 82
Way Down East, 20, 23–4, 26–7, 33
Wells, H. G., 184, 186, 192
Whiteness, 4, 7, 19, 24, 27, 29, 84–5, 90
Williams, Esther, 82, 103, 132
Women, The, 41, 44–5
Women's magazines, 7, 13, 17, 98, 122, 131, 135–6
Wright, Ellen, and Phyll Smith, 230
Wulfman, Clifford, 14, 97

X-ray photography, 186–7

Yiddish language, 180, 256–72
Young at Heart, 79, 82–3

EU representative:
Easy Access System Europe
Mustamäe tee 50, 10621 Tallinn, Estonia
Gpsr.requests@easproject.com

www.ingramcontent.com/pod-product-compliance
Lightning Source LLC
Chambersburg PA
CBHW052103230426
43671CB00011B/1919